American

Cut and Engraved

Glass

Books by Albert Christian Revi

Nineteenth Century Glass—Its Genesis and Development

American Pressed Glass and Figure Bottles

American Cut and Engraved Glass

American Art Nouveau Glass

American
Cut and Engraved
Glass

by

Albert Christian Revi

Schiffer Publishing Ltd

Box E, Exton, Pennsylvania 19341

REVISED AND ENLARGED EDITION, JULY 1967

Eighth Printing

© 1965, by Albert Christian Revi

All rights reserved under International and Pan-American Conventions.
Published by special arrangement with Thomas Nelson, Inc., Publishers.
Nashville, Tennessee. Address inquiries to Schiffer Publishing, Ltd.,
P.O. Box E., Exton, PA 19341

DESIGNED BY HAROLD LEACH

ISBN 0916838579

Library of Congress Catalog Card No.: 65—22016

MANUFACTURED IN THE UNITED STATES OF AMERICA

To my wife

Acknowledgments

The author wishes to acknowledge the kind assistance of the following people: Mrs. Henrietta Andriette, Maywood, Illinois; Miss Gladyce Blackmer, New Bedford, Massachusetts; Mr. Frank Blake, Painted Post, New York; Mrs. Marion Campbell, Fairhaven, Massachusetts; Mr. Gustave S. Carlson, Minneapolis, Minnesota; Mrs. P. M. Chamberlain, Pittsford, New York; Mr. John D. Clower, Cherry Hill, New Jersey; Mrs. Letitia C. Connelly, Goshen, New York.

Mr. Robert G. DeGoey, Providence, Rhode Island; Mr. Jackson T. Dobbins, Warsaw, Indiana; Mr. and Mrs. John C. Dorflinger, Hawley, Pennsylvania; Mr. Raymond H. Fender, Quakertown, Pennsylvania; Mr. J. Fletcher Gillinder, Port Jervis, New York; Mrs. Maxine Godsey, Toledo, Ohio; Mr. Carl Gustkey, Bellaire, Ohio; Mr. Otto Heinz, St. Charles, Illinois; Mr. August Keiser, Egg Harbor City, New Jersey; Mr. William J. Kokesh, Seattle, Washington; Mr. Lynn A. Kosht, Lansing, Michigan.

Mr. William E. McIlvain, Rancocas, New Jersey; Mrs. Martin Mellin, Walkerton, Indiana; Mr. Ashton Merrill, Towanda, Pennsylvania; Mrs. Clark Morton, Geneva, Illinois; Mrs. Mollie C. Nolan, Meriden, Connecticut; Mrs. Elmer Nuber, Lafayette Hill, Pennsylvania; Mr. Donald C. Parsche, Chicago, Illinois; Mr. Harry C. Pfeiffer, Egg Harbor City, New Jersey; Mr. J. "Eddie" Pfeiffer, Pitman, New Jersey.

Mrs. Marie H. Roberts, St. Louis, Missouri; Mrs. Beatrice G. Rosenblum, Middletown, New York; Mrs. John Rothfus, Hammonton, New Jersey; Mr. T. E. Salmon, Meriden, Connecticut; Mr. Daniel Smith, Medford, New Jersey; Mr. Don E. Smith, Findlay, Ohio; Mrs. Lillian Stehlin, Pasadena, California; Miss Irma L. Tilton, Hammonton, New Jersey; Charlie and Eleanor Vetter, Elmira Heights, New York; Mr. Claude B. Wilson, Jeannette, Pennsylvania; Mrs. Charles Zulich, Valparaiso, Indiana.

We also wish to acknowledge the use of the historical sources found at the following public and private institutions: Falmouth Public Library, Falmouth, Massachusetts; The Public Library of the City of Somerville, Somerville, Massachusetts; Sandwich Historical Society, Sandwich, Massachusetts.

Providence Public Library, Providence, Rhode Island; Rhode Island Historical Society, Providence, Rhode Island.

The Custis Memorial Library, Meriden, Connecticut; The Howard Whittmore Memorial Library, Naugatuck, Connecticut; The International Silver

Company, Meriden, Connecticut; The Meriden Historical Society, Meriden, Connecticut.

Brooklyn Public Library, Brooklyn, New York; Buffalo and Erie County Public Library, Buffalo, New York; Buffalo Chamber of Commerce, Buffalo, New York; Corning Museum of Glass, Corning, New York; Corning Public Library, Corning, New York; Goshen Library and Historical Society, Goshen, New York; The Green Free Library, Wellsboro, New York; The New York Public Library and The New York Historical Society, New York City; Rochester Public Library, Rochester, New York; Saugerties Public Library, Saugerties, New York; Syracuse Public Library, Syracuse, New York; Thrall Library, Middletown, New York.

Camden Free Library, Camden, New Jersey; Free Public Library, Trenton, New Jersey; The New Jersey Historical Society, Newark, New Jersey; The Public Library of Newark, Newark, New Jersey; Vineland Historical and Antiquarian Society, Vineland, New Jersey; Woodbury Public Library, Woodbury, New Jersey.

Carnegie Library of Pittsburgh, Pittsburgh, Pennsylvania; Columbia Public Library, Columbia, Pennsylvania; The Free Library of Philadelphia, Philadelphia, Pennsylvania; Lancaster Free Public Library, Lancaster, Pennsylvania; Pittston Public Library, Pittston, Pennsylvania; Wayne County Historical Society, Honesdale, Pennsylvania.

Carnegie Public Library, Marion, Ohio; Cleveland Public Library, Cleveland, Ohio; Findlay Public Library, Findlay, Ohio; Greater Cleveland Growth Board, Cleveland, Ohio; The McClean Public Library, Fostoria, Ohio; The Public Library of Cincinnati and Hamilton County, Cincinnati, Ohio; Toledo Museum of Art, Toledo, Ohio; Toledo Public Library, Toledo, Ohio; Tiffin Public Library, Tiffin, Ohio.

Carnegie Public Library, Anderson, Indiana; Public Library of Warsaw and Wayne Township, Warsaw, Indiana; Walkerton Library, Walkerton, Indiana.

Maywood Public Library, Maywood, Illinois.

The Detroit Public Library, Detroit, Michigan; The Lansing Libraries, Lansing, Michigan.

Olmstead County Historical Society, Rochester, Minnesota; Minneapolis Public Library, Minneapolis, Minnesota; Rochester Public Library, Rochester, Minnesota.

Contents

American

Cut and Engraved

Glass

The Development of the Cut Glass
Industry in America

As with all the glass arts, when viewed in retrospect, we find that cut and engraved glass had a very ancient origin. Cut glass, which is simply blown or pressed glass ground upon a wheel, goes back at least to ancient Rome. Pliny once wrote that after it was fashioned into the required shape by the blowpipe, it was "cut, as we term it, although 'ground' (*teriture*) is a more accurate phrase; or engraved with a sharp tool, like silver." Egyptian cut glass has been put forth as being as early as the fifteenth century B.C., when fairly large vessels and small cups were cut and decorated with what is believed to have been metal drills.

Glass cutting is recorded in Constantinople in the twelfth century. After the Turks overran Constantinople in 1453, there was a revival of the art in Italy. By the end of the sixteenth century Rudolph II introduced Italian glass cutters from Milan in his glassworks in Prague.

L. M. Angus-Butterworth, in *The Manufacture of Glass*, says that there is no proof that any cut glass was made in England before the beginning of the eighteenth century. Previous to 1850 in England, cut designs were confined mostly to flat panel fluting, large diamond cutting, splits and olives, flutes

Cut glass decanters made by Lloyd & Summerfield of Birmingham, Eng., *ca.* 1851.

1

Cut and engraved glass produced by W. Naylor, London, Eng., 1851.

Cut glass decanters made by Richardson's of Stourbridge, Eng., *ca.* 1851.

and fringe, prisms, hobnails, and the popular "Strawberry-Diamond" pattern; there were also some engraved decorations of various designs. Several English glass concerns exhibited their cut glassware at the Crystal Palace Exhibition in London in 1851—Molineaux, Webb & Company of Manchester; Lloyd & Summerfield, Birmingham; W. Naylor and Apsley Pellatt & Company of the Falcon Glass Works, both of London; and Messrs. Richardson of Stourbridge. Illustrations of wares from these glasshouses show the beginning of a trend toward more intricately cut designs in crystal and flashed colored and crystal glass.

Continental glasshouses in Bohemia and Belgium also exhibited cut glass at the Crystal Palace, and the articles illustrated in the exhibition catalogue evidence an even more elaborate style of cut decorations than those shown by conservative English and American firms at that time.

Cut glass covered dish made by M. Dierckx of Antwerp, Belg., *ca.* 1851.

Cut glass articles produced at Gilliland's Brooklyn Flint Glass Works, *ca.* 1851.

Many of the glass cutters employed in American factories about the middle of the nineteenth century originally came from Europe, and because of this, American cut glassware of this period bears a marked resemblance to cut crystal wares from abroad; however, John L. Gilliland's stand in the American department at the Crystal Palace Exhibition showed cut glass articles of a distinctive design which could be called purely American in character. The cut glass articles made at Gilliland's Brooklyn Flint Glass Works won an award both for the purity of the metal and the novelty of the decoration.

English, Irish, and Continental cut glass patterns influenced the designs produced in American cut glass factories until about 1880, when fan-scallops, rosettes, and curved miter cut patterns were introduced in America. In 1882, Phillip McDonald designed the "Russian" pattern for T. G. Hawkes & Company of Corning, New York, and from this point on American cut glasswares became richer and richer, both in design and in the quality of the glass and workmanship. John S. O'Connor's "Parisian" pattern (patented 1886) was the first cut glass design to utilize a curved line in cutting and it greatly influenced American designs for many years thereafter. Up to that time all cuttings had been in straight lines.

In 1812 an Englishman named Thomas Caines came to work for the South Boston Crown Glass Company, Boston, Massachusetts, a firm engaged principally in the manufacture of window glass. Caines induced this firm to produce a fine grade of flint glass, and it is believed that this metal was used in the production of some of the first cut glasswares ever made in America. The supposition that cut wares were made in this factory at that time is within the realm of possibility and probability, since the War of 1812 had stopped the importation of fine cut glass from abroad. By 1820, Caines had opened his own flint glassworks in South Boston (Suffolk), the Phoenix Glass Works, which was located across the street from the South Boston Crown Glass Company. In 1852, the Phoenix Glass Works were known as Caines & Johnston—William Caines (son of Thomas Caines) and William Johnston, proprietors. By 1859 the style of the firm had changed again to Thomas H. Caines & Son; and in 1867 the name was again changed to William Caines & Brother (Joseph Caines). This factory continued manufacturing flint glass tablewares until sometime after 1870.

In 1843, Patrick Slane took over the abandoned works of the South Boston Crown Glass Company and manufactured cut and pressed glassware along with the usual staple items produced by glasshouses of this period. In 1848 he took a partner into the firm and the company was then known as Slane & Burrell until 1853, when Slane again was listed as sole owner; the last listing for Slane's glassworks in Boston was in 1858; the factory was wiped out by a fire and afterward Slane built and operated a glasshouse in Brooklyn, New York, but was unsuccessful from the start.

In 1815 Messrs. Emmet, Fisher, and Flowers, former employees of the South Boston Crown Glass Company, started a small six-pot furnace in East Cambridge, Massachusetts, which, after two years, was sold at auction and ultimately became the New England Glass Company. This firm started in 1817 with a capital of $40,000. The original six-pot furnace, which produced only 600 pounds of glass each, was manned by 40 employees and manufactured not more than $40,000 worth of glass a year. In 1818 the output of the factory was increased by an additional furnace producing glassware of every description, some of which was cut on their 24 cutting frames (the technical term for cutters of glassware). By 1823 they were averaging a weekly output of 11 tons of glass, which was sold through their Boston showrooms. In 1852 five furnaces were operating at the New England Glass Company, averaging about a ton of glass each, and necessitating the employment of around 500 men and boys. By 1878 losses from various causes forced the retirement of the company and it was finally leased to William L. Libbey, whose son nine years later moved the plant to Toledo, Ohio, where it became famous as the Libbey Glass Company, manufacturers of rich cut glass.

Deming Jarves, formerly associated with the New England Glass Company, started a glassworks in Sandwich, Massachusetts, which later became a stock company known as the Boston & Sandwich Glass Company. This concern started with a modest eight-pot furnace producing about $75,000 worth of glass yearly. In time this was substantially increased until the Boston & Sandwich Glass Company was one of the largest glass-producing factories in America. They finally ran into labor trouble and financial difficulties in the late 1880's and were closed.

When Deming Jarves retired from the Boston & Sandwich Glass Company in 1858, he built another glass factory in Sandwich known as the Cape Cod Works. This plant had 12 cutting frames and produced cut wares similar to those made in England during this same period. Unfortunately, Jarves's new company lasted only a very few years and was never a successful business venture.

Before associating himself with the Boston & Sandwich Glass Company, Jarves built the Mt. Washington Glass Works in South Boston for his son. The factory operated a large cutting department in connection with their other glass productions, but in 1850 it was transferred to Jarves & Commerais, who increased the business greatly for a time. By about 1860 it was being operated by Capt. Timothy Howe, who was later joined by William L. Libbey. After Howe's death in 1866, Libbey managed the Mt. Washington Glass Works alone.

In 1861 a new factory was built in New Bedford, Massachusetts, for the manufacture of flint glass. The firm failed within a few years of its establishment and was finally taken over by William L. Libbey, who moved his business from South Boston and renamed the New Bedford factory the Mt. Washington Glass Company. Several changes in ownership of this works occurred during its long history and in the end it was taken over by the Pairpoint Corporation. In 1869, when Libbey first took over the works, they were operating only 15 cutting frames.

The *Boston Almanac & Business Directory* for 1889 listed the following glass cutters and engravers: Jones, McDuffee & Stratton, 59 Federal Street, Boston, retailers of fine china and glassware; M. T. J. Keenan, 71 Sudbury Street,

Boston; Kelley & Company, 118½ Milk Street, Boston; J. G. McConnell, 19 Harvard Place, Boston (listed as an engraver); Redding, Baird & Company, 83 Franklin Street, corner of Arch Street, Boston, manufacturers of stained-glass memorial windows, ground and cut glassware; John E. Rice & Company, 55½ Sudbury Street, Boston; E. E. Sweeney, 19 Harvard Place, Boston; P. H. J. Loan & Company, 28 Sudbury Street, Boston, listed as agents for the Central Glass Works (probably of Wheeling, West Virginia), and as P. H. J. Loan & Company, manufacturers of cut glassware.

It is believed that cut crystal was first produced in New York City by Joseph Stouvenal about 1837. At one time Stouvenal had a retail store on lower Broadway in New York City. At the same time the Williamsburgh Flint Glass Works also produced flint glass, cut and plain. A French family by the name of Walter (Walther) established the Williamsburgh factory with a man named Berger, and in 1845 this shop won a silver medal for an exhibit of colored and cut wares at the annual fair of the American Institute of the City of New York, and another in 1850 for cut, plain, and colored glass. By 1879 the Williamsburgh Flint Glass Works had been taken over by John and Nicholas Dannehoffer and was operated as Dannehoffer & Brothers until about 1886, when Nicholas Dannehoffer was listed in the city directories as the sole owner of the glassworks at 260 Boerum Street, Brooklyn, New York.

The early cutting shops in New York City and Brooklyn cut principally shades and globes for oil lamps; only a few shops cut table glass, E. V. Haughwout and Joseph Stouvenal & Company being the largest producers of such wares. At Gilliland's South Ferry Glass Works, 40 cutting frames were in operation producing a fine grade of richly cut crystal tablewares in addition to lighting fixtures and globes. About 1854 Messrs. Hoare, Burns & Dailey started their cut glass shop, later moving into the South Ferry Glass Works, and again in the early 1860's moving to Greenpoint, Brooklyn; finally they moved to Corning, New York, where they joined with the Corning Flint Glass Works, established by Amory Houghton, Sr. in 1868. Previously Houghton had built the Union Glass Works in Somerville, Massachusetts, and operated it from 1852 to 1864. After he sold his interest in the Somerville works, he went to Brooklyn, New York, and purchased the South Ferry Glass Works, where he stayed from 1864 to 1868. In 1868, Houghton established the Corning Flint Glass Works in Corning, New York. In 1872, Amory Houghton, Jr. was made president of the Corning Flint Glass Company, and in 1875 a reorganization of the company was effected and the style of the firm was changed to the Corning Glass Works, with Amory Houghton, Jr. as president.

The establishment of the Corning Glass Works made possible the many cutting shops that were scattered about in the Corning area between 1870 and 1900—J. Hoare & Company, T. G. Hawkes & Company, O. F. Egginton Company, H. P. Sinclair & Company, Hunt & Sullivan, and many others; Corning became one of the great cut glass centers in the United States.

In 1852, Christian Dorflinger started his Concord Street works in Brooklyn, New York, and by 1854 he began to manufacture crystal blanks for cutting shops in the New York City area. Several years later he started a much larger glassworks, the Plymouth Street shop in Brooklyn, and commenced manufacturing cut glass himself. Hoare & Dailey established their cut glass shop at Dorflinger's Plymouth Street works soon after it was erected. From 1856 to 1860 the cut glass trade had been doing very well and there was a demand for cut crystal wares from Cuba and some South American countries, which was largely supplied by the Dorflinger works. E. V. Haughwout & Company, Ebenezer Collamore and Davis Collamore were the principal dealers in cut glasswares in New York City around the middle of the nineteenth century.

When the Civil War broke out between the states, the cut glass business was hard hit. In 1863, Dorflinger moved to his farm in Pennsylvania and two years later established his large glassworks and cutting shop in White Mills, Pennsylvania. Meanwhile the two Brooklyn factories had been leased to former employees who met with but a little success at first and finally failed. In 1870 Fowler, Crampton & Company purchased the Plymouth Street glassworks; previous to that they had been for many years importers of glassmaking materials which they supplied to the trade. Fowler, Crampton & Company operated the former Dorflinger plant and cutting shop consisting of some 35 frames for about four years. After losing a great deal of money, they finally gave up the business. Elliot P. Gleason, Charles F. Gleason, and John P. Gleason leased the Greenpoint Flint Glass Works from Dorflinger and operated it for some years, producing gas and electrical wares; evidently they were active as late as 1902, for William Dorflinger speaks of them in a contemporary vein in his report to the American Association of Flint and Lime Glass Manufacturers in Atlantic City, New Jersey, in 1902.

James D. Bergen, in an article he wrote for the *Jeweler's Circular Weekly* in 1915, mentioned the following cut glass manufacturers operating in New York City in the last half of the nineteenth century:

Mr. Bloomer, whose shop was located on Elm Street, near Grand Street; Cavanaugh & Hatton, Grand Street; Connelly & Murtagh of Brooklyn; the Co-Operative Cut Glass Company of Brooklyn (John J. McCue, president); Fowler & Crampton who operated the Plymouth Street Glass Works formerly owned by Christian Dorflinger; J. B. Dobelmann operated the Greenpoint Flint Glass Works in Brooklyn; Joseph(?) Marrett worked a shop on Columbia Street in Brooklyn and later moved into Thill's Glass House on Kent Avenue, Brooklyn; thereafter Marrett moved to the premises of Meyer & Koelsch's Glass House. Quinnell & Harris produced cut glass at their shop on Broadway and Broome Street in New York City.

About 1824 the brothers George Dummer and Phineas C. Dummer, with Joseph K. Milner and William G. Bull, built the Jersey Glass Company in Jersey City, New Jersey. George Dummer had been in business in Albany, New York, before this time and had already established a glass and china business in New York City, known as George Dummer & Company, at 110 Broadway. Before going into the glass business for himself, Dummer had imported all his cut crystal from Europe, but as soon as he began producing

Cut glass table lamp 33¾ in. high, in the residence of Mary Baker Eddy, discoverer and founder of Christian Science, Chestnut Hill, Mass. The lamp was a gift to Mrs. Eddy from Mrs. Emilie B. Hulin of Brooklyn, N.Y., in Dec. 1899.

cut flint glass, he stocked his New York City outlet with his own wares from the Jersey City glassworks. In 1826, Dummer's works received an award for their cut glass at the Third Exhibition of the Franklin Institute; they continued exhibiting at this fair until 1845. By 1856, after a few changes in the style of the firm, it was being operated by Augustus O. Dummer; he was not listed after 1862/63.

In the early years of the Jersey Glass Company's operations, George Dummer went to England, where he procured the services of a number of skilled glass cutters and glassworkers for his factory. He constructed a large cutting department in connection with the glass factory and for many years the Jersey City Glass Company, Joseph Stouvenal & Company, and Gilliland's Brooklyn Flint Glass Works supplied the crystal blanks for cutting shops operating in their area at that time.

The establishment of the Meriden Flint Glass Company in Meriden, Connecticut, preceded the opening of a host of cut glass shops in that city and surrounding communities—J. D. Bergen & Company; J. J. Niland & Company; Meriden Cut Glass Company; and several others. Meriden's silver plate concerns supplied many of the cut glass shops in the area with handsome silverplated complements for their finely cut wares, and created a need in return for cut glass fittings for their own silverplated service pieces for the table.

The earliest cut and engraved glass produced in America was probably manufactured (during the last half of the eighteenth century) at Henry William Stiegel's glass factory in Manheim, Pennsylvania, and the works established in Fredericktown, Maryland, by John Frederick Amelung. Aside from the engraved designs which have been identified as being peculiar to these late eighteenth-century factories, we would be hard pressed to make a positive attribution of some of the simple cut glass patterns—flutes, panel cutting, and some diamond cutting—because they are identical to wares made in Europe during this same period.

About 1780, Robert Morris and John Nicholson established a glasshouse (in Philadelphia) at the falls of the Schuylkill, and in 1793 employed a German glass cutter named William Peter Eichbaum as their superintendent. Eichbaum left their employ soon after and became superintendent of the O'Hara & Craig glassworks in Pittsburgh, Pennsylvania, which was started in 1797. It would appear that the first recording of cut glass manufacturing in Pennsylvania can be attributed to Eichbaum while he was in the employ of Morris and Nicholson.

In 1817 an Englishman reported in *Sketches of America*:

At Messrs. Page & Bakewell's glass ware house I saw chandeliers and numerous articles of cut glass of every splendid description. Among the latter was a pair of decanters cut after an English pattern, the price of which will be eight guineas. It is well to bear in mind that the demand for these articles of elegant luxury lies in the western states, inhabitants of eastern America being still importers from the old country.

Left: Covered sugar bowl; *ca.* 1815–35; U.S., Pittsburgh, possibly Bakewell, Page and Bakewell; height with cover 8⅝ in. *Right:* Tumbler; *ca.* 1830–40; U.S., possibly Philadelphia (Kensington), Union (Flint) Glass Co.; height 4⅜ in.

Collection of Corning Museum of Glass

Although the cutting of flint glasswares was confined mostly to eastern factories, the first flint glass made for cutting was produced and cut in Pittsburgh, Pennsylvania.

In 1820 former employees of the New England Glass Company built a glass factory in Philadelphia (Kensington), Pennsylvania, known as the Union (Flint) Glass Company. A three-story brick building was erected for the cutting shop and by 1827 they had won recognition for their cut wares which were shown at the Fourth Exhibition of the Franklin Institute. In later years the company won awards also for their colored glassware. In 1831, Charles B. Austin & Company were noted as agents for the Union Glass Company in Kensington, with warehouses at 10 Minor Street and 23 Dock Street; Charles B. Austin & Company exhibited at the Franklin Institute in 1831, showing cut crystal and colored glassware. Hartell & Lancaster operated the glassworks in 1848, and McKearin, in *American Glass*, reports that ten years later it was known as Hartell, Letchworth & Company. The latter firm exhibited at the Franklin Institute's Twenty-seventh Exhibition in 1874.

The Dithridge Flint Glass Company, which started in Martins Ferry, Ohio, moved to New Brighton, Pennsylvania, in 1887. They made pressed and blown wares and crystal blanks for cutting. They also cut glass, utilizing some 75 cutting frames, and employing about 250 hands in all facets of the business.

In Monaca, Pennsylvania, in 1884, the Phoenix Glass Company were manufacturing fine flint glass for cutting. Their own cutting shop of about 70 frames was largely employed in the manufacture of lamp shades and globes, and some decorative and tablewares. Difficulties with the glassmakers' union curtailed their cut glass operations greatly after 1890, and for a time they produced only cut, engraved, and etched lamp shades, globes, and ceiling light shades.

Christian Dorflinger's glassworks and cutting shop in White Mills, Pennsylvania, was begun in 1865. As a result of this, numerous cutting shops were established in nearby Honesdale, Pennsylvania—T. B. Clark & Company; Krantz & Smith; Gibbs, Kelly & Company; the Irving Cut Glass Company; Herbeck & Demer; Feeney & McKanna; John S. O.'Connor; and several others. Honesdale became one of the largest cut glass manufacturing centers in America by the turn of the century.

In Wheeling, Virginia (now West Virginia), in the early nineteenth century, Sweeney & Company and Ritchie & Wheat cut glass in the traditional designs copied from contemporary English cut glasswares dating about 1829.

In 1883 the Census Report for that year indicated that there was a cutting shop operating in Kentucky in 1840, but its source of supply for crystal blanks was unknown.

Left to right: Wine glass, cut; Dithridge Flint Glass Co., New Brighton, Pa.; *ca.* 1888; height 4¾ in. Salt dish, cut; probably English or Irish; *ca.* 1780; height 2¼ in. Cut glass dish; Dithridge Flint Glass Co., New Brighton, Pa.; *ca.* 1888; length 6⅞ in.

The Smithsonian Institution

Perhaps the greatest impetus the American cut glass industry experienced in its early days was the reception American cut wares received at the Centennial Exposition in Philadelphia in 1876. Showings by Christian Dorflinger, the New England Glass Company, the Mt. Washington Glass Company, Gillinder & Sons, J. B. Dobelmann, and a few others brought the elegance of American cut glass to the public's attention rather forcefully. Up to this period there had been very little demand for fine cut glass products from the south and western sections of the country. The innovation of cut glass perfume and scent bottles produced a rage for these articles among the distaff members of the nation, and in time cut glass tablewares, lighting fixtures, and lamps were making their appearance in the finer homes in western and southern communities.

The Libbey Glass Company's magnificent exhibition factory at the World's Columbian Exposition in Chicago, Illinois, in 1893, produced a market for richly cut American crystal such as the industry had never known before. The contents of Libbey's Crystal Art Room established cut glass as a god in American households for many years thereafter. With some semblance of truth, one Edwardian wit declared that no table of his time was socially correct unless it had cost a million and weighed a ton (he was referring to cut glass, its weight and expense). The thick blanks needed for the production of fine cut glass did make for ponderous table pieces, but this did not prevent Edward D. Libbey and others from realizing a fortune from such wares. In its day cut glass was considered the most correct gift for weddings and anniversaries, and a great quantity of fine cut glass found its way into the nation's homes, where it enriched dining tables set with heavy damask, and drawing rooms hung with lace curtains.

Shortly before the turn of the century there were more uses found for cut glass articles than was ever thought of previously, and everything from knife rests and napkin rings to enormous punch bowls and floor lamps were made, besides cologne and perfume bottles, hair receivers, jewel boxes, and other accessories for a lady's or gentleman's use.

Before 1893 the wholesale and retail dealers in cut glass refused to recognize the product they were selling as American-made and very often presented it to their clients as imports from English and Continental cut glass factories. This so enraged the American cut glass manufacturers that they began to advertise "American Rich Cut Glass" in all the trade papers, national magazines, and newspapers. William Dorflinger reported in 1902 that before this gigantic advertising campaign on the part of American cut glass manufacturers, the dealers were showing inferior European cut glass to customers who asked to see some of the domestic cut glass products. After many months of educating the American public to an appreciation of the fine quality of American cut glassware, at an expense far above their usual dole for advertising, the American cut glass manufacturers were given their rightful place in this expression of the glass arts. The National Association of Cut Glass Manufacturers, founded in 1911, was established to maintain the highest standards in the cut glass industry.

William H. Hawken cutting a bowl in his "White Rose" pattern. Photograph taken in Irving Cut Glass Co. shop, *ca.* 1922.

In time the cut glass industry began moving westward, and cut glass shops were opened in Cleveland, Toledo, Findlay, Fostoria, and Cincinnati, Ohio; Anderson, Warsaw, and Walkerton, Indiana; Detroit and Lansing, Michigan; Chicago, Illinois; St. Louis, Missouri; Minneapolis, St. Paul, and Rochester, Minnesota; and as far west as Seattle, Washington.

The cutting of glass gives expression to one of the essential qualities of this material, namely, its inherent brilliancy. To produce an article of cut crystal glass, the first step was to mark the pattern on the blank with white or colored pigment. The cutting was done on stone or steel wheels, upon which carborundum, sand, or some other abrasive dripped from a funnel-shaped hopper situated just above the cutting wheel. The deepest cuts were always made first, since these militated against the article remaining true and were the most difficult to produce. If the cutting of these deep incisions in the glass blank caused it to break in the early stages of its production, then less time and money were expended on the article and the loss was not so great. When the article comes from the cutting rooms, the cuttings are gray (matted) and must be polished on wooden wheels with rouge or some similar polishing agent. About 1890 the final polishing of the cut glass articles was accomplished by dipping them in an acid bath. The latter process was cheaper and quicker, and more healthful for the workmen. Its adoption increased the output of cut glass by 25 per cent, but old-timers in the trade despaired that the fine hand polishing techniques had been abandoned.

Several attempts to cut glass by machinery were made in the nineteenth century, but most of these efforts met with little success. However, in the American section of the Universal Exposition, held in Paris in 1878, samples of glass cut by machinery were exhibited by J. P. Colné, the result of a joint invention with Charles Colné, which was possibly the result of an earlier machine for cutting glass patented by John P. Colné of New York City on August 26, 1851. These were the only machine-cut articles in the exhibition and excited the curiosity of foreign manufacturers because of the beauty and regularity of the work. These samples consisted of decanters, goblets, sugar bowls, mustard pots, tumblers, and so forth, of different shapes and styles of cutting. The cutting machine itself was not on exhibition, but it was put to use in some French glass factories shortly after 1878. The machine was not entirely automatic, but was adapted to cut all geometrical shapes and patterns, as well as a great variety of styles of cuttings, and did not require any skill in the person operating it, as the penetration of the cutting wheels was perfectly regulated. The rapidity, regularity, and perfection of the cutting done with this machine ensured a great saving in the cost of producing cut glass articles. Nevertheless, for some reason Colné's cutting machine was not widely used in America.

There were many improvements in the production of cut glass. First came a change from cast-iron to soft-steel wheels; but the most important change was the adoption of what is known today as assembly line production. In the English cut glasshouses the workers were taught to cut an object from the very beginning to the final polishing process. Of necessity, this was a slow operation, and changing wheels and other equipment took a great deal of precious and costly time. In the early 1870's American craftsmen were taught one or more of the various steps to a finished article. Some became expert roughers of the pattern, while still others specialized in the smoothing and polishing of the cut glass articles. In this way each phase of the work was carried on by one or more men and there was no need to change over from one operation to another. By 1880 feeding-up brushes for polishing cut glass were introduced, which saved the wages of one man's work. Until 1854 the English practice of working a night and a day shift had been largely abandoned by American cut glass shops and day work only was adopted. With the advanced techniques used in the industry, it was possible, about 1890, to increase the work schedule again whenever necessary, especially during the busy Christmas season.

Engraving is the production of ornamental designs on glassware by a fine grinding, mostly done with copper disks revolving on a lathe. This technique was sometimes used in combination with the deep-cut designs, and usually was left in a mat (gray) finish.

Rock crystal is the name given to an all-polished cutting copied from early Bohemian rock crystal designs and does not refer to the quality of the glass at all. The metal itself could be flint or soda lime glass. This type of engraving, or cutting, dates from about the turn of the century in American cut glass, but it had manifestations in England a few years earlier.

The introduction of pressed blanks for cutting came rather late in the cut glass era, but even this technique had an ancient origin in Egypt or Rome. Fragments of ancient cut glass have been found which showed that mold-blown articles had been touched up by linear wheel cuts carried out in the molded depressions. The use of pressed or figured blanks was one of the contributing factors to the decline of the cut glass business in America. The cheapening of the product made cut glass available to even the poorest household in the early part of this century, but soon it degenerated into the pressed cut wares produced by the McKee Glass Company and the Imperial Glass Works.

One cut glass distributor suggested the following means for cleaning cut glass wares: "Tepid water and the best castile soap, applied with a stiff brush. After washing and rinsing place the cut glass in boxwood sawdust. This will absorb the moisture in the cuttings. Next remove the sawdust from the plain surfaces with a soft cloth or camel's hair brush." Modern detergents make this long and tedious method unnecessary.

Between 1890 and 1918 there were many small cut glass shops located in homes, cellars, and barns, and operated by independent glass cutters who purchased their blanks from various sources in and around their locale; usually these blanks were seconds, or rejects, made by glassworks and ordinarily these would have been consigned to the cullet heap. The equipment needed for this work was very simple and easily got together from bits and pieces that a glass cutter might have on hand, or be able to acquire without much trouble. The cut glass made in these little "cribs," as they were called in England, makes it more and more a problem to attribute cut glass articles to any one locale, let alone to a certain manufacturer. Unless the cut glass object is signed, or has been decorated with a design patented by a known cut glass manufacturer, it is quite difficult to make a positive attribution; and even this latter means of identification could be misleading, as is evidenced by the several similar "Rose" patterns produced in Honesdale, Pennsylvania, and the widespread use of the "Russian" pattern throughout the trade.

The fabric of the cut glass industry in America is as intricately woven as a Gobelin tapestry. The paths of cutters and entrepreneurs in this industry cross and crisscross so often that it is difficult to keep track of them. Glass cutters, like the modern migrant farmworkers, followed their trade from place to place, hoping that each move would enrich their lot. Some of these men made their fortune in the cut glass business, and others never aspired to anything more than the great joy they derived from their art. They cut more or less the same patterns wherever they were working, and for this reason it is impossible to say that one common, or favorite, cut glass pattern is indigenous to a particular cutting shop or a certain area in America. We have endeavored in our illustrations to give our readers as many means for identifying their cut glass pieces as is possible. There is such a similarity in many of the patented designs for cut glass that we suggest a really close comparison be made before an attribution is attempted. A listing of trademarks used by many of the cut glass manufacturers will be found in the Appendix.

The American cut glass industry took great pride in their products and every effort was bent to make American cut glass the finest cut crystal in the world. This goal was achieved by American glass cutters, and the appellation "American Rich Cut Glass" was not an empty boast—it was a superb reality that is patently obvious in the many public and private collections of cut glass throughout the United States.

Cut Glass Manufacturers in Massachusetts

The New England Glass Company
W. L. Libbey & Son Company
The Libbey Glass Company

The New England Glass Company was established in 1817 in East Cambridge, Massachusetts, by Amos Binney, Edmund Monroe, Daniel Hastings, Deming Jarves, and their associates. The company was incorporated on February 16, 1818, and maintained offices in Boston at 67 Federal Street, where their wares were shown to the trade. The original capital stock amounted to $40,000. The factory occupied facilities formerly used by the Boston Porcelain & Glass Manufacturing Company of East Cambridge, Massachusetts.

Henry Whitney succeeded Deming Jarves in 1825, when the latter left the New England Glass Company to establish the Boston & Sandwich Glass Company. In 1826, Thomas Leighton was made superintendent of the works and he continued in this capacity for almost 20 years.

William L. Libbey joined the company in 1872, having first served in various positions with the Mt. Washington Glass Company of New Bedford, Massachusetts, and earlier with Jarves & Comerais in Boston. Two years later, in 1874, Edward Drummond Libbey joined his father in the New England Glass Company, and together they managed the firm until its dissolution. In 1880 the name of the company was changed to the New England Glass Company, W. L. Libbey & Son, Proprietors. The *Boston Almanac and Directory* for 1889 listed the "W. L. Libbey & Son Company, New England Glass Company, with offices at 155 Franklin Street, Boston; A. F. Putney, agent, W. H. Munroe, treasurer." This would seem to indicate that the works reopened some time after the strike of 1888, but this was not the case. On July 18, 1890, the company surrendered its charter in Massachusetts.

The early cut wares produced at the New England Glass Company are indistinguishable from other cut crystal and colored glassware made in America and abroad from about 1825 to 1850. During this period their wares were decorated with simple flute or panel cutting and the popular "Strawberry-Diamond" and "Prism" patterns, which were also universally employed by most every cut glass shop in Europe and America, and they continue to be popular cut glass patterns today.

In 1853 a visitor to the New England Glass Company noted in *Gleason's Pictorial*: "We were repeatedly struck by the fact, new to us, that most of the exquisite, highly coloured and decorated glassware, which is so much admired under the name of Bohemian glass, is manufactured at these works." Some examples of cut glassware executed on cased colored blanks were imported as

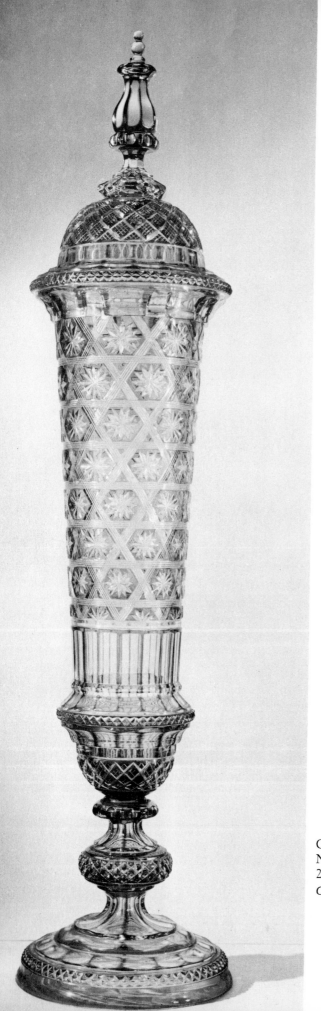

Covered urn; ruby over clear glass; made by New England Glass Co., *ca.* 1845; height 29¾ in.

Collection of Toledo Museum of Art

models from Bohemian factories; Louis Vaupel and Henry Fillebrown were the artist-engravers usually associated with this type of work at the New England Glass Company. Both Fillebrown and Vaupel were European craftsmen who had been brought to America especially for this type of engraving by the Cambridge works. The New England Glass Company's engraved glass after the fashion of Bohemian models was produced on blanks of crystal glass plated or stained with color—ruby, blue, violet, amber, and green. On occasion such pieces were gilded or painted with transparent stains, which was an inexpensive substitute for cased blanks. After 1875 the more brilliant miter-cut patterns were preferred by the public, and it can be said with some degree of certainty that the so-called "Brilliant Period" in American cut crystal dates from 1875 to 1925.

Some old factory records listed the following glass cutters working in the New England Glass Company's cutting shop: John L. Hobbs, glass cutter

Cut glass articles from an illustrated New England Glass Co. catalogue, *ca.* 1885.

during the 1820's; he was foreman of the cutting department around 1825. Oliver T. Leighton, cutter. Joseph Burdakin cut glass in the factory from 1831 to the day it closed in 1888; Burdakin was foreman of the cutting shop in the latter years of the company's existence. John Lowry, cutter, worked in the shop from about 1850; he was foreman of the cutting department in the 1870's and early 1880's. Samuel Fillebrown, cutter. Robert P. Tuten was listed as foreman of the cutting department (no date given).

We found a great many brilliantly cut patterns in an illustrated catalogue issued by the New England Glass Company about 1885. Pattern names included "Cut Hob and Star," "Cut Hobnail Diamond," "Cut Strawberry-Diamond," "Cut Belgian," and "Cut Russian." Several cut glass designs were patented for the company. Among the earliest were two designs for oval-shaped dishes registered by George W. Lowry of East Cambridge, Massachusetts, on February 23, 1875. Lowry's patterns were rather simple for this late period, but they reflect the conservative taste of the New England glass manufacturers of this era who were still catering to a sophisticated clientele wanting wares similar to those that could be purchased in England. The first design is one of horizontal and parallel incisions forming squares, the edge of the dish having what is known as a "dental" design. The other design consisted of a series of depressed ogivals (olives) around the mid-section of the sides of the dish, with simple cut patterns about the top and the bottom edges. Lowry stated in his patent papers that these designs could be applied to "either cut or pressed glassware."

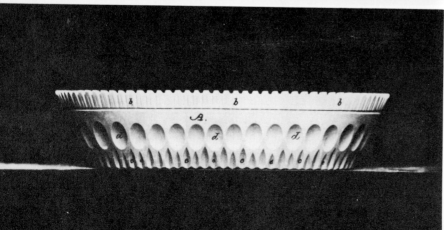

G. W. Lowry's designs for cut glass dishes; patented Feb. 23, 1875; New England Glass Co.

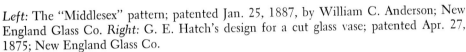

Left: The "Middlesex" pattern; patented Jan. 25, 1887, by William C. Anderson; New England Glass Co. *Right:* G. E. Hatch's design for a cut glass vase; patented Apr. 27, 1875; New England Glass Co.

While he was associated with the New England Glass Company, George E. Hatch patented a design for cut glassware on April 27, 1875. Here again the pattern is a very simple one of "channels or grooves" extending from the top of the article to the base. In his patent illustrations Hatch showed a trumpet-shaped vase which was inserted in a silver or white metal base.

On January 25, 1887, William C. Anderson patented the New England Glass Company's "Middlesex" pattern. This appears to be the last design patent for cut glass issued to the firm while it was in Massachusetts.

In 1888 the Cambridge works were closed after a prolonged strike forced the company out of business. Edward D. Libbey moved his business to Toledo, Ohio, and on June 21, 1888, a charter was authorized for the establishment of the W. L. Libbey & Son Company. (William D. Libbey had died in Newton, Massachusetts, in 1883.) The new company had a capital stock of $100,000, which was raised through local businessmen. The name of the firm was changed to the Libbey Glass Company on February 3, 1892.

In 1893 the Libbey Glass Company erected a large exhibition factory on the World's Columbian Exposition fairgrounds in Chicago, Illinois. It was located on Midway Plaisance and was 150 feet wide and 200 feet long. The height of the central dome, which served as a smokestack for the furnaces, was 100 feet. The structure resembled a palace, with two imposing towers flanking either side of the main entrance. Inside the main doorway visitors were

greeted by the sight of a huge semicircular room with a complete glass furnace, around which men and boys plied their ancient trade of blowing glass. The furnace in the center of the blowing room, in the form of a truncated cone, was 100 feet high, with a base diameter of 25 feet.

The sides of the building, the enormous dome, and the ceiling of the exhibition factory were made of glass, somewhat after the fashion of the magnificent Crystal Palace erected in London in the mid-nineteenth century. Crystal blanks made at the exhibition factory were cut and polished before the eyes of an admiring public who eagerly purchased thousands of dollars' worth of Libbey's magnificent cut glass. In full view of thousands of visitors daily, the entire process of spinning glass fibers and weaving them into glistening glass cloth was performed. The spun glass material was used for upholstering divans, chairs, and ottomans, as well as draperies, cushions, lamp shades, and so on, all of which were for sale in the exhibition showrooms.

The "Crystal Art Room" was the main attraction in Libbey's imposing exhibition building. It was resplendent with prismatic hues thrown from myriads of deep incisions in the cut glassware display, and was highlighted by the soft sheen and luster of the spun glass cloth coverings on the furniture, lamp shades, and draperies. The glitter of the cut glass shown in this room was reflected in the huge plate-glass mirrors surrounding the walls, softened somewhat by the ceiling which was bedecked with glass cloth. The whole effect was toned down only slightly by the somber black ebony paneling and encasements. In the center of the room, protected from the curious by a rope of glass link chains, were the most exquisite furnishings manufactured by the spun glass department of the "Crystal Palace." The attention of visitors was drawn particularly to the spun glass cloth *tapisseries* and ceiling decorations, whose value was estimated at $10,000. Wall coverings, lamp shades, and fire screens of spun glass material were decorated with paintings of flower and fruit subjects, and it was pointed out to the visitors that all the woven fabrics could be easily sponged clean without the least detriment to the colors or the goods.

All about the room were examples of the glass cutter's art—ice-cream sets of thirteen pieces encased in brassbound Morocco boxes, sherbet and punch jugs of Roman design, quaint decanters of Venetian shapes, graceful celery trays, ice tubs, novel honey dishes, a high banquet lamp, and richly cut dishes of every conceivable use and pattern. At the entrance to the Crystal Art Room was an old Henry Clay punch bowl of pressed glass (supposedly of the 1812 period, according to a small brochure published in 1893 by the Libbey Glass Company), placed in contradistinction to an elegant cut glass punch bowl manufactured by Libbey and priced at $200, which was no small price in those days.

Cut glass table lamps made by Libbey Glass Co. *Left:* "Sunburst" pattern; *ca.* 1900; height 40 in. *Right:* "Prism" pattern, made in 1892 for the World's Columbian Exposition, height 33 in.
Collection of Toledo Museum of Art

Engraved punch bowl and six cups made by Libbey Glass Co.; copperwheel engraved with hunting scenes; height of bowl 13½ in., of cups 3⅜ in.; gold medal award, World's Columbian Exposition, 1893.

On Saturday, June 10, 1893, Princess Eulalia and Prince Antoine, with their entourage, visited Libbey's Crystal Palace. The princess examined the spun glass dress made for the actress Georgia Cayvan and the magnificent display of cut glass, saying repeatedly, "I am so fond of this cut glass; it is excellent." A few hours after her visit to the exhibition glass factory, she ordered a spun glass dress for herself and appointed the Libbey Glass Company "Glass Cutters to Her Royal Righness Infanta Doña Eulalia of Spain."

The proceeds realized from the sale of cut glass and pressed and blown glass souvenirs and novelties more than justified the expenditures made by the Libby Glass Company to erect their "Crystal Palace." Their cut glass

Left: The "Florence" pattern; patented Apr. 23, 1889; *right:* The "Rhomb" pattern; patented May 7, 1889; both by William A. Anderson; W. L. Libbey & Son Co., Toledo, Ohio.

Left: The "Stratford" pattern; patented Dec. 3, 1889; *right:* The "Wedgemere" pattern; patented July 7, 1891; both by William C. Anderson; W. L. Libbey & Son Co., Toledo, Ohio.

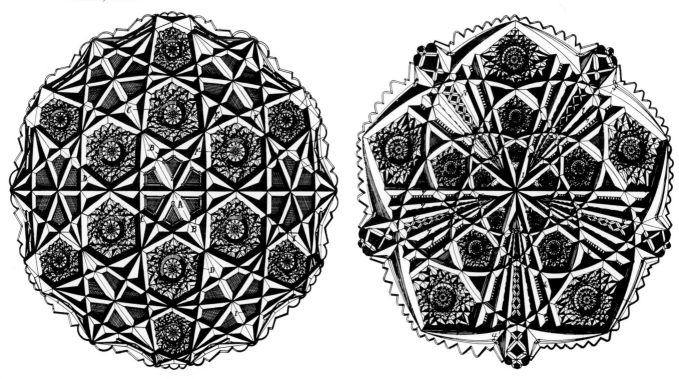

Left: The "Kimberly" pattern; patented Mar. 8, 1892, by William C. Anderson; W. L. Libbey & Son Co., Toledo, Ohio. *Right:* The "Isabella" pattern; patented Jan. 2, 1893, by William C. Anderson; Libbey Glass Co., Toledo, Ohio.

Left: The "Stellar" pattern; patented Feb. 14, 1893; *right:* The "Kite" pattern; patented May 9, 1893; both by William C. Anderson; Libbey Glass Co., Toledo, Ohio.

display was undoubtedly responsible for placing them in the first position in this country as manufacturers of rich cut glassware, and they retained this high station for the entire run of the popularity of this ware.

William C. Anderson continued to design cut glass for W. L. Libbey & Son Company after they moved to Toledo, Ohio. On April 23, 1889, Anderson registered their "Florence" pattern. What we have designated the "Rhomb" pattern was patented by Anderson for W. L. Libbey & Son Company on May 7, 1889.

The "Stratford" pattern was registered by Anderson on December 3, 1889. Anderson's "Wedgemere" design was patented by him on July 7, 1891. On March 8, 1892, his magnificent "Kimberly" pattern was patented.

Anderson's first patent for the newly formed Libbey Glass Company was issued on January 3, 1893, and was known as the "Isabella" pattern. We have given the name "Stellar" to a pattern for cut glass patented by Anderson for the Libbey Glass Company on February 14, 1893. The patent

Left: The "Pentagon" pattern; patented Apr. 23, 1895; *right:* The "Imperial" pattern; patented June 4, 1895; both by William C. Anderson; Libbey Glass Co., Toledo, Ohio.

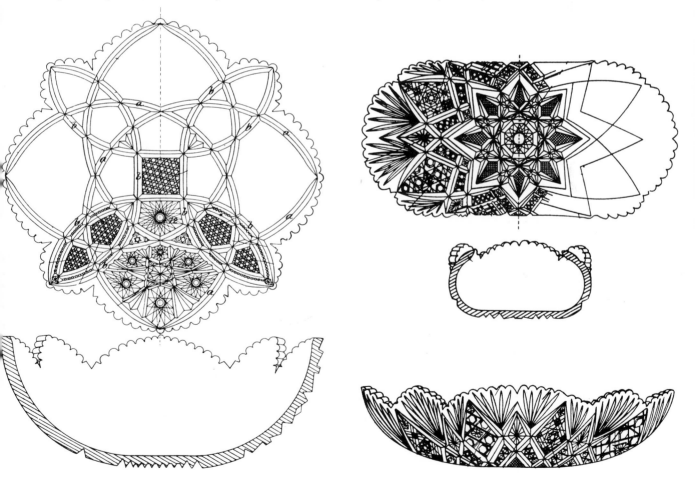

Left: The "Princess" pattern; patented Nov. 12, 1895; *right:* The "Mathilda" pattern; patented May 19, 1896; both by William A. Anderson; Libbey Glass Co., Toledo, Ohio.

Left: The "Corinthian" pattern; patented June 2, 1896; *right:* The "Neola" pattern; patented Apr. 1, 1902; both by William C. Anderson; Libbey Glass Co., Toledo, Ohio.

illustration shows an unusual open handle nappy in this design with the most beautiful and intricate cutting forming a pattern of brilliant rosettes around the edge of the dish.

On May 9, 1893, Anderson patented a design for cut glass which we have named "Kite" because this appellation has been given to certain portions of the design in his patent specifications. Still another pattern for which we have had to supply a common name for the sake of identification was Anderson's "Pentagon" design, patented on April 23, 1895.

The "Imperial" pattern was registered by William Anderson on June 4, 1895, and assigned to the Libbey Glass Company. His handsome "Princess" pattern was registered at the patent office on November 12, 1895. A pattern which we have designated "Mathilda" was registered by Anderson on May 19, 1896. On June 2, 1896, he patented a lovely cut glass design that the Libbey catalogues identify as the "Corinthian" pattern.

"Neola" was the name given to a design for cut glassware which Anderson patented on April 1, 1902. One of the finest examples of this pattern exists in a fabulous cut glass table now in the collection of the Toledo Museum of Art. On April 7, 1903, Anderson registered a design for a cut glass vessel in which he described the design as consisting of "circles and arcs"; in lieu of a proper name for the pattern, we suggest that it be called "Circles and Arcs." A design named "Star and Feather" was the last cut glass pattern patented by Anderson for the Libbey Glass Company: the papers are dated May 8, 1906. Before 1906, and for some time thereafter, William C. Anderson patented

Left: The "Circles and Arcs" pattern; patented Apr. 7, 1903; *right:* The "Star and Feather" pattern; patented May 8, 1906; both by William C. Anderson; Libbey Glass Co., Toledo, Ohio.

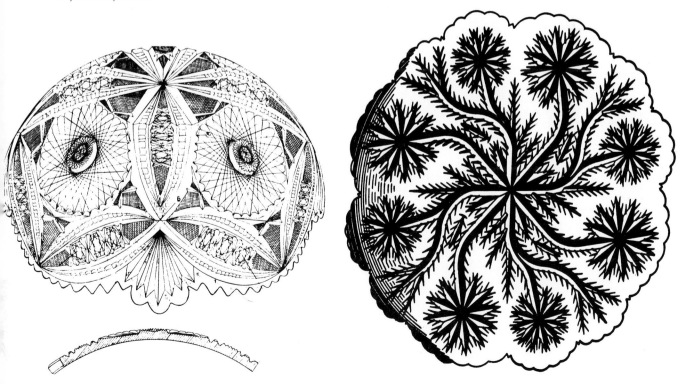

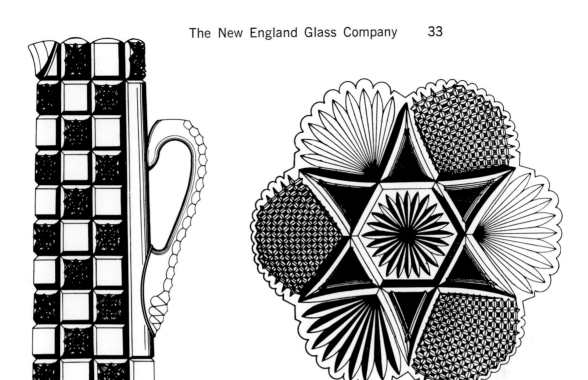

Left: The "Starred Blocks" pattern; patented June 18, 1889; *right:* The "Star and Fan" pattern; patented Nov. 12, 1895; both by Solon O. Richardson, Jr.; Libbey Glass Co., Toledo, Ohio.

several beautiful cut glass designs for the American Cut Glass Company of Chicago, Illinois, and Lansing, Michigan.

Solon O. Richardson, Jr., patented a very chaste cut glass design for the Libbey Glass Company on June 18, 1889. The design consisted of a series of beveled blocks alternating with starred squares of the same proportions. No name for this design could be found in the patent papers, nor could we find it illustrated in any old Libbey cut glass catalogues. We suggest the name "Starred Blocks" be given this pattern until its true name can be discovered. On November 12, 1895, Richardson patented another cut glass design of a rather simple style. The main features of the design appear to be a star in the center of the dish and the fan-shaped edges; this suggests the name "Star and Fan," since the real name for the pattern could not be found in any of the old records.

The over-all pattern of William Marrett's cut glass design, patented on May 25, 1897, suggests a chrysanthemum; in lieu of the real name for this design, we have designated it Libbey's "Chrysanthemum" pattern. In his

Cut glass table in the "Neola" pattern; height 32 in., diameter of top 28 in.; produced at Libbey Glass Co., *ca.* 1902.
Collection Toledo Museum of Art

Left: The "Chrysanthemum" pattern; patented May 25, 1897; *right:* The "Silver Diamond" pattern; patented Jan. 15, 1901; both by William Marrett; Libbey Glass Co., Toledo, Ohio.

Left: The "Sultana" pattern; patented Jan. 15, 1901, by William Marrett; Libbey Glass Co., Toledo. *Right:* Cut glass plate in the "Sultana" pattern; diameter 12 in.

Collection of Toledo Museum of Art

patent enumerations for still another cut glass pattern, dated January 15, 1901, Marrett used the descriptive term "silver diamond" when referring to his design, and since no proper name has yet been found for this design, we have dubbed it the "Silver Diamond" pattern. Libbey's "Sultana" pattern was patented by Marrett on January 15, 1901.

Ornamental bars of different cut glass designs alternating with plain flutes comprised another cut glass pattern patented for the Libbey Glass Company

Left: The "Ornamental Bars" pattern; *right:* The "Festoons and Prism Bands" pattern; both patented Apr. 7, 1903, by William Marrett; Libbey Glass Co., Toledo, Ohio.

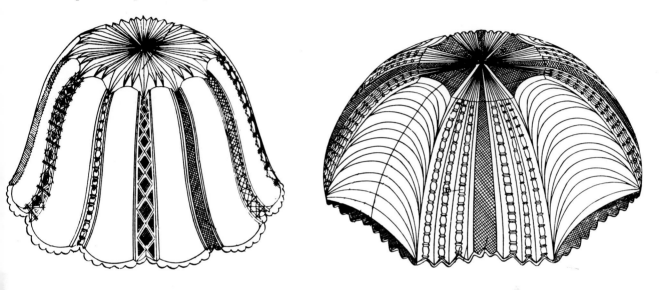

Left: The "Marrett" pattern; patented Apr. 7, 1903, by William Marrett; *right:* The "Wicker" pattern; patented May 8, 1906, by D. F. Spillane; both for Libbey Glass Co., Toledo, Ohio.

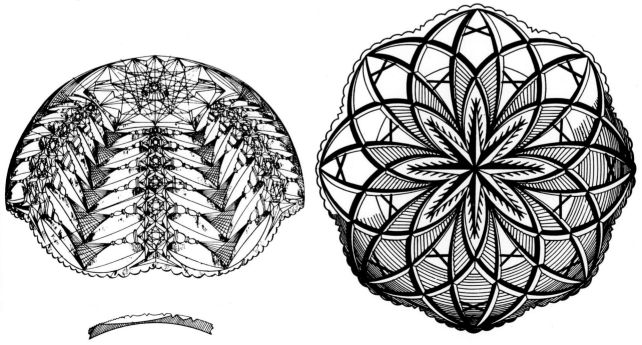

The "Trefoils with Rosettes" pattern; patented
May 8, 1906, by D. F. Spillane; Libbey Glass
Co., Toledo, Ohio.

Cut glass floor lamp; height 4 feet 9½ in.;
Libbey Glass Co., Toledo, Ohio; *ca.* 1904.
Collection of Toledo Museum of Art

by William Marrett on April 7, 1903. We suggest it be called "Ornamental Bars" until its proper name can be determined by further research. On April 7, 1903, Marrett patented a cut glass design which he described in his patent papers as consisting of "festoons and prism bands." Since we cannot find this pattern's name in any old catalogues, it appears best to call it the "Festoons and Prism Bands" design, at least until its original name can be found. The last cut glass design registered by Marrett for the Libbey Glass Company was also patented on April 7, 1903. Once again no name for the design could be found in any old catalogues; we suggest it be called the "Marrett" pattern in honor of its designer.

Dennis F. Spillane patented two designs for cut glassware on May 8, 1906; both were assigned to the Libbey Glass Company. Neither of the designs could be found in any old pattern books or illustrated catalogues and so we have named the first one "Wicker," since it is a relatively simple pattern suggesting wickerwork; the other design is composed of trefoils and rosettes, and this naturally suggested the name "Trefoils with Rosettes."

A great many spectacular pieces of cut glass were made by the Libbey Glass Company. In this list of their noteworthy art works should be included a large cut glass punch bowl presented to President William McKinley by J. D. Robinson, secretary of the Libbey Glass Company. It was designed by William Marrett and required the united efforts of two expert glass cutters

The "St. Louis" punch bowl; height, with base, 24 in.; diameter 25 in.; with 23 matching punch glasses; Libbey Glass Co., Toledo, Ohio; *ca.* 1904.

Collection of Toledo Museum of Art

Collection of Mrs. Vernon E. Cook

Cut and engraved bowl, signed "Libbey"; diameter 10¾ in.; height 3½ in.; *ca.* 1910.

for about four weeks. The two parts, a bowl and a pedestal base, were most appropriately cut in a pattern known as "Stars and Stripes." Six shields composed of thirteen stars and stripes adorned the bowl, while four shields of the same design were carried out on the base; each shield was separated by a group of stars. An elaborately cut floor lamp almost five feet tall was produced about 1904; and a cut glass table in the "Neola" pattern, standing 32 inches high, was made in 1902. The "St. Louis" punch bowl, standing 25 inches high and with 23 matching punch glasses, was cut by Rufus Denman for the World's Fair held in St. Louis, Missouri, in 1904. An engraved punch bowl and matching cups won the Gold Medal award at the World's Columbian Exposition in Chicago in 1893. Fortunately, almost all of these treasures are now in the permanent collection of the Toledo Museum of Art for all to see and enjoy.

Until 1896, Libbey's cut glassware was marked with a paper label displaying an eagle with spread wings and holding in each of its claws three arrows. Around this trademark, in a circular band, were the words "Libbey Cut Glass, Toledo, Ohio," and "Trade Mark." (We have also found these labels on Libbey's painted opal glass novelties and their "Maize" pattern tablewares.) On April 21, 1896, the Libbey Glass Company registered a trademark consisting of the name "Libbey," underscored by a sword with a curved blade. Only the name "Libbey" appeared in their trademark representation which was validated on June 19, 1906. On October 2, 1906, they again reverted to their trademark "Libbey," with a sword beneath the name. A beautiful cut glass plate in the collection of the Toledo Museum of Art attests that "This Trade Mark [was] Cut on Every Piece." The human factors being what they are, we can be almost certain that not every piece of cut glass made at the Libbey factory was etched or engraved with their identifying trademark; however, these instances of unmarked pieces would be relatively few, and would be more likely to occur on an occasional goblet or punch cup from a set, rather than on large and important pieces.

On April 16, 1901, a trademark for wares produced from "shaped (pressed) blanks intended to be made into cut-glass articles" was issued to the Libbey Glass Company. The trademark consisted of "a star inclosed within a circle." The preponderance of pieces so marked verifies the fact that pressed and cut wares were, unfortunately, a major production at the Libbey Glass Company. Their works in Toledo, Ohio, also supplied pressed and blown crystal blanks to cutting shops all over the country.

Three-handled sugar bowl signed with Libbey's pressed-cut trademark—a star within a circle.

Collection of Mrs. Wilbur Griffin

In 1893 the following concerns were agents for the Libbey Glass Company's cut glasswares:

William Arnold, Ann Arbor, Michigan
M. Alexander, Asheville, North Carolina
James Allan & Company, Charleston, South Carolina
C. H. Ankeny & Company, Lafayette, Indiana
D. Abraham, Montgomery, Alabama
E. P. Allan, Newport, Rhode Island
Aler & Garey, Zanesville, Ohio
Baltzell Bros., Altoona, Pennsylvania
E. J. Born & Company, Ashland, Wisconsin
Bartlett Bros., Bradford, Pennsylvania
I. R. Brayton, Buffalo, New York
Bour Bros., Canton, Ohio
C. H. Baddeley, Champaign, Illinois
Burley & Company, Chicago, Illinois
Frank F. Bonnet, Columbus, Ohio
Blackman & Lunkenheimer, Evansville, Indiana
Bloch Queensware Company, Ft. Smith, Arkansas
E. Bixby, Ironton, Ohio
Henry Birks & Sons, Montreal, Quebec, Canada
M. A. Bell, Morenci, Michigan
John Bright, New Haven, Connecticut
Black, Starr & Frost, New York, New York
L. C. Bradley, Norwalk, Ohio
Bell Bros., Ogdensburg, New York
Samuel Burns, Omaha, Nebraska
Bailey, Banks & Biddle, Philadelphia, Pennsylvania
J. B. Blickle, Rochester, Minnesota
Boyd & Stahel, San Diego, California
S. S. Brooks, Tacoma, Washington
M. W. Beveridge, Washington, D. C.
Isaac Bennett, York, Pennsylvania
E. H. Carpenter, Burlington, Iowa
T. Z. Cook & Laurance, Cedar Rapids, Iowa
O. D. Chapman, Coldwater, Michigan
Cooke & Hendricks, Danville, Illinois
O. E. Curtis & Brother, Decatur, Illinois
E. M. Caldcleugh & Brother, Greensboro, North Carolina
Wm. Crawford, La Porte, Indiana
Joseph Coleman, Massillon, Ohio
N. V. Cole, Michigan City, Indiana

Davis Collamore & Company, New York, New York
S. Chapin & Son, Oneida, New York
Callaway, Hook & Co., Salt Lake City, Utah
P. M. Church & Company, Sault Sainte Marie, Michigan
The Clark-Sawyer Company, Worcester, Massachusetts
R. Douglas Crockery Company, Denver, Colorado
J. C. Decker, Flint, Michigan
J. Dolfinger & Company, Louisville, Kentucky
The Dickinson Company, Minneapolis, Minnesota
George W. Dillaway, Muscatine, Iowa
William Dearden, Northampton, Massachusetts
John F. W. Decker, Oshkosh, Wisconsin
S. J. Dutton Company, Oskaloosa, Iowa
The Daudt & Watson Company, Saginaw, Michigan
J. G. DePrez, Shelbyville, Indiana
I. G. Dillon & Company, Wheeling, West Virginia
S. H. Dodge, Ypsilanti, Michigan
A. E. Elbe, Bloomington, Illinois
L. Emery, Jr. & Co., Bradford, Pennsylvania
E. L. Entrikin, Findlay, Ohio
Charles Emerson & Sons, Haverhill, Massachusetts
S. L. Erwin & Company, Honey Grove, Texas
E. E. Ewing, Portsmouth, Ohio
Abram French Company, Boston, Massachusetts
Thomas Fassitt, Easton, Pennsylvania
Funke & Ogden, Lincoln, Nebraska
Ford & Company, Paris, Kentucky
W. R. Farrington, Poughkeepsie, New York
C. B. Fischer, Springfield, Ohio
J. W. Forney, Steubenville, Ohio
Farnsworth & Brinsmaid, Topeka, Kansas
John Goldstone, Alameda, California
George Greyer, Anderson, Indiana
Gluck & Black, Birmingham, Alabama
W. Gros, Delphi, Indiana

Gowans, Kent & Company, Hamilton and Toronto, Ontario, Canada

C. D. Gardner, Manistee, Michigan

Benjamin Guider, Vicksburg, Mississippi

W. F. Hoppe, Alton, Illinois

J. Seth Hopkins & Co., Baltimore, Maryland

T. M. Hemphill & Co., Erie, Pennsylvania

T. F. Heffner, Fremont, Ohio

Harris, Underwood & Doering, Jamestown, New York

C. Hornaday, Keokuk, Iowa

Hope Bros. & Co., Knoxville, Tennessee

Harman & Bell, Lima, Ohio

H. Harroun & Co., Mansfield, Ohio

Frank Haviland, New York, New York

Higgins & Seiter, New York, New York

P. Heliagers, Passaic, New Jersey

Hardy & Hayes, Pittsburgh, Pennsylvania

B. Hinrichs, Racine, Wisconsin

Charles Hall, Springfield, Massachusetts

W. H. Hill, Sunbury, Pennsylvania

A. L. Hall, Titusville, Pennsylvania

George Harris, Vincennes, Indiana

J. C. Illig & Brother, Reading, Pennsylvania

Adam Imig, Sheboygan, Wisconsin

A. K. Jobe, Jackson, Tennessee

T. M. James & Sons, Kansas City, Missouri

A. Jeanneret, Kansas City, Missouri

W. & S. Jack Company, Memphis, Tennessee

Jackson & Ethell, Muncie, Indiana

S. N. Jenkins, Richmond, Indiana

S. R. James, Schenectady, New York

Jessup & Henderson, Troy, New York

Kline & Company, Hazleton, Pennsylvania

C. L. Knapp & Company, Leavenworth, Kansas

A. Kaye, Louisville, Kentucky

Kinnier, Montgomery & Co., Lynchburg, Virginia

A. Kahn, Shreveport, Louisiana

J. C. Klaholt, Springfield, Illinois

Jens Lorenzen Crockery Co., Davenport, Iowa

C. H. Little, Bruce & Co., Dubuque, Iowa

C. H. Little & Co., Freeport, Illinois

H. Leonard, Sons & Co., Grand Rapids, Michigan

A. W. Luckhardt, Johnstown, Pennsylvania

John Larson & Co., Madison, Wisconsin

Louis Bros., Piqua, Ohio

E. Lobe Company, Seattle, Washington

Lucke & Mitchell, Sherbrooke, Quebec, Canada

William Lawton, Wilmington, Delaware

James Mooney & Co., Bangor, Maine

A. S. Miner, Binghamton, New York

McKell & Co., Chillicothe, Ohio

A. Matthews, Colorado Springs, Colorado

W. A. Maurer, Council Bluffs, Iowa

H. P. Mead & Co., Hillsdale, Michigan

Charles Mayer & Co., Indianapolis, Indiana

T. W. Martin, Joliet, Illinois

W. E. McCann & Co., Lexington, Kentucky

George W. Meyer, Meridian, Mississippi

F. Mueller, Muskegon, Michigan

A. & A. F. McMillan, Ottawa, Ontario, Canada

J. McClelland, Peterborough, Ontario, Canada

A. A. Mills, Pittsfield, Massachusetts

Moxie, Sawyer & Co., Portland, Maine

Mermod & Jaccard Jewelry Co., St. Louis, Missouri

George Marshall, Sandusky, Ohio

A. Newsalt, Dayton, Ohio

Nathan, Dohrmann & Co., Fresno, Oakland, San Francisco, Sacramento, Stockton, and Santa Cruz, California

A. D. Norton, Gloversville, New York

M. Nelson & Sons, Marion, Ohio

Ovington Bros., Brooklyn, New York

Olds & Whipple, Hartford, Connecticut

E. Offner, New Orleans, Louisiana

O'Neil Bros. & Co., Port Huron, Michigan

Olds & Summers, Portland, Oregon

D. C. & E. M. Peck, Bridgeport, Connecticut

Pool & Son, Clinton, Iowa

Perkins & Brinsmaid, Des Moines, Iowa

Peters & Herr, Goshen, Indiana

C. Preusser Jewelry Co., Milwaukee, Wisconsin

J. Prugh & Co., Ottumwa, Iowa

B. T. Pace, Salem, Indiana

Oscar Promis, San Jose, California

J. K. Prugh & Co., Sioux City, Iowa

H. S. Pew, Warren, Ohio

W. W. Pearce, Wichita, Kansas

Thomas C. Parker, Wilkes-Barre, Pennsylvania

Charles Reizenstein, Allegheny, Pennsylvania

R. Riddell, Ashtabula, Ohio

Regnier-Shoup Crockery Co., Atchison, Kansas, and St. Joseph, Missouri

Allan Raymond, Battle Creek, Michigan

Roediger Bros. & Co., Belleville, Illinois

G. S. Read & Co., Charlotte, Ohio

The Rathbun Co., Deseronto, Ontario, Canada

Robbins Bros. & Co., Fostoria, Ohio

H. H. Rand, Oil City, Pennsylvania

Robins Glass & Queensware Co., Paducah, Kentucky

Robbin's Crystal Hall, Pueblo, Colorado

Richmond China Co., Richmond, Virginia

D. Rosenberg, Rochester, New York

George M. Rigden, Streator, Illinois

W. M. Ragland & Son, Waco, Texas

Wm. M. Sheldon, Adrian, Michigan

J. P. Stevens & Bro., Atlanta, Georgia

Wm. Schweigert, Augusta, Georgia

Silva & Abbot, Chattanooga, Tennessee

F. Schultze & Co., Cincinnati, Ohio

C. A. Selzer, Cleveland, Ohio

F. G. Smith Sons & Co., Detroit, Michigan

The Smith Bros. Crockery Co., Eau Claire, Wisconsin

W. A. Skinner, Elgin, Illinois

A. Spence & Son, Fond du Lac, Wisconsin

W. H. Spooner, Harrisburg, Pennsylvania

Charles S. Stifft, Little Rock, Arkansas

Snider & Alber, Logansport, Indiana

Charles H. Solomon, Macon, Georgia

E. Schertzinger, Mahanoy City, Pennsylvania

The B. H. Stief Jewelry Co., Nashville, Tennessee

W. H. Sperry & Co., North Adams, Massachusetts

Sohm, Rocker & Weisenhorn, Quincy, Illinois

W. K. Snyder, Shamokin, Pennsylvania

Joseph Seymour, Sons & Co., Syracuse, New York

J. E. Somes, Terre Haute, Indiana

L. Seewald, Tiffin, Ohio

Sherwood & Golden, Utica, New York

James A. Skinner & Co., Vancouver, British Columbia, Canada

Seitz Bros., Williamsport, Pennsylvania

S. A. Schloss & Co., Wilmington, North Carolina

W. G. Smith, Youngstown, Ohio

C. H. Trask, Galesburg, Illinois

Tredick & Co., Kingman, Kansas

J. W. Toms China Co., La Crosse, Wisconsin

Tiffany & Co., New York, New York

R. H. Trask, Ottawa, Illinois

Tilden—Thurber Co., Providence, Rhode Island

W. H. & R. S. Tucker & Co., Raleigh, North Carolina

George F. Tilghman & Co., Spokane Falls, Washington

E. T. Turner & Co., Waterbury, Connecticut

Ueberroth & Co., Bay City, Michigan

Ullrich Bros., Evanston, Illinois

The Van Heusen, Charles Co., Albany, New York

H. F. Vollmer & Co., Los Angeles, California

Weeks & Kingsbury, Akron, Ohio

Williamson & Lipscomb, Danville, Virginia

George H. Wheelock & Co., Elkhart and South Bend, Indiana

H. N. Ward, Ft. Wayne, Indiana

Weise & Holman, Green Bay, Wisconsin

W. E. Wygant, Jackson, Michigan

W. G. Wheelock, Janesville, Wisconsin

G. A. Woodford, Menominee, Michigan

Wilhelm & Graef, New York, New York

J. Wendall and Son, Oswego, New York

J. Wetherall & Son, Parkersburg, West Virginia

C. E. Wheelock & Co., Peoria, Illinois

Wright, Tyndale & Van Roden, Philadelphia, Pennsylvania

H. C. Wisner, Rochester, New York

A. W. Wheelock, Rockford, Illinois

Thomas West & Co., Savannah, Georgia

Wemott, Howard & Co., St. Paul, Minnesota

Weichel & Millar, Scranton, Pennsylvania

G. Judd Williams, Urbana, Ohio

A. Wiggenhorn, Watertown, Wisconsin

The Winn Furniture Co., Winchester, Kentucky

L. H. Yeager & Co., Allentown, Pennsylvania

B. Yehley, Delaware, Ohio

J. A. Zang & Co., Alliance, Ohio

Zimmerlin Bros., Lyons, New York

The following cut glass pattern names were noted in several Libbey Glass Company catalogues:

Catalogue dated June 1, 1896

Corinthian

Empress

Eulalia

Florence (pat. by W. C. Anderson, April 23, 1889)

Harvard (unlike any other pattern bearing this name)

Imperial

Kimberly (pat. by W. C. Anderson, March 8, 1892)

Marcella

Princess (pat. by W. C. Anderson, November 12, 1895)

Prism

Puritana

Star

Toledo

Wedgemere (pat. by W. C. Anderson, July 7, 1891)

Catalogue 24 (undated)

Engraved 0458 Line

Adela (prism cut and engraved floral pattern)

Adela (a variant of the above, with oval cuts and engraved hob-star and floral patterns)

Alma

Anita

Brilliant

Bristol (honeycomb cutting all over)

Carnation

Cherry Blossom (engraved pattern)

Corona

Delphos

Emblem

Floreus (floral and leaf engraved)

Flute (also plain and engraved)

Flute and Mitre Line (#541)

Gem

Glenda

Gloria

Iola

Lorena

Loretta Matt (mat finished)

Melrose (cut and floral design)

Mignon

Orient (prism cutting and engraved work)

Premier (cut and engraved design)

Primrose (cut and engraved with flowers)

Radiant

Regis

Rock crystal (various engraved patterns)

Roslyn (shallow cut floral and leaf designs)

Silex (Libbey's)—Light blown stemware, engraved. Sold at lower prices than their rock crystal. Each piece marked with a paper label reading "Libbey Silex."

Star and Feather (pat. by W. C. Anderson, May 8, 1906)

Sylvan (fine cut and floral engraved designs)

Venetia

Vesta

Victor

Wisteria (engraved with wisteria blossoms and a pair of lovebirds. Rims are diamond-cut.)

Designs from several catalogues dated ca. 1910

Azora

Aztec

Corena

Corinthian (pat. by W. C. Anderson, June 2, 1896)

Ellsmere

Elmore

Estrella

Fern

Iona

Kenmore

Kensington

Libbey (floral cut with mat finish)

Lorraine

New Brilliant

Oriena (floral cut with hob-star motifs)

Ozella

Savona

Sultana (pat. by W. Marrett, January 15, 1901)

Sunset

Waverly

Bay State Glass Company

Incorporation papers for the Bay State Glass Company of East Cambridge, Massachusetts, were dated 1857, but the company was first organized around 1849. Norman S. Cate, Mason Teasdale, and Jacob K. Dunham operated the concern as Norman S. Cate & Company. By 1851 the firm was operating as Cate & Phillips, with Linas A. Phillips as president and Norman S. Cate as treasurer. Amory Houghton, later founder of the Corning Glass Company in Corning, New York, was once a director of the Bay State Glass Company. Stock to the value of $30,000 was divided into 60 shares held by 21 stockholders.

In 1869 the company advertised "Cut Flint Glass Ware in all its varieties," along with other glasswares—"Engraving on glass done with Neatness and Dispatch." In February, 1863, the firm was dissolved, the property and buildings being sold to John P. Squires of Arlington, and William W. Kimball of Boston, Massachusetts.

Boston & Sandwich Glass Company
N. Packwood & Company
Packwood-Northwood Cutting Shop

The Boston & Sandwich Glass Company in Sandwich, Massachusetts, produced a considerable quantity of fine cut glassware beginning soon after its opening in 1825. The Cape Cod factory cut glass in the traditional designs

Pair of cut and engraved decanters presented to Deming Jarves in 1857 at the time of his leaving the Boston & Sandwich Glass Co.; height 14¾ in.

Collection of Henry Ford Museum

common to most English cut glass factories of this same period, and it continued to do so until the day it was closed in 1888. Nehemiah Packwood, an expert glass cutter and designer, was placed in charge of the cutting shop shortly after the Civil War. Packwood had been cutting glass in Stourbridge, England, a great cut glass center in that country, for many years before Deming Jarves induced him to come to America. Many pieces of glass designed and cut by Packwood and his son Nehemiah Packwood, Jr., were once in the collection of Packwood's daughter, Mrs. Lena Clayton, a former resident of Sandwich.

Just when Packwood set up his own cutting shop in Sandwich is not quite clear, but presumably it was either shortly before, or after, the Boston & Sandwich Glass Company closed their doors. N. Packwood & Company were listed as cut glass manufacturers in the 1918 issue of the *American Glass Trade Directory*. The Sandwich Historical Society has two photographs showing this factory with the name clearly visible in a sign over the entrance, and with a group of workers posing in front of the factory. With the help of Mrs. Doris Kershaw of the Sandwich Historical Society, we were able to identify a number of the people shown in one of these photographs, as listed in the caption. Another old photograph of the factory showed that at one time it was known as the Packwood-Northwood Cutting Shop.

Some years ago several drawings for cut glass designs were found in an old trunk in the attic of the Packwood house in Sandwich. These have been presumed to be drawings of cut glass designs made by Nehemiah Packwood for the Boston & Sandwich Glass Company. We hesitate to make such an attribution positively, for the possibility does exist that these drawings were

Celery vase; free blown, cut and engraved; height 6½ in.; Boston & Sandwich Glass Co.; *ca.* 1869.
Collection of Corning Museum of Glass

A group of factory workers in front of N. Packwood & Co. cut glassware building, Sandwich, Cape Cod, Mass.; *ca.* 1890. *Left to right, front row:* Ace McConville, Amy Lovett, Dan Callahan, Eddie Brady, George Brady, Will Humphrey, Raymond Howland, William Smith, Alf Chevall. *Second row:* Phill Murphy, ———, Harry McNamie, Will Coffee, ———, Nicholas Smith, Lester Fish, Ed Humphrey, Al Cunningham. *Back row:* Jim Jennings, ———, Joe Brady, Michael Canary, Eddie McHugh, John Jones (who came from Stourbridge with Packwood), Nehemiah Packwood, Joe Humphrey, and Charlie Pike.

cut glass designs which Packwood may have brought from England, or they could have been sketched for his own cut glass company. For the most part the sketches are of early cut glass patterns—"Silver Diamond," "Nevins," "No. 25," "Prism" (which looks very much like the Bryce Brothers' "Maltese" or "Jacob's Ladder" pattern in pressed glass), "McLuvee Plaid," "Strawberry-Diamond," "Matonia," and "Strawberry"—and it is quite possible that these patterns were once cut at the Boston & Sandwich Glass Company. The aforementioned patterns were still very much in vogue when Packwood opened his own cut glass factory in Sandwich, and there is no reason to believe that he would not continue cutting the old patterns for a market already established for him by his former employer.

No closing date for the Packwood cut glass shop has been determined, but we believe it went out of business soon after 1920.

Mt. Washington Glass Company
Pairpoint Manufacturing Company
Pairpoint Corporation

The Mt. Washington Glass Company was established in New Bedford, Massachusetts, in 1869. The original factory, erected in 1837 by Deming Jarves, was located in South Boston, Massachusetts, between First and Second Streets, near Dorchester Street, and was under the supervision of Capt. Luther Russell. Russell operated the glassworks for Jarves's son George, who at that time was only twelve years old. In 1839, according to a historical account of the firm in the New Bedford Board of Trade's annual report for 1888, the business reverted to George D. Jarves and was carried on by him and John D. Labree, first as Labree & Jarves, and later with Henry Comerais under the firm name of Jarves & Comerais. Jarves & Comerais greatly increased the facilities of the factory by building new furnaces. In 1860, Jarves & Comerais closed the business, and subsequently the factory was rented by Timothy Howe, who proved to be a most energetic manager. Howe was joined by William L. Libbey, and together they managed a very successful glass business. On the death of Howe in 1866, his interest in the firm was purchased by Libbey, but in 1869, as the old factory had become dilapidated, Libbey purchased another glass factory on Prospect Street in New Bedford, Massachusetts, for $35,000. This had been built by the New Bedford Glass Company, a concern that had a short business life because of financial difficulties.

The newly acquired factory in New Bedford was designed by a practical glassmaker and was considered one of the most substantial and completely equipped in the country at that time. It was erected in 1861, and comprised a commodious glasshouse with a 10-pot furnace and an extensive water frontage for landing supplies and shipping goods. On the first floor were well-arranged annealing kilns, a selecting room, a mold room, and an office. On the second floor were a large machine shop and a cutting shop which produced some of the finest cut glass ever made in America. On the third floor were the stock room and the chandelier rooms, where hundreds of brilliantly cut chandeliers of every size and description could be found. The basement level was occupied by the mixing, packing, and engine rooms, and a complete carpenter shop. Two elevators, one for light and one for heavy goods, connected all four levels of the building.

Outside the main factory were several other large buildings. One, three stories in height, was occupied by the decorating shop and was fitted out completely with all the necessary adjuncts for this sort of work, including three large kilns for the firing of the decorated wares. There was a cooper's shop where all the packing cases for the goods were made, a large storage building for the packed glassware, also clay and pot rooms, a blacksmith's shop, and a boiler house. The company maintained stables on an adjacent lot.

After the business was transferred to New Bedford, it was conducted under its original name, the Mt. Washington Glass Works. Soon an increase of trade called for more capital, and Capt. Henry Libbey became associated with the business, the firm name being W. L. Libbey & Company. On March 25, 1871, the Libbeys sold out to a stock company—the Mt. Washington Glass Company—for cash and mortgages totaling $60,000, thereby realizing a profit of $25,000 on the original investment. The stock company was formed with a capital of $100,000, which afterward was increased to $150,000. William L. Libbey was appointed agent for the newly formed company and Capt. Henry Libbey was made superintendent of the works.

In 1872, William L. Libbey resigned to accept the agency of the New England Glass Company and Capt. Henry Libbey assumed the management of the New Bedford factory. On July 23, 1872, a patent for pressed glassware was issued to "William L. Libbey & Brother" of New Bedford, Massachusetts, indicating a business connection with the Mt. Washington Glass Company at that time. Although the business of the company at this period was quite diversified, the general depression of 1873 greatly reduced their capital. Capt. Henry Libbey resigned in 1874 and for a while the factory was closed.

In the fall of 1874 the Mt. Washington Glass Company resumed business, and the management was placed in the capable hands of Frederick S. Shirley. The company was reorganized in 1876, with A. H. Seabury as president, Frederick S. Shirley, as agent, and Robert G. Tobey as treasurer. Robert King was appointed glasshouse manager.

In 1881 the facilities of the factory were again greatly increased by the erection of an additional glasshouse on the south end, provided with an eight-pot furnace.

On July 17, 1887, Seabury died. He was succeeded by William J. Rotch. Andrew Snow, Jr., who had grown up in the business, was elected treasurer and took an active part in the management of the firm.

In 1880 the Pairpoint Manufacturing Company was organized; a three-story building was erected on land adjoining the Mt. Washington Glass Company, with power supplied from the latter concern, which was really the parent institution. Although the ground area was only 120 by 40 feet and the space necessarily limited, a complete line of staple and fancy articles in silver plate was produced and placed on the market. Edward D. Mandell was the first president of the new concern, and T. J. Pairpoint its superintendent. The capital stock was originally $100,000, but in July, 1887, this was increased to $400,000, and to $1,000,000 in 1896. Pairpoint resigned as superintendent on April 1, 1885, and was succeeded by Thomas A. Tripp. Seabury resigned as treasurer in May, 1885, and Tripp also succeeded him. In 1898 the officers of the firm were Clarence A. Cook, president; Thomas A. Tripp, general manager and treasurer.

On July 14, 1894, "in consideration of one dollar and other valuable considerations," the Pairpoint Manufacturing Company bought out the parent company, the Mt. Washington Glass Company, making it an integral part of the Pairpoint Manufacturing Company. This enlarged the floor area to an equivalent of an avenue 40 feet wide and one mile in length. Financial difficulties forced a reorganization of the two companies in 1900, which evolved into the formation of the Pairpoint Corporation. At this time the company was employing 350 glass cutters and about 100 men in the blowing room. In 1918 the *American Glass Trade Directory* listed A. G. Pierce, Jr., president; C. A. Cook, treasurer; and Fred R. Fish, factory manager. At this time only two furnaces were operating.

The company had been advertising "superior polishing brushes for glass cutters" since 1885 and had been marketing crystal blanks for cutting for some years before that date. Since the Mt. Washington Glass Company also produced pressed glass, it is conceivable that the firm went into the production of pressed, or figured, blanks for cutting when this practice came into general use around the turn of the century.

In 1929 the Pairpoint Corporation suffered severe business losses from which it never fully recovered. Thereafter the glassworks were used by J. & B. Kenner, Incorporated, a salvage company. In 1938 it was reopened as a glassworks by Robert M. Gundersen and was known as the Gundersen Glass Works. When Gundersen died in 1952, it became a part of the National Pairpoint Company and was known as the Gundersen-Pairpoint Glass Works.

Left: Design for a cut glass vase; patented Dec. 7, 1875; *right:* Design for cut glass dishes; patented Aug. 8, 1882; both by Frederick S. Shirley.

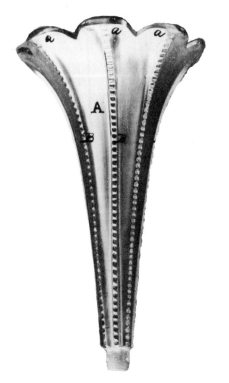

In 1957 the works were moved to East Wareham, Massachusetts, by Robert Bryden, its manager, where it was called the Pairpoint Glass Works.

According to the New Bedford Board of Trade's annual report for 1888, some of the richest cut glassware was manufactured at the Mt. Washington glassworks, which at that time boasted that it was the only factory in the country where crystal chandeliers were made complete. Cut glass was a specialty with the company and their patrons included some of the most celebrated dealers in cut glass in the world. In 1888 only about 50 men were employed in the cutting room, and in addition to the more common patterns, the company patented a number of special designs, including the "Electric," "Thurber," and "Dauntless" patterns. These designs were copyrighted to protect the company from pressed glass manufacturers of that period, who cribbed the popular patterns for their cheaper pressed wares. Among the hundreds of beautiful cut glass articles always on hand in their showrooms was a magnificent toilet table made almost entirely of cut glass. It was piped for gas or could be wired for electricity, and its value was fixed at that time at $500. At the Centennial Exhibition in Philadelphia in 1876, the Mt. Washington Glass Company exhibited a crystal fountain, crystal toilet bottles, prismatic candelabra, chandeliers, vases, and table glassware—all richly cut—for which they won an award.

Many patents for cut glass designs and cut glass articles were registered by members of the Mt. Washington Glass Company and their successor, the Pairpoint Corporation. On December 7, 1875, Frederick S. Shirley patented a lily-shaped vase with heavy ribs running from the base of the vase to its flared top. Each rib was notched or serrated throughout its length, and these notches were highly polished. The rest of the vase was ground down to a mat finish. The vase was intended to be mounted on a standard, such as the one patented by Frederick Ratcliff for the Mt. Washington Glass Company on June 12, 1883, which was in the form of an elephant. We have seen the same vase with an applied glass foot (called a "Tappan vase") in their advertisements in the *Crockery and Glass Journal* for this same period.

Shirley patented a design for cut glass dishes and other tablewares on August 8, 1882, which appeared in several illustrated catalogues issued by his company. A simple star-shaped motif was cut into the bottom of the vessel and the sides of the dish were fashioned with deep grooves, as is shown in the patent illustration. One of the main features of Shirley's design was the indentations, which were evenly spaced around the side of the dish. According to Shirley's patent enumerations, these dishes were produced in various sizes and in round, square, and oval shapes.

Dishes and bowls were beautifully cut from blanks shaped like the illustration which accompanied Frederick Shirley's design patent dated July 14, 1885. The scalloped edge of the dishes was separated by deeply cut grooves which extended from the base of the bowl to the rim. Illustrations of these bowls in trade catalogues showing the company's cut glass wares indicate that the panels between the deeply cut grooves were ornamented with bright cuts in

Left to right: Cut and engraved goblet with ruby-flashed plaque; presented to Frederick Shirley *ca.* 1880. Egg-shaped sugar shaker in "Strawberry-Diamond" pattern; Mt. Washington Glass Co.; *ca.* 1885.

conventional designs, such as the "Russian," "Strawberry-Diamond," and "Old English Diamond" patterns.

The "Electric" pattern was patented by Andrew Snow, Jr. on June 7, 1887. The main feature of the design was a circular band composed of angulated ribbons and fanlike figures, as can be seen in the patent illustration. A bowl in this pattern was shown in an old photograph of the Mt. Washington Glass Company's exhibition stand at the New Bedford Industrial Exposition in 1887.

On March 12, 1889, Frederick Shirley patented a cut glass pattern composed of cushion-shaped squares. Shirley suggested, in his patent specifications, that the table surface of the squares could be ornamented by crosscutting or star figures. The pattern appears in their illustrated catalogues in ice tubs, rose bowls, decanters, cream and sugar sets, stemware, cologne bottles, cruets, and dishes of every shape and size. In lieu of its original name, which is not known, we have designated this their "Cushion" pattern.

Thomas Singleton, Jr. assigned a patent to the Mt. Washington Glass Company on November 17, 1891, for a cut glass pattern which consisted of a series of fan-shaped and diamond-shaped figures combined with stars, as is shown in the patent drawings. The pattern was originally designed for cut glassware but Singleton states in his specifications that it was also applicable to pressed glassware. At this late date very little pressed glass was made at the New Bedford factory, but before 1886 it produced pressed glass in great quantities. (One of the finest examples of Mt. Washington pressed glass was their patented inkwell registered by Samuel Darling of Providence, Rhode Island, on August 30, 1887, which was pressed in jet-black glass. They also produced pressed black glass blanks for Darling's patented inkwell, which were cut and engraved with different patterns, another indication that they may have produced pressed and figured blanks for cut glass in the late period.) The character of Singleton's design is such that we feel certain it was confined entirely to the cut wares in which the Mt. Washington Glass Company excelled. For lack of a proper name, we have designated this design Singleton's "Diamond and Star" pattern.

Singleton registered another cut glass design on January 31, 1893, which he described as having "horseshoe shaped indentations" emanating from the center of the dish and forming apexes near the rim of the dish. Because this design's name is not known, we suggest it be called the "Horseshoe" pattern. Singleton's "Horseshoe" pattern was assigned to the Mt. Washington Glass Company on the day it was issued.

In describing another design for a cut glass dish patented by Singleton, the patentee spoke of the "rose" and "kite-shaped" figures he used as the main

Left: The "Electric" pattern ("Angulated Ribbon"); designed by Andrew Snow, Jr.; patented June 7, 1887. *Right*: The "Cushion" pattern; patented Mar. 12, 1889, by Frederick S. Shirley.

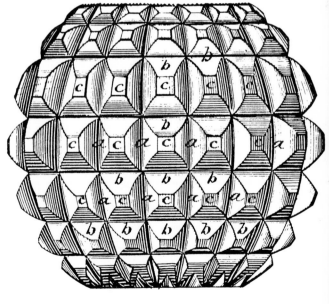

Left: The "Diamond and Star" pattern; patented Nov. 17, 1891; *right:* The "Horseshoe" pattern; patented Jan. 31, 1893; both by Thomas Singleton, Jr.

Left: The "Rose and Kite" pattern; patented Jan. 31, 1893; *right:* The "Daisy" pattern; patented Feb. 7, 1893; both by Thomas Singleton, Jr.

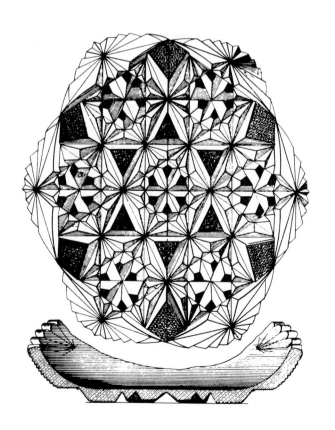

features of the design. Since the original name is unknown, we call it the "Rose and Kite" pattern; it was patented on January 31, 1893. Although the specifications refer to this lovely design as being applicable only to glass dishes, it was most certainly adaptable to many tablewares, bowls, vases, and other cut glass fancies of the late nineteenth century.

Singleton's "Daisy" pattern was patented by him on February 7, 1893. Throughout his patent enumerations Singleton referred to the design as a "daisy shaped figure, the points of which extend nearly to the rim of the dish." And although the patent states that this was a design for a glass dish, it is obvious that it could have been used for stemware and decorative articles of almost every description.

The common nomenclature "Bristol Rose" has already been applied to another cut glass design for a dish patented by Thomas Singleton, Jr. on March 14, 1893. In this design the central motif is a large seven-pointed star, each point ending in a fan-shaped ornament. Between the points of the star a large brilliantly cut rosette has been placed, as is shown in the patent illustration.

By 1894 Singleton's designs for cut glassware had taken on a different character. The patterns were less elaborate and more easily interpreted in stemware and other table glassware. On July 24, 1894, Thomas Singleton, Jr.

Left: The "Bristol Rose" pattern; patented Mar. 14, 1893; *right:* The "Fan and Diamond" pattern; patented July 24, 1894; both by Thomas Singleton, Jr.

patented a rather ordinary cut glass design which depends largely on a series of fan-shaped and diamond-shaped ornaments arranged around the edge of dishes and goblets, as is shown in his patent illustration. In the case of dishes and bowls, the center of the vessel was ornamented with a large scintillating rosette. This "Fan and Diamond" pattern resembles some pressed glass patterns of this same period, and because it lacks any really distinctive feature, it will be difficult to identify in antique shops.

Singleton made several references to the "ox-bow curves" he used in his design for a cut glass vessel patented on July 24, 1894. As a means of identification, and because the original name for this pattern is unknown, we have applied this appellation to this design. The "Ox-bow" pattern was another design which lent itself well to stemmed glassware, plates, and bowls for table use. The kite-shaped figures in the design were cut with diamonds to add brilliance, and softness was achieved with fan-shaped motifs, which are shown along the rim of the bowl in the patent illustration. This was the last design patent Singleton assigned to the Mt. Washington Glass Company.

On November 6, 1894, Thomas Singleton, Jr. assigned a cut glass design patent to the Pairpoint Manufacturing Company. The main feature of this design was a diamond-shaped figure ornamented by a series of crosscuts that produced small diamond-shaped heads, thereby giving each figure a marked

Left: The "Ox-bow" pattern; patented July 24, 1894; *right:* The "Priscilla" pattern; patented Nov. 6, 1894; both by Thomas Singleton, Jr.

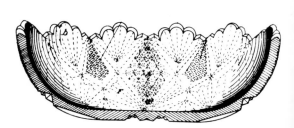

Left: The "Bull's-eye" pattern; patented Jan. 18, 1898; *right:* The "Punties and Prisms" pattern; patented Sept. 10, 1901; both by Andrew Snow, Jr.

and ornamental appearance. These ornamented motifs were arranged around the body of an article in connection with a series of kite-shaped and fan-shaped figures, as is shown in the patent illustration. The old "Strawberry-Diamond" cut is given a new twist in this, Singleton's only design for the Pairpoint Manufacturing Company. It was illustrated in an original Pairpoint catalogue as their "Priscilla" pattern.

Late in the cut glass era the patterns produced at the Pairpoint Manufacturing Company became less and less complicated. The firm explained this change in style as the result of a natural tendency on the part of the public to want less fussy designs. The truth of the matter was that the cutters demanded more money for their time spent on a piece, and patterns had to be designed for quicker execution. One of these less complicated designs was patented by Andrew Snow, Jr. on January 18, 1898; it consisted of a many-pointed star in the middle of the base of the dish, surrounded by a circle of upwardly extending rays; added to this was a marginal row of plain-surfaced depressions, or punties, arranged on the outer sides of the dish. On this same date Snow was issued another design patent for a similar design in which the

Left: The "Tulip" pattern; patented Oct. 27, 1908; *right*: The "Late Daisy" pattern; patented May 11, 1909; both by Albert Steffin.

punties were arranged up and down a glass receptacle intended as a bottle or vase. Between the rows of graduated punties were rows of prismlike ribs, as the patent illustration shows. This has been given the common name of "Bull's-eye" pattern.

On September 10, 1901, Snow patented still another design composed of punties and prisms arranged in a pattern of simple lines, as is shown in his patent drawings. We have named this design "Punties and Prisms" because the factory name for this pattern is unknown at this time.

Albert Steffin, the manager of the old Mt. Washington Glass Company's decorating department, stayed on with the firm after it was absorbed into the Pairpoint Corporation. On October 27, 1908, he designed a very beautiful cut glass pattern which we have named "Tulip." The design of tulips and leaves have been engraved in a masterful way, the leaves of the plant being notched with many prisms to reflect the light, while the flowers have been engraved with tiny hatch cutting and outlined with deep miter cutting, as is shown in the patent drawing. Steffin also designed the pattern which we have named "Late Daisy." In his specifications, dated May 11, 1909, Steffin relates that portions of the "daisy flowers reach the top of the rim of the vessel, the rim taking on the shape of the outer edge of the flowers," as can be seen in the patent drawings. Simple miter-cut leaves completed the design.

The "Rose" pattern, another Steffin design for cut glass, was patented on May 18, 1909. Realistically engraved wild roses, with buds and leaves on a thorny stem, have been crossed with branches of deeply cut leaves, as is shown in the patent illustration that accompanied Steffin's registration. Along the stems are short branches terminating in buds, and there are also short stems and leaves.

On June 22, 1909, Carl E. Morde patented his "Anemone" pattern and assigned it to the Pairpoint Corporation. The design consisted of a combination of leaves and stalks with "anemone shaped flowers," as the patent illustration shows.

A design patent for a gas and lamp shade was issued to Frederick S. Shirley on July 5, 1881. In the photographic illustration accompanying this design patent, there were shown two cut and engraved lamp shades with a design of flowers, punties, and fanciful scrolls. Although the patent covered the form of the shade, and not the decoration, still they both illustrate another of the Mt. Washington Glass Company's cut glass designs.

On January 30, 1883, Shirley registered the trademark "Russian Crystal." This mark was used on the Mt. Washington Glass Company's cut glassware for several years after this date. It was usually affixed to cut glass articles in the form of a paper label, consequently very few pieces of Mt. Washington's cut glassware will be found with this original identification still adhering to the article.

In a catalogue issued by the Pairpoint Manufacturing Company in 1894 were many cut glass pieces shown with their silver- and gold-plated utensils and tablewares. Most of the inkwells, cruets, celery holders, pickle jars, and small dishes were cut with designs common to many American and foreign manufacturers of cut glass. There were a few large bowls and dishes which were set in silver-plated frames and epergnes that were very brilliantly cut, but again, the designs were not positively attributable to the New Bedford glassworks, and since the catalogue did report that some of the inserts were "imported," it would be difficult to distinguish between the imported

Left: The "Rose" pattern; patented May 18, 1909, by Albert Steffin. *Right:* Pairpoint's "Anemone" pattern; patented June 22, 1909, by Carl E. Morde.

Grape juice bowl in Pairpoint Corp.'s "Garland" pattern; *ca.* 1900.

cut glass pieces and those supplied by their own cutting shop. At this time foreign imports of cut glasswares were making serious inroads on domestic products because they could be purchased much cheaper than American-made cut glass.

Several photographs used as illustrations in the Mt. Washington Glass Company's cut glass catalogues were found some years ago. Most of the articles shown in these photographs were cut in the "Russian," "Harvard," "Strawberry-Diamond," " Strawberry-Diamond and Fan," "Flat Diamond," "Nailhead Diamond," "Step Cut," and "Shell" patterns. There were also

Syrup jugs in Pairpoint Corp.'s (*left to right*) "Wheeler," "Sultan," and "Newton" patterns.

The "Caldonia" pattern; Pairpoint Corp.; *ca*. 1900.

several examples of etched and engraved glassware decorated with designs of fern fronds and other plants and flowers indigenous to the marshy area around New Bedford at that time. Hanging cornucopia vases and three-part bird-shaped relish dishes were among the most bizarre items shown in these old photographs, but there were also many odd-shaped nappies and bowls, some formed like a star, a crescent, or a scallop shell; still others were round, or square, or boat-shaped. Punch bowls in many sizes and very large trays were also included, along with stemware in several patterns, with pitchers, finger bowls and plates to match, salt and pepper dispensers, mustard pots and individual salt dishes, celery vases, sectioned relish dishes, baskets, covered cheese and butter dishes, covered cooky jars, candlesticks, compotes, and many beautiful vases and centerpiece bowls.

Smith Brothers

The brothers Alfred E. Smith and Harry A. Smith established a glass decorating shop in New Bedford, Massachusetts, about 1878. Their factory was located at 30 William Street, and for many years they produced a fine quality of decorated opal glass shades, vases, lamps, and tablewares. When the rage for cut glasswares began to manifest itself, they opened a glass cutting shop of their own, using crystal blanks supplied by the Mt. Washington Glass Company and their successor, the Pairpoint Corporation. Those cut glass designs attributable to Smith Brothers bear a striking resemblance to cut wares produced at the Mt. Washington glassworks. We are able to illustrate a few pieces from the collection of some of Alfred E. Smith's descendants; these articles date from about 1885.

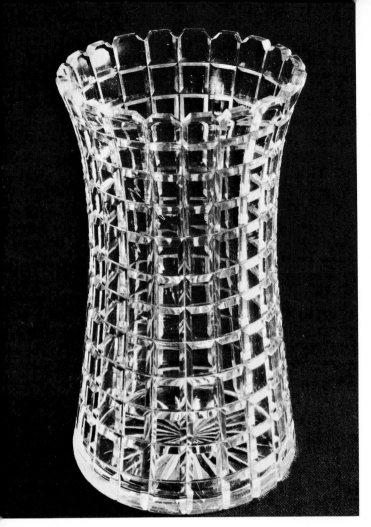

Collection of Miss Ethel A. Tripp
Left: Celery vase cut at Smith Brothers factory, New Bedford, Mass. *Right:* Rose bowl cut at Smith Brothers factory, New Bedford, Mass.
Collection of Mrs. Helen Smith McKenzie

Smith Brothers won several awards for their cut glass at the New Bedford Exhibition of 1889; they were represented in the Libbey Glass Company's fabulous exhibition factory during the World's Columbian Exposition of 1893, where they showed decorated opal glass novelties and souvenirs, and a few cut glass pieces of their own design.

Blackmer Cut Glass Company
A. L. Blackmer Company, Incorporated

In 1894, Arthur L. Blackmer founded the Blackmer Cut Glass Company in New Bedford, Massachusetts. The cutting shop was located at 169 North Second Street and was complete with large showrooms and an office. A second building, acquired later, was located on a lot adjoining the original factory. In the beginning Blackmer was listed in the business archives as sole owner and manager of the cut glass company. After the turn of the century, perhaps about 1902, the business had become a corporation, A. L. Blackmer Company, Incorporated, with John H. Lawrence as president and Arthur L. Blackmer as treasurer and manager. Blackmer was also very active as a salesman for his company, and his daughter Gladys remembers how very often her father was on the road selling his fine cut glass to jewelry shops, department and specialty stores. At the time the business was liquidated, in 1916, the factory occupied the original pair of two-story wooden frame buildings on North Second Street; in fact, the buildings were still standing in 1964.

Arthur L. Blackmer was born in Rochester, Massachusetts, on March 18, 1865. His ancestors on both his father's and mother's side were among the founders and most prominent settlers in the old Wareham and Rochester townships in colonial Massachusetts. After his father died the family moved to New Bedford, where Arthur completed his elementary and high school education. Later he took a business course in Scoffields Commercial College in Providence, Rhode Island. For about one year he was employed by the Old Colony Railroad, and later he engaged in various mercantile pursuits until 1885, when he went into the employ of the Mt. Washington Glass Company. During the nine years of his employment at the Mt. Washington glassworks (four years in the shipping department, and five years as paymaster and general assistant), he gained a thorough knowledge of the manufacture and sale of fine cut glass. Blackmer represented Ward 2 in the New Bedford Common Council from 1894 to 1897. In 1896 he was elected to the presidency of this body and was a member of different boards and committees of the city government. In 1887 he married Susan A. Gardner of Acushnet, Massachusetts, and they had one daughter, Gladys, who still resided in New Bedford in 1964. At the time of his death, February 12, 1937, Blackmer was a trustee of Trinity Methodist Church in New Bedford and a life member of Aleppo Temple (Shriner), Boston, Massachusetts.

After he established his cut glass business, Blackmer traveled extensively both as salesman for his company and as a representative of the National Association of Cut Glass Manufacturers. His territory covered nearly the whole of the United States. In the factory and showrooms in New Bedford he employed about 24 men, the majority being skilled mechanics and cutters. His foreman was a Scotsman named MacManus, and most of the workers were also from the British Isles, where glass cutting along the traditional lines had been a well-founded profession for more than a century. The office staff consisted of two girls, Ada the stenographer and typist, and Mabel, who assisted the bookkeeper. Both girls washed and wrapped glass in the interim of clerical duties and the bookkeeper served as acting manager during the weeks when Blackmer was on the road. Blackmer employed a regular designer, but his daughter reports that her father worked alongside this man, giving him suggestions. Some of the cut glass patterns were designed in accordance with the demands of Blackmer's customers for cheaper wares, and these do not come up to the high standards he prescribed for his products; however, he had several superbly cut patterns, such as "Constellation," "Superba,"

Blackmer cut glass. *Left to right:* vase, "Constellation" pattern; lemonade glass, "Columbia" pattern;
champagne glass, pattern unknown.

A compote in Blackmer's "Sultana" pattern.

"Roman," and "Sultana," that are classic examples of American cut glass of the Brilliant Period. The "Columbia" pattern was by far the most popular design cut by this factory. Two catalogues loaned to the author by Gladys Blackmer illustrated many of the company's cut glass patterns, but undoubtedly these were not the only designs produced at the Blackmer works.

For a few years after he closed his own cut glass factory, Blackmer was employed as a salesman for the Hunt Glass Company of Corning, New York. Blackmer was a good salesman, but the popularity of cut glass was on the wane by that time, and being in poor health, he retired from the business entirely.

The following cut glass patterns were produced by the Blackmer Cut Glass Company:

Acme	Marlo
Abington	Mavis
Aetna	Medina
Albemarle	Milton
Almont	Myrtle
Clarendon	Newport
Cleveland	Newton
Clifton	Norma
Columbia	No. 5000
Concord	No. 5005
Constellation	Oregon
Corsair	Oswego
Crescendo	Oxford
Criterion	Pansy
Crystalba	Plymouth
Derby	Portia
Dictator	Prudence
Doris	Quincy
Edith	Quinton
Elite	Radcliffe
Estelle	Rambler
Eudora	Richmond
Faustina	Roman
Fern	Ruby
Floral	Selma
Florence	Starling
Gem	Sultana
Gothic	Superba
Hanover	Thora
Hawthorne	Triton
Homer	Troy
Iola	Vesta
Irene	Violet
Iris	Waverly
Lyndale	Weyland
Magnet	Worthy
Marlborough	Wylie

Thatcher Brothers

In 1880, George T. Thatcher left the employ of the Boston & Sandwich Glass Company after ten years of service there, and went to the Mt. Washington Glass Company in New Bedford, Massachusetts. It is believed that he also worked for a Dr. Flowers at the Vasa Murrhina Art Glass Company's works on Cape Cod, Massachusetts. About 1883 there was a strike at the Mt. Washington glassworks and Thatcher and four or five of his glass cutter friends went to work in the cutting department of Smith Brothers in New Bedford. Thatcher was made foreman of the Smith Brothers cutting shop.

In 1886, George Thatcher bought out the cutting department of Smith Brothers and started a place of his own on Purchase Street in New Bedford. Later, in 1888, he moved to the old Hathaway & Soule shoe factory building on Second and North Streets in New Bedford, and then he sent for his brother Richard to join him about 1891. Richard Thatcher had been working for the Corning Glass Works in Corning, New York, until he joined his brother George in a partnership as Thatcher Brothers. George Thatcher was the head of the business and his brother Richard was general superintendent. They employed only 18 men in 1891.

In 1894, Thatcher Brothers built a large factory in Fairhaven, Massachusetts, a suburb of New Bedford. The building was three stories high, 100 feet long and 40 feet wide, and was painted dark red. It was located just south of Pease Street and ran from Main to Middle Streets. Besides this three-story factory there was a large two-story glass blowing room, with engine and boiler rooms added in 1896. Six pots with 300-pound capacities were later enlarged with the addition of four more pots of 50-pounds capacity each. A carload of tools and equipment was purchased from the defunct Boston & Sandwich Glass Company by George Thatcher and these additional facilities made Thatcher Brothers one of the largest producers of cut glass in the northeast.

By 1900 there were about 75 people in the employ of Thatcher Brothers; many of them came from Sandwich. They maintained a large showroom on the first floor of their building, where all kinds of cut glass articles were displayed for the public and the trade. No salesmen were employed by this company; instead, the goods were submitted as samples to various retail outlets, and many buyers came to their showrooms in Fairhaven. Crystal canes, known as "friendship canes," were one of the novelties made at this factory. The canes were shaped like a man's walking stick, and friends were supposed to tie a bow of pretty ribbon on the handle; thus decorated, the friendship cane was hung on the wall of one's sitting room or bedroom. Thatcher Brothers' glass was sold all over the United States and some was shipped abroad. The factory operated until the panic of 1907, when nearly $70,000 worth of goods were in the process of being made; almost every order was canceled and the com-

Thatcher Brothers cut glass lamp;
height 22 in.

Collection of Mrs. Elizabeth Maud

Thatcher Brothers cut glass. *Left to right:* vase 13 in. tall; bowl, diameter 8¼ in.; vase 10½ in. tall.

pany had to close down the business. The factory building burned down on June 21, 1918.

On December 31, 1895, a trademark was issued to Thatcher Brothers which included the legend "Diamond Finish"; it had been used on their products since about August, 1894. The trademark labels, printed in red ink, were affixed to each piece of cut glassware before it left the factory.

Mackey Cut Glass Works

The *American Glass Trade Directory* of 1918 listed the Mackey Cut Glass Works of New Bedford, Massachusetts, but an exhaustive search of that city's records and directories failed to reveal any information on this company. Long-time residents of New Bedford could not remember this cut glass concern; however, some of them reported that a Mr. Mackey was employed by the Pairpoint Corporation for a short period on two different occasions.

Union Glass Company

The Union Glass Company was established in Somerville, Massachusetts, in 1851 by Amory Houghton and his associates. At this time the area around Cambridge and Somerville was considered one of the largest glass-producing centers in America. Later Houghton sold his interest in the firm and eventually formed the Corning Glass Works in Corning, New York. Julian De Cordova took over the Union works and the business steadily increased. New equipment was installed and about 200 men were employed by the factory.

The *Somerville Journal* on November 27, 1875, reported

the gathering of thirty people to watch the blowing of a glass shade to be sent to the Centennial Exposition in Philadelphia (1876). Thomas Degnan was the principal man in the work of blowing shades, the first of which was five feet in height and 63 inches in circumference. The second one was 43 inches high and 63 inches in circumference. But neither of these was satisfactory. A third and fourth had flaws, but the fifth attempt was a successful one, and the Centennial shade for the Philadelphia Exposition was 48 inches high and 74 inches in circumference, and weighed nearly 75 pounds. One of the company's greatest feats was the forming of a giant cut glass bowl on a high standard ordered by Tiffany & Company of New York City, and when cut [was] valued by them at $3,000. Many other unique pieces have been turned out by the company and may be found in the most palatial hotels and residences in the United States.

Its vases and bowls, tumblers, pitchers, all sorts of bric-a-brac and tablewares in cut glass are distributed all over the country. Orders came from the greatest art establishments for particular pieces of glass, sometimes colossal, sometimes dainty and delicate.

The specialty of the company was cut glass blanks, and they were cut into glittering objects of beauty at leading establishments for this particular branch of work, but there were some exquisite specimens of mold-blown vases and dishes, as well as beautiful opalescent and enamel glass.

In the making of the best cut glass ware, the Union Glass Company had no competitor nearer than Virginia or Pennsylvania. All the fine art, the exquisite touches of color and decoration were brought to a high state of development at this factory. Not infrequently a large piece of cut glass had to be done over several times before a perfect result was obtained. This is one of the reasons why cut glass was expensive; but considering the education and skill required from the moment the melted glass is taken from the pot until the cutter has given the last touch, the wonder is that the price was kept down so low.

The work of the Union Glass Company has contributed in no small measure to the triumph of American cut glass over European wares. Only 20 years ago (1855) imported cut glass was considered the superior of the American, but conditions were reversed. American cut glass is the best and is so recognized even in Europe.

In 1885, David Walsh operated a cutting shop in conjunction with the Union Glass Company, using their blanks. The Somerville factory issued several large illustrated catalogues showing their crystal blanks for cutting: baskets, bowls, vases, bottles, and all kinds of tablewares were available from this factory and they did a brisk business in these wares until they closed in 1927; the buildings were razed in 1933.

In 1918 the *American Glass Trade Directory* listed the following officers of the Union Glass Company: Julian De Cordova, president; W. T. Rich, vice president; J. M. Hill, secretary; W. S. Blake, treasurer and general manager; J. Shaughnessy, factory manager; and Charles H. Glazier, sales manager. In 1918 they were operating three furnaces with a capacity of 33 pots of molten glass.

David Walsh

David Walsh operated a cutting shop in connection with the Union Glass Company's plant on Webster Street below the Union Square Station in Somerville, Massachusetts. Beginning in 1885, Walsh occupied two floors of the building, with 75 cutting frames which turned out a large variety of cut glasswares. The large proportion of Walsh's business was wholesale, and he shipped his wares to the best houses in New York City and Chicago, and as far west as Portland, Oregon. In Tiffany's magnificent showroom in New York City, many of David Walsh's finest examples of cut glass were to be found on exhibition.

In connection with his cutting shop, Walsh maintained a retail salesroom where Somerville residents and tourists could choose from a varied assortment of cut glass—punch bowls, finger bowls, vases, pitchers, tea sets, plates, spoon holders, bonbon trays, loving cups, tumblers, champagne glasses, and every variety of tableware. In December, 1905, David Walsh announced that the

Small basket cut by David Walsh on blank produced by Union Glass Co., Somerville, Mass.; *ca.* 1905.

"latest novelty," cut glass baskets for flowers, cake, or fruit, could be had at his shop in all sizes and shapes. If a customer had an original idea, or wanted something a little out of the ordinary, the glass was cut to order at this shop on blanks supplied by the Union glassworks.

David Walsh was born in Portland, Maine, and learned the glass cutting business at the Portland glassworks in that city. His apprenticeship in this field of the glass arts took four years to complete. In 1870 he came to Somerville and worked in the New England Glass Company in East Cambridge, Massachusetts. In 1885 he opened his shop in the Union Glass Company's building and operated it until the factory closed in 1927.

Old Colony Cut Glass Corporation

About 1914, Samuel Ginsburg of Providence, Rhode Island, Harry I. Magid, of Fall River, Massachusetts, and George D. Dinkel of Jeannette, Pennsylvania, formed the Old Colony Cut Glass Company. On June 20, 1917, these men formed a corporation, changing the name of the firm slightly, to read the Old Colony Cut Glass Corporation. In 1914, the firm was located at 436 Pleasant Street in Fall River, Massachusetts. By 1918 they had moved to 638 Second Street, Fall River. From 1919 to 1924 their address was 25 Bowers Street, Fall River. Evidently the business changed hands, for on March 24, 1924, an abstract of certification of condition was issued to the firm under the laws of the Commonwealth of Massachusetts, listing the following members of the company: Harold E. Clarkin, president and treasurer; George F. Arsnow, clerk; and William C. Crossley, a director. No closing date for the firm could be determined, but we estimate that it probably closed shortly after 1925, for no subsequent corporation reports were filed with the secretary of state of the Commonwealth of Massachusetts after 1924.

Lowell Cut Glass Company

There was a cut glass factory in Lowell, Massachusetts, in the early 1900's, but we were unable to find any recording of the works or its products in local listings of business enterprises. The company obviously did not operate for more than a few years at the most.

Cut Glass

Manufacturers

in Rhode Island

Hope Glass Cutting Works
Hope Glass Works

The Hope Glass Cutting Works of Providence, Rhode Island, was founded in 1872 by Martin L. Kern. In that year Kern was listed in the *Providence Directory* as a glass engraver. In 1873 the firm was listed for the first time, being located at 75 Clifford Street, Providence.

In 1880 the company advertised in the city directories: "Cut and engraved goblets, castor bottles, and table glassware of every description; particular attention given to matching broken pieces and sets; also wreaths, initials and monograms done to order."

In 1883 the Hope Glass Cutting Works moved to 23 Eddy Street, Providence, but returned to the Clifford Street address in 1888. The 1890 directory shows it at 44 Page Street in Providence.

Martin L. Kern died on May 1, 1891, and was succeeded by his son, Martin W. Kern, who must have been quite young at the time, since the 1891 directory described him as "a student." Young Kern evidently took John B. Stanley into partnership, as both of their names appear in the firm's advertisements. Stanley had been with the company since 1874, when he worked at 75 Clifford Street as a glass cutter; at that time he was living in East Greenwich. For one year, 1880, he boarded with the Kern family.

Left to right: star cut dish, diameter 7 in.; "Carnation" plate, diameter 7 in.; miter cut cream pitcher 4½ in. high; all cut at Hope Glass Works.

Collection of Robert G. De Goey

In 1893 the company was listed at 77 Page Street, possibly only a change in street numbering. The same year they advertised: "Rich cut glass for doors, cut and engraved glass globes, shades, etc., etched work of every description; table glassware of every description; particular attention given to matching broken pieces and sets." In 1894, "Rich cut glass for silversmiths" was added to their advertisements.

Stanley does not appear in the 1894 directory, and in 1895, George H. Eiswald's name replaces his in the advertisements. A year previously Eiswald had been listed as a student, living with his mother at 179 Chestnut Street, Providence. In 1895, Eiswald became sole proprietor of the business, and the name of the company was changed to the Hope Glass Works. Kern became a partner in Rhodes, Kern & Company, wholesalers of boots and shoes.

The Hope Glass Works was apparently sold to John R. De Goey and his brother William de Goey in 1898 or 1899. In 1900, Eiswald was in the advertising business. (We should explain here that the father of John R. De Goey and William de Goey emigrated to America from Holland. For convenience, John R. De Goey adopted the capital "D" for the spelling of his name; his brother William de Goey retained the original spelling of the family name and so did his descendants.)

We found the following report in a special edition of the *Providence News* (February, 1900):

> There is nothing more attractive to the eye than artistic cut glassware, and nowhere can finer specimens be found than among the productions of the Hope Glass Works. This concern, which was founded in 1872 by M. L. Kern, has an established reputation for splendid productions that is not confined to Rhode Island, but extends to many of the larger cities of the east and south. The present manager is Mr. William de Goey, an expert in his line, and during the time he has been at the head of the concern he has largely increased its business, and improved the quality of its products. Cut glass for silver mounting, large quantities of which are used by the Gorham Manufacturing Company, and also unmounted tableware and ornaments are the chief productions. Etching and plate glass grinding is also an important feature of the business, as well as the modeling and replacing of articles in cut glass. In the twenty-seven years the Hope Glass Works has been doing business its trade was never more prosperous than at present, nor its prospects for future expansion brighter.

In 1901 the company moved to 161 Dorrance Street, Providence, where it remained until 1930, when they moved into new quarters on Massasoit Avenue, corner of Curtis Street, in East Providence. John R. De Goey retired from active participation in the business in 1925; he and his brother William retained their executive positions in the company. At one time William P. H. Freeman was employed as factory foreman.

After 1901 the company was no longer listed in the Providence city directories, though John R. De Goey and William de Goey and his son W. Edmund de Goey were listed there as cut glass manufacturers. Evidently the

Signed Hope Glass Works cruet; height 5 in.
Collection of Mrs. E. F. Langham

firm was going downhill—it was taxed for real estate in East Providence valued at $80 in 1948. The Hope Glass Works appeared now and again in the East Providence directories in the latter years of its existence; in 1949 its address was given as 6 Curtis Street, along with the name of W. Edmund de Goey. Thereafter it could not be found in the directories.

John R. De Goey, "cut glass manufacturer," is listed in the *Providence City Directory* through 1949, as living at 64 Mt. Hope Avenue. His son reported that he died on November 17, 1950.

The two sons of William de Goey, Sr. joined him in the business; first W. Edmund de Goey and later Cornelius de Goey. The senior de Goey relinquished his control of the business to his sons at a later date. Still later, Cornelius de Goey sold his interest in the business to his brother W. Edmund de Goey. In 1951, W. Edmund de Goey liquidated the business. Cornelius de Goey operated a glass shop in Providence and was once listed as a "tumbler manufacturer" located at 400 North Main Street during the last few years of the Hope Glass Works' existence; he moved his shop to Laconia, New Hampshire, where he still operates (1964) under the name of "C. R. de Goey," manufacturing fine crystal, plain, carved, and engraved.

There was another cut glass manufacturer using the name of Mt. Hope Glass Works and operating in the vicinity of Fall River, Massachusetts, but the de Goey family had no connection with this firm.

Two trademarks were used by the Hope Glass Works: the first consisted of a representation of a Maltese cross with an anchor in the center and the name of the firm, "Hope Cut Glass Works"; the second trademark was a representation of an anchor and the words "Hope Glass Works, Prov. R.I."

Cut Glass Manufacturers in Connecticut

Parker & Casper

In 1867, Charles Parker and Charles Casper operated a glass cutting shop in Meriden, Connecticut, located on Pratt Street, corner of Catlin Street. This shop manufactured cut glass caster bottles, decanters, sugar, salt and mustard glass liners, and other tablewares used in combination with silver-plated fittings. When the shop closed in 1869, their equipment and workers were absorbed into the Wilcox Silver Plate Company and the Meriden Silver Plate Company. In 1892 the *Meriden City Directory* listed Albert Turner, a glass cutter, as an employee of the Charles Parker Company, and apparently Parker had again engaged in the cut glass business. Unfortunately no further record of the Charles Parker Company could be found in any of the public or historical sources in Meriden, Connecticut.

In 1869, Casper organized the Meriden Silver Plate Company and about 1895 he established the Meriden Cut Glass Company, which subsequently was incorporated into the International Silver Company.

Meriden Flint Glass Company

The Meriden Flint Glass Company was established in Meriden, Connecticut, in 1876. Ground breaking for the buildings was commenced on May 14, 1876, and the fires were lighted on November 10, 1877. The firm was started by glass blowers and glass cutters who were formerly associated with the New England Glass Company in East Cambridge, Massachusetts. The factory was situated north of Cambridge Street. After the Boston & Sandwich Glass Company was closed by a strike in 1888, many of their workers migrated to Meriden and were employed by the Meriden Flint Glass Company.

William W. Lyman was president of the company from its inception; other officers were Horace C. Wilcox, Joseph Bourne, and George Hatch. The factory employed about 130 workers, including glass cutters and decorators. Thomas B. Clark also worked for this company in their office, and later he and George Hatch formed their own glass company in Honesdale, Pennsylvania. (The *American Glass Trade Directory* listed T. B. Clark & Company as having a cutting shop in Meriden, Connecticut, in 1918, but we were unable to find any record of it at all.)

In 1888 the *Meriden Directory* listed the "Meriden Flint Glass Company, James J. Murray & Company, proprietors, Cambridge n. Griswold." This was the last entry for the firm and indicates that it had been reorganized just before its closing. The company also ran an advertisement which appeared in another section of the directory: "Meriden Flint Glass Company, Meriden, Conn., Manufacturers of the best flint glass ware in all its varieties. Opal goods, both plain and decorated a specialty. Rich cut glass ware. Kerosene goods. New York Offices, 46 East 14th Street, 37 Barclay Street, and 78-80 Murray Street."

William W. Lyman was apparently an energetic man and had an inventive turn of mind. He was a pewterer in Meriden in the 1850's, and in 1852, when the Meriden Britannia Company was formed, he merged his business with theirs. He was born in Vermont, March 29, 1821, and died in Meriden, November 15, 1891. He was buried in the East Cemetery. At one time Lyman was president of the Meriden Cutlery Company.

The Meriden Flint Glass Company continued until about 1896, but occasional batch failures and other complications, such as improper fuel and shortages of material and equipment, piled up losses and the business was discontinued. A fire destroyed part of the building. The highly skilled cutters and engravers employed by the Meriden Flint Glass Works, sometimes called "The Old North Shop," went to work for other glass cutting shops in and around Meriden.

Joseph Bourne was the company's first superintendent. In 1879 he was listed as being employed by the Meriden Malleable Iron Company, but by 1880 he was back at "The Old North Shop" and remained with them until his death in 1882. Bourne originally came from the New England Glass Company with George Hatch. Hatch was the firm's traveling salesman until he withdrew to form a company with T. B. Clark. Later Hatch established his own cut glass business, Hatch & Company, in Brooklyn, New York.

The Meriden Flint Glass Company produced crystal blanks for cutting shops in the area and also cut a great deal of their own wares. From diaries

Designs for cut glass fruit bowl and flower bowl; patented Sept. 19, 1882, by George E. Hatch for Meriden Flint Glass Co.

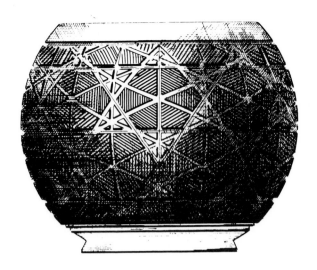

The "Cobweb" pattern; patented July 24, 1883, by George E. Hatch for Meriden Flint Glass Co.

kept by Bourne while he was superintendent of the glassworks, we learned that the firm also produced opal glass and other similar items in a full line of wares; they made a lot of caster bottles for the Meriden Britannia Company, Meriden Silver Plate Company, and Wilcox Silver Plate Company. Bourne's diaries show that they produced quite a sizable amount of glass tubes for thermometers and barometers, and water closets; one entry in his diary credits a man by the name of McCabe with making 52 water closets. Shades and lamp chimneys were another of their staples; some of these wares were made especially for Bradley & Hubbard. Skilled glass cutters such as Fillebrown, Leighton, and others from the New England Glass Company cut and engraved a superb line of table glassware for the Meriden Flint Glass Company.

George Hatch was a designer of cut glass for the New England Glass Company and he lent his talents in this direction when he came to the Meriden Flint Glass Company. On September 19, 1882, Hatch assigned two very handsome designs for two-part fruit and flower bowls to the Meriden Flint Glass Company. The first of these was a beautifully cut fruit bowl set into the top of the flower bowl base, each part capable of performing a decorative function by itself. The edge of the fruit bowl was scalloped and its outer surface was cut to represent "rose-" and "lozenge-shaped" figures, as is shown in the illustration which accompanied the design patent. The bowl base was similarly decorated and prismatic step cutting embellished the central standard. The second design, which was a combination flower vase and bowl base, was engraved with the same pattern of "rose-" and "lozenge-shaped" cutting. The main portion of the vase is shaped like a ball (rose bowl) and sets into the bowl base. As in the case of the previous design, both pieces served a dual purpose, according to the need.

On July 24, 1883, Hatch patented another cut glass design which has since been designated as the Meriden Flint Glass Company's "Cobweb" pattern. The patent illustration shows a lamp shade in this pattern, but Hatch stated in his patent specifications that the design could also be applied to decorative articles and tablewares.

Bergen & Niland
J. D. Bergen Company

In 1880, James D. Bergen and Thomas A. Niland formed a partnership in Meriden, Connecticut, under the style of Bergen & Niland; their shop was located on Miller Street, between State and Pratt Streets. In 1885, Bergen purchased Niland's interest in the firm and formed a stock company known as J. D. Bergen Company. Niland continued working for Bergen, for the city directories listed him as a glass cutter working for this firm from 1885 to 1901; after 1901, Niland joined his brother James J. Niland in another cut glass business in Meriden. In 1906 the J. D. Bergen works were moved to more spacious quarters in a large five-story factory building at Britannia and Center Streets in Meriden. A private spur track leading from the factory to the New York, New Haven, & Hartford Railroad made excellent accommodations for their shipping needs. At this time the company employed more than 400 people. In 1909, Bergen was listed in the directories as the manager of the J. J. Niland Company at 16 Miller Street in Meriden; but in 1912 J. D. Bergen's name was listed along with the Bergen Cut Glass Company and their factory on Britannia Street.

In 1916, R. V. Lamberton was listed as president of the J. D. Bergen Company, with A. M. Bradley, treasurer; W. H. Pooley, secretary; and James D. Bergen, manager. In 1917, Bergen's name was dropped from the list of officers of this firm. From 1918 to 1922 the only change in the principals of this firm was the omission of Lamberton as president of the company. After several changes in ownership and management, the plant was closed in 1922.

James D. Bergen learned his trade at the Co-Operative Cut Glass Company in Brooklyn, New York, where his uncle, John J. McCue, was president.

Left: The "Cornucopia" pattern; patented Sept. 22, 1891; *right*: The "Empress Eugenie" pattern; patented July 5, 1892; both by James D. Bergen.

Bergen also worked for other cut glass shops in New York City and Brooklyn before going to New Bedford, Massachusetts, where he cut glass for the Mt. Washington Glass Company. From New Bedford he went to East Cambridge, Massachusetts, where he continued his career with the New England Glass Company. In 1877 he entered the employ of the Meriden Flint Glass Company in their cutting department and worked there for about three years before opening his own shop.

Several designs for cut glass were issued to this firm: On September 22, 1891, James D. Bergen registered a design for cut glass which we have named "Cornucopia." Bergen's "Empress Eugenie" pattern was patented on July 5, 1892 and assigned to J. D. Bergen Company.

A pattern which we call "Sunflower" was registered by Bergen on May 29, 1894. It was a simple design reminiscent of the old "Strawberry-Diamond" pattern which had been in use for more than a century. Dorothy Daniel, in *Cut and Engraved Glass, 1771–1905*, gave the name "White Rose" to another cut glass design patented by Bergen. This design was also registered on May 29, 1894.

Paul Seitlinger and James D. Bergen filed a joint design patent for another cut glass pattern on March 19, 1895. The design consisted mostly of sharp angular cuts in combination with fan-shaped motifs. We call it "Elegance" because its proper name is as yet unknown. On July 30, 1895, Bergen registered a typical cut glass pattern of the Brilliant Period which we have named "Ozone." "Dauntless" is the name we have given to a cut glass design patented by Bergen on August 3, 1897.

Left: The "Sunflower" pattern; *right*: The "White Rose" pattern; both patented May 29, 1894, by James D. Bergen.

Left: The "Elegance" pattern; patented Mar. 19, 1895, by Paul Seitlinger and James D. Bergen. *Right:* The "Ozone" pattern; patented July 30, 1895, by James D. Bergen.

Left: The "Dauntless" pattern; patented Aug. 3, 1897, by James D. Bergen. *Right:* Bergen's "Prism Flowers"; patented Oct. 31, 1922, by William B. Bartley.

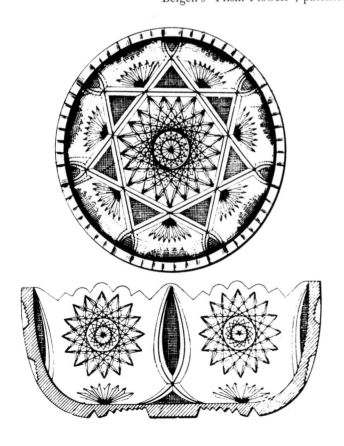

Two-part punch bowl, signed "Bergen"; height 16⅛ in.

Covered box, signed "Bergen," in the "Chair Bottom" ("Harvard") pattern.
Collection of Mrs. H. E. Taylor

The trend toward very simple cut glass patterns is mirrored in a design registered by William B. Bartley for the J. D. Bergen Company on October 31, 1922. We call it "Prism Flowers" in lieu of its unknown original name. A design for the shape of a carafe was registered by James D. Bergen on January 29, 1901.

Bergen's trademark consisted of the name "Bergen" stretching across a representation of two world globes, with the legend "Cut Glass"; this mark, and the name "Bergen" in script, were lightly etched into the glass, usually in some conspicuous place.

J. J. Niland & Company
J. J. Niland Company
Niland Cut Glass Company

In 1902, James J. Niland established a cut glass shop in Meriden, Connecticut, at 16 Miller Street, corner of Miller and State Streets. James Niland and his brother Thomas had learned their trade in Birmingham, England; their mother paid a half crown a week for their apprenticeship. James Niland came to America in 1882 and settled in Meriden, where he worked for the Bergen & Niland cut glass company.

James Niland's business prospered, and in 1906 it was incorporated as the J. J. Niland Company. In 1909 the city directories listed James D. Bergen as manager of the J. J. Niland Company, and we can assume from this that Bergen was financially interested in this concern. In 1904, Thomas Niland, James D. Bergen's former partner in Bergen & Niland, moved to Toronto, Canada, but returned the following year to become manager of the J. J. Niland shop. In 1909, Thomas Niland was listed as a commerical traveler for the Niland cutting shop. In 1907 the business directory listed James J. Niland as president and treasurer of his company; in 1916 E. T. [Mrs. James J.] Niland was listed as secretary of the company. The *American Glass Trade Directory* in 1918 shows the firm as the Niland Cut Glass Company in their compilation of cut glass manufacturers. After 1935 the business was operating on a small scale and in 1959 the corporation was dissolved.

In the early days of this concern's existence they manufactured heavy cut glass and copperwheel engraved caster bottles, cruets, sugar dredgers, salt and pepper shakers, and so forth; also a complete line of tableware, vases, decanters, and serving pieces. They were noted for their excellent quality and workmanship. A huge four-piece vase, 62 inches tall, was made in 1906 for Tiffany & Company, New York jewelers, costing $1,000. The vase was considered one of the most outstanding articles of its kind ever produced at an American cut glass factory. By 1929 rock crystal was a specialty at the Niland shop.

From an old photograph in the possession of Mrs. Mollie C. Nolan of Meriden, Connecticut, we learned that the following men cut glass at the J. J. Niland cut glass shop: Leo Maguder, John Dunnigan, Thomas Callahan (foreman and nephew of James J. Niland), James Roark, Jr., Frank Schmidt, and Walter Gurtowski.

Four-part cut glass vase produced by J. J. Niland Co. for Tiffany & Co., 1906. Reproduced from an original cut used on Niland Co. letterhead.

Thomas A. Niland & Company
Niland Cut Glass Company

Thomas A. Niland emigrated to the United States about 1876, having learned his trade of glass cutting in Birmingham, England. He worked at the Boston & Sandwich Glass Company on Cape Cod, and then moved to East Cambridge, Massachusetts, where he was employed as a glass cutter with the New England Glass Company. Niland came to Meriden, Connecticut, in 1879 and associated himself with the Meriden Flint Glass Company for a short time before entering into a cut glass business with James D. Bergen as Bergen & Niland. After five years he sold his interest in the business to Bergen, and for a while he worked as a salesman for another firm (possibly in Toronto, Canada). It has been reliably reported that Thomas Niland went to England to manage a branch of the J. D. Bergen Company in Stourbridge; however, we feel that he may have represented J. D. Bergen's interest in a Stourbridge cutting shop at that time.

Niland returned to Meriden from England in 1894; in February, 1896, he established Thomas A. Niland and Company in Deep River, Connecticut, with James A. Jones and his son Ansel R. Jones and Edward T. Burgess (subsequently of Corning, New York). Shortly after the company was established, Niland sold his interest in the firm to James and Ansel Jones; thereafter it was known as the Niland Cut Glass Company.

The Niland Cut Glass Company occupied the factory and buildings, located on the banks of Rogers Pond in Deep River, in which Calvin B. Rogers conducted his ivory novelty business for many years. The factory was of two stories and a basement; power to operate the cutting frames was furnished principally by a turbine waterwheel though when occasion demanded, steam was used, the factory being equipped also with a powerful horizontal engine.

The company manufactured cut glass goods of every description. Most of their designs were worked up by Thomas Niland himself; however, a "Butterfly" pattern in cut glass, designed by Thomas Mortensen, was one of their most popular patterns. The Niland Cut Glass Company maintained a New York City showroom where a complete assortment of their cut glass wares was to be found at all times. They also had a dazzling array of their cut glass on view at their factory showroom in Deep River. According to an article in the *New Era* (published in Deep River, Connecticut, August 25, 1899) the Niland factory did a considerable export trade through their New York City office.

The Niland cutting shop did not have a great many employees in 1899, but the dollar value of their production was purported to be very high at that

A group of cut glass articles produced at the Niland Cut Glass Co., Deep River, Conn. The low bowl, decanter, and footed glass are cut in Thomas Mortensen's "Butterfly" pattern.

time. The factory was closed around 1902 and in 1906 their tools and machinery were sold to a firm in Buffalo, New York. Some years later the factory building burned down, but as late as 1957 their office building in Deep River was being used as a private residence.

James A. Jones and his son Ansel R. Jones were not glass cutters themselves. The *New Era* article reported that James A. Jones was born in Tremont, Tazewell County, Illinois, in 1845, and came to Deep River, Connecticut, five years later. He was essentially a business man and "a man of affairs all his life." In 1891 he represented the town of Saybrook in the legislature and was for two years State Auditor. He also served as Sheriff for five years and held various town offices, including that of Selectman and of Town Agent. In 1871 he married Miss Hannah S. Rogers. They had two children, a son and a daughter.

Ansel R. Jones, described as "the junior member of the firm" in the *New Era* article, was born in Deep River, Connecticut, in February, 1875. He was educated at the Deep River High School and Hannum's Business College, and before joining his father in the cut glass business, he was employed by Pratt, Read & Company. He became associated with the Niland Cut Glass Company at its founding in 1896 and was in charge of the mechanical department.

After he sold his interest in the Deep River cut glass works to the Joneses, Thomas Niland returned to Meriden, Connecticut, in 1897 to become superintendent of the J. D. Bergen Company, but in that same year he actively joined his brother's company (J. J. Niland & Company) as a designer and salesman. While he was in Toronto, Canada (reportedly from 1904 to 1905), he represented J. J. Niland cut glassworks.

C. F. Monroe Company

In 1880, Charles F. Monroe operated a glass shop at 36 West Main Street in Meriden, Connecticut, primarily for the selling of imported glassware. By 1882 he had started a glass decorating shop and in the following year he was noted in the Meriden directory as maintaining "Art Rooms and Glass Company's Show Rooms, Oil Paintings, Artist's Materials, Art Goods, Decorative Vases &c. Art Glassware and a choice and varied line of Bric-a-Brac Articles"; he also advertised that "orders [were] taken and lessons given in glass and china decorating. Orders also received for Rich Gold Frames." In 1884 M. Rick was the manager of the decorating department at the C. F. Monroe Company and Charles F. Monroe was the president of the concern.

In 1903 a glass cutting department was added to the C. F. Monroe Company. The plant, located at Main Street and Capital Avenue in Meriden, employed over 200 hands, most of whom were experienced glass cutters, apprentices, and designers.

The "Monroe" pattern; patented May 13, 1902, by Carl V. Helmschmied for C. F. Monroe Co.

Before he opened his own glass establishment in 1880, Monroe was a designer for the Meriden Flint Glass Company, traveling to Europe on company business. In 1891 a group of buildings on West Main Street and Capital Avenue were converted into his glass decorating works; and in the late 1890's a five-story building was erected for his use. In 1903, Monroe added to his business properties by constructing a three-story building at an angle to the main building, and this was used as his cutting shop. Some of the best cut glass produced in this area came from the C. F. Monroe shop. The business was liquidated about 1916. E. Miller & Company, manufacturers of gas and electric fixtures, occupied the factory site until about 1923. Monroe was listed in the Meriden directories as foreman of E. Miller & Company's plant until 1920, when he moved to New Hampshire.

On May 13, 1902, Carl V. Helmschmied assigned a cut glass design patent to the C. F. Monroe Company. Since we could not find the name of this pattern, we have called it "Monroe." This appears to be the only cut glass design patented by this firm.

The International Silver Company
Meriden Silver Plate Company
Meriden Cut Glass Company
Wilcox Silver Plate Company
Meriden Britannia Company

The International Silver Company in Meriden, Connecticut, was formed by a merger of several large and small silver plating concerns. Among the more important names in this enterprise were Meriden Britannia Company, Rogers Brothers, Roger Smith & Company, William Rogers Manufacturing Company, and the Meriden Silver Plate Company; International can trace its lineage as far back as 1825, when Church & Rogers were producing coin silver in Hartford, Connecticut. Today it stands out as perhaps the most important firm of its kind in the world.

In 1869, Charles Casper organized the Meriden Silver Plate Company. The firm was incorporated in 1870 by Charles Casper, Isaac H. Cornwall, William E. A. Bird, and William Mackay, with a capital stock of $30,000, and from its inception they produced a fine line of cut glass—salt and pepper shakers, pickle and berry dishes, sugar dredgers, and so forth. About 1895 they added cut tablewares to their list of products; at that time it seemed advisable to market their cut glass goods under another name, and the style Meriden Cut Glass Company was adopted. The Meriden Silver Plate Company and their subsidiary the Meriden Cut Glass Company became a part of the International Silver Company in 1898. (They were known as "Factory N" and "Factory T," respectively.) The Meriden Cut Glass Company was moved from their position in the Meriden Silver Plate Company's building on Colony Street at Cross Street, into the Wilcox Silver Plate Company's building on Pratt Street at Myrtle Street, in Meriden. The Meriden Cut Glass Company operated from 1895 to 1923, when a lack of high-grade crystal blanks for cutting forced them to close their doors.

The Wilcox Silver Plate Company was organized in 1865. In 1869 they bought out Parker & Casper's glass cutting shop and continued making cut glass in connection with their silver-plated fittings. Charles Parker was one of the directors of the firm, with Horace C. Wilcox, Samuel Dodd, and several associates who were connected with the silver plate and banking business in Meriden. The factory was located at the corner of Pratt and Myrtle Streets.

Horace Cornwall Wilcox was also president of the Meriden Britannia Company, which was established about 1860 and employed 320 hands producing more than half a million dollars' worth of electroplated wares annually. On July 1, 1863, ground was broken for the new Meriden Britannia building and the company continued to grow. They maintained offices in New York City, Chicago, San Francisco, London, and South America. Dorothy Daniel, in *Cut and Engraved Glass, 1771–1905*, reported that this firm used "lead glass with 35 cutters to make pickle dishes, castor bottles, etc.," but a local authority on the cut glass industry in Meriden, Mrs. Mollie C. Nolan, said that the Meriden Britannia Company never made cut glass.

The Wilcox Silver Plate Company was absorbed into the International Silver Company just before the turn of the century. Mrs. Nolan recalled that the Wilcox works were supplied with cut glass for their silver-plated fittings by the Meriden Flint Glass Company, and later by Bergen & Niland.

Cut glass articles, such as caster bottles, mustard pots, jars, and other wares were supplied to the International Silver Company and their associated firms by cut glass shops in the Meriden area for several years. In this connection many cut glass designs were patented for them. On February 13, 1900, William R. Eliot of Meriden, Connecticut, patented two intricately devised designs, each for a "Glass Receptacle," which were assigned to the International Silver Company. His first design, which we have named "Byzantine," was described in his patent specifications as consisting of "four bands, festooned, the surface of the bands being checkered [hatchwork], and on each band a series of punties differing in size." Alternately arranged with respect to the bands were "other bands or festoons to points over the center of the festoons, these latter bands being surfaced with fine cuttings." The bottom of the vessel was adorned with a brilliantly cut star center surrounded by a number of smaller stars; still other stars were cut between the points of the festoons.

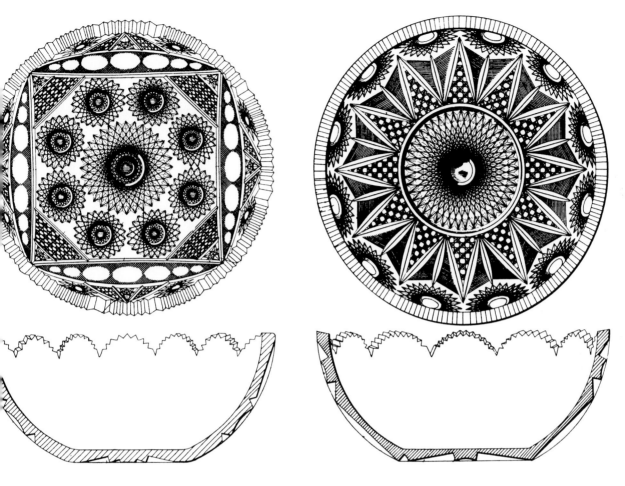

Left: The "Byzantine" pattern; *right:* The "Theodora" pattern; both patented Feb. 13, 1900, by William R. Eliot for International Silver Co.

Eliot's second design, called "Theodora" for want of its actual name, was registered on the same date, February 13, 1900, and consisted of a many-pointed star having a hob; radiating from this central star are "feathers," each comprising a finely lined body and a hob-star tip having a punty, which gave them the semblance of "peacock feathers."

William R. Eliot's name is first listed in the *Meriden City Directory* for 1895, where he was identified as a general agent for the J. D. Bergen Company. In 1897 and 1898 he was listed as a salesman for the Meriden Cut Glass Company. By 1900, though his employment did not change, he had moved from his home at 78 Wilcox Avenue to "board at the Winthrop Hotel." After 1900 his name no longer appeared in the directories.

Although Eliot's designs were assigned to the International Silver Company, they were undoubtedly cut at the Meriden Cut Glass Company's shop from blanks provided by the Pairpoint Corporation of New Bedford, Massachusetts. Their trademark label consisted of the words "Meriden Cut Glass Company, Meriden, Conn., U.S.A.," surrounding a representation of an elaborately cut glass plate.

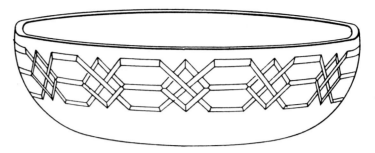

The "Chain" pattern; patented Oct. 10, 1911, by Albert Turner for International Silver Co.

A design assigned to the International Silver Company on October 10, 1911, was issued to Albert Turner of Meriden, Connecticut. The rather simple pattern, which we call "Chain," may have been used in connection with other cut glass patterns of this period. Turner was listed in the *Meriden City Directory* in 1892 as an employee of the Charles Parker Company (formerly associated with the Parker & Casper cut glass shop). From 1893 to 1896, Turner's residence is given as South Meriden, Connecticut, but no place of employment is mentioned. Between 1897 and 1899 he was employed by the Wilcox Silver Plate Company as a glass cutter, and in 1900 he joined the Meriden Britannia Company. The records show that Turner was a foreman at the Wilcox Silver Plate Company between 1906 and 1920, residing at 62 North Hanover Avenue in Meriden. Presumably his design was cut for the International Silver Company at the Wilcox Silver Plate Company's cutting shop.

Thomas A. Shanley was a foreman at the Meriden Cut Glass Company from 1904 to 1918. Several home addresses are listed for him in the Meriden city directories, but he did not change his employer until 1919, when he was working for the New Method Laundry, an unlikely occupation for a glass cutter. Shanley was formerly a resident of Honesdale, Pennsylvania, and presumably he worked for one of the several cut glass factories in that part of the country.

On January 17, 1911, Shanley patented a design for the International Silver Company, known as their "Alhambra" pattern. Brilliantly cut rosettes alternate with vertical bands of bright diamond cutting to form the main feature of the pattern, with a chainlike border of a simple design around the top. The edge of the bowl was cut with square scallops all around, known in the trade as a "dental edge." A plate in this pattern was given to the Wayne County Historical Society by Shanley.

A floral motif constituted the main feature of Shanley's design for a cut glass vessel which he patented on May 27, 1913. We call this pattern "Flora." This too was assigned to the International Silver Company. Brilliantly cut rosettes and elliptically shaped ornaments alternate between the fan-shaped design of flowers and leaves, as is shown in the patent drawings.

Another floral pattern was designed and patented by Shanley for the International Silver Company on June 19, 1917. This pattern we call "Diadem."

Collection of Wayne County Historical Society
Left: Plate in the "Alhambra" pattern produced *ca.* 1911 by International Silver Co.;
designer, Thomas A. Shanley; cutter, John C. Reilly (both former residents of Honesdale,
Pa.). *Right:* International Silver Co.'s "Flora" pattern; patented May 27, 1913, by
Thomas A. Shanley.

Left: The "Diadem" pattern; patented June 19, 1917; *right:* The "Othello" pattern;
patented Apr. 2, 1918; both by Thomas A. Shanley for International Silver Co.

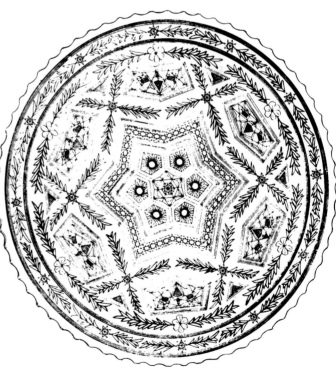

In this design a wreath of flowers and leaves flows around the mid-section of the vessel. In the base of the bowl a hob-star motif was cut, surrounded with a ring of diamond-cut buttons. The top of the bowl was cut with a stylized chain design, and the rim ornamented with sharp-pointed scallops all around.

On April 2, 1918, Shanley patented his "Othello" pattern, and in our estimation this is one of the most beautiful cut glass designs ever made; it too was assigned to the International Silver Company. The center of the bowl, or dish, is decorated with a six-pointed star, within a star, within a star, in a variety of intricately cut designs. Small garlands of leaves and flowers are engraved around the central motif, and between these garlands are pentagon-shaped shields cut in a brilliant pattern. The top of the dish, or bowl, is ringed with garlands of flowers and leaves, and the edge is scalloped.

It seems obvious that although the designs for Shanley's cut glass articles were assigned to the International Silver Company, they must have been cut at the Meriden Cut Glass Company, and perhaps many of these pieces will bear this firm's label or trademark.

Silver City Cut Glass Company
Silver City Glass Company

In 1905 three practical glass cutters—Percy Phoenix, A. Abercunos, and Joseph Schick—founded the Silver City Cut Glass Company in Meriden, Connecticut. The firm first occupied a building on Hicks Street, later moving to larger quarters on North Colony Street. The partners added additional cutters and apprentices, and began in earnest the production of some very good cut glass tablewares and ornamental items. In 1918 the firm was listed in the *American Glass Trade Directory* as a cut glass manufacturer. The company prospered, adding relative lines to their cut glass products and combining these with silver decorations.

In 1920, Carl A. Schultz, at that time foreman of the cutting shop, bought out the business and continued working the factory at the North Colony Street address. Later Schultz purchased the Delaney Building on Charles Street in Meriden (formerly the Meriden Curtain Fixture Company), where the business is still carried on as the Silver City Glass Company.

Aetna Cut Glass Company

The Aetna Cut Glass Company was located in Meriden, Connecticut, at 91 Veteran Street. It was a small cut glass shop operated by Alfred Pelerin and Joseph Pelerin for about three years, from 1907 to 1909.

Webster & Briggmann

The first reference to Webster & Briggmann appears in the 1910 Waterbury-Naugatuck (Connecticut) city directory under the heading of cut glass manufacturers as follows: "Webster & Briggmann (Wallace W. Webster and George F. Briggmann) cut glass manufacturers, Naugatuck (Connecticut)." Webster was boarding at 140 Hillside Avenue in Millville, while Briggmann resided in nearby Meriden. From 1911 to 1917 the listing for this firm is the same except that Briggmann is listed as living in Millville, Connecticut. The 1918 directory shows that both had moved to Meriden, Connecticut, where they operated a cutting shop from 1917 to 1923. Webster & Briggmann produced a good line of tableware, ornamental pieces, serving dishes, plates, and so forth. George Briggmann, a practical glass cutter, was in charge of the cutting shop from the time it opened until it closed in 1923.

H. C. Baldwin Cut Glass Shop

Herbert C. Baldwin had a small cut glass shop in Meriden, Connecticut, from 1911 to 1914. The business was located on Veteran Street. After 1914, Baldwin moved to Wallingford, Connecticut, where the business was in operation until at least 1918, for at that time he was listed as a cut glass manufacturer in the *American Glass Trade Directory*.

Hall & Callahan

John Hall and Thomas F. Callahan entered into a partnership in 1914 to produce high-grade stone-engraved glassware; their shop was located on Sherman Avenue, in Meriden, Connecticut, and it operated from 1914 to 1917. After Hall died, Callahan moved their equipment to Hawley, Pennsylvania, where he operated a division of the Monoghan Brothers cut glassworks; Callahan was their manager and chief designer. In 1918, Callahan returned to Meriden and entered the employ of the J. J. Niland Company as their designer and foreman of the cutting department.

Cut Glass Manufacturers in New York State

John L. Gilliland & Company
The Brooklyn Flint Glass Works

John Loftus Gilliland established John L. Gilliland & Company in October, 1823, after severing his connection with John and Richard Fisher, proprietors of the New York Glass Works, in the fall of 1822. In 1826, Gilliland won a medal for his flint glassware at the Third Exhibition of the Franklin Institute and in 1831 he showed cut and pressed glassware. From 1830 to 1850 he received various awards for his glassware, showing them at the fair of the American Institute of the City of New York. By 1843 the plant was known as the Brooklyn Flint Glass Works.

Gilliland exhibited his cut crystal glass at the Crystal Palace Exhibition in London in 1851 and won a prize medal for his wares. He also showed at the New York Crystal Palace. Gilliland was a very successful man for some years, and at one time was reputed to be a very rich man. He stayed in England for an extended period shortly before 1854, and during this time his business deteriorated and he returned to find himself penniless and his business and credit rating seriously impaired.

In 1864, Amory Houghton and his son, Amory Houghton, Jr., acquired the controlling interest in the Brooklyn Flint Glass Works (sometimes known as the South Ferry Glass Works), and in 1868 the business was moved to Corning, New York, where it was re-established as the Corning Glass Company.

During the time that Gilliland operated the Brooklyn Flint Glass Works he registered two patents: the first, dated January 11, 1853, was for a tool for fire polishing glassware; the second, dated January 5, 1863, was a patent for a glass furnace.

Joseph Stouvenal & Company
Joseph Stouvenal & Brothers

In 1837, Joseph Stouvenal established a glass factory in New York City and from the beginning this firm cut glassware for the table. Stouvenal was listed in the city directories as a glass cutter from 1837 to 1841. The firm first appeared in the public records in 1841. In 1838, Stouvenal received an award for a glass cutting machine which he exhibited at the annual fair of the American Institute of the City of New York. On September 16, 1833, Joseph Stouvenal and Francis A. Martin of Philadelphia, Pennsylvania, were issued a joint patent for "Glass Blowing Machines." In 1842, Joseph Stouvenal & Company was given second place in an award for cut glassware; by 1843, Joseph Stouvenal & Brothers—as the firm then became known—had gained first place, and a diploma for their superior cut glass was recorded.

In 1843 the style of the firm became Joseph Stouvenal & Brothers (Francis and Nicholas). In 1853, as Joseph Stouvenal & Company, they exhibited pressed and cut glassware at the New York Crystal Palace.

Francis Stouvenal was operating the factory by 1870, and at that time advertised that they were taking special orders for cut glass for homes, railroad cars, offices, steamboats, and so on. In 1915, James D. Bergen reported that this works operated in New York City during the 1870's on Center Street, near Canal Street.

Turner & Lane

From 1841 to 1850, "William Turner, glasscutter, 43 Duane Street, New York City," was listed in the *New York City Directory*. In 1844, Turner & Lane, William Turner and M. H. Lane, were listed as cut glass manufacturers at 117 Attorney Street, New York City. An advertisement in the *New York City Directory*, dated 1857/58, confirmed that Turner & Lane were

> Importers and manufacturers of Cut Glass Ware, 44 & 46 Duane Street, have constantly on hand a general assortment of Cut Glass Tumblers, Goblets, Wines, Decanters, Celleries, Fruit, Finger & Sugar Bowls, Pitchers, &c. All articles cut and matched to patterns. Also, Gas, Solar, and Fluid Shades and Globes, all of the latest style and pattern. Window Glass Cut, frosted, and stained. All of which we [Turner & Lane] offer at reduced prices.

Before the Civil War, John S. O'Connor worked for Turner & Lane. The firm was not in business after 1864.

Empire State Flint Glass Works
Francis Thill Sons & Company

In 1857, Francis Thill established his Empire State Flint Glass Works on Kent Avenue, corner of Taylor Street, in Brooklyn, New York. Henry Reed Stiles, *History of Kings County, Including Brooklyn, from 1683 to 1884* (New York, W. W. Munsell & Co., 1884), reports: "Houses engaged in hollow glass ware manufacturing are Empire State Flint Glass Works of Francis Thill; he makes all kinds of flint and colored glass ware and has been in the business since 1857." The Brooklyn directories listed Francis Thill in 1865 as a "glass manufacturer"; in 1866 "Thill & Company, Empire State Flint Glass Works" is listed. From 1891 to 1892 the directory showed "Francis J. Thill and Francis J. Thill, Jr., glass, Kent Avenue, corner Taylor Street"; and "F. Thill Sons & Company, glass merchants" at the same location. The directory also listed "Harry Thill, glass" at the same address. This must be Francis Thill's youngest son, who joined his father and brother in the business about this period. Carl Dreppard reported, in *A.B.C.'s of Old Glass*, that the firm produced glass until the 1890's. Although we found no record of this firm as a cut glass manufacturer, this is quite possible. Dorothy Daniel, in *Cut and Engraved Glass, 1771–1905*, reported that this firm manufactured "fine lead glass, clear, colored, engraved, cut."

E. V. Haughwout & Company

In 1859 the New York City directories listed E. V. Haughwout & Company as "dealers," not manufacturers of any kind of merchandise. In 1860 the firm was listed as "importers and manufacturers of sterling silver, china, glassware, mirrors, bronzes, silver plate ware, gas fixtures, cutlery, and parian statuary. 488, 490, 492 Broadway and 24 Rue de Paradis, Paris, France. Eder V. Haughwout, president; home 100 East 21st Street." In 1913, Haughwout was living at 150 Schermerhorn Street, Brooklyn, but was not active in the cut glass business.

In the Bella C. Landauer Collection in the New York Historical Society there is an invoice issued by this firm, dated May 15, 1868, which reads: "Bought of E. V. Haughwout & Company, Nos. 488, 490, & 492 Broadway; Broadway and Broome Streets, New York City, Importers & Decorators—

French China and Manufacturers Silver Plated Ware—Cut Glass and Table Cutlery—Wholesale and Retail Dealers in Chandeliers & Gas Fixtures, French Clocks & Silver Plated Ware & Cut Glass." Another bill in this same collection had the same billhead except that on one side it had "Brooklyn Cut Glass." At one time John S. O'Connor was employed by E. V. Haughwout & Company, obviously as a cutter of glass tablewares; O'Connor went to work for Christian Dorflinger just about the time E. V. Haughwout & Company was going out of business, about 1870.

The Lafayette Flint Glass Works
East River Flint Glass Works

A. Stenger & Company established the Lafayette Flint Glass Works in Brooklyn, New York, on North 11th Street and Second Avenue. Notice was taken of the firm in the city directories (1868/69) but the works were operating as early as 1865. Many changes in ownership took place before it became known in 1880 as the East River Flint Glass works; at that time the glass factory was under the supervision of P. Schneider's Sons. Francis Storm was the proprietor of the East River Flint Glass Works from 1882 to 1895, the date it is believed the works ceased operating.

George and Helen McKearin, in *American Glass*, reported that this glassworks produced flint tablewares and colored glass of all kinds. Dorothy Daniel, in *Cut and Engraved Glass, 1771–1905*, suggested that this firm also produced cut crystal in the French style, rock crystal cutting, and cut glass bottles for perfume and cosmetics.

Lum & Ogden
William H. Lum & Son

For many years William H. Lum represented glass manufacturers in his shop in New York City. From 1869 to 1880 his place of business was variously listed at 40 Barclay Street, 24 Barclay Street, 20 College Place, 90 College Place, and 42 Murray Street. About 1875 the firm was also known as Lum &

Ogden. In *New York's Great Industries: Exchange and Commercial Review, Embracing also Historical and Descriptive Sketch of the City—Its Leading Merchants and Manufacturers* (New York and Chicago, Historical Publishing Co., 1885) we found the following reference to this firm:

> William H. Lum, Manufacturer of Glass and agent for [the] Mt. Washington Glass Company, &c. office and salesroom at 46 Murray Street, N.Y.C.; Factory, Port Jervis, New York. It is now over 20 years since Mr. Lum founded his present extensive concern . . . factory fitted with improved modern furnaces, machinery, and appliances. Manufactures various lines of medium and cheap glassware . . . his finer goods being produced at the Mt. Washington Works. Specialties: castor, pickle and cologne bottles, berry dishes, lamp pegs, fonts, etc. Mr. Lum is agent for the Mt. Washington, celebrated for its rich cut glass and opal goods. . . . Another department of his business is the cutting and engraving of glass in all its branches. Special attention to jobbing orders, expert operatives only at his factory at No's. 201 and 203 East 12th Street. All work guaranteed to give entire satisfaction.

The *Pottery and Glass Directory* listed this firm as cut glass manufacturers from 1920 to 1925. William T. Bonner, *New York: The World's Metropolis, 1623/4–1923/4*, confirmed that William H. Lum & Son were manufacturers of cut glass and at that time (1923/24) they were located at 508–510 Broome Street. The New York City directories showed Lum's business address from 1910 through 1912 to be 46 Murray Street. From 1913 through 1919 the address appeared in these directories as 508–510 Broome Street, and for the first time, in 1913, we found his son's name listed, Elmer R. Lum. From 1920 to 1929, William H. Lum & Company was listed as a cut glass manufacturer in the New York City and Brooklyn directories; their address was still 508 Broome Street, New York City.

On December 16, 1884, William H. Lum registered a design for a caster bottle shape which his firm manufactured and sold in crystal and colored glass, both plain and engraved.

Constitution Flint Glass Works

The only mention of the Constitution Flint Glass Works we could find in the public records in Brooklyn, New York, confirms that this factory was located at Delevan and Van Brunt Streets between 1867 and 1869. Dorothy Daniel, in *Cut and Engraved Glass, 1771–1905*, reported that this Brooklyn, New York, firm had ties with Augustine Thiery and Company in the manufacture of lead glass perfume bottles, cut and colored.

George and Helen McKearin, in *American Glass*, noted that in 1876 the name was changed to the LaBastie Works, and at that time it was operated by

Ernest De La Chapelle & Company. In 1884 they advertised that their glass was annealed "in oil to make them indestructible" and were "importing [wares] also to meet the demand." The last listing for the LaBastie Works was dated 1886.

Hibbler & Rausch
George H. Hibbler & Company
J. S. Hibbler & Company

Henry Reed Stiles, *History of Kings County, Including Brooklyn, from 1683 to 1884,* reported that:

> about 1850 a Mr. Dorflinger [Christian Dorflinger] established a large glass house on or near Concord and Prince Streets [Brooklyn, New York]. Snyder, Storms, Brookfield, Dannenhoffer and Huwer were engaged in the business at different points within the next ten or twelve years. About 1866 Mr. Hibbler [George Hibbler], who had been in the employ of Mr. Dorflinger, purchased the works at Concord and Prince Streets, a brother of Mr. Dorflinger being his partner. On the death of Mr. Dorflinger in 1879, Mr. Rausch took his place and the firm is now Hibbler and Rausch, largest in Brooklyn, makes globes and chimneys.

In the International Publishing Company's *Half-Century's Progress of the City of Brooklyn, New York, 1886 (The City's Leading Manufacturers and Merchants)* we found the following:

> Hibbler & Rausch, Concord Street Glass Works, glass manufacturers, corner of Concord and Prince Streets. Originally established in 1835, and, after several changes in style and title of the firm, in 1877 Messrs. Hibbler and Rausch became sole proprietors, in 1886 Mr. B. Rausch died, being succeeded by his partner under the firm name of Hibbler and Rausch. 350 skilled operators, manufacturing largely all kinds of lantern globes, lamp chimneys, battery jars, lamp bowls, milk and lager bottles, etc.

Still there is no specific mention of cut glass being made by this firm.

The *Brooklyn Directory* for 1891/92 listed "Joseph S. Hibbler, glass, 212 Concord Street; J. S. Hibbler & Company, glass manufacturer, 212 Concord Street." The directories for several years after 1892 were thoroughly examined but we found no further mention of this firm. We can only assume that they went out of business soon after 1893.

On February 8, 1887, Daniel Forbes patented a cut glass design which we have designated "Hobnails and Rosettes," since these terms were used by Forbes in his descriptive explanation of the design he registered. The patent

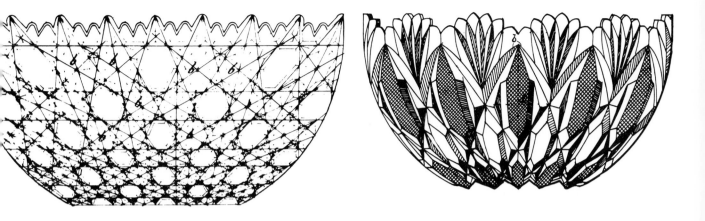

Left: The "Hobnails and Rosettes" pattern; patented Feb. 8, 1887; *right:* The "Macbeth" pattern; patented Feb. 11, 1890; both by Daniel Forbes for George H. Hibbler & Co.

Left: The "Star of David" pattern; *right:* The "Rose Point" pattern; both patented Aug. 1, 1893, by Daniel Forbes for George H. Hibbler & Co.

was assigned on that same date to George H. Hibbler. On February 11, 1890, Forbes registered a design for cut glass, assigning it to Hibbler. It has been named the "Macbeth" pattern by Dorothy Daniel. Forbes's "Star of David" pattern was patented on August 1, 1893; and on this same date he registered a design which we have named "Rose Point."

Long Island Flint Glass Works
Huwer & Dannenhoffer

The International Publishing Company's *Half-Century's Progress of the City of Brooklyn, New York, 1886* (*The City's Leading Manufacturers and Merchants*) listed the "J. N. Huwer, Long Island Flint Glass Works, manufacturers of every description of glassware, etc., [had an] office and factory [at the] corner of Maujer Street and Morgan Avenue [Brooklyn, New York]. Mr. Huwer founded his works in 1877 . . . [the] building is two stories in height and has a frontage of 250 feet and a depth of 100 feet. . . . 180 operatives." (No specific mention of cut glass is made here.) The firm was listed in the *Brooklyn Directory* for the years 1891/92 at the same address. Henry Reed Stiles's *History of Kings County, Including Brooklyn, from 1683 to 1884* revealed that Messrs. Dannenhoffer and Huwer were associated with the Dorflinger glass works on the corner of Concord and Prince Streets in Brooklyn before establishing their own glassworks. Although we could find no positive indication that the Long Island Flint Glass Works produced cut crystal, it is quite probable that a firm of this size, and operating in this period, did manufacture cut glassware of some kind. Dorothy Daniel, in *Cut and Engraved Glass, 1771–1905*, reported that there may have been a tie with the Greenpoint Flint Glass Works. Stiles noted in his book that "the Greenpoint Glass Works, now owned and run by the E. P. Gleason Manufacturing Company, engaged in the manufacture of globes, chimneys, as well as decorated and engraved bottles, vases, etc."

The *Brooklyn Directory* (1913/14) listed the Dannenhoffer Glass Works at 330–336 Himrod Street, Brooklyn, New York.

E. J. S. Van Houten
Williamsburgh Flint Glass Company

In 1886, Erskine J. S. Van Houten, cut glass manufacturer, was listed in the *New York City Directory* at 29 Murray Street. From 1887 to 1896 the firm was located at 18 College Place, New York City. By 1900, Van Houten had moved their showrooms to 74 Park Place, where the firm remained until 1915, when it again moved up the street to 96 Park Place.

In 1912, Van Houten's Williamsburgh Flint Glass Company was listed at 260 Boerum Street in Brooklyn; the glassworks were so listed until 1919.

In 1911 the public records showed that Erskine J. S. Van Houten was president of the company. In 1915, Erskine B. Van Houten was listed as secretary of this concern. M. Bach was vice president of the E. J. S. Van Houten Company in 1917. Erskine J. S. Van Houten and Erskine B. Van Houten retained their positions in this firm as president-treasurer and secretary throughout the many listings of their firm in the directories, along with the Williamsburgh Flint Glass Company, until 1919. From 1920 to 1923 we found E. J. S. Van Houten listed as a manufacturer's agent at 123 Chambers Street, New York City. William T. Bonner's *New York: The World's Metropolis, 1623/4—1923/4* listed the business address for this firm as 290 Broadway, New York City.

Van Houten's trademark label consisted of a representation of an American flag surrounded by the words "Van Houten, Cut Glass, New York." It was in use from about 1896 to 1919.

Hatch & Company

George E. Hatch established a glass cutting shop at 212 Concord Street in Brooklyn, New York, around 1886 (it was listed in the *Brooklyn Directory* for 1886/87). This was also the location given for the J. S. Hibbler cutting shop in 1891, and presumably one or more cutting shops were operating in this location to avail themselves of the glass blanks produced by the old Dorflinger glasshouse on the corner of Concord and Prince Streets in Brooklyn.

Before 1886, Hatch had been associated with the New England Glass Company of East Cambridge, Massachusetts, the Meriden Flint Glass Com-

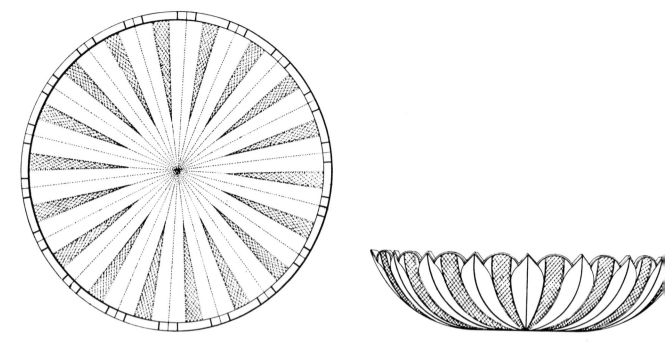

The "Hatch" pattern; patented Oct. 26, 1886, by George E. Hatch.

pany, Meriden, Connecticut, and with Thomas B. Clark as Hatch & Clark in Honesdale, Pennsylvania. Hatch had registered several cut glass designs for some of the concerns he worked for in the past, but only one such design was patented for his own company. On October 26, 1886, Hatch registered a simple cut glass pattern which we have named the "Hatch" pattern in his honor. The design consisted of deeply cut grooves alternating with panels of hatch cutting, as is shown in the patent illustration. A design of this character demands the finest quality crystal, otherwise it would have very little sparkle or reflective powers.

We could find no mention of Hatch or his cut glass shop in any of the New York City or Brooklyn directories after 1891, and presumably he went out of business at this time, and may have been succeeded by J. S. Hibbler & Company, who occupied this location at 212 Concord Street in 1891/92.

L. Straus & Sons

Lazarus Straus and Sara Straus came to America from Rhenish Bavaria in 1852 with their two sons, Isidor and Nathan. The family settled in Talbotton, Georgia, where Lazarus Straus engaged in the business of importing and selling fine china and glassware. In 1865 the family moved to New York City, and the firm of L. Straus & Son was organized, which in 1872 became L. Straus & Sons.

When Isidor Straus was sixteen years of age, and a graduate of Collingsworth Institute preparing to enter the Military Academy at West Point, the Civil War broke out. Isidor was caught up in the war fever, as were many other men and boys at that time, and he wished to enter the service of the Confederate Army. He assisted in the organization of a company of young men and boys and was chosen their lieutenant. The governor of Georgia told them that they did not have enough guns for men, and they therefore could not arm boys. In 1863, Isidor Straus went to England for an importing company organized to build ships for blockade-running. In 1888 he and his brother Nathan entered the New York City firm of R. H. Macy & Company, and in 1892 he became a partner in the Brooklyn dry goods firm of Abraham & Straus. Isidor and Nathan Straus were generous men and donated much of their time, energy, and money to many worthwhile charities, among which was the distribution of sterilized milk to the poor of New York City.

L. Straus & Sons operated a cut glass factory in New York City in a loft building on Jay Street, where three entire floors were given over to the production of richly cut glassware of every description. L. Straus & Sons began cutting glass in 1888, and by 1892 they were employing over 100 expert cutters. According to reports in the *Pottery and Glass Reporter* and the *Jeweler's Circular Weekly*, they displayed their wares in their shop at 42–48 Warren Street, and over 40 original designs, not made by any other cut glass manufacturer, were attributed to this firm.

L. Straus & Sons affixed their trademark label on each piece of glass that left their shop. The trademark consisted of a representation of a round diamond and the words "Straus, Cut Glass." According to their trademark papers, this designation had been used on their cut glasswares prior to 1894. The papers are dated October 2, 1917. Lee Kohn, a member of the

The "Encore" pattern; patented Dec. 11, 1888, by Benjamin Davies for L. Straus & Sons.

firm at that time, testified in the papers that the mark had been in actual use as a trademark of the copartnership (the firm at that time was composed of Nathan Straus and Lee Kohn) for ten years next preceding February 20, 1905; in other words, since February, 1895.

Presently, the name of the company is Straus-Duparquet and they are located at 33 East 17th Street in New York City; china and glassware is still their stock in trade and they maintain a long tradition for fine merchandise.

Several cut glass designs were patented for L. Straus & Sons by Benjamin Franklin Davies, Hermann Siegel, and Herman Richman. On December 11,

Left to right: "Americus"; "Ulysses"; "Peerless"; patterns designed by Hermann Siegel; *ca.* 1891.

Left: The "Imperial" pattern; patented Feb. 2, 1892, by Hermann Siegel for L. Straus & Sons. *Right:* The "Inverted Kite" pattern; patented Mar. 14, 1893, by Benjamin Davies; L. Straus & Sons.

1888, Davies patented Straus's "Encore" pattern, which was a combination of "Strawberry-Diamond" cutting, fine hatch cutting, and fan-shaped motifs.

Seigel's "Peerless" pattern, produced at the Straus factory from about 1891, consisted of a combination of the old "Russian" pattern with diagonally cut panels and fans. The "Americus" and "Ulysses" patterns are from the 1890 period of Straus's productions.

The "Imperial" pattern was patented by Hermann Siegel on February 2, 1892. The essential features of this design were a large central star, the longer points of which were enclosed by grooves convexed toward each other and meeting at points outside the star points, and oppositely curved grooves crossing each other beyond these points. The spaces bounded by the grooves have alternate fields of stars and crossed lines, as is shown in the patent illustration.

On March 14, 1893, Benjamin Davies registered his design for a pattern which we have named "Inverted Kite" because this term of reference was used in the patent specifications to describe a portion of the design.

The "Golden Wedding" pattern was so named by Dorothy Daniel. It was patented by Davies on May 8, 1894.

Davies' "Tausend" pattern was also registered on May 8, 1894. The design consists of a central six-pointed star surrounded by circular designs which were cut in typical patterns of the Brilliant Period.

"Tassel" is the name we have given to still another Straus cut glass design which was patented by Benjamin Davies on May 8, 1894. The leading feature

Left: The "Golden Wedding" pattern; patented May 8, 1894, by Benjamin Davies for L. Straus & Sons. *Right*: The "Tausend" pattern; patented May 8, 1894, by Benjamin Davies.

Left: The "Tassel" pattern; patented May 8, 1894, by Benjamin Davies. *Right:* The "Athena" pattern; patented Oct. 23, 1894, by Hermann Siegel.

Left: The "Perrot" pattern; patented Apr. 16, 1895; *right:* The "Bontemps" pattern; patented June 4, 1895; both by Benjamin Davies.

of this design resembles tassels depended from diamond-shaped motifs at equal distances about the object and further embellished with cut glass motifs resembling flowers and pinwheels.

Straus's "Athena" pattern was registered by Hermann Siegel on October 23, 1894. The pattern is a combination of several cut glass designs—stars, fans, and prismatic cutting. The patent illustration shows only a portion of this pattern, but it was noted in the specifications that the design was to be repeated in the unoccupied spaces shown in the drawings.

On April 16, 1895, Davies patented a handsome cut glass design which we have named "Perrot." The design resembles the handsome rose windows found in medieval cathedrals in Europe. Stars, fans, and small diamond cutting are arranged in the pattern to form one of the most scintillating cut glass designs ever made in the late nineteenth century.

A combination of the "Strawberry-Diamond" pattern, fans and small diamond cutting, was used by Benjamin Davies in a cut glass design which we

Left: The "Sterling" pattern; patented Oct. 13, 1896; *right:* The "Puntie" pattern; patented May 31, 1898; both by Benjamin Davies.

Left: The "Bijoux" pattern; patented Oct. 31, 1899, by Benjamin Davies. *Right:* The "Stars and Banners" pattern; patented Nov. 26, 1901, by Herman Richman.

Left: The "Beatrice" pattern; patented Nov. 15, 1904, by Herman Richman. *Right:* The "Joan" pattern; patented Feb. 28, 1905, by Hermann Siegel.

have named "Bontemps," in honor of that great French glassmaker of the mid-nineteenth century. The patent was dated June 4, 1895.

On October 13, 1896, Davies registered a design for cut glass which we have designated the "Sterling" pattern. An arrangement of brilliantly cut rosettes and fans were featured in this design.

Punties and notched ribs formed a rather simple but elegant cut glass design patented by Davies on May 31, 1898. Since no proper name for this pattern can be found, we have named it the "Puntie" pattern. (It is similar to a design registered by Andrew Snow, Jr. for the Pairpoint Corporation, January 18, 1898.)

A very handsome cut glass design was registered by Benjamin Davies on October 31, 1899. Since this too lacked a proper name, we have called it "Bijoux." Bands of stars and diamond cutting were arranged with brilliant rosettes and fine hatch cutting in this, one of Davies' best cut glass designs.

On November 26, 1901, Herman Richman registered a design which we have named "Stars and Banners." The design is rather massive in character and shows a trend toward simplicity in cut glass patterns that ultimately led to their final degradation. Still, Richman's first design for L. Straus & Sons has all the earmarks of quality for which this firm became famous in the cut glass business.

Left: The "Avon" pattern; patented Apr. 4, 1905, by William R. Schaffer. *Right:* The "Turandot" pattern; patented May 8, 1906, by Benjamin Davies.

On November 15, 1904, Richman patented another cut glass design for L. Straus & Sons which combines several motifs of the Brilliant Period very tastefully. Since we could find no name for this pattern either, we have called it "Beatrice."

Hermann Siegel patented the "Joan" pattern on February 28, 1905. This design is beautifully arranged with large rosettes, fans, and prismatic cutting.

William R. Schaffer of Fort Lee, New Jersey, assigned his design for a cut glass pattern to L. Straus & Sons on April 4, 1905. The patent illustration indicates that it consisted of deeply cut grooves and panels in a flashy pattern of rosettes and prismatic cutting. We call it the "Avon" pattern.

Straus's "Turandot" pattern was registered at the patent office by Benjamin Davies on May 8, 1906. The main feature of this design was a large stylized rose, brilliantly cut, and combined with other motifs of a similar character.

Richman's "Manon" pattern was patented on June 11, 1907, and assigned to L. Straus & Sons. This pattern consisted of a geometrically arranged design of rosettes and diamond cutting, as is shown in the patent illustration.

On June 28, 1910, Benjamin Davies registered a cut glass design which consisted of stylized roses surrounded by a pattern known to collectors as "Daisy and Button." Since we could not discover the name of this design, we have designated it "Daisy and Button with Roses."

Herman Richman patented three cut glass designs for L. Straus & Sons on October 24, 1916. The first one, Design Patent No. 49,805, we have called "Daisies and Diamonds" because no proper name for the pattern could be

Left: The "Manon" pattern; patented June 11, 1907, by Herman Richman. *Right:* The "Daisy and Button with Roses" pattern; patented June 28, 1910, by Benjamin Davies.

Left: The "Daisies and Diamonds" pattern; *right:* The "Carnations and Diamonds" pattern; both patented Oct. 24, 1916, by Herman Richman.

Left: The "Songbird with Flowers" pattern; patented Oct. 24, 1916; *right:* The "Festoon and Urn" pattern; a cut and engraved design patented July 10, 1917; both by Herman Richman.

found. "Carnations and Diamonds" is the name we have given to the second patented design, No. 49,806; and "Songbird with Flowers" seems to fit the last cut glass design, No. 49,807, very well.

On July 10, 1917, Richman registered three more cut glass patterns. The first one we have named "Festoon and Urn"; the second, "Maltese Urn"; and

Left: The "Maltese Urn" pattern; *right:* The "Festoon and Wild Rose" pattern; both patented July 10, 1917, by Herman Richman.

Straus's "Lily of the Valley and Pansy" pattern; patented July 24, 1917, by Herman Richman.

the third, "Festoon and Wild Rose." Richman's last design patent, dated July 24, 1917, was a tasteful arrangement of "Lily of the Valley and Pansy"; hence the common nomenclature for this design.

On November 24, 1925, Abraham & Straus, Incorporated, of Brooklyn, New York, registered a trademark for "cut glass of all kinds, sheet glass, glass tablewares, ornamental glassware, glass bottles, and glass jars." The trademark was applied to their cut glass articles with a paper label, on which was represented a house and the words "Better Homes Bureau." The store records (it is still operating today) did not reveal whether this firm imported their cut glass or purchased it from domestic sources; however, we feel that since the Straus family was prominently associated with this department store, they probably purchased at least a portion of their wares from L. Straus & Sons.

Becker & Brisbois

The first mention of Becker & Brisbois as manufacturers of "rich cut glass" appears in the 1912 Brooklyn directories. Benjamin H. Becker was formerly associated with Becker & Wilson, cut glass manufacturers in New York City and Montrose, Pennsylvania. The Becker & Brisbois cut glass shop was located at 123–133 Middleton Street in Brooklyn. In 1913, Benjamin H. Becker of 414 Hooper Street, Brooklyn, and Victor Brisbois, art glass manufacturer, of 123 Middleton Street, Brooklyn, were listed as Becker & Brisbois, manufacturers of rich cut glass. The *American Glass Trade Directory* listed Becker & Brisbois as cut glass manufacturers in 1918.

In 1920 the *Pottery and Glass Directory* noted Victor Brisbois as a manufacturer of cut glass, located at 65 Varick Street, New York City. By 1923, Brisbois' shop was at 514 Johnson Avenue, Brooklyn, where he remained as a cut glass manufacturer until at least 1930, the date of the last listing for Victor Brisbois. During this period Brisbois produced cut glass lamps and girandoles. In 1924, Victor Brisbois, Incorporated, was listed as an agent, with showrooms at 200 Fifth Avenue, New York City.

Benjamin Becker continued in the cut glass business at the old address on Middleton Street, Brooklyn. In 1920, Charles Becker took over the business, and by 1923 he had added another cutting shop in Glendale, Long Island, which he ran in conjunction with the original shop on Middleton Street. In 1900/01 Charles Becker & Company was selling glassware at 59 Park Place, New York City.

John A. Boyle

In 1912, John A. Boyle was listed in the *Brooklyn Directory* as a "cutter" of glassware, living at 1747 73d Street. Boyle was a member in good standing in the National Association of Cut Glass Manufacturers at this time. The shop must have been a very small one, for we could find nothing more about it in the various New York City and Brooklyn directories either before 1912 or for several years after that date. We did find a listing for Boyle Brothers, manufacturers of cut glass in Somerville, Massachusetts, in 1923, and we have reason to believe that this is a continuation of John A. Boyle's cutting shop.

Thomas B. Campbell & Company

In 1905, Thomas B. Campbell was listed as a "glasscutter" in the *Brooklyn Directory*, with a home address given at 51 Rodney Street. From 1909 to 1913, "cut glass" is placed after his name and his business location was listed at 42 South 8th Street; his home address remained the same. Thomas B. Campbell & Company moved to 2 East 23d Street in Manhattan around 1913, and remained at that location in New York City until 1916. Campbell was a member of the National Association of Cut Glass Manufacturers and was listed in the *American Glass Trade Directory* for 1918. Thereafter we could not find any mention of the firm in any of the business or trade directories.

On March 30, 1915, a patent was issued to Thomas B. Campbell, of New York City, covering his design for a cut glass vessel. The pattern is so simple

Thomas B. Campbell's design for a cut glass vessel; patented Mar. 30, 1915.

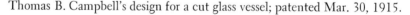

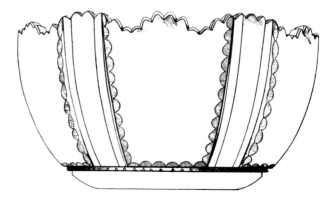

124

that we must assume it was further embellished with light cutting, which was so popular at this late period in cut glass production. The basic idea, that of sectioning the article off into large and small panels, seems to be the main feature of Campbell's design patent.

Colonial Cut Glass Company

From 1910 to 1914, the Colonial Cut Glass Company was located at 47 Warren Street in New York City. In 1914 the company was incorporated and the names of C. B. Warner and J. Warner appear in the public records as principal owners of the business. From 1914 to 1916, the last year this firm was recorded, they had moved to 54 West 23d Street in New York City, with a branch office at 90 Nassau Street.

Crystolene Cut Glass Company

On November 11, 1919, Louis Stanner and Hugo Engelke, copartners of the Crystolene Cut Glass Company of 117–119 Himrod Street, Brooklyn, New York, registered their trademark for cut glass products. The mark consisted of the name "Crystolene" in connection with the representation of a tall glass vase cut in a pattern that was known to the trade as "Chair Bottom" (sometimes called the "Harvard" pattern by collectors). This trademark was applied to cut glass articles comprising dishes, vases, bowls, nappies, jugs, tumblers, puff boxes, and hair receivers, in the form of a paper label. Most of these identifying labels have been washed off over the years, and it would be almost impossible to identify Crystolene cut wares from those produced by their contemporaries. Stanner and Engelke reported in their trademark papers that this mark had been in use by their firm since October 18, 1918, thus indicating the time they first established their cut glass business. The firm was listed in the *Pottery and Glass Directory* for 1920/21, but thereafter their name was not included in the roster of cut glass manufacturers.

Diamond Cut Glass Works

In 1900 the *New York City Directory* listed "Abraham Diamond, glass, 67 Columbia Street." The first listing of the Diamond Cut Glass Works appeared in 1910, when the company was situated at 87 Nassau Street, in lower Manhattan. The firm remained at this address until at least 1917, but after that date it disappeared from the public recordings. In 1915, Lawrence I. Cohn and Minnie Cohn were listed as principal owners of the Diamond Cut Glass Works.

German Plate and Cut Glass Company
German Rich Cut Glass Company

In 1912, Richard German was listed as the manager of the German Plate and Cut Glass Company at 240 Franklin Street, Brooklyn, New York. We are assuming that the German Rich Cut Glass Company of Brooklyn, which was listed in the *American Glass Trade Directory* in 1918, is this same firm under a different style.

Ferstler & Christian

In 1912 the *Brooklyn Directory* listed "Christopher Ferstler, glass, 635 Kent Avenue. Home address 72 St. Nicholas Avenue" and "M. D. Christian, glass, home address Pulaski." In 1913, Christopher Ferstler was listed separately as a glass cutter at 71 Clymer Street, Brooklyn. Ferstler & Christian were included in the 1918 issue of the *American Glass Trade Directory* as cut glass manufacturers. This is the last mention of this firm we were able to find. Their address on Kent Avenue in Brooklyn was quite near the site of the Empire State Flint Glass Works, which operated some years before 1912,

126

and there is a strong possibility that Ferstler & Christian operated a small cutting shop near their source of supply of blanks for cutting.

In 1933/34, a Phil Ferstler, crystal cutter, was working at this trade in a shop at 90 Nassau Street, New York City.

J. Halter & Company
Halter Cut Glass Company, Incorporated

Joseph Halter was listed as a "glasscutter" in the *Brooklyn Directory* in 1905. In 1909, J. Halter & Company, glass cutters, 850 DeKalb Avenue, Brooklyn, is listed in the directories, along with Halter's name as a glass cutter. From 1910 to 1913, J. Halter & Company was located at 68 West Broadway, (Brooklyn) and the Halter Cut Glass Company, Incorporated, was listed at 963–965 Kent Avenue, Brooklyn. Halter maintained a showroom on West Broadway and operated his manufactory at the Kent Avenue address in Brooklyn. The *Pottery and Glass Directory* listed this firm at 489 DeKalb Avenue, Brooklyn, in 1920/21; thereafter we could find no mention of Halter's cut glass company in any of the public or trade directories. The last secretary of the National Association of Cut Glass Manufacturers, Raymond H. Fender, confirmed that J. Halter & Company was a member of that organization.

E. W. Hammond Company

Although the E. W. Hammond Company was listed as a cut glass manufacturer in the *American Glass Trade Directory* in 1918, we could find nothing else to indicate that they actually produced such wares. Apparently Hammond was a manufacturer's representative and a retail and wholesale outlet for china and glassware. From 1910 to 1916 his business was located at 65 West Broadway in New York City, and was known as the E. W. Hammond Company. In 1917 the firm moved to 23 West 23d Street, New York City. At this period Edward W. Hammond was the president of the concern; Clarence D. Vail, secretary; and James M. Stewart, treasurer. No changes were made in the listings of the firm until 1920, when they moved to 10 West 23d Street, New York City.

Max Herbert Company, Incorporated
United Cut Glass Company
Herbert & Neuwirth Company

From 1911 to 1914, Max Herbert was listed variously as manager, president, and agent for his firm, the Max Herbert Company, Incorporated, of 26 Murray Street, New York City. In 1916, Herbert was president and treasurer of the company; Samuel Neuwirth, vice president; and Harry S. Wallenstein, secretary. The firm's address at this time, and until at least 1919, was at 8 West 22d Street, New York City.

In 1917 they were listed as an outlet for "novelties"; however, on March 18, 1913, Herbert registered a design for an unusual cut glass dish in the form of a cart with wheels. The patent illustration obviously shows only the pressed blank for such an article, with simple cutting on the edge and sides of the dish; the wheels were cut to resemble daisylike flowers. The dish was, in all probability, further embellished on the plain portions of the blank with various cut patterns popular at the time the patent was issued.

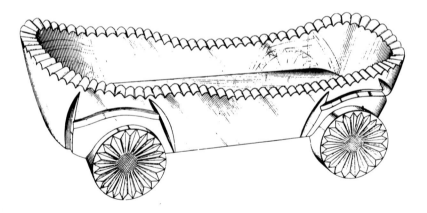

Max Herbert's design for a cut glass dish; patented Mar. 18, 1913.

There was a connection between the Max Herbert Company and the United Cut Glass Company. In 1910 the United Cut Glass Company was located at 42 West Broadway, New York City. From 1911 to 1915 their address was the same as the Max Herbert Company, 26 Murray Street. From 1916 to 1919 the firm was operating at 8 West 22d Street in Manhattan.

The list of officers of the United Cut Glass Company from 1915 to 1919 were Max Herbert, president-treasurer; Samuel Neuwirth, vice president; and John Halpin, secretary. In 1918 Harry Wallenstein replaced Halpin as secretary.

128

Both the Max Herbert Company, Incorporated, and the United Cut Glass Company were listed as manufacturers of cut glass in the *American Glass Trade Directory* from 1914 to 1918. Some years later they were merged into the Herbert & Neuwirth Company (Max Herbert and Samuel Neuwirth, proprietors). At this time they gave up the production of cut glass and carried both domestic and imported wares. The Herbert & Neuwirth Company went out of business when Herbert died. Sam Neuwirth formed his own company, the Neuwirth Company, Incorporated, which is still presently operating in New York City at 225 Fifth Avenue.

S. Herbert Cut Glass Company
Herbert Glass & Import Corporation

Sigmund Herbert operated a cut glass shop in New York City at 48 West Broadway and was first listed in the city directory in 1910 as "S. Herbert Cut Glass Company, Sigmund Herbert, president." In 1912 the firm was operating at the two locations at one time, 26 Murray Street and the old address at 48 West Broadway. The S. Herbert Cut Glass Company was connected with the Max Herbert Company, Incorporated, at this time, and both firms were housed under the same roof until 1915, when the S. Herbert Cut Glass Company moved to a new location at 37 West 23d Street. The connection between the two firms remained the same, for we find John J. Halpin's name listed as secretary of the S. Herbert Cut Glass Company from 1915 to 1919. Sigmund Herbert was president and treasurer of the company throughout its business life, and David L. Wise was vice president. The *Pottery and Glass Directory* for 1920/21 listed the firm as a manufacturer's agent at 35 West 23d Street, and also listed the Herbert & Neuwirth Company at 25 West 23d Street as wholesale distributors of "lamps, metal and wood novelties, cut glass."

In 1900 the New York City directories listed "Herbert & Hollis, glass, 64 Murray Street and 605 West 39th Street. Sigmund Herbert, president. Business address 66 Murray; home 142 West 73rd Street. Sigmund H. Herbert, secretary." Herbert was also associated with the Rock Crystal Glass Company of Jersey City, New Jersey, in 1918; and was listed as a manufacturer of cut glass in the *American Glass Trade Directory* for that same year.

In 1926 the name of the firm was changed to the Herbert Glass & Import Corporation, manufacturers of cut glass and importers of glassware. The association with the Herbert & Neuwirth Company was confirmed again in the 1927 directories. By 1928 only the Herbert & Neuwirth Company was listed in the business records.

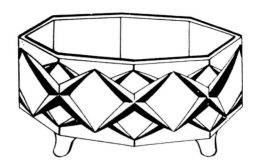

Sigmund Herbert's design for a footed cut glass bowl; patented Aug. 2, 1910.

On August 2, 1910, Sigmund Herbert registered a design for a footed cut glass bowl, known in those days as a "fernery."

J. H. Herrfeldt & Company

In 1909 the *Brooklyn Directory* listed "J. H. Herrfeldt, glass, 67 Clymer Street"; and again in 1910, "J. Hugo Herrfeldt, glass, 71 Clymer Street, Brooklyn." Since we could not find an earlier entry for Herrfeldt, we believe he started his small cut glass business not earlier than 1908. In 1913, Herrfeldt was located at 72 Grand Avenue in Brooklyn. In 1918, J. H. Herrfeldt & Company was listed as cut glass manufacturers in the *American Glass Trade Directory*; and in 1920/21 the firm was noted in the *Pottery and Glass Directory*, with a new address at 48 Lexington Avenue, Brooklyn. The last entry for this firm was in 1923 at its Lexington Avenue address.

L. Hinsberger Cut Glass Company

Louis Hinsberger's name first appears in the New York business directories in 1895; at that time his shop was located at 39 Barclay Street. In 1898 an address at 300 Oakland Street was given where Hinsberger manufactured beveled glass until at least 1910; the cut glass shop was still operating all this while at 39 Barclay Street. Hinsberger was listed as the president of his firm throughout the life of the business. On May 19, 1908, Louis Hinsberger

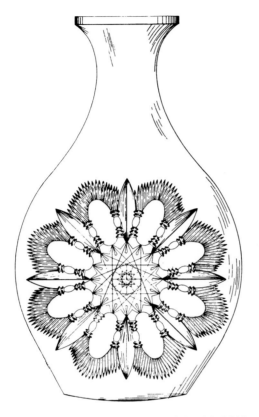

Louis Hinsberger's "Radiant Star" pattern; patented May 19, 1908.

patented a cut glass design which we have named "Radiant Star." The firm's trademark label read "Hinsberger Cut Glass Co., N.Y." The last directory entry for Hinsberger was dated 1913, and he was living in Brooklyn at 710 Leonard Street.

Jansen & Wells

John Jansen, "cutter," was listed in the 1891/92 *Brooklyn Directory* at 107 Warwick Street. In 1905, John A. Jansen, "cutter," and Edward F. Wells, "cutter," were both listed as Brooklyn residents. No business address for the firm could be found; but in 1918 the *American Glass Trade Directory* listed the firm of Jansen & Wells as cut glass manufacturers in Brooklyn, New York.

Thomas G. Jones

On April 13, 1920, Thomas G. Jones registered a beautiful cut glass design which was a combination of "Chair Bottom" cutting with broad perpendicular flutes and a wreath of flowers and leaves around the rim of the bowl, as is shown in the patent illustration. We named this pattern the "Beauchamp" design.

The "Beauchamp" pattern; patented Apr. 13, 1920, by Thomas G. Jones.

We discovered that Jones was listed in the East Orange, New Jersey, directories from 1910 through 1936, and his occupation was given as "glass, N.Y." or "glassware, N.Y.," indicating that his shop or firm was located in New York City; but we were unable to locate him there. Apparently Jones died some time between 1936 and 1938, for his widow was listed in the East Orange, New Jersey, directories from 1938 to 1942.

Kellner & Munro Rich Cut Glass

Angus Munro and Frank Kellner established a small cut glass factory in Brooklyn, New York, at 308 Graham Avenue, corner of Ainslie Street. The company operated from 1908 to 1918, according to Munro's son Duncan, who presently is associated with the Shelburne Museum, Incorporated, in Shelburne, Vermont. We are indebted to Duncan Munro for the illustrations of

Covered jar in the "Chair Bottom" ("Harvard") pattern produced by Kellner & Munro; *ca.* 1913.

Collection of Duncan Munro

Spoon holder cut at Kellner & Munro.

Collection of Duncan Munro

Small cut glass bowl produced by Kellner & Munro; *ca.* 1913.

cut glass made by his father's concern, all of which were cut on crystal blanks imported from Belgium.

At the peak of their business the firm employed about 21 cutters and two dippers (acid dippers) or polishers. The product was of a very high quality and was sold through such retail stores as Tiffany & Company and Weinburg's in New York City.

We found a listing in the *Brooklyn Directory* for a Thomas Munro, cut glass manufacturer, at 308 Graham Avenue, Brooklyn, in 1913, along with a listing of Kellner & Munro. On this same date George Kellner was listed as a cut glass manufacturer living at 128 Ainslie Street in Brooklyn.

Kiefer Brothers Cut Glass Company

George Kiefer was listed as a purveyor of "glassware" in the *Brooklyn Directory* for 1909. In 1912 this same source listed Charles Kiefer and Edward J. Kiefer, and the Kiefer Brothers, manufacturers of cut glass, at 805 Lexington Avenue, Brooklyn. The *Pottery and Glass Directory* indicated that the firm was located at 4 Ralph Avenue, Brooklyn in 1920/21. Kiefer Brothers appeared as cut glass manufacturers in the *American Glass Trade Directory* in 1918.

In 1913/14 Charles Kiefer, "glass merchant," was located at 949 Broadway, New York City. By 1924 Kiefer was listed as an agent for the Johnson-Carlson Cut Glass Company of Chicago, Illinois; also as the Kiefer Products Company, cut glass manufacturers, 4 Ralph Avenue, Brooklyn, New York.

Kings County Glass Works
Kings County Rich Cut Glass Works

The Kings County Glass Works were operating in Brooklyn, New York, in 1905, at 176 North 4th Street. In 1909 the name of the firm was changed to Kings County Rich Cut Glass Works, 174 North 4th Street; the company was still operating under this name and at the last address given on North 4th Street as late as 1923, when it was listed as a manufacturer of cut glass in the *American Glass Trade Directory*, and the *Pottery and Glass Directory*. The firm was a member of the National Association of Cut Glass Manufacturers.

Emil F. Kupfer, Incorporated

In 1912, Emil F. Kupfer, Incorporated, cut glass manufacturers, were operating a small factory in Brooklyn, New York, at 239 Greenpoint Avenue. A. Kupfer was listed as a "cutter" under this listing, with a home address at

128 Noble, Brooklyn, New York. In 1911, Emil F. Kupfer was noted as an agent for manufacturers at 65 West Broadway, Brooklyn. From 1912 to 1916 he was located at 66 Murray Street, and dealt primarily in "glassware," and later he was listed as a "glassware manufacturer." From 1917 to 1918 the firm's address was given as 116 Nassau Street, New York City, and at this time they were designated as "importers."

The *American Glass Trade Directory* listed Emil F. Kupfer, Incorporated, as a manufacturer of cut glass from 1918 to 1920. From 1920 to 1929, Emil F. Kupfer, Incorporated, manufacturer of cut glass, 132 Greenpoint Avenue, Brooklyn, was listed in the Brooklyn directories. In 1889/90, Emil Kupfer, clerk, was residing in New York City at 206 East 102d Street.

The "Good Luck" pattern; patented July 29, 1913, by Francis R. Smith for Emil F. Kupfer, Inc.

Francis R. Smith of New York City assigned one half of a design patent to Emil F. Kupfer, Incorporated, of Brooklyn, New York, on July 29, 1913. The design consisted of a representation of a horseshoe in the center of the article and the words "Good Luck."

Louis Levine Cut Glass Company

Aside from a listing in the 1918 issue of the *American Glass Trade Directory* for the Louis Levine Cut Glass Company, very little information could be found on this firm. From 1910 to 1912, Levine was located at 294 Delancey Street, New York City, as a glass merchant. The M. J. Levine Glass Company appears in the New York City directories from 1912 to 1914 at 327 Spring Street and then at 255 Spring Street. By 1915/16, Louis Levine is listed as a "glazier," and it would appear that he was manufacturing both cut plate glass and cut glass tablewares.

The Louis Levine (Levien) Cut Glass Company, 164 Fifth Avenue, New York City, was listed as a distributor and jobber of cut glass products. This listing continued until 1923.

Metropolitan Glass Works
Metropolitan Cut Glass Company
Metropolitan Pottery Company

The Metropolitan Glass Works, located at 95 Commercial Street, Brooklyn, New York, and Garrison and Flushing Avenue, Maspeth, Long Island, New York, was first listed in the *Brooklyn Directory* in 1912. The name of the firm again appeared in the 1918 listing of cut glass manufacturers published by the *American Glass Trade Directory*, as the Metropolitan Cut Glass Company.

By 1927 the name of the firm was changed to the Metropolitan Pottery Company, with locations at Maspeth, Long Island, and Meriden, Connecticut; the last listing for this concern was dated 1930.

Theodore Meyer

In 1911 and 1912 Theodore Meyer, a glass importer with shops at 508 Fifth Avenue and 50 Union Square, sold cut glassware in New York City, but we could not determine if his cut glasswares were imported or domestic.

S. F. Meyers Company

The S. F. Meyers Company, a jewelry concern located in New York City at 50 Maiden Lane and 33 Liberty Street, was listed in the *New York Directory* for the year 1900 as a cut glass manufacturer. Actually, we believe this firm was a wholesale and retail outlet for another company's cut glass products.

McCue & Earl
James H. McCue
Co-Operative Cut Glass Company

The Brooklyn directories for the years 1891 and 1892 listed McCue & Earl, glass cutting, at 22 Morton Street; James H. McCue, glass cutter, and John Earl, glass cutter, were listed separately under this heading also. From 1905 to 1909 James McCue, glass cutter, was reported as residing at 370 Euclid Avenue, and John J. McCue at 515 Kent Avenue. In 1912/13 only James McCue was listed as a glass cutter.

In an article written for the *Jeweler's Circular Weekly* in 1915, James D. Bergen of Meriden, Connecticut, mentioned the McCue & Earl cutting shop as one operating in Brooklyn between 1860 and 1870; and the Co-Operative Cut Glass Company of Brooklyn, New York, John J. McCue, president. The *American Glass Trade Directory* listed James J. McCue as a manufacturer of cut glass in the 1918 compilation.

138

John A. Nelson

John A. Nelson was a member of the National Association of Cut Glass Manufacturers, and this would indicate that his shop was not a one-man operation; however, the few recordings of this man's name in various sources never showed that it had been a company at any time. In 1912, John A. Nelson was listed in the *Brooklyn Directory* as a glass cutter located at 320 Driggs Avenue. Nelson was among the names listed in the 1918 issue of the *American Glass Trade Directory* as a manufacturer of cut glasswares.

Pope Cut Glass Company, Incorporated

In 1916/17, Frederick J. Grace was the president of the Pope Cut Glass Company, with Frank C. Hastings as secretary-treasurer. Shortly thereafter the firm was incorporated and the name changed to the Pope Cut Glass Company, Incorporated, with Benjamin I. [J.] Ward, president; Hastings was still secretary-treasurer. In 1916 the business was located at 66 Murray Street, New York City; in 1917 it was situated at 170 West Broadway. From 1918 to 1920 it was operating at 23 Worth Street. The address changed again in 1924 to 27 Thames Street.

The firm was listed as a manufacturer of cut glass in the *Pottery and Glass Directory* between 1920 and 1923. On September 20, 1916, they filed their trademark papers for the "Diamon Kut" mark with which they identified their cut glass products. The trademark, issued on December 26, 1922, was affixed to their cut glassware with a paper label, or lightly etched in the surface of the glass.

Reyen & Schaning

In 1912, Nicholas Reyen and G. Schaning were operating a cut glass shop at 65 Varick Street in Brooklyn, New York. Nicholas Reyen was listed under "glassware" in 1913, with a shop at 146 Kingsland Avenue, Brooklyn. Reyen & Schaning were listed as cut glass manufacturers in the 1918 *American Glass Trade Directory*.

Max Schaffer Company

In 1910, Max Schaffer was listed as president and treasurer of his company, which was located at 256 Grand Street, New York City. By 1911 the firm had moved to 298 Grand Street. In 1915, the Max Schaffer Company was listed as an importer and supplier of glassware located at 26 Warren Street. The firm remained at that location until at least 1921, when its advertisements were noted in the *Pottery and Glass Directory*. In 1918 the firm was known as a cut glass manufacturer, according to the *American Glass Trade Directory*. The Max Schaffer Company had a shop at 31 West 15th Street, New York City, from 1923 to 1928.

George Schneider Cut Glass Company

The George Schneider Cut Glass Company was listed in the Brooklyn directories from 1905 to 1913 as cut glass manufacturers located at 61 Clymer Street. Between 1910 and 1912 they also maintained a shop at 25 West Broadway, Brooklyn, probably as a showroom. The firm was a member of the National Association of Cut Glass Manufacturers for several years.

C. P. Schuller Cut Glass Company
Charles P. Schuller Cut Glass & Lamp Company

The C. P. Schuller Cut Glass Company was listed as a manufacturer of cut glasswares in the *American Glass Trade Directory* for 1918. In 1918/19, Charles P. Schuller Cut Glass & Lamp Company was listed in the New York City business directory at 25 West 23d Street. Charles P. Schuller was president of the firm; Louis I. Schuller, secretary; and William F. Hayes, Jr., treasurer.

Thomas Shotton Cut Glass Company
Shotton Cut Glass Works
Thomas Shotton & Sons

James D. Bergen once described the Shotten Cut Glass Works as a "very large glass cutting shop in Brooklyn, New York," and reported that Shotton employed hundreds of cutters manufacturing, for some time, some fairly good cut glassware. According to Bergen, the firm went into the more popular-priced cut glass and cheap figured (pressed) wares before going out of business some time after World War I.

We found Thomas Shotton listed in the Brooklyn directories from 1905 to 1912, where his shop was noted as being at 482 Driggs Avenue. From 1910 to 1914, Thomas Shotton Cut Glass Company maintained a shop at 48 West Broadway, New York City, to display their cut glasswares. The Thomas Shotton Cut Glass Works advertised in the *Pottery and Glass Directory* in 1920 and 1921, with a location at 345 Eldert Street, Brooklyn; and in 1922 and 1923, Thomas Shotton & Sons were operating out of their shop at 128 Wythe Avenue, Brooklyn; no mention of this firm could be found after this date.

Standard Cut Glass Company

The Standard Cut Glass Company was established in New York City some time before 1895 by Harry T. Broden. The shop was located at 549 West 22d Street. In the *New York City Directory* for 1895 Broden was listed as president of the concern.

Harry T. Broden registered two designs for cut glass on September 24, 1895; both patterns are typical designs of the Brilliant Period. The leading feature of the first design, which we call "Bruce," consisted of "lune prisms" crossing one another at different angles and substantially forming the outline of a many-pointed star. Minute prisms arranged in conjunction with cross-hatching and checkering presented a Gothic fenestrated appearance. The

Left: The "Bruce" pattern; *right*: The "Tartan" pattern; both patented Sept. 24, 1895, by Harry T. Broden for Standard Cut Glass Co.

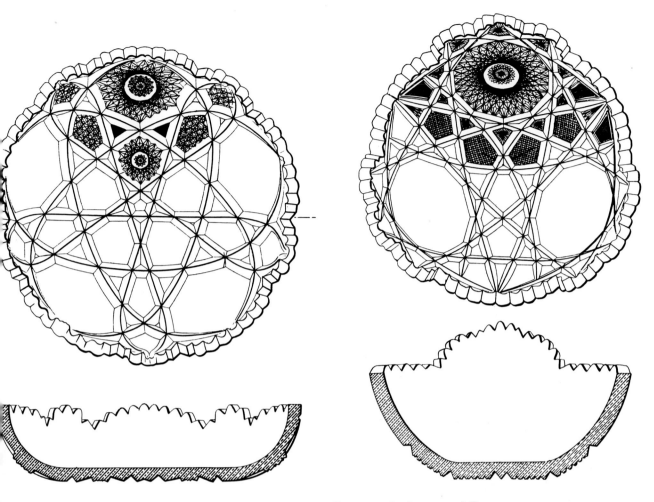

Left: The "Lazarre" pattern; *right:* The "Prismatic Stars" pattern; both patented Dec. 10, 1895, by Henry T. Broden for Standard Cut Glass Co.

The "Pinto" pattern; patented Dec. 10, 1895, by Henry T. Broden for Standard Cut Glass Co.

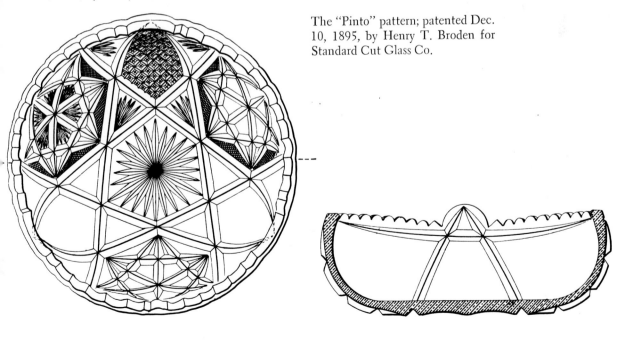

second design, called "Tartan" here, was described by Broden as consisting somewhat of oval prisms connected to form a starlike chain. In the center of the dish a "button" of prismatic character was formed.

On December 10, 1895, three cut glass designs were patented by Henry T. Broden and assigned to the Standard Cut Glass Company. The first two, which we have named "Lazarre" and "Prismatic Stars," are somewhat similar in character and appear at first glance to be alike because of the large prismatic rosette used in each as the main feature of the design. However, differences in the patterns show clearly in the patent drawings. The third design, "Pinto," registered by Broden on this date, consists of starlike formations of prismatic quality bounded with hatchwork cutting alternating with panels of "Strawberry" cutting. The center of the dish is ornamented with a prismatic radiating design.

The Standard Cut Glass Company's trademark label consisted of their name and a representation of the American flag.

Steinfeld Brothers

The Steinfeld Brothers were listed as cut glass manufacturers in the *American Glass Trade Directory* in 1918, but quite obviously this was not their only product. In 1900 the *New York City Directory* listed them as purveyors of "woodenware," and in 1911/12 this same source noted that they were a retail outlet for "toys," located at 620 Broadway. The *Pottery and Glass Directory* (1920/21) listed this firm at 116 West 32d Street.

J. M. Uniack

The first listing of J. M. Uniack, a cut glass company, was found in the *New York City Directory* for the 1911/12 period. At this time James M. Uniack was listed as vice president of the firm, which was located at 200 Fifth Avenue. In 1918, J. M. Uniack was among the names of cut glass manufacturers listed in the *American Glass Trade Directory*.

C. G. Alford & Company

In 1872, C. G. Alford & Company were jewelers and watch jobbers, located at 12 Maiden Lane, in the heart of what was then New York City's jewelry center. By 1874, Charles. G. Alford moved his business to 183 Broadway. From 1889 to 1891 their shop was noted at 200 Broadway, and in 1900 it was listed at 185 Broadway. In 1910 Alford again moved his business, this time to 11 John Street, in lower Manhattan. In 1913 he was listed as president of the concern, and J. Warren Alford was treasurer. At this period they had their shop at 192 Broadway, and it remained at this address until 1918, according to the city directories.

Signed "Alford" plate; diameter 7¼ in.

Collection of Mr. and Mrs. Jack Walker

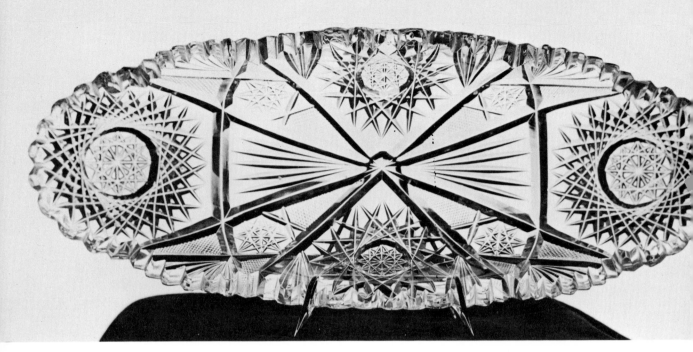

Celery dish, signed "Alford"; length 12 in.

Obviously C. G. Alford & Company were not a cutting shop at all, but a manufacturer's agent, or retail outlet, for some cut glass factory's products. Alford's trademark consisted of their name in block letters within a diamond-shaped field.

George Borgfeldt & Company
George Borgfeldt Corporation

George Borgfeldt & Company were wholesale distributors of all kinds of household goods, including some fine cut glass. Their showrooms were located at 16th Street and Irving Place in New York City. On May 5, 1914, Borgfeldt registered a trademark "for use on cut glass," which consisted of a crown with rays of light emanating from a point just above the coronet. Ekko Sollmann was secretary of the firm in 1914; at one time D. C. Tracy, another member of this firm, was on the board of directors of the National Association of Cut Glass Manufacturers. The firm was established in 1881 and is still in existence as the George Borgfeldt Corporation, 21 East 26th Street, New York City. At no time did they actually manufacture their own cut glass. Some members of their firm believe that their cut glassware was imported from abroad.

Duncan & Dithridge

In the early 1900's, J. Duncan Dithridge was an agent for cut glass manufacturers and other glass-producing companies, with a shop at 25 West Broadway in New York City. The firm of Duncan & Dithridge did not operate a cutting shop of their own, though they have been reported to have been cut glass manufacturers. The Dithridge Flint Glass Company in New Brighton, Pennsylvania, did manufacture a very high grade crystal blank for cutting in the first quarter of the twentieth century.

Higgins & Seiter

For many years the firm of Higgins & Seiter in New York City were wholesale distributors of fine china and glass. They issued several illustrated catalogues showing their fine selection of brilliantly cut glass; unfortunately, without naming the actual manufacturer of these wares. One thing is certain—they sold Libbey's cut glass for many years and were listed as an agent for the Libbey Glass Company in Libbey's Columbian World's Fair brochure issued in 1893.

Charles Levin

Matt Hanse, owner of the Lotus Glass Company of Barnesville, Ohio, told the author that Charles Levin was a wholesale distributor of cut glass in New York City and not a manufacturer of this product. Since Hanse was speaking from his vast experience in the trade, we are inclined to accept this information as fact; however, Charles Levin did obtain a patent for a cut glass design on November 9, 1915. The registration covered a design for a celery or relish dish with a rather simple floral design, as is shown in the patent illustration.

147

Design for a cut glass dish patented Nov. 9, 1915, by Charles Levin.

Lazarus & Rosenfeld

Lazarus & Rosenfeld, importers of Bohemian glass, operated a showroom and shop in New York City during the last quarter of the nineteenth century and the first quarter of the twentieth century. They were listed as cut glass manufacturers by the *American Glass Trade Directory* in 1918, but we have reason to believe that they did not actually cut their own wares. At the end of World War I, a brisk trade in cut glass developed with foreign factories, which was a contributing factor to the curtailment of this industry in America; the simple fact was that foreign factories could, and did, produce cut glasswares much cheaper than it was possible for American manufacturers to do.

Bawo & Dotter

Bawo & Dotter of 26 Barclay Street, New York City, were wholesale distributors of Bohemian glass and china. They operated their own glass and china factories in Europe and it is not likely that they sold any domestic cut glass in their New York showrooms. Carl F. Prosch, who later worked for Christian Dorflinger in Honesdale, Pennsylvania, was once Bawo & Dotter's New York representative.

C. G. Tuthill & Company
Tuthill Cut Glass Company

Among the finest pieces of American cut glass ever produced were the products of the Tuthill Cut Glass Company of Middletown, New York. This factory was first established as C. G. Tuthill & Company by Charles Guernsey Tuthill in 1900, and it operated as such until around 1902, when Charles Tuthill was joined in the business by his brother James F. Tuthill and his sister-in-law Susan C. Tuthill. Originally the factory was located on North Street at the corner of Wisner Avenue. Thereafter it was moved to 36 Little Avenue. The business closed in 1923. Its equipment, patterns, and photographs were sold to the Henry Guyard Company in Honesdale, Pennsylvania.

Charles Tuthill was a most talented designer of cut glass patterns and was responsible for most of the company's designs. The man who made some of their finest pieces was Harry Holmbaker, a former police chief of Middletown. Perfection was the keynote in this factory, and Susan Tuthill was its chief priestess. She insisted on punctuality, and would call in any worker who was even a few minutes late, for a protracted lecture on the virtues of being "on time." She insisted on every piece of glass being perfect in design and cutting before it left the factory. She would measure the depth of the cutting, scallops, and dentil edges of every article; with calipers she would check the alignment of the design. After 1915 each piece of Tuthill cut glass was marked with their trademark—the name "Tuthill" in flowing script. This work was originally done by Grace Vail Clark, who was succeeded by Fannie Temper Green. Susan Tuthill's husband, James Tuthill, has been credited with taking the excellent photographs of their wares for their salesmen's catalogues in a specially fitted darkroom in the factory building. When the lint from a dress factory on the top floor of their building began to filter down and impair the cutting and polishing of their cut glass, Susan Tuthill asked them to move. Charles E. Rose of Corning, New York, was once associated with the Tuthill Cut Glass Company.

The Tuthill Cut Glass Company won many awards for their wares; among these was the Bronze Medal of Honor and a plaque presented to them for the finest cut glass exhibited at the 1915 Panama-Pacific International Exposition in San Francisco. Among their most important pieces of cut glass was a

Signed "Tuthill" plate; diameter 7 in.

vase, 36 inches tall, which was made as a farewell gift for the Chinese ambassador; it was engraved by Harry Holmbaker in a design of coiled dragons which wrapped themselves around the vase. Holmbaker is the proud owner of a small dish in the "Rex" pattern which won Tuthill their award in the San Francisco exposition. The factory made use in their products of all the usual cut glass designs common to the Brilliant Period—stars, fans, shells, hob-star, buzz-star (pinwheel), strawberry-diamond, fine saw tooth, checkering, beaded columns, and so on.

Among their flower and fruit designs, Tuthill had such patterns as "Orchid," "Phlox," "Cosmos," "Wild Rose," "Forget-me-not," "Tiger Lily,"

"Daisy and Festoon," "Grape," "Grapefruit," and "Tomato." "Egypt," "Madrid," "Yale," and "Florence" were names given to still more cut glass patterns. A unique example of Tuthill cut glass was exhibited at the Thrall Library in Middletown some years ago; this was a dish engraved with a speckled trout in gray tones (mat finish) and with a border of fine diamond cutting. Tuthill's line ran the full gamut from small bottles and trifles to large vases and punch bowls, lighting fixtures, and boxes. At one period they supplied the White House in Washington with beautiful cut crystal inkwells with sterling silver tops.

Tuthill's "Wild Rose" pattern; diameter of plate 13 in.

Collection of Lynn Parker

Van Heusen & Charles
Van Heusen, Charles & Company

Theodore V. Van Heusen and D. D. T. Charles formed Van Heusen & Charles, a wholesale china and glass store in Albany, New York, in 1843. They bought out the firm of Wardwell & Bordwell, then doing business in an old building at 66 State Street. Van Heusen & Charles occupied one half of

Plate, signed "Van Heusen, Charles Co."; diameter 6 in.

Collection of Mr. and Mrs. Jack Walker

the shop and J. & A. McClure, druggists, the other half. In 1884, **Van Heusen & Charles** moved to 62 and 64 State Street, to a site formerly occupied by Lewis Benedict & Company, hardware merchants. In 1856 they bought the property on Broadway then known as the Mansion House, for many years an old hotel, and on this site they built the store which they still occupy at 470 Broadway. In 1886 the shop extended through the block from Broadway to James Street, and was 250 feet deep.

In 1864, George W. Pierce, who had been in their employ for several years, became a partner, and the style of the firm was changed to Van Heusen, Charles & Company. From 1920 to 1930 Charles M. Van Heusen was president of the concern; Rustam K. Kermani became president in 1945.

In 1893, Van Heusen, Charles & Company were agents for the Libbey Glass Company and were so designated in Libbey's list of agents published that year. A former general manager of the Van Heusen, Charles Company, confirms that they did not cut their own glassware; however, articles of cut glass bearing this firm's name etched lightly in the metal have been found, and we can only conclude from this that they purchased their cut wares from one or more small cutting shops and had their own trademark placed on these articles. The Libbey Glass Company's wares, of course, would in every instance bear their own identifying trademark.

American Cut Glass Company

The American Cut Glass Company was a small cutting shop operated in Port Jervis, New York, by Arthur E. O'Connor for his father John S. O'Connor of Hawley, Pennsylvania, and Goshen, New York. The American Cut Glass Company was active for only a very short period—perhaps not more than two years—1902 to 1904. (See J. S. O'Connor, Hawley, Pennsylvania.)

Edward W. Mayer—Glass Cutters

About 1910, Michael Mayer started a cut glass shop in Port Jervis, New York, which was located adjacent to the Gillinder Brothers' glass factory. The business was started some years earlier in Brooklyn, New York. Edward W. Mayer, Michael Mayer's only son, took over the business when his father died, and named it Edward W. Mayer—Glass Cutters. Anton (Tony) Meyer, a cousin of Edward Mayer, came to America from Alsace-Lorraine at the age of twenty-one years and was foreman of this shop. Edward Mayer died in 1933, and at the request of his widow, Gillinder Brothers operated the shop for her until they purchased the propery a year or so later, perhaps in 1935, and moved the equipment into their own factory.

In the beginning the Mayer cut glass factory employed about 30 expert glass cuttters and used heavy crystal blanks imported from Belgium. Their cut glass was considered very fine at that time. The shop cut glass for Gillinder Brothers for many years, but by 1920 they had only 10 cutters working their frames. Before 1930 the number of cutters had been reduced again to just five in number and the firm was producing only cut glass lighting fixtures for Gillinder Brothers.

Century Cut Glass Company

The Century Cut Glass Company was located on Jane Street in the village of Saugerties, New York, in 1918, the year it was listed in the *American Glass Trade Directory*. It was operated by Daugherty (Dougherty) Brothers for only a short time, not more than two years according to existing records, after which the owners moved to Brooklyn, New York. Some families in Saugerties still possess pieces of Century's cut glass which, for the most part, are indistinguishable from other brilliantly cut patterns of the 1918 period.

Kelly & Steinman
Peerless Cut Glass Company

After they had severed their connection with the Gibbs, Kelly cut glass shop in Honesdale, Pennsylvania, Michael J. Kelly and Frank Steinman opened their own cut glass works about 1905 on West 11th Street, and were known as Kelly & Steinman. Not long afterward they opened the Peerless Cut Glass Company in Deposit, New York, and operated it for about eight years.

Elmira Cut Glass Company
Elmira Glass Cutting Company

In 1899 the Elmira Cut Glass Company, also known as the Elmira Glass Cutting Company, was located at 158 Fox Street in Elmira, New York. At this period they shared their premises with Frederick J. Schweppe and Henry C. Schweppe, painting and decorating contractors. The large two-story red brick building is still standing (1964) and is currently occupied by the Machinist Union Hall. In 1909 the factory was moved to the corner of DeWitt and East Water Street in Elmira. The last entry for this firm in the city directory was in 1911.

The officers of the Elmira Cut Glass Company were John C. Ferris, president; Joel Ferris, treasurer; and B. F. Levy, secretary. In 1899, George R. Ferris was listed as foreman of the shop, and in 1911 Frank E. Ferris appeared in the city directory as a "glass worker."

The Elmira *Star Gazette* for Friday, November 4, 1910, had a headline: "Cut Glass Plant Idled." Forty employees walked out, demanding that the American Flint Glass Workers' Union be recognized as their bargaining agent. The president of the company, John C. Ferris, said the men asked for a 55-hour week instead of the usual 59 hours, and a posted price list so that the workers might know what they were to receive by the piece for each job. At the time the men were earning from $12.00 to $18.00 a week and they demanded a 10 per cent raise. The company claimed to be paying higher wages than any other glass factory at that time. On the following day, November 5, 1910, Ferris reported in the papers that his plant in Corning, New York, would start operating the following Monday with 40 hands. Later editions of the Elmira *Star Gazette* indicated that both plants were operating with but 16 employees each, and that Ferris had still refused to recognize the union or make any compromise on the wage scale. Obviously, Ferris had anticipated the labor trouble and had established his cutting shop in Corning to open as soon as labor troubles in Elmira caused a shutdown of the factory there. Ferris was also associated with the Arcadia Cut Glass Company of Newark, New York.

The Elmira Cut Glass Company was not listed in the 1918 issue of the *American Glass Trade Directory* and we believe it was out of business a few years before that date.

Majestic Cut Glass Company

Wolf M. Spiegel and his son Saul S. Spiegel, owners of a salvage and metal works in Elmira, New York, founded the Majestic Cut Glass Company in that city about 1900; it was closed down shortly before World War I. The glass cutting factory was located in Elmira at the corner of Madison Avenue and East Clinton Street and was housed in a two-story building of wooden construction. The Spiegels employed between 25 and 30 glass cutters at the height of their business career.

Majestic's wares were cut on heavy blanks imported from Belgium, but they did produce some light cut glassware too. The leading stores throughout the eastern half of the United States were the retail outlets for Majestic's

Left: Cut glass lamp made by Majestic Cut Glass Co.; height 18 in. *Right:* Cracker jar cut at Majestic Cut Glass Co.; height 9½ in.
Collection of Mrs. Beatrice Perling

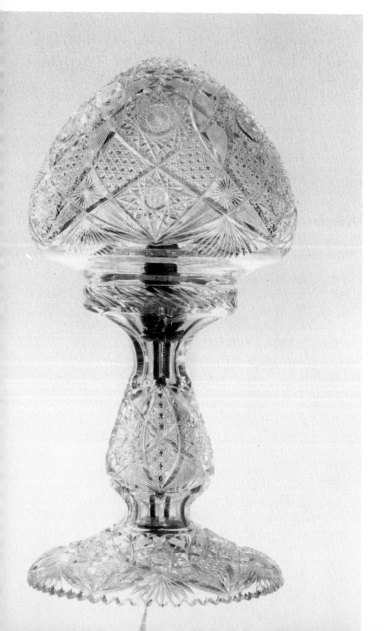

Cut glass decanters 8 in. tall; celery vase 9¾ in. tall; produced by Majestic Cut Glass Co.

products, which were all of the very highest caliber. During the weeks preceding the Christmas holidays, Spiegel rented a downtown store and sold his wares as gifts. Wolf Spiegel's daughter, Mrs. Beatrice Perling, told us that they used a trademark on their glass; she thought it was the letter "M."

A full-time designer was employed at the Majestic Cut Glass Company, but his name has long since slipped from everybody's memory. The designs he created are all beautiful and representative of the best patterns of the Brilliant Period. Majestic's wares covered the entire field of cut glass articles—lamps, candlesticks, bowls, nappies, covered boxes, jars, perfume bottles and decanters, punch bowls and cups, stemware, ice buckets, vases, compotes, and so forth.

The Enterprise Cut Glass Company

The Enterprise Cut Glass Company of Elmira Heights, New York, was established about 1905 by George E. Gaylord, formerly of Honesdale, Pennsylvania. It was a small concern housed in a two-story building on College Avenue, almost directly across from the end of West 10th Street. On the lower floor were two rooms occupied by the roughing department, under the supervision of Courtney B. Boucher, and a small office. Boucher's men were responsible for the rough cutting of the patterns on plain crystal blanks. After the initial deep cutting was done, the roughed blanks were sent upstairs to the smoothing and finishing room, and ultimately scrutinized for perfection in the inspection room. If a blank passed inspection, the object was washed thoroughly, placed in huge vats of hardwood sawdust to dry, and then dusted with a fine camel's-hair brush, which made it sparkle like a diamond. From 1910 to 1917, James Lamb was in charge of the smoothing and finishing department. According to Lamb, the factory employed about 75 men at that time, and many of the cutters were splendid craftsmen who turned out a finished article of a very high quality.

In 1907 the Elmira city records show that George E. Gaylord was the president of the firm. He lived in a large house on the corner of 12th Street and Glenwood Avenue in Elmira Heights. James W. Bennett was treasurer, and at that time he resided in Elmira Heights, on 12th Street between Glenwood and College Avenues.

In 1908, Gaylord and Bennett occupied the same positions in the firm as president and treasurer, but the records indicate that Frank C. Farnham was vice president, and William Loring secretary of the company. Farnham was the inventor of a spindle brush which made the polishing of deep miter-cut designs much easier. James Bennett assumed the position of vice president and treasurer of the company in 1909. In 1910, P. D. Peterson was named to fill the vice presidency, and Charles Spencer was secretary; Gaylord was still president of the company. From 1911 to 1914, the officers of the firm were George Gaylord, president; James Bennett, vice president; and Courtney B. Boucher, secretary. In 1915 only Gaylord and Boucher were listed in the business directories.

The plant closed in 1917, as did many other cut glass factories, because World War I had made it impossible to secure blanks from Belgium, their main source of supply. Some of the articles made at the Enterprise Cut Glass Company were cut on blanks supplied to them by the Union Glass Works of Somerville, Massachusetts, but even this source was cut off when the United States entered the war in 1917. During a blizzard in 1917, the roof of the factory building was badly damaged and this was probably the last straw in the attempt to keep the business going. In 1935 the building occupied by the Enterprise Cut Glass Company was completely destroyed in a windstorm.

George Edwin Gaylord was born in Clinton, Wayne County, Pennsylvania, on June 4, 1873. He started his career in the cut glass business with T. B. Clark & Company of Honesdale, Pennsylvania. From about 1902 to 1905 Gaylord was with the Quaker City Cut Glass Company in Philadelphia; he returned to Honesdale for a short time before starting the Enterprise Cut Glass factory in Elmira Heights. On March 23, 1894, he married Rachel Ordnung. His two daughters report that they were a close-knit family and that their father "was a delightful person, with great *joie de vivre*, and exquisite taste." The latter quality is reflected in Gaylord's many beautiful cut glass designs. George Gaylord died on February 25, 1924.

In an interview with James Lamb, the author was assured that no marks of any kind were used on the Enterprise cut glasswares during his term of employment; because of this, identification of their products is extremely difficult. The illustrations shown in this book were obtained from original catalogues issued by the firm and from the collections of Gaylord's two daughters, and Lamb's daughter. Several pieces shown here are from local collections, and each piece was purchased directly from the Enterprise Cut Glass Company many years ago.

One common, but fine, pattern produced at the Enterprise works was patented by George Gaylord on October 24, 1911. It consists of a flower with about ten petals, each petal so finely engraved that it appears frosted until closely examined. The center of each flower is engraved with fine hatch cutting, while the leaves and stems of the flowers are miter cut in a simple

Left: "Rambler Rose" plate; diameter 8¼ in.; Enterprise Cut Glass Co. *Right:* "Daisy" tankard pitcher; height 7 in.; Enterprise Cut Glass Co.
Collection of Mrs. Louise Mosher

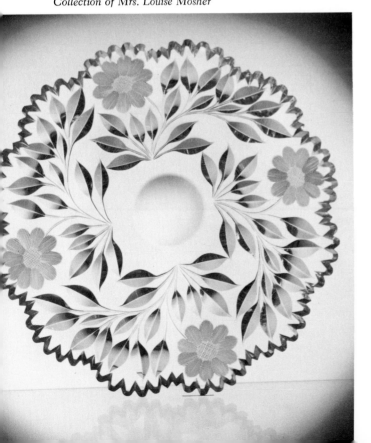

"Rose" celery tray, diameter 12½ in.; Enterprise Cut Glass Co.

Left to right: Sugar bowl in the "Stellaris" pattern; nappy in the "Tidy Tips" pattern; vase in the "Wild Flower and Butterfly" pattern; all Enterprise Cut Glass Co.

fashion. Gaylord described the flower as a "rambler rose" in his patent enumerations, and the pattern was sold under this name for many years.

Another "Rose" pattern was produced at the Elmira Heights cutting shop. The celery tray shown in the illustrations bears a marked similarity to the "White Rose" pattern illustrated in a catalogue issued by the Irving Cut Glass Company of Honesdale, Pennsylvania. The roses cut at the Enterprise works have fewer petals than those engraved by the Irving Cut Glass Company.

A simple floral design known as their "Daisy" pattern was cut at the Enterprise works on light wares; that is, the blanks were not as thick and heavy as those used for deep miter cutting. The "Daisy" pattern usually has ten petals, each engraved with fine straight lines, as is shown in the illustration of a tankard pitcher. Wild grasses are combined with the flowers to complete this simple and harmonious design. The "Daisy" pattern suite included tumblers in several shapes and sizes, handled mugs, covered and uncovered pitchers of different shapes and capacities, cream and sugar sets, a full line of stemware, including hollow stem champagnes, water carafes, a teapot, jam jars, and many other useful tablewares.

We have given names to three unidentified patterns found in an old Enterprise catalogue: "Stellaris," "Tidy Tips," and "Wild Flower and Butterfly."

Enterprise's "Star" pattern follows a more or less conventional design common to many cut glass factories of the time. Small intricately cut rosettes and buttons are combined in an elegant way with deep miter cutting to simulate the form of an eight-pointed star. The "Buzz" pattern was another

"Star" pattern bowl; diameter 7½ in.; Enterprise Cut Glass Co.

Collection of Mrs. Louise Mosher

Left: "Buzz" pattern decanter; height 13 in.; Enterprise Cut Glass Co.
Collection of Mrs. Louise Mosher

design common to many cut glass factories in America. William P. Feeney, of Feeney & McKanna, Honesdale, Pennsylvania, was credited by one of his contemporaries with promoting the popularity of the "Buzz" pattern. The brilliance of the design is beautifully illustrated in a decanter produced at the Enterprise cut glassworks about 1910.

A large bowl shown in the illustrations was cut by Gaylord for his wife. His daughter, Helen Gaylord, said he cut it "just for fun—a busman's holiday sort of thing." The sides of the bowl are engraved with large brilliant rosettes placed so as to form a six-pointed star. A tall vase in the Gaylord collection combines many intricately cut designs common to many cut glass shops of this period. The brilliance of the design is a credit to the engraver and the manufacturer.

Cut glass vase made at Enterprise Cut Glass Co.; height 13 in.
Collection of Misses Helen and Margaret Gaylord; photo by Higbie

Cut glass bowl executed by George E. Gaylord; Enterprise Cut Glass Co.
Collection of Misses Helen and Margaret Gaylord

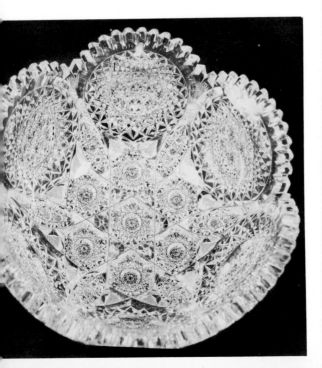

The "Royal" pattern; from an original Enterprise Cut Glass Co. catalogue; *ca.* 1915.

Pitcher in the "Imperial" pattern; cut at Enterprise Cut Glass Co.; height 13½ in.; *ca.* 1915.
Collection of Mrs. Helen Lamb Wieneke

Punch bowl and standard in the "Majestic" pattern manufactured at Enterprise Cut Glass Co.; height 11 in.; diameter of bowl 10 in.; *ca.* 1915.

Collection of Mrs. Helen Lamb Wieneke

Pitcher in the "Sunburst" pattern; produced at Enterprise Cut Glass Co.; *ca.* 1910; height 8 in.

Collection of Mrs. Robert Biddle

Fortunately, we were able to find a page from an old Enterprise Cut Glass Company catalogue showing their "Royal" pattern. The design is a simple one, composed of stylized flowers and leaves. Two tall vases in this pattern were further embellished with representations of butterflies flitting among the flowers.

Vandermark, Brace & Hall Cutting Shop

A year after the Enterprise Cut Glass Company closed their shop in Elmira Heights, New York, three men—George Vandermark, Adelbert B. Brace, and Harry Hall—opened their cutting shop, which was known as the Vandermark, Brace & Hall Cutting Shop. Operations began in 1918 but by 1921 the three men went out of the cut glass business. About a year after the firm was established, Brace sold his interest to Fred Nintz; and a year and a half later the business failed. Vandermark, Brace & Hall purchased some equipment from the defunct Enterprise Cut Glass Company when they started their small shop. Vandermark designed one pattern, the "Rex" pattern, which this small shop cut in great quantities. A wholesale glass and china store in Chicago purchased their entire production. Special lead glass blanks were purchased for their cut wares from the Libbey Glass Company in Toledo, Ohio.

Elmira Window Glass Works

There was another glass factory operating in Elmira Heights, New York, from 1896 to 1908. The Elmira Window Glass Works manufactured only window glass, but the workers, many of whom were from Belgium, often made paperweights and six-foot-long glass canes in their spare time. These were presented to spectators who came from near and far to stand on the balcony overlooking the work area to see how glass was made. Some of these canes have been in local collections for many years. They are straight, with a large knob for a handle, and spiraled with different colors. They differ in no way from similar canes made in European and American glass factories in the latter part of the nineteenth century.

Hoare & Burns
Gould & Hoare
Hoare & Dailey
J. Hoare & Company

The cut glass industry in Corning, New York, was transplanted from Brooklyn, New York, where James Hoare and his son John Hoare, with others, had become established in the business as the Brooklyn Flint Glass Company. In 1868 that company was induced to locate in Corning, and later, as the Corning Glass Works, became large and prosperous. John Hoare was associated with Amory Houghton, Sr. and Amory Houghton, Jr., both in the Brooklyn Flint Glass Company and in the Corning Glass Works, and his son James Hoare 2nd became widely known as a cut glass manufacturer. Both the senior James Hoare and his son John were born in Cork, Ireland; the grandson, James Hoare 2nd, was born in Birmingham, England. All were glass manufacturers, men of great skill and ability, successful in their trade and experts in the art of glass cutting and manufacturing.

The senior James Hoare followed his trade as a glass cutter in Cork, going thence with his family to Birmingham, England, where he remained in the glass cutting trade until he joined his son John Hoare in Brooklyn, New York, where he spent his declining years and died. His son John Hoare also learned his trade in glass cutting in Cork, and moved from there to Belfast and then Birmingham, where in 1842 he entered the employ of Rice Harris & Company of the Five Ways Glass Works. Later he was employed by Thomas Webb & Sons of Wordsley, England, becoming foreman of their cutting shop. He also worked for Lacey & Son of Birmingham as a traveling salesman. John Hoare was foreman of the cutting department of Lloyd & Summerfield, and for a time was associated with the Park Glass Company, one of the oldest and largest glasshouses in England. In 1848, John Hoare established a business in England for himself, and for five years had some degree of success. In 1853 he closed his factory and with his wife and children came to the United States, locating in Philadelphia, Pennsylvania, with a cash capital remaining of a half sovereign.

John Hoare went to New York City and worked for a year with E. V. Haughwout & Company in Brooklyn; then with five other men he formed a partnership to conduct a glass cutting business, Hoare being the active head of the firm. Two years later he bought the interests of three of his partners and with the remaining partners he formed the firm of Hoare & Burns. In 1855, Hoare bought from the Brooklyn Flint Glass Company its glass cutting department, stock and machinery, and established the firm of Gould & Hoare, who operated that business until 1861, when Gould & Hoare were succeeded by Hoare & Dailey.

James D. Bergen reported in the *Jeweler's Circular Weekly* in 1915 that

in the late 1850's or early 1860's Gould & Hoare were on the premises of the Columbia Street Glass Factory. Later Hoare & Dailey were at Greenpoint, New York, circa 1865. Afterwards John Hoare started a cutting shop on Centre Street in New York City and from there went to Corning, New York, where the firm J. Hoare & Company was formed.

John Hoare's family told the author that in 1867, Thomas G. Hawkes was brought over from Ireland (John Hoare paid his passage). He lived with Hoare before going into business for himself in Corning as T. G. Hawkes & Company.

In 1868, Amory Houghton and his son, Amory Houghton, Jr., the principal owners of the Brooklyn Flint Glass Company, were persuaded to move their plant to Corning; Hoare & Dailey also made the move at the same time, Hoare becoming connected with the Corning Flint Glass Company but retaining the cut glass department under the style of J. Hoare & Company. He continued active in the cut glass business in Corning during the remainder of his life, and was recognized as one of the pioneers of the American cut glass business. Hoare was the first man to turn glass on a lathe, and was also the first to make cut glass for store windows. His workmanship won awards at various exhibitions in Boston, Philadelphia, and Baltimore, and in 1893, Hoare won a gold medal at the World's Columbian Exposition in Chicago. Captain Hoare, as he was known in those days, died on June 17, 1896, at the Everett House in New York City. He was seventy-four years old.

James Hoare 2nd was born in Birmingham, England, on March 6, 1847, and was still a child when he came to America with his father. He grew to manhood in Brooklyn, New York, was educated there, and learned his trade of glass cutting under the tutelage of his famous father. He came to Corning with his family in 1868 and was associated with John Hoare in the firm of J. Hoare & Company. After the death of John Hoare the business was continued under the same name by James Hoare 2nd and his son John S. Hoare, the latter being a member of the firm also. The business was later sold to H. W. Baldwin and others, but in 1906 James Hoare 2nd repurchased it and continued its operation in a factory on Cortlandt Street in Wellsboro, Pennsylvania, the management being in the hands of his son John S. Hoare. At this time they employed 200 men.

Horace Taynton of Wellsboro was next in importance in the firm. The following men and women were also associates and workers in the Hoare factory while it operated in Wellsboro: William Langindorfer, Rome Bixby, Liner Bixby, Rose Bixby, Leon Watkins, Edward Wingate, Lewis Wingate, Harry Wingate, Charles Price, Lloyd Price, Homer Campbell, Charles Closs, Buster Spencer, George Landis, Leon Swope, Jack Skidmore, A. C. Edwards,

Frank Kriner, Jack Mattox, James Kimball, Harry Kimball, Alvin Tinker, Frank Farrell, Clyde Campbell, Arthur Dartt, Archie Ealey, Louis Grosjean, Stella Haight, Mary Moran, Will Davis, Layton Spraker, and Earl Spencer.

In 1916, J. Hoare & Company closed their Wellsboro factory and moved back to Corning, locating their shop on Bridge Street, where they operated until about 1921. James Hoare 2nd, died on November 4, 1921, the business was conducted by John S. Hoare until a short time before his father's death.

On April 4, 1871, John Hoare of New York City registered a design for caster bottles. The base of the bottle was formed to fit into a caster stand. In his patent specifications Hoare suggested that these bottles be cut or engraved in part as was desired. Hoare patented another design for a caster bottle on June 3, 1879; again suggesting that the upper portion of the bottle be decorated with engraving or cutting. Still another design patent for cut and engraved caster bottles was registered by Hoare on January 3, 1882.

John Hoare's first patented design for cut glass articles was registered on January 25, 1875, from Corning, New York. The patent covered a new design for a shell-shaped "Bouquet-Holder or Vase," which was formed in a contact mold. Afterward the article was cut on certain portions of the design to produce an effect of dull and bright finished lines converging toward a peg at the base of the vase.

Left: Design for a cut and engraved caster bottle; patented Jan. 3, 1882, by John Hoare. *Right:* John Hoare's molds for the manufacture of blanks for glass baskets; patented Apr. 8, 1884.

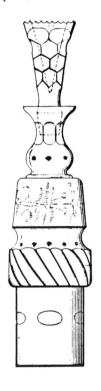

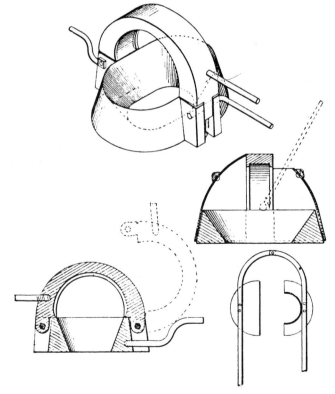

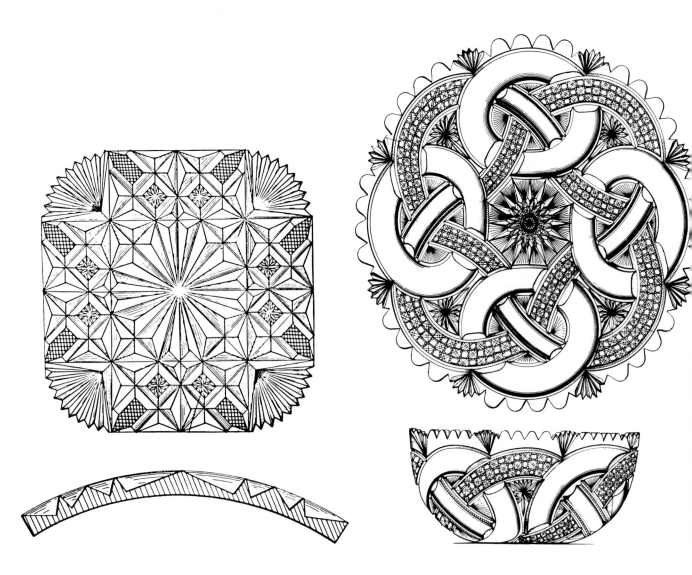

Left: The "Abbott" pattern; patented Feb. 15, 1887, by George L. Abbott. *Right:* The "Wedding Ring" pattern; patented Feb. 3, 1891, by John Hoare.

A mold for producing blanks for glass baskets was patented by Hoare on April 8, 1884. The idea was to produce a handled basket from a mold-blown blank, obviating the need for applying a handle to the body of the basket.

George L. Abbott was Hoare's first partner after he came to Corning. On February 15, 1887, Abbott filed a design patent for cut glass dishes which we have designated the "Abbott" pattern in his honor. The design consists of several cut glass motifs common to the Brilliant Period in cut glass—fans, checkered diamond, and star button.

On February 3, 1891, John Hoare patented a design which we have called "Wedding Ring." The pattern consisted of plain and brilliantly cut rings interlocking, and a pattern of stars and fans, as is shown in the patent illustration.

The Hoare shop furnished cut glass to the White House during the administration of President Grant.

J. Hoare & Company registered a trademark—their name and the date 1853 within concentric circles—on May 12, 1914, explaining that they had used this mark on their cut glass since early in the year 1895. The date "1853" refers to the time the firm was first founded in Philadelphia. This mark can be found on almost every piece of cut glass made by J. Hoare & Company since 1895. The trademark papers were signed by E. Haldeman Finnie as secretary of the company.

Pair of engraved bottles; *ca.* 1890; Corning Glass Works blanks; cutting done at J. Hoare & Co., Corning, N.Y.; height 7⅛ in. to top of stoppers.

Collection of Corning Museum of Glass

T. G. Hawkes & Company
Steuben Glass Works

T. G. Hawkes & Company of Corning, New York, was founded in March, 1880, by Thomas Gibbons Hawkes. The original name of the firm was Hawkes Rich Cut Glass Works, and it was located on West Market Street, a site it occupied until the company was dissolved in the winter of 1962. About 1887, Oliver F. Egginton and Henry P. Sinclaire, Jr. became Hawkes's partners— at this time the name of the company was changed from Hawkes Rich Cut Glass Works to T. G. Hawkes & Company. Some of Hawkes's associates soon opened cutting shops of their own. Oliver F. Egginton founded the Egginton Rich Cut Glass Company, and H. P. Sinclaire, Jr. who was once vice president of T. G. Hawkes & Company, operated as H. P. Sinclaire & Company. The Hunt Glass Company was established by Thomas Hunt and Daniel Sullivan; Hunt was a former employee of T. G. Hawkes & Company.

Thomas G. Hawkes was born in Surmount, Ireland, in 1846. He was descended from the Hawkes family of Dudley, England, and the Penrose family of Waterford, Ireland. In 1863, Hawkes came to America and settled in Brooklyn, New York, where he plied his family's trade of glass cutting with John Hoare. Within a few years thereafter he moved to Corning, where in 1871 he filled the position of superintendent at the old Hoare & Dailey cut glass shop. Only a few people are aware of the fact that Thomas G. Hawkes was also a graduate civil engineer. On July 7, 1913, Thomas Gibbons Hawkes died at the age of sixty-seven years. His obituary described him as "successful in business, a man of culture, of kindly disposition, who prized the good will of trustworthy employees."

Thomas Hawkes's son Samuel was apprenticed to the trade in his father's cutting shop about the turn of the century, thus carrying on the family name in the business until his death in 1959. The last vice president of the company, Penrose Hawkes, came from Dublin, Ireland, to Corning about 1916. The dissolution of the family business was, for him, a painful task. In 1964 Penrose Hawkes still occupied the old Hawkes showrooms on West Market Street in Corning, where he was a wholesale distributor for fine cut glass imported from Ireland.

From 1880 to 1904, Hawkes purchased their crystal blanks from the Corning Glass Works, then directed by Amory Houghton, Jr. On March 9, 1901, Thomas G. Hawkes purchased the B. W. Payne foundry and machine shops, which were in part occupied by the Allen Foundry Company. The premises were used by the Steuben Glass Company, which was founded on March 9, 1903, by Thomas G. Hawkes, Samuel Hawkes, Townsend de M. Hawkes (Samuel Hawkes's cousin), and Frederick Carder. The Steuben Glass Works

Collection of Lynn Parker   *From an original photo given to the author by Fred Carder*

Left: Vase, signed "J. Hoare & Company"; height 18 in. *Right:* Large vase in ruby flashed on crystal cut glass; Steuben Glass Works, 1917.

produced art glass of all kinds and cased colored and crystal blanks for the Hawkes cutting shop. As soon as the Steuben works was established, Carder began designing many fine cut glass patterns for Hawkes. Carder illustrated some of his original cut glass designs on small brochures which were distributed by T. G. Hawkes & Company. Around 1917 cut and engraved designs of sailing ships, flowers (the most common being thistle flowers and leaves), and simple flute and diamond patterns were issued by Hawkes in console sets consisting of a footed centerpiece bowl and matching candlesticks, and vases in various shapes and sizes. Engraved crystal vases in shapes especially designed

From an original photo provided the author by Fred Carder

Vases, footed bowls, and candlesticks in flashed ruby and crystal cut glass; Steuben Glass Works, 1917.

Left to right: Engraved crystal vase ("Duveen" pattern); oval crystal vase ("Elaine" pattern); covered jar ("Wield" pattern).

From an original Steuben catalogue ca. 1918

by Carder were also popular at this time. Beautifully cut crystal pheasants were made in pairs as mantel ornaments.

In reminiscing with the author, Fred Carder revealed that many times a good portion of blanks supplied by the Steuben works were returned to him because of bubbles or small flaws in the glass which the Hawkes cutting shop found objectionable. Rather than break the blanks for cullet (scraps of refuse glass suitable for remelting), Carder hired cutters who fashioned the rejected blanks into cut glass articles of his own design. None of these articles were marked in any manner which would identify the maker.

One of the rarest pieces in cut glass ever made was a policeman's "billy" club; it was designed and executed by workers in the Steuben Glass Works cutting shop about 1910. The club was especially ordered by the chief of police of Painted Post, New York, to be given to his friend, the chief of police of Corning, but the gift was never delivered for some reason and the club remained in the possession of the buyer's family in Painted Post until just a few years ago.

In 1918, when the Steuben Glass Works became a subsidiary of the Corning Glass Works, Hawkes purchased their heavy blanks for cut glass from the Libbey Glass Company. Later on they sold their molds and patterns to the United States Glass Company in Tiffin, Ohio. This firm supplied Hawkes with crystal blanks for cutting until just shortly before Hawkes went out of business in December, 1962. A short time thereafter the public demand for Hawkes patterns in cut crystal resulted in an affiliation of the old Hawkes name with the Tiffin Art Glass Corporation of Tiffin, Ohio. For many years this latter firm had supplied Hawkes with blanks, and they were thoroughly familiar with their standards of quality in glass and designs. Fortunately for those people still using Hawkes fine cut crystal, the merger of the two com-

Pair of cut crystal pheasants made by Steuben Glass Works, 1932; height 6¾ in.; length 11½ in.

Collection of Rockwell Gallery, Corning, N.Y.

panies has opened up a source of supply which promises to be of a long duration.

In September, 1885, an order was filled for 600 pieces of richly cut table glassware for the White House in Washington. The set included numerous examples of art work of the richest class cut in Philip McDonald's design known as the "Russian" pattern, which he patented for Hawkes on June 20, 1882. The original order was placed by President Grover Cleveland, and the magnificently cut crystal service was to be used at state dinners. The suite was enlarged by Presidents Benjamin Harrison and Theodore Roosevelt and was in continuous use at the White House until 1938; at that time President Franklin D. Roosevelt ordered the less expensive "Venetian" pattern. The "Venetian" pattern was in use at the White House during the Truman and Eisenhower administrations. The Hawkes factory also produced cut crystal for President William McKinley.

McDonald's "Russian" pattern was formed by six sets of parallel lines extending directly across the article. The lines so crossed to form rows of large stars, with intervening hobnails. On each of the hobs a fine sixteen-point star was cut. The brilliancy of this pattern is wonderful, the countless angles catching and reflecting light, till the whole piece glistens like diamonds. The small stars, which appear white when seen through from the smooth side of the glass, look like pearls set in the midst of jewels. As soon as McDonald's patent had run its term of seven years, it came into the public domain and was produced by several cut glass factories. Dorflinger's added pieces to the White House set during the administration of Theodore Roosevelt.

Hawkes's "Grecian" pattern (patented October 25, 1887) and "Chrysanthemum" pattern (patented November 4, 1890) won the Grand Prize at the Paris Exposition of 1889, giving additional impetus to the company's rising star in the cut glass industry. The local newspapers reported that the news of the award caused public rejoicing in Corning.

The *Elmira Telegram*, on October 16, 1962, reported that Hawkes's *pièce de résistance* at the St. Louis Exposition of 1904 was a four-poster bed made entirely of cut glass. It was subsequently sold to a wealthy Indian who had it sent to his palatial home in Calcutta, India. (Carder could not remember such a bed being made at Hawkes and suggested that it was probably supplied to Hawkes by F. & C. Osler of Birmingham, England.)

During the first half of the twentieth century some of the greatest families of the nation purchased cut table glassware for their sumptuous homes from T. G. Hawkes & Company, including Rockefeller, Whitney, Astor, Vanderbilt, Armour, Frick, and Chauncey M. Depew. When Mrs. Joseph Davies fitted out her magnificent yacht *Sea Cloud*, a special crystal service was designed and manufactured for her by Hawkes. Internationally known personalities such as Chiang Kai-shek, the Crown Prince of Sweden, Sir Thomas

Cut glass "billy" club produced by workers in Steuben Glass Works; *ca.* 1910.
Author's Collection

Plate in the "Russian" pattern; patented June 20, 1882, by Philip McDonald for T. G. Hawkes & Co.

Table lamp cut in the "Persian"
pattern, probably by T. G. Hawkes
& Co.; *ca.* 1890; height 28 in.
Collection of Lynn Parker

Left: The "Grecian" pattern; patented Oct. 25, 1887; *right*: The "Chrysanthemum" pattern; patented Nov. 4, 1890; both by T. G. Hawkes.

Lipton, and President Diaz of Mexico were also numbered among their patrons.

Hawkes gained an international prominence during the Brilliant Period of cut glass (1880 to 1910) and from that time until the factory closed in Corning, they had been recognized as masters in the cut glass art. Of the 50 or more most important cut glass patterns produced in the Brilliant Period, Hawkes created 15; and at one time the factory produced 322 patterns of stemware necessitating the employment of several hundred glass cutters. T. G. Hawkes's nearest competitor in volume business at the turn of the century was the Libbey Glass Company.

On January 17, 1893, Walter E. Egginton patented his "Valencian" pattern, which has since been rechristened the "Lattice" pattern by another author. In view of the fact that Egginton specifically mentioned the design in his patent specifications as "Valencian," we think it meet that it should be given its proper name in these pages. The leading feature of the "Valencian" pattern consists of the large central figure having radiating lines representing extending and withdrawing rays; there are also pelecoid figures, and double-pointed figures between the pelecoids. The beautifully designed pattern makes excellent use of large and small rosettes and fine hatch cutting (sometimes referred to in the trade as "checkered" cutting) so popular with glass cutters

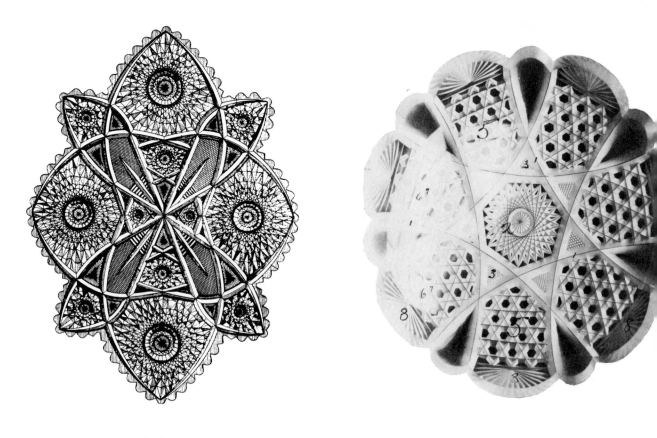

Left: The "Valencian" pattern; patented Jan. 17, 1893, by Walter Egginton for T. G. Hawkes & Co. *Right:* The "Old-fashioned Hobnail" pattern; patented Apr. 24, 1888, by T. G. Hawkes.

Left: The "Star Rosette" pattern; patented Apr. 24, 1888; *right:* The "Devonshire" pattern; patented May 8, 1888; both by T. G. Hawkes.

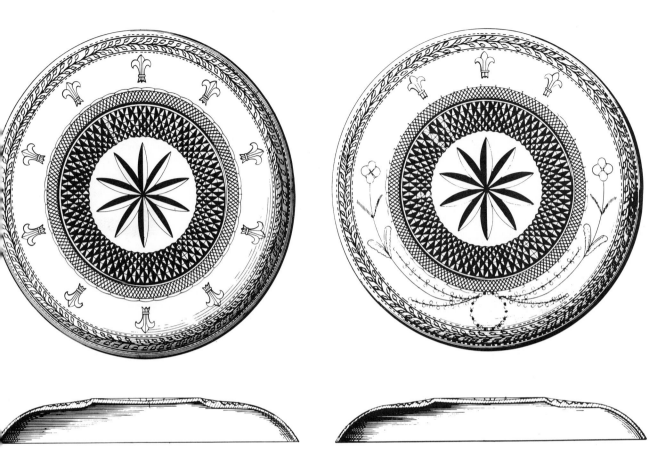

Left: The "Louis XIV" pattern; *right:* Variant of the "Louis XIV" pattern; both patented May 21, 1889, by Richard Briggs; cut by T. G. Hawkes & Co.

of the Brilliant Period. At the time of his patent, Egginton was working for T. G. Hawkes & Company.

Besides those already mentioned, T. G. Hawkes & Company patented the following cut glass designs:

"Russian and Pillar": patented on October 25, 1887, by Thomas G. Hawkes. This was a combination of the McDonald "Russian" pattern separated with plainer cut designs in spirals.

"Old-fashioned Hobnail": patented by Thomas G. Hawkes on April 24, 1888.

"Star Rosette": patented by T. G. Hawkes on April 24, 1888.

"Devonshire": patented by T. G. Hawkes on May 8, 1888.

"Louis XIV" (Pattern 14): patented by Richard Briggs of Boston, Massachusetts, on May 21, 1889. Cut only at T. G. Hawkes & Company.

"Louis XIV" (variant): patented by Richard Briggs of Boston, Massachusetts, May 21, 1889. Cut only at T. G. Hawkes & Company.

"Brazilian": patented by T. G. Hawkes on May 28, 1889.

Three illustrations of the "Brazilian" pattern showing the design as it was adapted to the form of the article on which it was cut; patented May 28, 1889, by T. G. Hawkes.

Left: The "Venetian" pattern; patented June 3, 1890; *right:* The "Maltese Cross" pattern; patented Sept. 2, 1890; both by T. G. Hawkes.

Left: The "Coronet" pattern; patented June 12, 1892; *right:* The "Aberdeen" pattern; patented Apr. 14, 1896; both by T. G. Hawkes.

Left: The "Nautilus" pattern; patented Aug. 18, 1896; *right:* The "Nelson" pattern; patented Mar. 9, 1897; both by T. G. Hawkes.

Left: The "Festoon" pattern; patented Mar. 9, 1897, by T. G. Hawkes. *Right:* The Gravic "Carnation" pattern; patented Nov. 2, 1909, by Samuel Hawkes.

Plate in the "Panel" pattern; patented Aug. 3, 1909, by T. G. Hawkes.

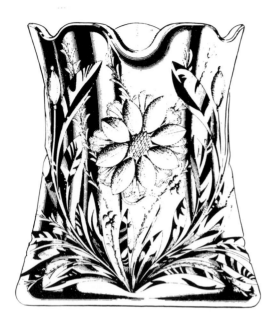

Left: The Gravic "Floral" pattern; patented Nov. 2, 1909, by Samuel Hawkes. *Right:* The "Tiger Flower" pattern; patented Nov. 29, 1910, by T. G. Hawkes.

Left: The "Latticed Rosettes and Ribbons" pattern; patented Feb. 7, 1911, by T. G. Hawkes. *Right:* Townsend de M. Hawkes's French dressing bottle; patented Oct. 6, 1914.

"Venetian": patented by T. G. Hawkes, June 3, 1890.

"Maltese Cross": patented by T. G. Hawkes, September 2, 1890.

"Coronet": patented by T. G. Hawkes on June 12, 1892.

"Aberdeen": patented by T. G. Hawkes on April 14, 1896.

"Nautilus": patented by T. G. Hawkes on August 18, 1896.

"Nelson": patented by T. G. Hawkes on March 9, 1897.

"Festoon": patented by T. G. Hawkes on March 9, 1897.

"Panel": patented by T. G. Hawkes on August 3, 1909.

"Carnation": A Gravic glass pattern patented by Samuel Hawkes on November 2, 1909.

Left: The "Edenhall Goblet"; engraved by William H. Morse in 1920. *Right:* Table lamp in the "Majestic" pattern; illustrated from an original catalogue issued by T. G. Hawkes & Co.

Photo courtesy of T. G. Hawkes & Co.   *Photo courtesy of Corning Museum of Glass*

Signed "Edenhall" bowl; diameter 9 in.

"Floral": A Gravic glass pattern patented by Samuel Hawkes on November 2, 1909.

"Tiger Flower": patented by T. G. Hawkes on November 29, 1910.

"Latticed Rosettes and Ribbons": patented by T. G. Hawkes on February 7, 1911.

On October 6, 1914, Townsend de M. Hawkes registered a design patent for a new French dressing bottle. On the body of the bottle were engraved markings to show the proper amounts of oil and vinegar to be used for this type of salad dressing. Hawkes's French dressing bottles were made in the form shown in the patent illustration, and in more pleasing shapes, and were decorated with various cut and engraved designs—"Gravic," "Satin Engraved," deep miter cutting, and light etching and engraving. Most of these bottles have mushroom-shaped stoppers made of glass, or glass and sterling silver.

On March 3, 1903, T. G. Hawkes & Company registered their trademark—three segmental lines connected together to form a trefoiled ring enclosing a central ornament (a fleur-de-lis) and the pictorial representation of two hawks placed within the lower parts of the trefoiled ring. The papers stated that this mark had been used by Hawkes since July 1, 1890. On December 26, 1905, and again on July 13, 1926, this same mark was registered by T. G. Hawkes & Company as their trademark for cut glasswares. According to their advertisements, every piece that left the factory could be identified by their trademark, which was lightly etched in the surface of the glass.

Hawkes's trademark for their Gravic glass was also registered on March 3, 1903. Their Gravic glass was a combination of light cutting and deep engraving, primarily intended to produce a quality ware at the least amount of cost. Gravic glass was made in several patterns: "Carnation," "Wild Rose," "Iris," "Cosmos," "Strawberry," and "Floral." The trademark "Gravic" was reissued to the firm on March 20, 1906, and both trademark registrations revealed that the firm had been producing these wares since December 13, 1902. All pieces of Gravic glass are so marked, sometimes in combination with their regular trademark.

Hawkes's "Satin Engraved Glass" appeared in their catalogues and brochures about 1903. This glass was a finely engraved line of wares with the designs left in a mat, or satin, finish.

For a while T. G. Hawkes & Company produced another cut and engraved line of glassware under the name "Edenhall." Undoubtedly this cheaper line took its name from the handsome "Edenhall Goblet," which was engraved for Hawkes by William H. Morse in 1920. We can assume that Hawkes's "Edenhall" line dates from about this 1920 period.

The following patterns were found in illustrated catalogues issued by T. G. Hawkes & Company between 1905 and 1915:

Alberta	Elba	London
Alexandria	Elk	Lustre
Atlantic	Electric	
Avon	Elite	Majestic
	Empire	Manhattan
	Ethel	Manilus
Baltic	Eureka	Maple
Bolton		Mars
Bordon		Maxim
Borneo	Favorite	Mildred
Brighton	Felton	Milo
Brilliant	Flutes and Greek Key	Milton
Bussaw		Minerva
	Grant	Mocha
Cairo	Gravic Carnation	Model
Canton	Gravic Cosmos	
Caroline	Gravic Floral	Napier
Celeste		Napoleon
Colonial	Hanover	Nevada
Concave	Harold	Norman
Concord	Harvard	
Constance	Hilda	Oakland
Cordova	Holland	Olympic
Cornell	Hudson	Oregon
Crescent		Ormond
Cuba		Othello
	Japan	
	Juliet	Palmyra
Daisy	Juno	Panel
Devon		Pekin
Diana		Pembroke
Domestic	Kaiser	

Persian	St. Regis	Union
Persian and Pillar	Satin Engraved	Utopia
Plymouth	Silvia	
Priscilla	Sonora	Venus
Prudence	Star	Vermont
Puritan	Starlight	Viking
	Stepped	Violet
Queens	Sultana	
		Warsaw
		Weston
Raleigh		Whirlwind
Rathbone	Tartan	Wilbert
Reese	Teutonic	
Rio	Tyrone	Yale

(There were also several patterns identified only by numbers.)

Egginton Rich Cut Glass Company
O. F. Egginton Company

In 1899, Oliver F. Egginton and Walter F. Egginton established the Egginton Rich Cut Glass Company in Corning, New York. The factory was located at 152–174 West 5th Street. Oliver Egginton was the firm's first president and was succeeded in this position by Walter E. Egginton in 1905. Before establishing his own cut glass business, Oliver Egginton was employed by T. G. Hawkes & Company in Corning, and in 1893 he was manager of the Hawkes cutting department. From 1895 to 1899, Oliver Egginton was a partner in the firm of T. G. Hawkes & Company.

Old records indicate that Walter E. Egginton and Walter F. Egginton were glasscutters employed at T. G. Hawkes & Company from 1893 until the time they joined Oliver Egginton in the family business.

The Egginton cutting shop bought their blanks from the Corning Glass Works. They operated until about 1920; after this date there was no mention of the firm made in the city records and there was no indication of its final dissolution to be found in any of the old archives or newspaper files.

Walter E. Egginton patented his "Magnolia" pattern on February 24, 1903, and we can be certain that this design was made especially for the O. F. Egginton Company. The leading features of this design were the magnolia blossoms (so designated by Egginton in his patent enumerations) alternating with brilliantly cut rosettes, as is shown in the patent drawings.

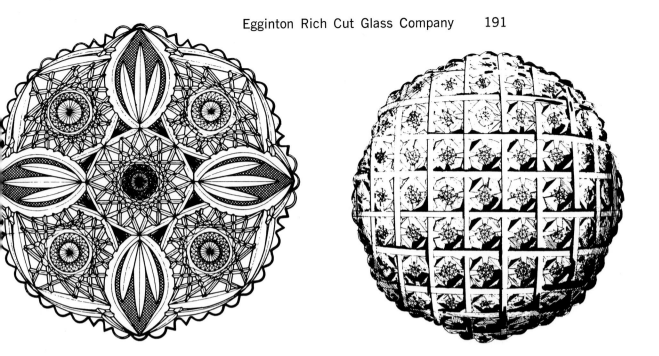

Left: The "Magnolia" pattern; patented Feb. 24, 1903; *right:* The "Trellis" pattern; patented Feb. 4, 1908; both by Walter E. Egginton.

Signed "Egginton" punch bowl with matching ladle and champagne glasses; height of bowl 15½ in.

Collection of Lynn Parker

Signed "Egginton" epergne; height 30 in.
Collection of Miss Janel Neiman

A very handsome geometric pattern in cut glass was designed and patented by Walter E. Egginton on February 4, 1908. The design is one of small intricately cut roundels set within squares, as is shown in the patent illustration. The regularity of the pattern has given rise to its common nomenclature "Trellis," and its similarity to H. P. Sinclaire, Jr.'s "Bird-in-a-Cage," the "Harvard" pattern (also known as "Chair Bottom"), and T. B. Clark's "Quilt Block" pattern is apparent.

On January 23, 1906, Egginton's trademark—a star arranged within the horns of a crescent moon and the name "Egginton"—was issued to them. This mark appears on most of their wares, lightly etched in the surface of the glass.

H. P. Sinclaire & Company

The first recording of H. P. Sinclaire & Company appears in Hanford's *Corning Directory* in 1905, but it is quite possible that the firm was established as a cutting shop a year or two earlier, possibly in 1903. In 1905 the officers of the company were Henry P. Sinclaire, Jr., president, and Marvin Olcott, vice president. The business operated under the name H. P. Sinclaire & Company until 1929, with little change in its principals. The names of Henry P. Sinclaire, Sr., Henry P. Sinclaire, Jr., and William Sinclaire are found here and there in the old records from 1893 to 1912. H. P. Sinclaire, Sr. was the secretary of the Corning Glass Works from 1893 until his death some time before 1903 (the time of his death was determined by a listing of his widow, Anna Sinclaire, in the 1903 edition of the *Corning City Directory*). Henry P. Sinclaire, Jr. was the secretary of T. G. Hawkes & Company from 1893 to 1903, and presumably he left that firm to establish his own company in 1903 or 1904. William Sinclaire is listed as a "glassmaker" from 1893 to 1899. In 1899 he was elected assistant secretary of the Corning Glass Works, and from 1905 to 1912 he served as secretary of this firm.

H. P. Sinclaire & Company probably purchased their blanks from the Corning Glass Works, as did many other cutting shops in this area, and the marked similarity in the shapes of their wares as compared with other manufacturers in the vicinity of Corning is at once apparent. The standard cuts indigenous to most of the American cut glass factories can be found in many of the Sinclaire designs—"Strawberry-Diamond and Fan," "Rosettes," and the ever-popular "Russian" pattern—but some of their designs showed a tendency

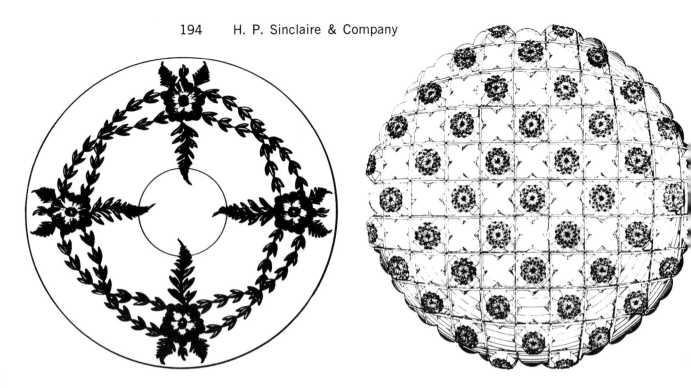

Left: The "Wreath and Flower" pattern; patented May 4, 1909; *right:* The "Bird-in-a-Cage" pattern; patented Aug. 3, 1909; both by H. P. Sinclaire, Jr.

Left: The "Greek Key and Laurel" pattern; patented Apr. 5, 1910; *right:* The "Holly" pattern; patented Feb. 28, 1911; both by H. P. Sinclaire, Jr.

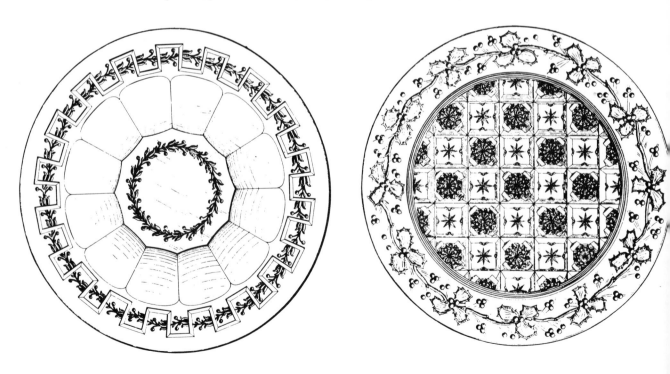

to deviate from the usual patterns, and this is evident in several patents for cut glass designs registered in Washington by Henry Sinclaire, Jr. from 1909 to 1911.

On May 4, 1909, Henry P. Sinclaire, Jr. patented his "Wreath and Flower" pattern. The design consists of a wreath of laurel leaves tastefully interlaced at equal distances with a flower-and-leaf motif.

Sinclaire's "Bird-in-a-Cage" pattern was patented by Henry P. Sinclaire, Jr. on August 3, 1909. The close pattern of brilliant rosettes is evenly spaced in a checkered design of crosses within a square, as is shown in the patent illustration of a bowl in this design.

By 1910 cut glass patterns were tending more toward the simpler designs, and in keeping with this trend Sinclaire registered his design patent for their "Greek Key and Laurel" pattern on April 5, 1910. A vine, or wreath, of laurel leaves and berries overcut with a Greek key motif is the basic idea for this design, which was produced in crystal and colored glass—amber, blue, green, and ruby. Sinclaire's pattern, as applied to the several pieces in this suite of glassware, takes its cue from the flat panel cutting and the simple Greek key

Cut and engraved olive dish made by H. P. Sinclaire & Co.; diameter 9 in.

Author's collection

and laurel wreath shown in the center of the plate illustrated in the patent specifications. The pitcher in this pattern has already been mistaken for a much earlier design in another cut glass book. At the time Sinclaire's "Greek Key and Laurel" pattern was being made, the firm was purchasing much of their colored glass for cutting and engraving from the Steuben Glass Works and many of their forms were designed by Fred Carder. Occasionally a piece of Sinclaire glass can be found with their trademark signature (the letter "S" enclosed within a laurel wreath) and Steuben's trademark (a fleur-de-lis), lightly etched in the pontil mark or some other inconspicuous place on the article.

The following year, on February 28, 1911, Sinclaire patented the firm's "Holly" pattern. The design reverts somewhat to the more elaborate cutting of a previous era, but with a bit more restraint in the over-all effect. The pattern derives its name from the wreath of holly leaves and berries that surround the border of a plate used in their patent illustration. In the center of the plate a variation of their "Bird-in-a-Cage" pattern is used as a brilliant and very effective balance in the over-all design.

Sinclaire's cutting shop and showroom was located in Corning on Conhocton Street for many years. About 1921 they built their own glass factory in Bath, New York, which was located just off West Morris Street. Many of Carder's workers were induced to leave the Steuben Glass Works and took up their trade in Sinclaire's new glass factory. Much to Carder's chagrin, some of his best color formulas were used in the Sinclaire works; previous to this the Sinclaires had purchased colored wares from Steuben to sell along with their own cut wares.

Sinclaire also featured a fine line of hand-painted china which they decorated themselves, possibly using imported blanks. The china was marked "Ravenwood" in black letters, surmounted with a representation of a raven. Sinclaire's glassworks in Bath, New York, closed around 1929, according to Frank Blake, whose father once worked for this company.

Hunt & Sullivan
The Hunt Glass Company

The Hunt Glass Company of Corning, New York, operated as a cutting shop from about 1895 and is still in business. Originally the style of the firm was Hunt & Sullivan, with Thomas T. Hunt and Daniel S. Sullivan as principal stockholders. Harry S. Hunt, the son of Thomas T. Hunt, was also associated with the firm at its inception and was the company's first salesman.

Engraved crystal gramophone or early crystal radio set; Hunt Glass Co.; *ca.* 1920; height 14½ in.

Thomas Hunt and his son Harry came to America in 1880 from England and settled in White Mills, Pennsylvania, where the elder Hunt was employed as a glass cutter by some of the old firms located there, possibly Dorflinger and others. Later they came to Corning, where both Hunts cut glass for T. G. Hawkes & Company. Hanford's *Corning Directory* listed Harry Hunt and Thomas Hunt as glass cutters as early as 1893.

The elder Hunt started the family business in a small cutting shop which he built onto his house located at the corner of Washington and West Sixth Streets. They gradually enlarged this structure and continued to manufacture their wares here even after Thomas Hunt passed away. Harry S. Hunt took over the factory at his father's demise and did quite a thriving business in old miter-cut glass; he died in November, 1935. In 1949 the business was moved to a modern factory with all new machinery and is still operating as the Hunt Glass Company, with Walter J. Sullivan (Harry Hunt's son-in-law) and his wife Dorothy B. Sullivan (Harry's only child) as president-secretary and vice president, respectively.

In 1905 the officers of the firm were listed as Thomas T. Hunt, president; Harry S. Hunt, secretary and treasurer; and J. T. Sullivan, vice president.

In 1907 the company's style changed from Hunt & Sullivan to the Hunt Glass Company, with Thomas T. Hunt, president; Mary E. Hunt (the wife of Thomas T. Hunt), vice president; and Harry S. Hunt, secretary and treasurer. The list of officers changed again in 1909: Harry S. Hunt, president; N. E. Fuller, vice president; and Cassie L. Hunt (Harry's wife), secretary and treasurer.

The Hunts purchased their blanks for cutting from the Corning Glass Works, T. G. Hawkes's Steuben Glass Works (operated by Frederick Carder in partnership with members of the Hawkes family), and from the Union

Left: "Rosettes and Stars" cut glass bowl, signed "Hunt"; diameter 7 in. *Right:* The "Royal" pattern; patented July 11, 1911, by Harry S. Hunt.
Collection of Mrs. E. F. Langham

Glass Company in Somerville, Massachusetts. There are only a very few distinctive patterns in cut glass peculiar to the Hunt cutting shop, and collectors will have a difficult time identifying their wares unless they are marked with their trademark "Hunt," which was lightly etched into the glass in various locations (depending on the cut and the shape of the article). This mark will appear on pieces made after 1907; before 1907 some pieces may have been marked "Hunt & Sullivan," or "H & S," but so far, we have been unable to find pieces with these marks.

The only patented design for cut glass acquired by this firm was issued to Harry S. Hunt on July 11, 1911. The rather heavy, handsome design, which the company named their "Royal" pattern, more closely resembles the English cutting of this same period than their American contemporaries, who were inclined to make their cutting more intricate, and therefore more brilliant. Hunt's "Royal" pattern was cut and polished from pressed blanks made by the Union Glass Company. The relative simplicity of the pattern makes it at once elegant and beautiful.

Other cut glass articles produced by the Hunt Glass Company exhibit their talent for manufacturing brilliantly cut patterns, and affirm their concessions to the popular taste in cut glass.

George Drake Cut Glass Company

George Washington Drake was born in Atlanta, Georgia, in June, 1870, and died in Corning, New York, in December, 1910. He first established his cut glass business in 1900 in a large barn on his property at the corner of

Cut glass bowls; made at the factory of George Drake; diameters 5 in. and 7 in.
Collection of Mrs. Myra Tillotson Todd Brown (George Drake's cousin)

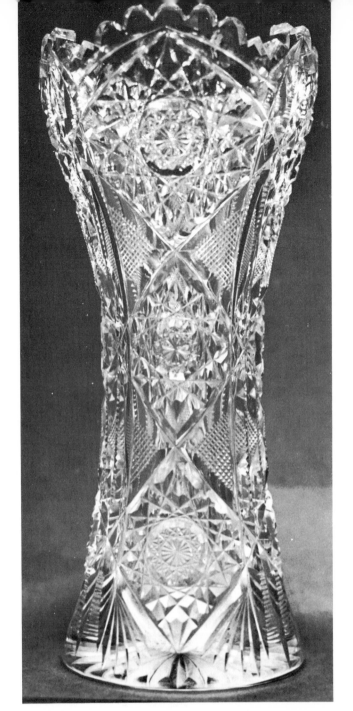

Vase in the "Ogontz" pattern; cut at
George Drake Cut Glass Co.; height 9 in.
Collection of Mrs. Martha Drake McCarty
(George Drake's cousin)

Fifth and Cedar Streets in Corning, New York. Later he moved to a large
factory on Bridge Street. At one period in his business he employed from 40
to 50 cutters. Drake was not a glass cutter by trade, but the quality of his
wares was on a par with the best of his contemporaries.

George Drake was at one time postmaster of Corning, New York, having
been appointed to this post by President Grover Cleveland. His paternal
grandfather, Franklin N. Drake, was a man of great prominence in Corning
and was at one time president of the Erie Railroad; he also owned mines in
Arnot, Pennsylvania, where George spent many years as a child.

Edward T. Burgess

On July 18, 1882, Edward T. Burgess registered three designs for cut glassware. Each of them seems to be a variation of the old "Rose and Diamond" pattern used by many cut glass manufacturers in the early years of the Brilliant Period. Burgess described his design No. 13,041 as consisting of "stars, octagons, or hobnails and diamonds formed by a series of parallel miter cuts into the surface of [the] glassware." Burgess' design No. 13,042 consisted of a combination of "stars, octagons, and irregular hexagons formed by three series of parellel miter cuts or grooves cut into the surface of the glassware." Burgess stated that his design No. 13,043 was a "combination of diamonds, hexagons and stars formed by a series of parallel miter cuts, . . . said figures being brought to a point or left with a flat surface, according to the depth of the cut."

Edward T. Burgess' Designs Patent No. 13,041 and 13,042; registered July 18, 1882.

201

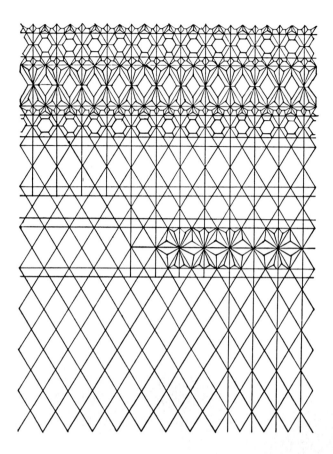

Edward T. Burgess' Design Patent No. 13,043; registered July 18, 1882.

Hanford's *Corning Directory* for the year 1893 listed a "Charles Burgess, glasscutter" boarding at 91 E. Erie Avenue in Corning, but we could uncover no record of Edward T. Burgess. In 1903 Mrs. Nina C. Burgess lived in Corning at 214 W. Erie Avenue. It is quite possible that Edward T. Burgess operated a small cutting shop of his own in 1882, this being a common practice among glass cutters. Blanks were available from the Corning Glass Works and easily purchased for a few dollars each, or even less than that amount, depending on the size of the article.

In the 1890's E. T. (Tom) Burgess was associated with Thomas A. Niland & Company of Meriden, Connecticut. Burgess was considered to be a first-class designer and cutter. After his death, the family moved to Middletown, Connecticut, and nothing more is known of them after 1910.

Ferris Glass Company

The Ferris Glass Company was founded in Corning, New York, by John C. Ferris, in November, 1910. Originally Ferris operated the Elmira Cut Glass Company in Elmira, New York, and had an interest in the Arcadia Cut Glass Company of Newark, New York. The shop in Corning was established to offset the possible closing of the Elmira Cut Glass Company's facilities because of labor troubles. At first only 16 cutters were employed in Ferris' Corning shop, but business increased within a short time and consequently so did the number of workers.

The Ferris cutting shop was located in the old Heermans & Lawrence Building in Corning, at the corner of Cedar Street and East Erie Avenue (now Denison Parkway). On April 18, 1913, a fire damaged much of the building which housed several small cutting shops. The Ferris Glass Company reported $2,000 worth of damaged goods and equipment.

The date of this company's closing could not be determined from local records; presumably it went out of business soon after the fire, for no listing of the Ferris shops in Elmira and Corning could be found in the 1918 issue of the *American Glass Trade Directory*.

Giometti Brothers
Sebring Cut Glass Company

The Giometti brothers, Lazarus C. Giometti and Cherubino J. Giometti, operated a small cut glass shop on the north side of Corning, New York, according to Frederick Carder. The brothers did not have a great deal of capital, and within a few years their business was purchased by a lawyer named Sebring, who continued the business as the Sebring Cut Glass Company. The latter firm also had only a very short business life.

On July 8, 1924, design patents for glass dishes were issued to the Giometti brothers and assigned by them to the Corning Glass Works; obviously the brothers went to work for the Corning Glass Company after their cut glass business was sold to Sebring.

The Knickerbocker Cut Glass Company

The Knickerbocker Cut Glass Company was established in the Heermans & Lawrence Building in Corning, New York, in 1902. Within a few months after it had started, its production, equipment, and stock were purchased by Charles H. Almy and G. Edwin Thomas, who operated it thereafter as Almy & Thomas.

Almy & Thomas

On February 25, 1903, Charles H. Almy and G. Edwin Thomas purchased the short-lived Knickerbocker Cut Glass Company. The cutting shop was located in the old Heermans & Lawrence Building on East Erie Avenue (now

Signed "Almy & Thomas" cut glass decanter and glasses; height of decanter 7 in.
Collection of Mr. and Mrs. George S. Helm

Denison Parkway) and Cedar Street in Corning, New York. Almy & Thomas produced a fine grade of brilliantly cut glass and used blanks manufactured by the Corning Glass Works. Some of their wares are marked with their cipher "A & T" and "Almy & Thomas, Corning, N.Y." within a circle. No closing date for this factory could be determined, but it probably went out of business shortly after World War I.

Frank Wilson & Sons

Frank Wilson and his two sons, Robert and Joseph, worked eight cutting frames in their small cut glass shop on Sly Avenue in Corning, New York. Frank Wilson, Sr. first came to Corning in 1879 as a cutter in the newly established T. G. Hawkes & Company. Wilson was considered one of the finest engravers in the trade, capable of producing a piece of cut glass from the initial drawing of the pattern on the blank to the final polishing of the richly cut designs. He was born in Windy Nook, Gateshead, Durham, England, and learned his trade of glass cutting in the English cut glass factories. Wilson arrived in America with his family on the steamer *Hecla* on September 17, 1872, and worked for the New England Glass Company of East Cambridge, Massachusetts, before he came to Hawkes's shop in Corning.

Frank Wilson & Sons produced a very fine grade of rich cut glass and their wares were distributed through such well-known commercial houses as Tiffany & Company in New York City, Marshall Field & Company, in Chicago, Illinois, and many of the better specialty shops in the eastern half of the United States. Joseph Wilson and another son, Frank Wilson, Jr., were associated with cut glass shops of their own in Brooklyn, New York, Montrose, Pennsylvania, and New Brunswick, New Jersey.

Other Cutting Shops
in Corning, New York

Joseph Black

According to a report by the Corning Historical Society, Joseph Black operated a small cutting shop in Corning, New York, as a subsidiary of T. G. Hawkes & Company, about 1910.

Peter A. Eick

A report published by the Corning Historical Society in May, 1963, stated that Peter A. Eick specialized in engraving Pyrex teapots. The objects Eick engraved date his contributions to American cut glass at around 1917, when Pyrex wares were being produced by the Corning Glass Company.

William B. Eick

A William B. Eick assigned a cut glass design to the Genesee Cut Glass Company of Rochester, New York, in 1913.

Frederick Haselbauer

Frederick Haselbauer owned a small engraving shop in Corning, New York, around 1915, in which he produced nicely engraved light cut wares.

Illig Cut Glass Company

Fred Carder told the author that a man named Illig ran a small engraving business in his home in Corning, New York, in the first quarter of the twentieth century.

Ernest Mulford

The Corning Historical Society reported in May, 1963, that Ernest Mulford operated a small concern cutting glass as a subsidiary of T. G. Hawkes & Company.

Painter Glass Company

There was a Painter Glass Company operating in Corning, New York, around 1915, but no indication of their activities could be found in the public records.

206

Corning Cut Glass Shop

The Corning Cut Glass Shop operated in that city in the first quarter of the twentieth century.

Bronson Cut Glass Company

The Bronson family of Painted Post, New York, were prominently associated with this community and evidence of their influence is still quite obvious. Frank, Willard, and George Bronson operated a small glass cutting establishment about 1910 at the front, or Water Street end, of the Bronson Block, on the second floor over the present location of the Hall hardware store in Painted Post. George Bronson, the elder brother, operated the factory, which produced patented cut glass inkwells known as "Bronson's Ink Stand" and some other cut glass articles for decorative and table use. A glass cutter from Corning, New York, named George MacKay did most of the work with one or two assistants. The glass blocks for the inkwells were purchased from T. G. Hawkes & Company. The inkwells were about three inches square, according to a former employee, and were cut with various designs both popular and well known to most cut glass manufactories of this period.

No one seems to remember what the patented feature of the inkwell was, and we could find no record of such a patent in Washington. The Rev. D. D. Dilworth, George Bronson, and Frank Bronson (a banker who financed the enterprise for his brothers) often discussed their plans and hopes for the future of their inkwell business. Local wiseacres joked about it, and gave George Bronson the nickname "Inky Bronson." A former employee recalled that the business lasted about 18 months, during which he estimated that they produced approximately 100 inkwells. During the last few months, George Bronson and Jeffrey Smith operated the cutting shop.

Ellsworth C. Cowles of Corning, our source for most of the information on the Bronson Cut Glass Company, remembered that as a boy in Waverly, New York, he visited a local cut glass factory that made vases, bowls, decanters, glasses, and so forth, and employed perhaps 6 to 10 people. In his youth (around 1910), Cowles used to watch the cutters at work on heavy glass blanks. He became acquainted with one of the cutters, Harry Hall, and they were friends until Hall's death some years ago. The glassworks were located on South Fulton Street, in South Waverly, Pennsylvania, next to the Erie Railroad tracks, and Cowles believes it was in business for about six or eight years. Inquiries about this factory in South Waverly, Pennsylvania, and the adjoining town of Waverly, New York, have been unsuccessful; we were not able to discover even its name, or the name of the owner. It would appear that in a small community such as South Waverly, business records were not considered important enough to keep for posterity. Harry Hall's sister reported that he was a partner in the Vandermark, Brace & Hall Cutting Shop in Elmira Heights, New York.

Ideal Cut Glass Company

The Ideal Cut Glass Company of Canastota, New York, was established in 1904 by Charles E. Rose of Corning, New York, with Frederick Leonard Morecroft as its manager. The company's offices were located in Canastota in what was then known as the Pike Block, at 109 West Fayette Street. In 1908, Rose returned to Corning to join in a partnership with Messrs. Shepherd and Conover in a hardware and sporting goods store.

In 1909 the firm moved to 127 South Clinton Street in Syracuse, New York. Morecroft succeeded to the position of secretary in the Ideal Cut Glass Company in 1908; he remained secretary of the company until 1922, when he became president of the firm, a position he held until 1934.

The Ideal Cut Glass Company was listed in the *American Glass Trade Directory* for 1918 as a manufacturer of cut glass. (Another company bearing this same name was also listed in this directory with a location in Philadelphia, Pennsylvania, and this may have been a branch of Morecroft's business. A thorough search of the business records in Philadelphia failed to unearth any evidence of an Ideal Cut Glass Company having operated there in the first quarter of the twentieth century.) After 1934 the Ideal Cut Glass Company ceased to be recorded in the Syracuse city directories, and we can only assume from this that they went out of business about that time.

About 1921 the Ideal Cut Glass Company was associated with the W. P. Hitchcock Company, wholesale jewelers to the trade, with offices in Syracuse at 319 South Salina Street. At this time the Ideal Cut Glass Company was also listed at this address.

In 1894, Morecroft was a dashmaker for horseless carriages and boarded in Syracuse at 1810 E. Fayette Street. From 1895 to 1906 he was variously employed as a clerk, a bookkeeper, and a cashier. As late as 1907 he was still living in a boardinghouse on Allen Street in Syracuse. In 1917, Morecroft married, and Frederick and Minerva Morecraft resided at 700 Lancaster Avenue in Syracuse. In 1920 they moved to another house at 119 Victoria Place. At one time Morecroft was vice president of the National Association of Cut Glass Manufacturers.

Left: The "Star Flower" pattern; patented Nov. 11, 1913; *right:* The "Constitution" pattern; patented Dec. 6, 1927; both by Frederick L. Morecroft; Ideal Cut Glass Co.

Only two cut glass designs were patented by Morecroft for the Ideal Cut Glass Company. The first of these designs was registered on November 11, 1913. We have named it the "Star Flower" pattern. It is quite possible that the drawing accompanying the patent papers represents only the main feature of the design and that other decorative motifs may have been added to pieces in this set.

The second design was patented by Morecroft on December 6, 1927, and for obvious reasons we have designated this one the "Constitution" pattern. Here too it is possible that Morecroft's design of a sailing ship in full canvas formed only the main portion of the pattern, and that other cut designs may have been added to further embellish the pieces in this suite of glassware.

Empire Glass Company

We have been assured by an official of the Cleveland, New York, library that they have no evidence at all of the Empire Glass Company operating in their town, as was reported some years ago by Dorothy Daniel in *Cut and En-*

graved Glass, 1771–1905. According to their records, the American Glass Company, the Union Glass Company, and the United Glass Company all operated in Cleveland at one time or another, but none of these produced cut glass. Window glass was the principal product manufactured in the Cleveland glasshouses; the only exceptions noted were small pitchers, chains, darning eggs, and other small trifles called "friggers," which the workmen made for their own amusement. The Cleveland library cannot verify Mrs. Daniel's report that the Empire Glass Company was sold to J. Hoare & Company, stating that "the only thing sold to anyone in Corning was sand."

The Arcadia Cut Glass Company
American Cut Glass Company
Arcadian Cut Glass Company
The Spencer Cut Glass Company

The Arcadia Cut Glass Company was incorporated in Newark, New York, township of Arcadia, on September 30, 1901, by Caleb L. B. Tylee of Penn Yan, New York, George E. Tylee of Holliston, Massachusetts, John C. Ferris of Elmira, New York, and Ernest V. Peirson and Frank D. Burgess of Newark, New York, with a capital stock of $10,000. Actual production began in November, 1901. George Tylee was elected president of the new cut glass company, and Ernest Peirson, vice president; Caleb Tylee was made treasurer and manager of the factory, and Frank Burgess was the company's secretary.

In October, 1902, the corporation was reorganized and changed its name to the American Cut Glass Company. It increased its capital stock to the amount of $30,000, and William H. Tylee of Worcester, Massachusetts, replaced Ferris in the business. (Ferris was also associated with the Elmira Cut Glass Company, Elmira, New York, and the Ferris Glass Company in Corning, New York.)

The company was again reorganized in January, 1903; this time the name was changed to the Arcadian Cut Glass Company. There was no change in the list of owners.

When this factory was established, it was designed to employ only 10 hands, but instead of that number, 20 men were employed and the company soon found an urgent need for larger quarters and more cutters. In 1902 they moved from their original factory, a few rooms rented in the Fretch Building in Newark, to a small wooden building north of the West Shore Railroad on

North Main Street. In 1903 another two-story wooden building, 28 feet by 75 feet, was built for the growing concern. The company moved in 1908 to Lestershire, New York (the village name was changed to Johnson City, New York, in 1916), where it was continued by Tylee, Ferris, and Burgess. The city records confirm that it operated in Lestershire, New York, from 1909 to 1911 as the Arcadia Cut Glass Company. Formal dissolution papers for the firm are dated July 2, 1928, but it had gone out of business many years before then.

Caleb L. B. Tylee was a glassman who had originally come to Newark, New York, from Corning, New York, a few years before the Arcadia works were established. Ernest Peirson was a Newark banker, and Frank Burgess was coeditor and publisher of the local newspaper. At one time Caleb Tylee, Ernest Peirson, and Frank Burgess built a railroad linking Newark and the neighboring village of Marion, New York; with a length of but nine miles, it was one of the shortest railroads in the United States.

George Tylee and William Tylee were not residents of Newark, but presumably they were in the glass cutting trade; or they may have had a retail outlet in which the Arcadia wares were sold. Most of the cutters were admittedly "recruited" from cut glass factories in Corning and Elmira, New York. The blanks for cutting were of the "finest French glass," possibly from the Baccarat factory in France. Most of Arcadia's cut glass products were shipped to Boston and Worcester, Massachusetts, New York City, Chicago, Illinois, Rochester, New York, and other large cities throughout the country.

Peirson and Burgess gave up an active interest in the cut glass business after a time, and in 1906, Charles L. Crothers became financially involved in the firm. Crothers was a very wealthy man, and although he had no practical experience in the glass trade, he was very active in the affairs of the Arcadia Cut Glass Company while it remained in Newark.

In May, 1910, Arthur J. Spencer, for 12 years manager of the cutting department of the Arcadia Cut Glass Company, established the Spencer Cut Glass Company in Newark, New York. Spencer leased the second floor of the Arcadia Cut Glass Company building on North Main Street for a factory and showrooms. Spencer's specialties were vases, punch bowls, sugar and cream sets, napkin rings, water pitchers, tumblers, and center vases cut in the patterns formerly used by the Arcadia Cut Glass Company and some factories in Elmira, New York, where he worked for some years before his employment with the Arcadia works. Spencer once exhibited a center vase, weighing 42 pounds and measuring 16½ inches in diameter, which was reputed to be the largest vase ever cut in one piece in this country. Spencer's cut glass company was short-lived and soon after it was closed he went into a real-estate and insurance business which he operated until his death.

The Lyons Cut Glass Company

The Lyons Cut Glass Company of Lyons, New York, was incorporated on March 7, 1903, by George T. Getman, James D. Bashford, William H. Baltzel, William H. Burrell, Dr. Louis W. Smith, Albert E. Marshall, and Chester G. Blaine, with a capital stock of $12,000. The directors elected James Bashford president of the firm. Between 40 and 60 men were to be hired at first, many being formerly employed by cut glass factories in Corning, New York. The factory was located on the side of a hill on West Water Street (formerly the site of the New Haven Silver Plate Company), the cutting room being on a level with the street. This gave ample room on the floor beneath for storage and packing rooms. Power for the cutting wheels was derived from a five-horsepower electric motor. The blanks for cutting were purchased from the Union Glass Works in Somerville, Massachusetts, H. C. Fry Glass Company (possibly figured blanks only) of Rochester, Pennsylvania, the Baccarat factory in France, and from a few other glass factories

Bowl-vase, signed "Lyons"; height 5 in.

Collection of Mr. and Mrs. Jack Walker

supplying such articles. Most of the glass was purchased at a pound rate, 35 cents being the price at that time for good quality wares.

William H. Burrell, a former employee of the Arcadia Cut Glass Company of Newark, New York, was in charge of the plant and had worked in the cut glass business for 14 years. He learned his trade at the T. G. Hawkes factory in Corning, New York. In 1903, Burrell estimated the Lyons output at $40,000 a year. Considering that the Lyons Cut Glass Company employed no regular sales representatives, and that they sold direct from the factory to the trade, $40,000 annually was a tremendous amount of business.

In June, 1903, several of the glass cutters threatened to quit and return to their jobs in Corning because the Lyons directors refused to pay the customary 60 hours wages for 59 hours of work (the men usually stopped work one hour earlier on Saturday). Management held its ground and the men who left Lyons were immediately replaced. In October, 1903, Burrell left the company because of some disagreement with the directors. Thomas Durkin succeeded Burrell as foreman of the factory, and George W. Banks was made manager of the works.

In November, 1903, the company reported an increase in business, but a few days later, just before Christmas, the shop was closed. It reopened again in February, 1904, with a smaller staff of cutters. In March, 1904, a modern polishing room was added on the east side of the factory and the cutting machines and the staff of workers were increased by 40 per cent to handle a new spurt of business. On June 8, 1905, the Lyons Cut Glass Company offered their entire stock of cut glass to the public ($3,000 worth) at less than cost. The balance on hand, $2,130 worth, was finally sold to N. J. Ewer & Sons of Youngstown, Ohio, on August 17, 1905. The company went out of business shortly after 1905, but dissolution of the concern was not officially recorded until July 2, 1928.

The Lyons Cut Glass Company used a trademark showing two lions standing on their hind legs and supporting a small banner between them, all within a pentagon-shaped shield, and their name "Lyons."

Lyons Glass Manufacturing Company

According to the files in the Wayne County Clerk's offices, a glass company was incorporated in Lyons, New York, in 1846.

On April 17, 1867, corporation papers were issued to the Lyons Glass Manufacturing Company. This concern produced window glass and hollow wares. No mention of cut glass appears in any of the recordings of this company's products. Since no certificate of discontinuance was filed in the clerk's office, we cannot ascertain the closing date of this glass company. The members of the firm were William Van Marter, Miles S. Leach, John Layton, Caleb Rice, David Griffith, Amasa M. Medberry, and Silas Bashford.

Genesee Cut Glass Company

The Genesee Cut Glass Company first appears in the Rochester, New York, directory in 1911. In 1918, Goldsmith Tuthill is listed as treasurer. The firm appeared in the city directories, with Tuthill as treasurer, through 1925. After that year Tuthill is listed as vice president of Smith Ceramic Studios, Incorporated, and the Genesee Cut Glass Company's name no longer appears. Goldsmith Tuthill died in Rochester on February 17, 1962; he was eighty-three years old. His daughter operates her father's business, the G. B. Tuthill Lamp and Shade Shop, but could give us no information on her father's cut glass enterprise. We did learn that Tuthill was also associated with the Flower City Glass Company at one time. There was never any connection with the Tuthill Cut Glass Company of Middletown, New York.

Cut glass design patented Dec. 30, 1913, by William B. Eick for Genesee Cut Glass Co.

On December 30, 1913, William B. Eick patented a floral pattern in cut glass which was used in combination with other cut glass designs. The flower had eight petals formed of closely engraved lines, with a brilliantly cut button in the center, as is shown in the patent illustration.

The Buffalo Cut Glass Company

Originally 14 stockholders formed the corporation known as the Buffalo Cut Glass Company in 1902; the factory at that time was located on Swan Street in Buffalo, New York. In 1905 the *Buffalo City Directory* indicated that the company was located on Nichols Road. Within approximately three years after the firm was founded, three of the stockholders—Michael J. Kallighan, Daniel J. McGettigan, and Joseph H. Schmitt—acquired the interests of the others and moved the operation to Batavia, New York, on May 1, 1905. The Buffalo Cut Glass Company's new factory, located on Exchange Place in Batavia, was of heavy frame construction and entirely covered with tin sheets, with a brick-shaped design impressed thereon. The building was three stories high and had a hand-operated freight elevator in the rear. The location on Exchange Place was very accessible to the railroad freight houses. The factory was not large, as factories go, and the firm never employed more than 30 men at one time.

Kallighan, McGettigan, and Schmitt were equal owners of the business until January 15, 1914, when Schmitt retired from the partnership. When

Punch bowl in the "Fulton" pattern; from an original illustrated catalogue issued by Buffalo Cut Glass Co.

McGettigan died in February, 1914, his half interest in the company was sold to Schmitt; and on March 24, 1914, Schmitt purchased the other half interest in the company from Kallighan. Joseph Schmitt and his wife (as secretary of the firm) operated the factory as sole owners from 1914 until it went out of business in 1918. The company's assets were finally liquidated about 1920.

In the early days of the Buffalo Cut Glass Company's operations, Schmitt did most of the artistic work himself. He designed some of the company's best patterns, and even cut them in the rough. Schmitt also did the "dipping," which was the timely immersing of the finished cut glass article in acid to produce a high polish. Kallighan did some rough cutting but no designing; when he worked, it was mainly in the packing room. Most of the glass blanks used by this company were purchased from the Libbey Glass Company, and the H. C. Fry Company in Rochester, Pennsylvania. Resident salesmen were located in Chicago, New York, and other large cities in the east.

Joseph H. Schmitt was born in Berlin Township, Wayne County, Pennsylvania, on January 26, 1869, and died in Batavia, New York, on February 20,

Page from an original Buffalo Cut Glass Co. catalogue showing (*left to right*) the "Thistle," "Flower," "York," "Buffalo," and "Temple" patterns.

1948. He learned his trade at the Dorflinger Cut Glass Works in White Mills, Pennsylvania. Later he was employed by cut glass factories in New York, Toledo, Ohio, Meriden, Connecticut, and possibly other places.

Daniel J. McGettigan was born in Honesdale, Pennsylvania, on March 13, 1874. As a boy, he received his early training in the cut glass trade in factories located in and around Honesdale. He was one of several men chosen from the Honesdale area to go to Chicago's Columbian World's Fair in 1893 to display their handicraft. Later he worked in cut glass factories in Toledo, Ohio (possibly at Libbey's plant). McGettigan's efforts were considered to be largely responsible for the company's thriving business after it was moved to Batavia, New York. He was president of the concern until his death on February 21, 1914.

The Buffalo Cut Glass Company's trademark—a buffalo standing atop a map of the world, and the legend "Buffalo Cut Glass Company"—was found on their old stationery and on the first page of their illustrated catalogues, two of which are in the author's collection. We could not learn from Schmitt's widow and son if this mark had been registered in Washington, nor could we determine whether it was placed on their wares with etching or paper labels; more than likely, the trademark was affixed to their products in the form of a paper label, which in most cases has probably been removed from existing specimens. Identification of the Buffalo Cut Glass Company's products will not be an easy task for collectors. The "diamond-like finish," boasted of in their advertisements and illustrated catalogues, was achieved with the proper "dipping" of the finished article in acid to ensure a smooth surface on all the prismatic facets cut into the glass.

We found the following named patterns in two large illustrated catalogues issued by the Buffalo Cut Glass Company after 1905:

Akron

Aurene

Bedford

Belmont

Belmore

Boston

Brighton

Brilliant

Buffalo

C.B. ("Chair Bottom." A very similar pattern was their "Temple" design; this also resembles the popular "Harvard" pattern. "C.B." was probably produced on pressed blanks purchased from the H. C. Fry Glass Company.)

Clinton

Creston

Delaware

Delta

Diana

Duchess

Eclipse

Ellicott

Empire

Empress

Erie

Fan Star

Fargo

Flower

Freedom

Fulton

Gem

Gibson

Glenwood

Horizon
Hudson
Hunter
Huron

Iris

Jackson
Jewel
Jewel Special

Lafayette
Lily
Lincoln
London

Madison
Mage
Masse
Mayne
Milford
Mohawk
Monroe

Navarre
Newport
Niagara

Orient
Oxford

Perry
Phoenix

Pitchers numbered 281 to 288 ("No.
    283" was "C.B." or "Temple")
Planet
Plymouth
Porter
Prince
Providence

Reliance
Rome

Saxon
Seneca
Senior
Sultana
Superior
Supreme
Star

Temple (See "C.B.")
Thistle (Similar patterns produced by
    Max E. Schenk, Pitkin & Brooks, and
    F. X. Parsche & Son, all of Chicago,
    Illinois.)
Tokio
Troy

Waverly
Wayne
Wells
Winona

York

International Glass Company
International Cut Glass Company

The International Glass Company was established in Buffalo, New York, around 1904. At that time they maintained offices in the Ellicott Square Building, 295 Main Street. John C. Conway, Charles J. Carroll, M. J. Vallely, and John H. Vallely were associated with the firm at its inception. In 1905, Robert B. Adams became president and John C. Conway was listed as manager and treasurer. Evidently the glassworks itself was located at 59–61 Terrace Street in Buffalo, for the records indicate this fact in 1906. In 1907 the company moved their offices to 182 Main Street, Buffalo; and by 1910 their name had been changed to the International Cut Glass Company. All things remained the same until 1913, when John C. Conway was listed as president of the company in the Buffalo city directories.

The International Cut Glass Company was a member of the National Association of Cut Glass Manufacturers. No trace of the concern could be found in any of the Buffalo city records after 1913, and we can only assume from this that it went out of business about that time.

Niagara Cut Glass Company

The Niagara Cut Glass Company first appears in the Buffalo, New York, directories in 1906. Edward J. Eisle and Edward A. Eisle, father and son, were the proprietors of the business, which operated from 506–510 Genesee Street. By 1913, Edward A. Eisle was listed in the directories as president of the firm and Henry C. Van Anda (Edward J. Eisle's son-in-law) was secretary and treasurer. Messrs. Eisle and Van Anda remained in charge of the business until at least 1915, when it ceased to operate as the Niagara Cut Glass Company.

The Eisles were best known in Buffalo as manufacturing jewelers. Edward J. Eisle, the father, was born in the grand duchy of Luxembourg, where he was apprenticed to the jeweler's trade. He came to America and founded the firm of King & Eisle in 1870. Edward J. Eisle died in Buffalo at the age of eighty-nine years on October 18, 1919. His son, Edward A. Eisle carried on the family's jewelry business as Eisle & Company for 30 years before his death on October 2, 1939, at the age of seventy-eight years.

Didio Brothers Cut Glass Company

The brothers August A. Didio and John Didio founded their small cut glass shop around 1914; at that time they were located at 323 North Division Street in Buffalo, New York. In 1915, John Didio was listed in the city directory at this address as a glass cutter. By 1919 they had moved to 405–407 Clinton Street, Buffalo, and the owners were listed in the directories as John

Didio and Alexander Didio, Jr. The 1964 business directories list John Didio as sole owner of the business, which is now located at 1010 Niagara Street in Buffalo. Only light cut wares were produced by this shop.

Frontier Cut Glass Company
National Glass Manufacturing Company

John W. Murray was manager and treasurer of the Frontier Cut Glass Company, 180 Terrace Street, Buffalo, New York, in the early 1900's. He passed away about 1950, but his widow carried on as a consultant to the National Glass Manufacturing Company of Buffalo, New York, successors to the Frontier Cut Glass Company.

In the early days of the Frontier Cut Glass Company, some fine heavy cut wares were manufactured; however, shortly before World War I, they began producing light cut wares of a very good quality. On September 26, 1916, Murray received a patent for his "Star Flower" pattern for light cut wares. This beautiful design was further enhanced by lightly engraved parallel lines all over the object, as is shown in the patent illustration. In another design, which he patented for light cut wares, Murray again used the background decoration of parallel lines to set off his "Rose" pattern, patented on March 20, 1917; it is not unlike the "Rose" patterns produced by some cut glass shops in Honesdale, Pennsylvania.

Cream and sugar set produced by Frontier Cut Glass Co.

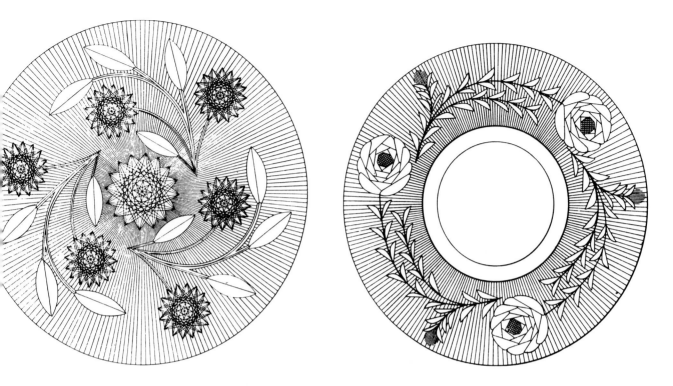

Left: The "Star Flower" pattern; patented Sept. 26, 1916; *right:* The "Rose" pattern; patented Mar. 20, 1917; both by John W. Murray; Frontier Cut Glass Co.

Ebenezer Cut Glass Company

The Ebenezer Cut Glass Company was started in Ebenezer, New York, in 1915, by Louis, Frances, and Earl Erckert. The factory was located on Mill Road until it burned down in 1957. After Louis Erckert's death in January, 1948, the business was continued by his widow, Mrs. Frances M. Erckert, who reports that only light cut wares were produced by this company.

Cut Glass Manufacturers in New Jersey

Crescent Cut Glass Company

The 1901 issue of the *Industrial Directories of New Jersey* listed the Crescent Cut Glass Company at 59 McWorter Street, Newark, New Jersey. By 1906 the firm had relocated at 38 Crawford Street in Newark, and remained there until some time after 1918, when it was again listed in the *American Glass Trade Directory* as a cut glass manufacturer. The firm was a member of the National Association of Cut Glass Manufacturers, according to that organization's records.

Unger Brothers

Unger Brothers, manufacturers of cut glass, were listed in the *Industrial Directories of New Jersey* from 1901 to 1918. They were also members of the National Association of Cut Glass Manufacturers, and were listed in 1918 as such in the *American Glass Trade Directory*, under cut glass manufacturers.

Tumblers, signed "Unger"; height 4 in.

Collection of Mr. and Mrs. Jack Walker

In 1901 their factory was located in Newark, New Jersey, at 412–418 Halsey Street. In 1912 the factory's address was listed as 32–38 Beecher Street, Newark; but by 1918 they were again listed at 412 Halsey Street.

Unger Brothers cut some very fine heavy wares early in their career, but as the demand for heavy cut glass diminished, they resorted to the cheaper pressed glass blanks and light cut wares. Some of their cut glass can be found with the name "Unger," lightly etched in script on some portion of the article.

C. H. Taylor Glass Company
Jewel Cut Glass Company

The C. H. Taylor Glass Company was established in Newark, New Jersey, just before 1906. On January 30, 1906, the firm was incorporated by Charles Henry Taylor, Edwin J. Lockard, and Henry R. Luckock. On June 24, 1907, the certificate of incorporation was amended and the name of the company changed to the Jewel Cut Glass Company. Charles H. Taylor, the president and treasurer of the concern, owned 92 per cent of the preferred stock; the rest was shared by Parker Wagner (1 per cent), Henry R. Luckock (5 per cent), J. C. Dahl, secretary of the company (1 per cent), and Edwin J. Lockard (1 per cent).

The company was first located at Sherman Avenue and Stanton Street in Newark. In 1911 they moved their retail store to 857 Broad Street; the cutting shop was in the rear of this two-story brick building, at 34 Treat Place. In 1917 they moved to 8 Academy Street in Newark. At this time Charles H. Taylor was listed as president; with Francis H. Taylor (C. H. Taylor's nephew) as secretary; and William Albert Elmhurst, as treasurer. Henry R. Luckock was the factory foreman and designer.

The company stayed at the Broad Street location until 1929, when they moved to 149–151 Halsey Street, Newark; as of 1964 they operated the Jewel Gift Shop at 147 Halsey Street under the management of Mrs. Francis H. Taylor. The firm discontinued the manufacture of cut glass about 1928 and has been in the greeting card business since then.

Charles Henry Taylor was born in Zanesville, Ohio, on May 27, 1866. He was not a practical glass cutter. His nephew, Francis H. Taylor, was also born in Zanesville, Ohio, on February 22, 1890; he too was not a glass cutter.

On March 19, 1912, Henry R. Luckock and Charles H. Taylor registered five designs for cut glass patterns. The first of these is a simple, but handsome, design representing a stylized flower, with petals formed of fine lines radiating

Left: The "Diamond Floral" pattern; *right:* The "Regency" pattern; both patented Mar. 19, 1912, by Henry R. Luckock and Charles H. Taylor for Jewel Cut Glass Co.

Left: The "Empire" pattern; patented Mar. 19, 1912; *right:* The "Primrose" pattern; both patented Mar. 19, 1912, by Henry R. Luckock and Charles H. Taylor for Jewel Cut Glass Co.

The "Primrose (Variant)" pattern; patented Mar. 19, 1912, by Henry R. Luckock and Charles H. Taylor for Jewel Cut Glass Co.

from the center, which was a brilliantly cut button; we have designated this design the "Diamond Floral" pattern, and it would appear that the plain, undecorated portions of the article, as shown in the patent illustration, was also engraved with cut glass designs of various kinds. Luckock and Taylor's second design, which we have named "Regency," is a superb blend of brilliantly cut rosettes and plain flutes. The third design is another triumph of simple elegancy, consisting of fine diamond cutting and flutes; we have named it "Empire." The last two designs are floral patterns which we have named "Primrose" and "Primrose (Variant)." In both instances Luckock and Taylor used smaller representations of their first design, "Diamond Floral," in combination with connecting stems and leaves. The only real difference between the last two patterns seems to be in the form of the plate and the decoration of the edge of the plates. Of course, in all instances the designs were modified to suit the article to be decorated—goblets, bowls, jugs, pitchers, and so on.

Newark Cut Glass Company

The *Industrial Directories of New Jersey* listed the Newark Cut Glass Company of Newark, New Jersey, from 1906 to 1918. From 1906 to 1912 the firm was located at 60–62 Arlington Street; from 1912 to 1918, the date of the last entry for this company, they were situated at 61 Arlington Street in Newark. The shop was listed in the *American Glass Trade Directory* for 1918 under cut glass manufacturers.

Signed "Newark" cut glass bowl; diameter 9 in.

Author's Collection

The Rock Crystal Glass Company

On April 17, 1916, the Rock Crystal Glass Company was incorporated under the laws of the State of New Jersey by Joseph Hinsberger, Abraham Gordon, and John J. Halpin, who at this time was also associated with the Max Herbert Company in New York City, indicating a direct connection with that firm. The amount of capital stock was $2,000. Their principal offices were located at 63 Irving Street in Jersey City, New Jersey. According to the certificate of incorporation, the company was primarily engaged in the manufacture of "cut glass, rock crystal, glassware and crystalware of any and all kinds and descriptions."

The company was listed in the *Jersey City Directory* for 1918, with Sigmund Herbert (see also S. Herbert Cut Glass Company, New York City) and Joseph Hinsberger named as principal owners, the factory or showrooms being located at 245 Cornelison Avenue. Elsewhere in the directory Herbert's home address was given as New York City, while Hinsberger's was shown as 77 Hague Street, Jersey City, New Jersey. In the 1922/23 issue of the *Jersey City Directory* there is no mention of the company, and Joseph Hinsberger at that time was listed as a "glass contractor"; he and his wife Mary were still living at 77 Hague Street, Jersey City. The Rock Crystal Glass Company's certificate of incorporation was voided on January 22, 1925, and presumably the company was no longer operating as such even earlier than 1925.

The Brooklyn, New York, directory for the years 1916/17 listed Joseph Hinsberger as president of the Peerless Cut Glass Company, Incorporated, 233 Mercer Street, Brooklyn. We could find no connection between this company and the one by the same name located in Deposit, New York.

Jersey City Glass Company

The Jersey City Glass Company of Jersey City, New Jersey, produced cut glass in the latter years of their existence. They were active from about 1824 to the early 1860's. Further details of this company will be found in the Introduction.

Jersey City Flint Glass Works

H. O'Neil operated the Jersey City Flint Glass Works of Jersey City, New Jersey, about 1861, according to George and Helen McKearin's compilation of glass-producing factories in the United States (*American Glass*). Dorothy Daniel reports (*Cut and Engraved Glass, 1771–1905*) that they produced lamps, bar accessories, fish globes, colored glass, and cut tablewares.

Empire Cut Glass Company
Flemington Cut Glass Company

The Empire Cut Glass Company was founded in New York City sometime before 1895, when it was first recorded in the New York City business records; it occupied a two-story brick building at 605 West 39th Street. Harry Hollis of Boston, Massachusetts, founded the firm, but in 1902 he sold the company to his employees and it was operated as a co-operative until 1904, when it was again sold, this time to the H. C. Fry Glass Company of Rochester, Pennsylvania. The factory's machines and equipment were moved to Flemington, New Jersey, in 1904, where the firm occupied a new building on Park Avenue which was built for them by the Flemington Board of Trade. In 1964 the building was used by the Flemington Auction Market for selling eggs, poultry, and livestock. At one time in its career the Empire Cut Glass Company employed about 100 men.

William E. Corcoran, who learned his trade at the Dorflinger works, was the president of the new company; Charles McMullen, the vice president, had learned his trade at the Hawkes cut glassworks in Corning, New York. The designer and assistant manager, Alphonse G. Muller, was apprenticed at L. Straus & Sons of New York City, and he also worked in Hoboken, New Jersey. The company was listed in the *Industrial Directories of New Jersey* as late as 1918, but it was no longer operating after 1925 or 1930, according to Muller. Most, if not all, of the blanks used at the Empire works in Flemington were purchased from the H. C. Fry Glass Company, and this would indicate that at least some of their cut glasswares were produced on pressed blanks.

The Empire Cut Glass Company's trademark label consisted of their name surrounding a representation of an eagle with spread wings.

Charles McMullen and Alphonse G. Muller started the Flemington Cut Glass Company in 1908, manufacturing fine cut glass in the old tradition. They purchased their blanks from the H. C. Fry Glass Company, Fostoria Glass Works, A. H. Heisey & Company, Duncan & Miller Glass Company, the Imperial Glass Company, the Libbey Glass Company, and the Union Glass Works in Somerville, Massachusetts. The factory is housed in a frame and cement block building located at 156 Main Street in Flemington, New Jersey, and is still operating today, manufacturing mostly light cut glassware, decorative cut glass articles, shades for lamps, and selling a line of crockery in conjunction with their own wares. In 1964 the firm's officers were: Alphonse G. Muller, chairman; R. J. Muller, president; P. S. Muller, vice president; and A. M. Reading, secretary and treasurer.

New Brunswick Cut Glass Company

From 1916 through 1919 entries for the New Brunswick Cut Glass Company, of 120 Eastern Avenue, in New Brunswick, New Jersey, appeared in that city's directories. The records show that a Louis Board was associated with the company. In 1920, Board was identified as being in the coal business, and presumably the cut glassworks were closed that same year.

Moses, Swan & McLewee Company

It is known that the firm of Moses, Swan & McLewee, Trenton, New Jersey, did produce cut glass in the late nineteenth century, but their wares, as far as we can determine, cannot be set apart from similar or same cut glass products produced by their contemporaries in the business. A design patent for a lamp shade was issued to a William S. McLewee of Trenton, New Jersey, on March 22, 1892.

Standard Lamp & Glass Company

Cut glass shades and lamp globes were manufactured by the Standard Lamp and Glass Company of Trenton, New Jersey, located at 15 Perrins Avenue. They were listed as lamp and glass manufacturers in the 1906 issue of the *Industrial Directories of New Jersey*.

George L. Borden & Company
Krystal Krafters

George L. Borden operated a small cut glass business in Groveville, New Jersey, between 1910 and 1920. His factory was listed in the *Industrial Directories of New Jersey* in 1918. By 1912, Borden had established another cut glass shop under the name of Krystal Krafters in Trenton, New Jersey. On July 25, 1922, Borden received his trademark papers; the mark consisting of the legend "Krystal Krafters—Trenton, N.J.—Genuine Cut Glass" encircling two large letters "K." The trademark was placed on all the wares with gummed labels. According to the trademark papers, he had been using this mark on his cut glass products since November 7, 1921.

Mercer Glass Company
Mercer Cut Glass Company

The Mercer Glass Company, also known as the Mercer Cut Glass Company, was situated at Lafayette Street, foot of Peace Street, in Trenton, New Jersey. It operated from about 1915 to 1920. In 1917 the city directories listed William C. Burrough as president and treasurer of the firm, with Robert Burrough as secretary. The company appeared in a list of cut glass manufacturers published in 1918 by the *American Glass Trade Directory*.

Merchant's Cut Glass Company
Merchant's Cut Glass Works
Merchant's Cut Glass Company, Incorporated

In August, 1896, the Merchant's Cut Glass Company of Philadelphia, Pennsylvania, moved its plant to the building of the Woodbury Manufacturing Company, which was located in the 100 block of North Broad Street in Woodbury, New Jersey. At this period the firm was connected with the John Wanamaker store in Philadelphia, and was supplying them with their fine cut and engraved glassware. In 1899 the firm's style was the Merchant's Cut Glass Works, but by 1906 this had been changed to the Merchant's Cut Glass Company, Incorporated.

In 1899 the factory was located at 31 South Broad Street in Woodbury. Samuel J. Merchant was listed as the manager of the company, and Jubal J. Merchant was a glass cutter. The company was started some years before 1896 by a father and two sons named Merchant, but no record of their Christian names could be found. Recordings of this firm in business and city directories continued until about 1909. Their name did not appear in the *American Glass Trade Directory* for 1918, and presumably they were closed before that date.

Excelsior Glass Works

The Excelsior Glass Works operated in Camden, New Jersey, from about 1841 to 1857, manufacturing cut glass and other tablewares. At this early period their wares would be indistinguishable from products made in other cut glasshouses in America and England.

Camden City Cut Glass Company
Camden Cut Glass Company

The Camden City Cut Glass Company first appeared in the city directory in 1911; at that time its address was on South Seventh Street, Camden, New Jersey. The principals listed were Bernard Gerety, Albert F. Priestley, and Bernard Weiner; in the early listings no information is given regarding the positions these three men held in the firm.

The same listing for this concern appeared regularly in the annual directories until 1917, when their address was changed to 818 Division Street in Camden. At this time Albert F. Priestley was noted as president, and Bernard Weiner as treasurer. This listing continued, year in and year out, until 1924, when the firm was not to be found in any of the directories.

The *Industrial Directories of New Jersey* took note of this concern under the style of the Camden Cut Glass Company, 818 Division Street, Camden, in 1918. Priestley was listed in one source as living in nearby Philadelphia; Weiner lived at 455 Haddon Avenue in Camden, New Jersey.

On November 15, 1921, Albert F. Priestley registered a design for the "ornamentation for a cut glass article of manufacture." His patent was illustrated with a drawing of a plate engraved with daisylike flowers of a type found on many late pieces of cut glass, and there is little to distinguish Priestley's design from those of his contemporaries. Obviously the daisylike flowers were used in combination with other cut or engraved motifs popular at this time (1921).

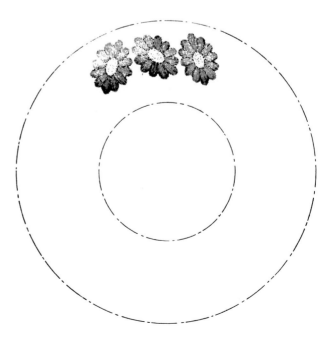

"Camden Daisy Chain" pattern; patented Nov. 15, 1921, by Albert F. Priestley for Camden City Cut Glass Co.

Frizlen Cut Glass Company

The Frizlen Cut Glass Company was started in Vineland, New Jersey, about 1907. At that time it was located at the corner of Fourth and Montrose Streets, but by 1908 it had moved to larger quarters on South Boulevard, corner of Montrose Street. In 1914 they relocated in Mt. Holly, New Jersey, in a factory on Water Street.

About 1918, William G. McIlvain rented a part of the Frizlen Cut Glass Company's factory and set up a showroom where he sold Frizlen's cut wares at wholesale. Later McIlvain moved his showrooms to a new location on Washington Street in Mt. Holly, but he continued to buy his cut glass from Frizlen. According to members of his family, McIlvain would order his own blanks and send them to the Frizlen Cut Glass Company to be cut and engraved to his own designs. This arrangement between Frizlen and McIlvain went on until the late 1920's, when cut glass lost its popularity.

William L. Frizlen was the president and manager of the Frizlen Cut Glass Company from the time it was founded until it closed around 1920. Wilbur F. Tower was listed in public records as treasurer. An account of the firm's activities in the Vineland *Evening Journal* of November 4, 1910, stated that they produced cut glass pitchers, vases, bowls, compotes, wine sets, cream sets, and some of the most handsome punch bowls on the market. The factory employed eight experienced glass cutters, and their annual production was in excess of $10,000 worth of cut glass, most of which was destined for markets in Philadelphia and New York City.

William G. McIlvain & Company

William G. McIlvain, who was born on October 27, 1882, began his mercantile career with the S. R. Justice Company in Philadelphia about 1907. This company sold mostly hotel silverware, but McIlvain persuaded them to take on a line of fine cut glass and novelties. McIlvain was with the Justice company until about 1918, when he rented part of the Frizlen Cut Glass Company's factory on Water Street in Mt. Holly, New Jersey, for his showroom. From there he sent salesmen out on the road selling cut glass and novelties. On September 27, 1920, he purchased a piece of property on Washington Street in Mt. Holly and moved his business there. McIlvain himself had nothing to do with the cutting of the glass, but he did buy his own blanks

236

Footed bowl 3⅞ in. high and pitcher 12¾ in. high; designed by William G. McIlvain; cut by Frizlen Cut Glass Co.

and sent them to the Frizlen cut glass works where they were cut to his own designs. This arrangement went on until the late 1920's, when cut glass went out of style.

William G. McIlvain & Company remained at their Washington Street location in Mt. Holly until the early 1930's, when McIlvain became the foreign buyer for George F. Bassett & Company, 225 Fifth Avenue, New York City. McIlvain was later made president of this company, and in 1935 he purchased it and remained there until his death in 1942.

Medford Glass House
Star Glass Works

From members of the families who were associated with the Medford Glass House, also known as the Star Glass Works at a later date, we learned that the business was established by 12 glass blowers in a small factory at the corner of South Main and Trimble Streets in Medford, New Jersey. The glassworks were formerly occupied by another glass company—Trimble & Yarnall—which manufactured only window glass. In time, John Mingin, Samuel Garwood, and Frank Reilly bought out their partners one by one, and they operated the works until it closed in 1922. What used to be the company store is still operated by Edward B. Wills, Jr. The factory site is now occupied by a modern dwelling.

Every effort was made to establish conclusively whether or not cut glass was ever produced in Medford, New Jersey. After many searches of the town's records and township tax records, also newspaper files in the area, and journals, we have finally concluded that only window glass and bottles were produced in the Medford glasshouses. The first glass company in Medford, Trimble & Yarnall, manufactured window glass. Later, the Star Glass Works made mold-blown bottles, and a star impressed in the base of each bottle was their trademark. Some bottles were engraved with the names of various kinds of liquors and medicines, on special orders from buyers, but they did not produce any cut glass table or ornamental wares, as was reported in another cut glass book.

It would appear that the attribution of cut glass to the Star Glass Works could be based on a misinterpretation of the trademark of a star within a circle found on some cut glass articles. This mark was registered in 1901 by the Libbey Glass Company for use on pressed (figured) blanks.

William Skinner & Son

William Skinner and his son Thomas came to America from England in 1887. In England the family had been glass cutters in the Coventry and Stourbridge glass districts for several generations. For a while the Skinners worked at the Dorflinger factory in White Mills, Pennsylvania; then they moved to New Bedford, Massachusetts, where they cut heavy glass for the Pairpoint Corporation. Skinner and his son went to Philadelphia and worked for the Henderson Cut Glass Company. In 1895 they opened their own cutting shop at the corner of 4th and New Streets in Philadelphia. In 1899 they moved to a small shop on Railroad Avenue, near the Pennsylvania Railroad Station, in Hammonton, New Jersey, and started to build their own factory in that town in 1901 at 317 North Egg Harbor Road, where it still stands.

William Skinner & Son was listed in the *Industrial Directories of New Jersey* from 1901 to 1918. They were also listed in the 1918 *American Glass Trade Directory* as manufacturers of cut glass. John Rothfus worked for them from 1902 to 1906.

William Skinner & Son employed as many as 140 workers at one time, though they started their business in Hammonton with only five men. They manufactured heavy cut glasswares until the beginning of World War I. After the war some cutters never came back to Hammonton, and the market for fine cut glass was definitely on the decline. In 1914 their business had been mainly that of jobbers to meet the demand of a lower quality market. By 1920 their production was at its lowest ebb, but they continued making stemware until around 1930. At one time the firm made mortuary boxes for crematories.

In the period between 1930 and 1940 the Skinner factory made mirrored picture frames and ash trays. As of 1964, they are making holders for desk pens for a large pen company and employ just a few workers. The factory is run by Thomas Skinner, Jr., the grandson of William Skinner.

Figueroa Cut Glass Company
Enterprise Cut Glass Company
Miskey-Reynolds-Rothfus Company
Rothfus-Nicolai Company

About 1914, Charles H. Strunk and John F. Rothfus formed the Figueroa Cut Glass Company in Hammonton, New Jersey. The works were located at West End Avenue and Pleasant Street in a two-story brick building along the side of the Reading Railroad tracks. Strunk was the president of the company, assuming the clerical and accounting duties; Rothfus was the vice president in charge of patterns and selling the merchandise to the retail outlets all over the country. At the height of its operations the factory worked 100 hands, but it ran into financial difficulties and terminated its activities about 1926. In the beginning the shop manufactured heavy cut glass. Toward the last it began producing both heavy and light cut wares.

Footed compote; height 8 in.; Figueroa Cut Glass Co.

Collection of John W. Clowar and Mrs. Emma Rothfus

The "Rose" pattern; diameter of bowl 8 in.; Figueroa Cut Glass Co. *Collection of John W. Clowar and Mrs. Emma Rothfus*

Strunk did not remain in the cut glass business, but Rothfus contined his career by purchasing the Enterprise Cut Glass Company from Mrs. Edward Reeves in 1926. The Enterprise cutting shop was located in Hammonton, New Jersey, across from the Pennsylvania Railroad Station and later Rothfus moved it to Walmer Street, where it occupied the former C. C. Small Shoe Company building. John Rothfus successfully managed the business until his death in 1944. In 1949 his widow, Mrs. Emma Rothfus, went out of the cut glass business, selling the factory building to a garment manufacturing firm. The Enterprise Cut Glass Company manufactured only light cut glassware.

Before entering into business in the Figueroa and Enterprise cut glass companies, Rothfus learned his trade with William Skinner & Son, cut glass manufacturers in Hammonton, New Jersey, beginning in 1902. Later he formed a partnership with Messrs. Miskey and Reynolds as the Miskey-Reynolds-Rothfus Company, which was located in the old mill building at the foot of Hammonton Lake, near the White Horse Pike, in Hammonton. The Miskey-Reynolds-Rothfus Company was founded in 1906 and operated as such until 1912. From 1912 to 1914 Rothfus joined Henry Nicolai, another practical glass cutter, in the firm of Rothfus-Nicolai Company. Their cutting shop was located on Egg Harbor Road (next to the Pennsylvania Railroad Station) in Hammonton. After John Rothfus left the concern Nicolai continued the operation as the Henry Nicolai Company.

The only design patent for cut glass registered by John Rothfus was dated November 17, 1914, and was assigned to the Figueroa Cut Glass Company. The pattern consisted of three stylized flowers and an undeveloped bud, with leaves appropriately placed along a slender stem. Rothfus referred to the design in his patent papers as "an ornamental spray of daisies exemplifying my new design for such vessels which comprise a floral pattern in imitation of

Footed flower bowl; height 6½ in.; Figueroa Cut Glass Co.
Collection of John W. Clowar and Mrs. Emma Rothfus

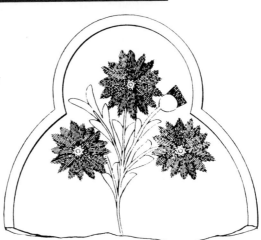

The "Daisy Spray" pattern; patented Nov. 17, 1914, by John F. Rothfus for Figueroa Cut Glass Co.

Table lamp in the "Chair Bottom" ("Harvard") pattern; height 24½ in.
Collection of John W. Clowar and Mrs. Emma Rothfus

a daisy, with the petals shown in opaque lines." Because of his reference to the design as representing a spray of daisies, we have named it the "Daisy Spray" pattern. The original name for the pattern is unknown at this time. Undoubtedly Rothfus' "Daisy Spray" design was used in conjunction with other cut glass designs, as this seems to have been a common practice throughout the cut glass industry during the first quarter of the twentieth century.

John Rothfus was born in Frankfort, Pennsylvania, on July 17, 1884, and died of a heart attack in Hammonton, New Jersey, in late June, 1944. He had come to Hammonton with his parents when he was just a small child and was a resident there until his death. He attended public schools in Hammonton and later studied at the Banks Business College in Philadelphia. Rothfus was a pioneer cut glass manufacturer in his area of New Jersey. He was a very active Mason and Kiwanian who took part in municipal affairs, having served on the town council of Hammonton, New Jersey, from 1929 to 1930, and on the Water Commission from 1931 to 1939. He was president of the Water Commission for one three-year term.

Henry Nicolai Company

The Henry Nicolai Company in Hammonton, New Jersey, was listed in the *American Glass Trade Directory* as a manufacturer of cut glass in 1918. The firm had been listed as such in the *Industrial Directories of New Jersey* from 1906 to 1909. From 1912 to 1914 Nicolai was in business with John W. Rothfus as the Rothfus-Nicolai Company; their shop was located on Egg Harbor Road, adjacent to the Pennsylvania Railroad Station, in Hammonton. When Rothfus left the concern in 1914, Nicolai continued the business under his own name.

Henry Nicolai also worked for the Figueroa Cut Glass Company in 1916; his son remembers that he was in business for himself as early as 1912, and while most people in this area agree that the Henry Nicolai Company was not in business for more than a few years, we cannot seem to reconcile his employment with another cut glass shop while apparently operating one of his own, as is indicated by the various listings in the two trade directories mentioned above.

Hammonton Cut Glass Company

In 1906 the *Industrial Directories of New Jersey* listed the Hammonton Cut Glass Company of Hammonton, New Jersey. Other than this scrap of information we could find nothing more in any business or historical sources. Apparently the firm was in business for only a very short time.

Zanes-Messina Glass Company

Michael Messina runs a small glass cutting shop in Hammonton, New Jersey, which he established about 1944. The firm, known as the Zanes-Messina Glass Company, does only light cutting, mostly to order. Messina was in the employ of William Skinner & Son in 1911.

Messina Cut Glass & Decorating Company

The Messina Cut Glass & Decorating Company, located on White Horse Pike in Elwood, New Jersey, is owned and operated by Thomas Messina and Irene Messina. (Thomas is the son of Michael Messina, but the two firms were never associated.) The Messinas currently manufacture only a small amount of heavy cut glass.

Fischer Cut Glass Company

The Fischer Cut Glass Company of Atco, New Jersey, was listed as a manufacturer of cut glass in the *American Glass Trade Directory* in 1918. Other than this information, we were unable to find additional material on this concern.

Acme Cut Glass Company
Aetna Cut Glass Company

George Link and Charles Link founded the Acme Cut Glass Company in Bridgeton, New Jersey, about 1916; the factory was located at 53 Atlantic Street. The Link brothers had learned their trade of glass cutting in nearby Hammonton, New Jersey, and produced a very fine grade of hand-cut crystal decorative ware and tablewares. In 1919 they changed the name of the con-

Advertisement from the *Evening Journal—Historical and Industrial Edition*, Aug. 20, 1917.

Acme Cut Glass

Is strictly hand cut glass. The perfect materials from which it is made, makes it rich in splendor, and need only be displayed to insure results. Do not be fooled by imitations.

Ask your dealer for "Acme Quality Cut Glass." Visit the factory and see how cut glass is made.

Acme Cut Glass Co.

53 Atlantic Street
BRIDGETON, N. J.

cern to the Aetna Cut Glass Company, but still maintained their cutting shop on Atlantic Street. The firm was dissolved in 1922 because fine cut glass had lost its popularity. George Link died in Gloucester, New Jersey, about 1943; Charles Link died in Bridgeton, New Jersey, in 1945.

The Evening Journal—Historical and Industrial Edition, for August 20, 1917 (published by the estate of B. F. Ladd, Vineland, New Jersey), showed an illustrated advertisement for the Acme Cut Glass Company, in which a pitcher and tumbler decorated with brilliantly cut rosettes and sprays of roses and leaves are combined in a design not unlike those produced by other cut glass concerns between 1915 and 1920. The pattern is so much like the rose designs produced by the Irving Cut Glass Company, McKanna Cut Glass Company, Libbey Glass Company, and others, as to be easily mistaken for a product of one or another of these firms.

Leeds Cut Glass Company

The Leeds Cut Glass Company operated in Bridgeton, New Jersey, in the first quarter of this century, but we were unable to find any indication of their activities in the local recordings of business enterprises. We did learn from our colleague, J. E. Pfeiffer of Pitman, New Jersey, that their wares could be identified by the "Cut Rose" and "Cut Thistle" designs they used extensively in their line of cut glasswares. Since these motifs were used by several other cut glass shops, we hesitate to suggest these designs as a means for identifying Leeds's cut glass products.

Bridgeton Cut Glass Company

In 1918 the *American Glass Trade Directory* listed the Bridgeton Cut Glass Company in Bridgeton, New Jersey, but we could never trace this firm through any of the usual channels and sources of information. No one we consulted in Bridgeton or the surrounding communities had even heard of this cut glass factory.

Liberty Cut Glass Works

In 1902, Thomas P. Strittmatter and his associates founded the Liberty Cut Glass Works in Egg Harbor City, New Jersey. Strittmatter was the president of the concern; Charles Cast, vice president; Albert C. Stephany, secretary; and Robert Ohnmeiss, treasurer. The board of directors consisted of John E. Marsden, John H. Diamond, and James Marsden. Cast, Stephany and Ohnmeiss were residents of Egg Harbor City; Marsden is given credit for being one of the principal organizers of the firm and was its general manager for many years. The rest of the men, it is believed, came from Philadelphia. The company's operation was financed with local capital.

In Alfred M. Heston's *Absegami: Annals of Eyren Haven and Atlantic City, 1609 to 1904*, the author states, in Volume one, page 278: "The Winterbottom, Carter & Company's bone knife-handle factory employs about fifty hands, while the same number is at present at work in the newly established Liberty Cut Glass Works." In Volume two, page 364, Heston writes:

> Glass—The cut glass factory at Egg Harbor City had been in operation less than a year in January, 1904, when the president of the company, Thomas P. Strittmatter, reported that $35,000 worth of cut glass had been sent out from the factory. The skilled labor is well paid, and the community profits by the circulation of the wages. Thirty-two cutters and polishers are now employed. The demand is increasing, and a five-year contract with a large house to take $20,000 worth of glass, at a fair profit, guarantees its success.

At the height of their production, the Liberty Cut Glass Works employed as many as 250 people, and their operation was for many years the major industry in Egg Harbor City. Their products ranged from simple cups, plates, and tablewares to fancy vases and decorative articles. At one time they made a huge cut glass electric floor lamp, consisting of many parts all joined together. Harry C. Pfeiffer, a long-time employee of the company, reported that it stood 10 or 12 feet high and was a magnificent example of the glass cutter's art. The lamp was sent around the country to be exhibited in various shops and department stores. Its whereabouts at this time are unknown, and no photographs of this piece exist today. Pfeiffer also confirms that Liberty's cut wares were noted for their allover cut patterns; it was their intention to cover every part of the article's surface with finely cut designs. Only toward the end of their business career did the Liberty Cut Glass Works begin to have uncut areas on their glass, usually with engraved, or otherwise applied, designs. In the late period figured (pressed) blanks were also used by this firm.

August F. Keiser, one of the workers in the Liberty Cut Glass Works, gave us the following list of glass cutters who were employed by the Egg Harbor City cutting shop: Henry Lehneis, William Kitz, Phillip Reinhard, Charles

Becker, Albert Roesch, William Roesch, Fred Doernbach, Frank Schoenstein, Frank Daddario, Bart Daddario, William Theilacker, John Husta, Joseph Slavinski, Edward Roesch, Frank Eckert, Jacob Klenk, Alex Flath, Jacob Kurtz, Fred Morgenweck, Adolph Joseph, Charles Winkler, Eugene Laielli, Tony Laielli, Jacob Futterer, Herman Regensberg, William Bercgtold, John Kamensky, Frank Ade, and, of course, August Keiser and Harry C. Pfeiffer. Keiser indicated that all these men were then still living, and that there were many more alive whose names he could not remember.

The Liberty Cut Glass Works was located at Buffalo Avenue and Atlantic Avenue, adjacent to what is now the Pennsylvania Reading Shore Lines. The original building, erected in 1903, was of wood construction and two stories high. It was 26 feet wide and 100 feet long, with an engine room attached to run the cutting frames. In 1905 an addition of 50 feet was added to the building, this of brick construction. In 1908 another two-story building, 40·feet by 150 feet, of brick construction, was added to the factory and adjoined to the original structure by a two-story connecting wing, 84 feet long by 30 feet wide. An office building was finally added to the complex; this was a two-story brick building, 50 feet by 40 feet. At this time the company started making their own metal parts for fixtures on lamps and other decorative articles.

In the beginning, the first floor of the shop housed the roughing and smoothing departments; the hand polishing was done on a part of the second floor, which also was shared by the acid polishing room and the washing and wrapping rooms. In the late 1920's, business began to slack off because of the declining interest in cut glass. Pfeiffer saw "the writing on the wall" soon after he returned from service in World War I, and realized that fine cut glass was fast becoming a thing of the past. The factory closed its doors in 1932, and as late as 1962 its buildings were occupied by the Nurre Company, manufacturers of mirrors.

In 1905 the Brooklyn, New York, directory listed the Liberty Cut Glass Works store at 239 Union Avenue, Brooklyn; by 1909 they had moved to 643 Kent Avenue, Brooklyn. From 1910 to 1911, they operated a shop and showroom in New York City at 25 West Broadway; thereafter, and until 1917, their showrooms in Manhattan were situated at 200 Fifth Avenue, under the management of Edward B. Dickinson.

The Liberty Cut Glass Works sold their wares through jewelers and a few department stores of high reputation. They also operated 21 crystal shops, and leased the glass departments in such stores as Lord & Taylor and James McCreery in New York City; R. H. White of Boston, Massachusetts; J. L. Hudson of Detroit, Michigan; the Bailey Stores in Columbus and Cleveland, Ohio; and several others. These crystal shops and departments sold all kinds of glassware, but Liberty manufactured only the cut glass, purchasing the other wares from domestic and foreign manufacturers. Pfeiffer's job after World War I, was to go around the country checking these 21 crystal shops and helping out wherever he was needed; his old position in the glassworks was taken over by Edward Meltzer. Liberty's salesmen covered the major

Edward Meltzer's design for a cut glass jug; patented Aug. 3, 1926, for Liberty Cut Glass Works.

cities in this country selling their fine cut glassware: Philadelphia, New York, Boston, Detroit, Toledo, St. Louis, Columbus, and many others. With this wide distribution, it should not be difficult for collectors to find objects made at the Egg Harbor City factory, but, unfortunately, they would be difficult to identify, since no catalogues or illustrations of their wares can be found. The only design patent issued to this firm for glassware was registered in the name of Edward Meltzer and is dated August 3, 1926. The patent covers Meltzer's design for a cut glass jug with a cover, and from the patent illustration it would appear to be a very simple cut pattern. Meltzer started with this concern as an office boy and worked his way up to the position of general manager. He succeeded Harry C. Pfeiffer after the latter went into the armed services around 1917. When Pfeiffer returned to the glassworks, Meltzer stayed in the factory and left the outside work to Pfeiffer and others. Meltzer tried desperately to keep the company alive—he even started to manufacture their own glass—but competition with the old established glass manufacturers was very keen and, around 1931, it was apparent that they could no longer stay in business.

Atlantic Cut Glass Company

The Atlantic Cut Glass Company of Egg Harbor City, New Jersey, operated rather late in the cut glass era, about 1925 to 1935. It was located at 120–128 St. Louis Avenue and its proprietor, Henry Theilacker, specialized in the wholesale and retail distribution of colored and crystal tablewares and some light cut wares in the early 1930's. Previous to that time the firm did cut some heavy brilliant pieces, but this had to be discontinued in the early 1920's because they were too expensive to manufacture. Theilacker's company was taken note of in Egg Harbor City's diamond jubilee booklet published in April, 1930.

An article in the Atlantic City *Sunday Press* on February 17, 1963, stated that "the area from Hammonton to Egg Harbor City was thick with glass-blowing and glass-cutting firms, but the industry virtually disappeared after World War Two ended."

Mays Landing Cut Glass Company

The Mays Landing Cut Glass Company was listed in the *Industrial Directories of New Jersey* in 1918. That same year it was also listed in the *American Glass Trade Directory* under cut glass manufacturers. In spite of these references to this firm, we could not find any listing of it, or even an indication of its size, in local directories.

Sam Neuwirth, formerly associated with the United Cut Glass Company in New York City, told us that a Joe Thorpe cut glass in Mays Landing, New Jersey, in the early part of this century. We could not find any definite connection between Thorpe and the Mays Landing Cut Glass Company, but this is a possibility.

Cut Glass Manufacturers in Pennsylvania

The Franklin Flint Glass Works
Gillinder & Bennett
Gillinder & Sons
Gillinder Brothers
Gillinder Brothers, Incorporated

William T. Gillinder founded his own glassworks in Philadelphia, Pennsylvania, the Franklin Flint Glass Works, in 1861. In 1863 he was joined by Edwin Bennett, a potter from East Liverpool, Ohio. Bennett brought in additional capital, with which the factory was expanded greatly, and the name was changed to Gillinder & Bennett. In 1867, Gillinder's two sons, Frederick and James, came into the firm and Bennett withdrew to form his own pottery business in Baltimore, Maryland. At this time the name of the company was changed from Gillinder & Bennett to Gillinder & Sons. William T. Gillinder died in 1871 and the firm was continued by his two sons under the name of Gillinder Brothers.

Gillinder Brothers built an exhibition factory on the Philadelphia Centennial Exhibition grounds in 1876, where they produced pressed glass and some cut and engraved wares. Primarily though, this company manufactured pressed glass tablewares, though at one time in their Philadelphia factory they main-

Cut and engraved decanters; Franklin Flint Glass Works; *ca.* 1870.

Photo courtesy of Gillinder Bros., Inc.

Cut and engraved celery holders and a pitcher; Franklin Flint Glass Works; *ca.* 1870.

Cut and engraved fruit bowls on standards; Franklin Flint Glass Works; *ca.* 1870.

tained a very large cutting department, making not only heavy cut glass items—lamps, shades, and so on—but punch bowls and a general line of cut table glassware. Shortly before the turn of the century, the factory was moved to Port Jervis, New York, where it now operates as Gillinder Brothers, Incorporated.

Illustrations from an original catalogue issued by Gillinder & Son's Franklin Flint Glass Works in Philadelphia show decanters, compotes, celery vases, and pitchers, as well as engraved lamp shades. All the cut designs reveal a restraint common to many English cut glass products of this same period, about 1870. Some members of the Gillinder family still possess some finely cut pieces resembling in many ways the beautifully cut designs of the Brilliant Period. We were unable to determine whether or not Gillinders marked their cut glasswares; consequently, attributions will be difficult to substantiate.

Imperial Cut Glass Company

The Imperial Cut Glass Company of Philadelphia (Wayne Junction), Pennsylvania, first appeared in the directories in 1896 as at 618 Chestnut Street. The following year it had moved to 709 Filbert Street in Philadelphia. By the turn of the century it had moved again to Wayne Avenue, near the Philadelphia and Reading Railway in the Germantown area of Philadelphia. In 1903 they relocated again to Wayne Avenue near Berkley Avenue in Germantown (Philadelphia). John T. White was listed as the president of the company in 1907. White was noted as president and treasurer of the concern in 1910, and Adelbert G. Lee was listed as secretary. From 1912 to 1913 the address of the Imperial Cut Glass Company was given as 411 Market Street, Philadelphia. After 1915 no further entries appeared for this company in the public records.

Left: The "Victoria" pattern; patented Dec. 15, 1896, for Imperial Cut Glass Co.; *right:* The "Maltese Crosses" pattern; patented Oct. 23, 1888; both by Joseph B. Hill.

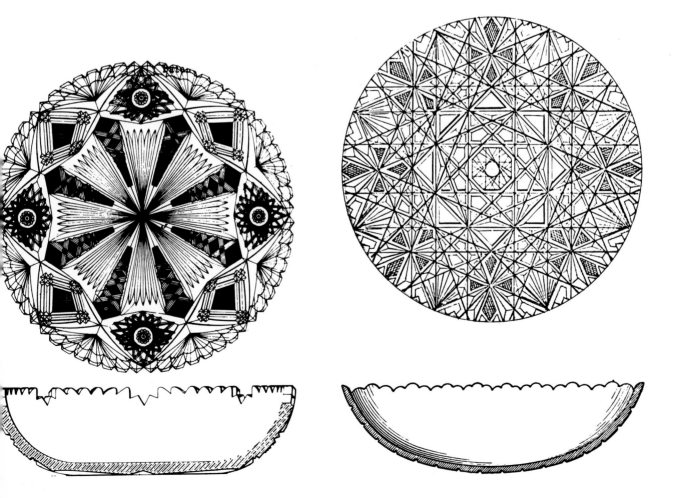

A design patent for cut glassware was issued to Joseph B. Hill on December 15, 1896 and assigned to the Imperial Cut Glass Company. Dorothy Daniel, in her book *Cut and Engraved Glass, 1771–1905*, designated this the "Victoria" pattern.

Some years earlier, on October 23, 1888, Hill patented another cut glass design which we have reason to believe was produced by the Phoenix Glass Company. One of the witnesses to Hill's patent papers, Joseph Webb, was associated with the Phoenix Glass Company at this time. However, the possibility does exist that the pattern, which we have named "Maltese Crosses," may have been registered by Hill for still another cut glass company.

Quaker City Cut Glass Company
Cut Glass Corporation of America

The Quaker City Cut Glass Company, also known as the Cut Glass Corporation of America, was first located in Philadelphia, Pennsylvania, at the corner of Montgomery Avenue and 9th Street, North, according to the city directories for the year 1902. In 1904, Gospill's *Philadelphia Business Directories* listed the firm's location as the corner of South 60th Street and Baltimore Avenue, where it remained until 1924, when it moved to 4945 Wakefield Street in Germantown (Philadelphia), Pennsylvania.

Thomas Wolstenholme was president of the company in 1907 and Thomas P. Strittmatter was secretary and treasurer. In 1909, Robert H. Hood was listed as vice president and Wolstenholme and Strittmatter appear in the records in their original positions in the company. In 1915, Isidore P. Strittmatter succeeded to the presidency. The firm did not appear in the city directories after 1927, and we assume from this that they were no longer in the cut glass business after that date.

Thomas' *Register of American Manufacturers and First Hands in All Lines* listed the Quaker City Cut Glass Company with an "A" rating, indicating that it had assets of over $100,000. Thomas P. Strittmatter was the president and cofounder of the Liberty Cut Glass Works of Egg Harbor City, New Jersey, in 1902; he was also the first treasurer of the National Association of Cut Glass Manufacturers.

After World War I, the Quaker City Cut Glass Company joined with the Laurel Cut Glass Company of Jermyn, Pennsylvania. A short time later they separated, and the Quaker City Cut Glass Company continued on their own in their old location.

Unfortunately, we have never found any marked pieces of the Quaker

City Cut Glass Company's wares, though they were issued a trademark—a bust of William Penn and their name—which they placed on their glassware with gummed paper labels. One of their old employees, Eber Burrough, told the author that he worked mostly on punch bowl sets, and one of the firm's favorite designs was the "Dewberry" pattern.

Taylor Brothers & Williams
Taylor Brothers Company, Incorporated

About 1902, Albert R. Taylor and his brother Lafayette Taylor, together with John H. Williams, formed Taylor Brothers & Williams, manufacturers of rich cut glassware. The business was then located at 3531 North Comac Street in Philadelphia, Pennsylvania. In 1903 their address was 968 North

Left: Signed "Taylor Brothers" vase; height 8 in. *Right:* Signed "Taylor Brothers" bowl; diameter 8 in.

Collection of Mrs. Wilbur Griffin   *Collection of Mr. and Mrs. Lee Schreiber*

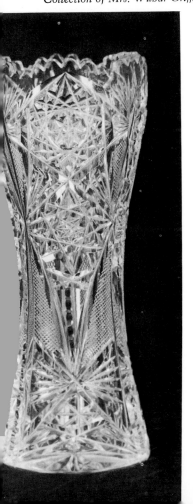

Franklin Street, Philadelphia. The style of the firm was changed in 1904 to Taylor Brothers, Albert R. Taylor and Lafayette Taylor, proprietors. Taylor Brothers moved in 1906 to Cambridge Street, corner of North 3d Street, in Philadelphia. The city directory for 1908 listed Lafayette Taylor as president; Albert R. Taylor, vice president; John R. Earnshaw, secretary; and Andrew McClay, treasurer. In 1911 Taylor Brothers Company, Incorporated, filed bankruptcy papers; their quarters at Cambridge and North 3d Streets were taken over by the Powelton Cut Glass Company. In 1912 the city records show Taylor Brothers still operating at 608 Keith's Theatre Building, 1116 Chestnut Street, Philadelphia. The company maintained these quarters until they went out of business entirely in 1915.

Round bowl made by Taylor Bros. Co., Inc. (signed); diameter 11½ in.

Collection of Charles P. Huber

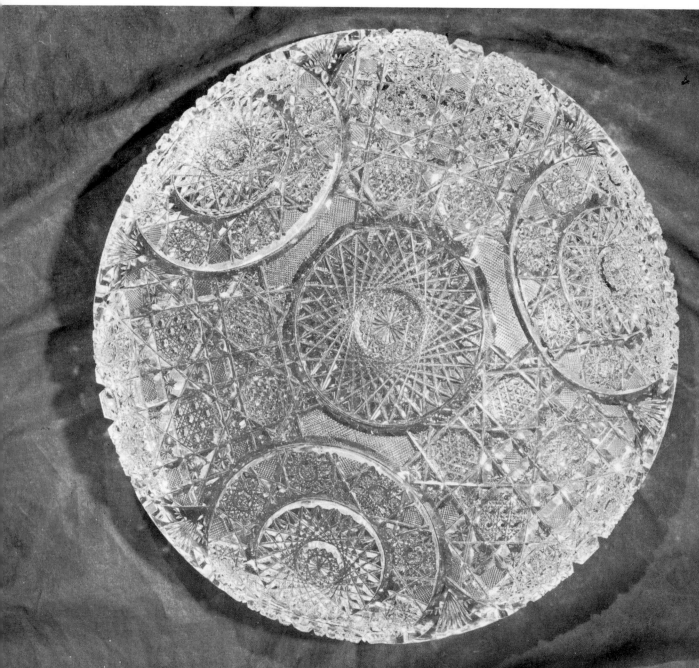

Handled nappy, signed "Taylor Brothers"; diameter 6 in.
Collection of Mr. and Mrs. Jack Walker

Taylor Brothers Company, Incorporated, produced a fine grade of cut glass, using designs that were typical of the Brilliant Period. Their wares are usually marked with a cipher of the letters "T" and "B," and the name "Taylor" or "Taylor Brothers."

Statt Brothers
Fred Statt Company

John W. Statt, James Statt, and Fred Statt founded the Statt Brothers cut glass shop in Philadelphia (Manayunk), Pennsylvania, about 1905. (We have found the name listed as "Stott Brothers" on one or two occasions, but this is in error.) Their cutting shop was located at 4450 Main Street in Manayunk. In 1910 the city records indicate that only James Statt and Fred Statt were operating the cut glass business; they continued as Statt Brothers, in the same location, until 1920. The 1918 issue of the *American Glass Trade Directory* listed Statt Brothers as operating in Manayunk that year. From 1930 to 1936, the Fred Statt Company, manufacturers of glassware, was located in Philadelphia at 1007 Filbert Street.

The Powelton Cut Glass Company

The Powelton Cut Glass Company was formed in 1910 with Iredell Eachus as president; James W. Jamison, vice president; and Raymond H. Fender, secretary and treasurer. E. Ellis Stalbird was superintendent (he withdrew from the firm during World War I). The shop was first located at 62d Street and Girard Avenue in Philadelphia, Pennsylvania. When Taylor Brothers failed, the company moved into their vacated quarters at North 3d and Cambridge Streets. In 1925, Powelton again moved to 67 Laurel Street, a part of the old Disston estate. When the Disston estate was dissolved in 1948, Fender purchased one of the buildings across the street from their Laurel Street shop, at 42–44 East Allen Street, where Powelton remained until they were dissolved in 1953. The company was incorporated in 1917.

From 1910 to the beginning of World War I, Powelton cut beautiful brilliant patterns on heavy blanks. After 1918 they produced only light cut wares and painted designs on glass. The company started in business about the time the floral designs came into vogue in cut glassware and their principal patterns were "Poinsettia," "Apple Blossom," and "Marigold."

The "Marigold" pattern; from an original catalogue issued by Powelton Cut Glass Co.
Photo courtesy of Raymond H. Fender

NO 56 JEWEL NO. 2 POINSETTIA 9 B JEWEL NO 25 JEWEL

Photos courtesy of Raymond H. Fender

Top: The "Jewel" and the "Poinsettia" patterns; *bottom:* Light wares in gray cut finish; both from an original catalogue issued by Powelton Cut Glass Co.; *ca.* 1915.

MARMALADE JAR DAISY NO. 14 DAISY NO. 30 POINSETTIA

NO. 105 NO. 504 NO. 73 DAISY NO. 71½ NO. 48 POINSET.

Conlow & Dorworth

Conlow & Dorworth maintained a sales agency for cut glasswares in the Roxborough section of Philadelphia, Pennsylvania, at 407 Walnut Lane from 1915 to at least 1920. Their cutting shops were located in New Jersey, in Mt. Holly and Palmyra. Augustus Conlow was president; George F. Dorworth, vice president; and William Nickels, secretary and treasurer. Conlow & Dorworth were members of the National Association of Cut Glass Manufacturers and were listed under cut glass manufacturers in the 1918 issue of the *American Glass Trade Directory*.

Diamond Cut Glass Company

The Diamond Cut Glass Company operated in Philadelphia, Pennsylvania, at 214 Dauphin Street, under the direction of Frederick E. Field. The public records indicate that it started business about 1915 and continued active until at least 1920. No further entries for this concern were found in the city directories after 1925.

Samuel H. French & Company

The Samuel H. French & Company, located at 4444 Main Street, Manayunk, Philadelphia, Pennsylvania, enjoyed a AAA rating (over $500,000) in Thomas' *Register of American Manufacturers and First Hands in All Lines* as cut glass manufacturers (1909/10). They were not listed in the *American Glass Trade Directory* for this period, so we cannot be certain that they actually manufactured their own cut glass. It is known that they handled the cut glass products of other manufacturers, and this too indicates that they were actually not in the glass cutting business themselves.

Philadelphia Cut Glass Company

The Philadelphia Cut Glass Company was a small cutting shop located about 1912 at 1419 North Franklin Street in Philadelphia, Pennsylvania. No entry for this concern could be found in the public records or in the Philadelphia city directories. The owners were members of the National Association of Cut Glass Manufacturers, though their name does not appear in any of the association's records still in the possession of Raymond H. Fender, the organization's former secretary. Fender told the author that the company was not in business for very long, and suggested that it may have closed around 1920 or 1925.

S. K. Bitner & Company

S. K. Bitner (Bittner) & Company of Lancaster, Pennsylvania, cut glass manufacturers, operated their shop from 1913 to 1928. According to city records, their address in Lancaster was 446–448 Lafayette Street. S. S. Bitner (not S. K. Bitner, according to the records) was president of the firm, and Hayes G. Shimp secretary and treasurer throughout their 15 years' existence.

Val Bergen Cut Glass Company

Valentine Bergen and a man named Cluny established the Val Bergen Cut Glass Company in Columbia, Pennsylvania, about 1907; the factory was located at the corner of Manor and Twelfth Streets. No notations concerning this firm could be found in the town's records, but local residents and former employees of the company agree that the factory closed down in the early 1920's. The Val Bergen Cut Glass Company produced brilliant cut patterns on heavy blown crystal blanks.

Columbia Cut Glass Company

The Columbia Cut Glass Company of Columbia, Pennsylvania, had a very short duration. It was located in Columbia at Second and Linden Streets and was owned and operated by Blanton Welsh. The shop opened in 1918 and closed the same year, according to the available records.

The Susquehanna Cut Glass Company
The Susquehanna Glass Company

In 1910, Albert Roye, assisted by Harry P. Glasser, organized the Susquehanna Cut Glass Company in Columbia, Pennsylvania. Roye was the firm's first president. The shop was begun in a shed in an alley between Locust and Walnut Streets, just above Seventh Street. Roye had learned the glass cutting trade in the Val Bergen Cut Glass Company. When Roye died, his brother Walter Roye assumed the presidency of the firm. It still does business in Columbia, Pennsylvania, as the Susquehanna Glass Company.

Dorflinger Glass Company
C. Dorflinger & Sons
Honesdale Glass Works
Honesdale Decorating Company

Christian Dorflinger was born on March 16, 1828, in Rosteig, Canton Bitsch, Alsace, France. His parents, Francis and Charlotte Clemens Dorflinger, apprenticed him to his uncle to learn glassmaking at the St. Louis Glass Works in St. Louis, France, where he soon mastered the fundamentals

Collection of Mr. and Mrs. John C. Dorflinger;
photo courtesy of Everhart Museum, Scranton, Pa.

Left to right: Cream pitcher; cut neck of "Hollow Diamond" design above two bands of "Strawberry-Diamond" separated by a band of "Hollow Flutes"; height 5¾ in. Pitcher with cut neck of "Hollow Diamond" design above two bands of "Strawberry-Diamond" separated by a band of "Hollow Flutes"; engraved "D"; made for Eugene and Clothilde Dorflinger; height 10½ in. Oval vegetable dish; cut and polished copper-wheel engraving; made for Fanny B. Bailey, wife of Nathaniel S. Bailey, Dorflinger associate in Brooklyn, N.Y.; made at Dorflinger's Greenpoint glassworks, Brooklyn, N.Y. *ca.* 1850; length 9 in.

of the trade. He was especially interested in the decorating techniques for glassware—etching, cutting, gilding, and enameling. After his father's death in 1845, he and his mother migrated to America in 1846, bringing with them his brothers and sisters. The rest of the family went on to Indiana, but Christian Dorflinger stayed in Philadelphia, where he worked as a journeyman glass blower for a firm which manufactured druggist's bottles and chemical wares. Later he worked in Camden, New Jersey.

Dorflinger met his future wife, Elizabeth Hagen, while he was on one of his many trips to Brooklyn, New York. He used to stop at the old Pacific Hotel, at that time operated by a former seafaring captain named Aaron Flower. About 1850, Captain Flower and several of his friends sent for Christian Dorflinger to establish a glass factory for the manufacture of kerosene oil lamps and chimneys, which had just begun to come into wide use in this country. Dorflinger's first factory, the Long Island Flint Glass Works, was established on Concord Street in Brooklyn in 1852. It consisted of only one five-pot furnace, but with industry and long hours of hard work, Dorflinger was able to buy out his backers and operate the business on his own. In 1858 he built another glass factory on Plymouth Street, Brooklyn, and in 1860 he built the Greenpoint glassworks on Commercial Street in Brooklyn, where he manufactured the fine glassware for which he became so famous.

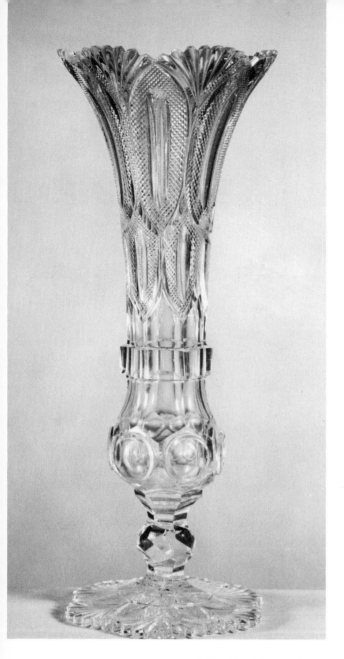

In Brooklyn Museum Collection, Brooklyn, N. Y.   *Collection of Corning Museum of Glass*
Left: Vase, blown and cut flint glass; made by Dorflinger glassworks, Brooklyn, N.Y. as presentation piece for Mrs. Dorflinger; inscribed "Presented by the Officers and Members of the Dorflinger Guards to Mrs. Dorflinger, January 14, 1859." *Right:* Pitcher; *ca.* mid-nineteenth century; Dorflinger glassworks, Brooklyn, N.Y.; height at handle 12⅛ in.

The Lincoln service for the White House was produced in this new factory in 1861. Here too Dorflinger produced the fine colored glassware which is now so sought after by collectors.

By 1863, Dorflinger's health would not permit him to continue the strenuous pace he had set for himself, and he was forced to retire from active participation in the business. He sold the Long Island Flint Glass Works to J. S. Hibbler, and entrusted the operation of the Greenpoint glassworks to two employees, John B. Dobelmann and Nathaniel Bailey. Later on, he leased the Greenpoint glassworks to E. P. Gleason and eventually, in 1902, it, too, was sold.

Christian Dorflinger accepted Captain Flower's invitation to spend some time at his farm in Wayne County, Pennsylvania, a lovely spot along the Lackawaxen River near the town of White Mills, through which the Delaware and Hudson Canal ran. Dorflinger fell in love with the whole area, and in 1865 he bought Captain Flower's 300-acre farm for his retirement. In a short time he was bored with his leisure and began plans for the construction of a glass factory. At first he built a small plant at Indian Orchard, Pennsylvania, a nearby farming center, and later in that same year, he built the Dorflinger Glass Company's works at White Mills, Pennsylvania.

The White Mills factory started with a five-pot furnace with seven houses constructed on the grounds for key personnel whom he brought from the Brooklyn works. In 1866 the number of employees mushroomed to 100 men and boys, most of whom had been farm help only a few months before. Under the tutelage of Dorflinger's expert workers from the Brooklyn factory, most of whom were glassmen from Europe, the green help developed into one of the finest groups of glassworkers in America. In 1867, Dorflinger opened his glass cutting shop with one frame and six expert glass cutters and engravers. At that time the works had added a two-story building for its cutting shop and a packing department. A three-story building was added in time, and also a building in which large clay pots and crucibles were made.

A basin was dug on the Delaware and Hudson Canal to facilitate shipping to and from the factory, and after 1868, when the Erie Railroad extended its tracks to East Honesdale, Pennsylvania, a railroad siding to the Dorflinger works supplemented their transportation needs. Dorflinger's glass found its way to every state in the Union and abroad by way of all the different mediums of transportation then available—canal, gravity railroad, steam railroad, and horse and wagon; the latter were horse-drawn wagons equipped with hay riggings which hauled barrels of lamp chimneys and lantern globes to the Delaware & Hudson freight station at Honesdale for transshipment to the company's supply warehouse at Colonie, New York. Some shipments were taken by wagon to the Pennsylvania Railroad facilities at Wilkes-Barre, Pennsylvania, for distribution along the company's route.

In the early 1870's over 75 workmen's cottages were built, along with some additional factory buildings. One of the new buildings was a large glasshouse with an enormous basement of iron and stone construction extending under the whole building; it contained one eight-pot furnace and three annealing ovens. A three-story gray stone building was erected to accommodate an increase in the cutting business. On the second floor of this building was a 75-horsepower engine to turn the hundreds of wheels in the cutting shop below.

The Honesdale Glass Works of Traceyville, Pennsylvania (near Honesdale), was established about 1840. The works failed and were taken over by R. F. Lord and T. H. R. Tracey, who were succeeded by James Brookfield. It finally ceased operating in 1861 when the plant was destroyed by a flood.

About ten years later, Christian Dorflinger rebuilt the factory and operated it under the same name in association with G. S. Minor, W. H. Ham, S. A. Tyrell, W. W. Weston, and William Weiss. The plant's two five-pot furnaces produced four tons of glass daily.

In 1881, Christian Dorflinger took into the business his three sons, William, Louis J., and Charles, and the name of the company was changed to C. Dorflinger & Sons. All three sons were active in their father's business from an early age and were well versed in every facet of the trade. It was during this period that the Dorflingers produced some of their finest wares. Louis J. Dorflinger's two sons, Dwight and Charles Dorflinger, entered the firm about 1900 and held supervisory positions.

In its long and illustrious existence the Dorflinger works employed many fine craftsmen: Nicholas Lutz, originally from St. Louis, France, who later distinguished himself in the glass trade at the Boston & Sandwich Glass Company; Ralph Barber, who produced some of the most beautiful rose paperweights at Millville, New Jersey; and Charles Northwood, Oscar Levine, Louis Aug, Alvin Falk, John Johnson, and the Larsen and the Lilequist brothers. In 1903 the White Mills factory employed 650 men and boys.

With the exception of gold decorating, all articles of glass made at the Dorflinger works were finished products, ready for sale at the time they left the factory. Dorflinger used to send some of his glassware to an Austrian decorator in New York City whenever gold decorations were to be added to the articles. When his business in such wares increased, he made an arrangement with Carl F. Prosch, an expert designer in etching and gold decoration, to operate a new factory Dorflinger built in Seelyville, Pennsylvania, known as the Honesdale Decorating Company. Prosch had studied at Melk on the Danube River in Austria, in a school operated by Benedictine monks. At the time he went into business with Dorflinger, he was the New York representa-

Left to right: "Water Lily" goblet; flower bowl in the "Biltmore" pattern; sherbet glass in the "Cornflower" pattern. Crystal glass decorated with gold and enamel by Carl Prosch of the Honesdale Decorating Co.

Collection of Wayne County Historical Society

Photo by Abbie Rowe—Courtesy National Park Service,
U.S. Department of the Interior

Cut and engraved goblet and wineglass with the coat of
arms of the United States of America; attributed to the
administration of Abraham Lincoln; produced at White
Mills, Pa., by Christian Dorflinger.

A wineglass engraved with the arms of New York State
from the Centennial Set; 5 in. high; made at Dorflinger
Glass Works in 1876 for the Centennial Exposition in
Philadelphia; the set consisted of a decanter and 38 wineglasses.

Collection of Wayne County Historical Society

tive for an Austrian wholesale glass agency, Bawo & Dotter, whose factories were located in Bohemia, with main offices at Kotzschenbroda bei Dresden. In 1915, Prosch bought out the Dorflinger interest in the Honesdale Decorating Company and continued the business under the old name until 1932.

Prosch made certain designs which were exclusively his own. His wares were sold through Tiffany and Ovington in New York City, and in Philadelphia by Wright-Lyndale and Van Roden. His decorative pieces were marked "Honesdale" (most of these in the style of the *art nouveau* cameo glasswares on cased colored blanks). Some tablewares are marked with his ciphers—a gold keystone with the letter "P" in the center; and a mark similar to one used by the A. H. Heisey Glass Company, from whom he purchased pressed glass plates—a diamond with the letter "H" in the center. The latter wares were usually decorated with gold designs and rims.

The Dorflinger glassworks supplied crystal and cased colored blanks for cutting and engraving to more than 22 cutting shops in their area. All their own cut wares were shipped to their shop and showrooms at 36 Murray Street in New York City. The goods were then sold to retailers—Gorham, Ovington, Tiffany, and other fine stores in New York City. Many shops in Washington, Boston, Chicago, Philadelphia, and San Francisco purchased their glass from

Rock crystal punch bowl and glasses made in 1917 for exhibition purposes only at Dorflinger Glass Works. The panels have been cut in full relief and engraved with rock crystal designs; height 17 in.; glasses are 3½ in. tall.

Collection of Wayne County Historical Society

Dorflinger's New York City outlet. Dorflinger's retail shop was located in New York City at 915 Broadway; later, about 1920, it was moved to 3–5 West 9th Street.

The death of Christian Dorflinger in 1915 was a great blow to the company. His personal supervision of the works ensured that only the finest glass would leave their hands. On top of this, World War I made it impossible for them to purchase the potash necessary for the manufacture of their fine crystal. The era of prohibition also cut into Dorflinger's production of stemware and bar accessories. In 1921 the family decided to close the factory rather than continue the business producing cheaper glassware. The decision was in keeping with Christian Dorflinger's tradition for excellence in workmanship and design. For many years after the factory closed, John Dorflinger of Hawley, Pennsylvania, kept the showrooms of the factory open at White Mills, exhibiting and occasionally selling some of the fine old glass still on hand at the time the company ceased operating. For the most part, John Dorflinger operated the place as a museum, and was often on hand to speak to visitors about the glass his family had made so famous. On February 5, 1964, John Dorflinger died, closing the final chapter on the Dorflinger glassworks.

During its long and distinguished career the Dorflinger works produced beautiful glassware for several presidents—Lincoln, Grant, Harrison, Wilson—and internationally known personages. The Prince of Wales (later King Edward VIII) ordered a set of fluted glassware from Dorflinger's for his use when he toured Canada and the United States in 1919. Henry Clay Pierce's fabulous ocean-going yacht, the *Yacona*, was outfitted with a cut glass service, valued at $60,000, from the White Mills factory. A suite of glass numbering 2,300 pieces was assembled for President Mario Menocal of Cuba and engraved with the coat of arms of the Cuban Republic. For the Centennial Exposition in Philadelphia, Dorflinger cut a magnificent wine service known as the "Centennial Set," which consisted of 38 wine glasses and a decanter engraved with three panels; on one was depicted the Goddess of Liberty, on another the United States coat of arms, and on the third panel the crest of the City of Philadelphia, together with the name of the mayor of that city and the date—"1876." Each wine glass bore the seal of one of the individual states, the name of its governor, and the date "1876." The Centennial Set is now in the collection of the Memorial Museum in Fairmount Park.

A copper-wheel engraved punch bowl and cups, now on exhibition at the Wayne County Historical Society in Honesdale, was produced at Dorflinger's works in 1917. It was designed by Charles O. Northwood, roughed by Fred Houth, smoothed by Arthur E. Firmstone, and copper-wheeled by Edward Basler. Since it was made for exhibition purposes only, there are no duplicates of this bowl.

Cut glass baseball bat presented to Eddie Murphy by John Dorflinger in Philadelphia, Oct. 8, 1913. The bat was produced at the Dorflinger factory at White Mills, Pa., and is of regulation size and shape.

Collection of Eddie Murphy

Design for engraved glass bottles, Design Patent No. 9,646, dated Nov. 21, 1876, by Christian Dorflinger of White Mills, Pa.

One of the most interesting novelties in cut glass ever produced was the baseball bat which Dorflingers made for their local hero, Eddie Murphy. The bat was of regulation size and shape and the blank for this masterpiece was made at the White Mills works by Peter Jones (who later went to Corning, New York, and subsequently joined the police force in that town). It was

Left: The "Parisian" pattern; patented May 4, 1886, by John S. O'Connor for C. Dorflinger & Sons. *Right:* The "Parisian" pattern adapted to the form of a cream jug; height 6 in. (Compare this pattern with the original design at left.)

Author's collection

Left: The "Florentine" pattern; patented Nov. 13, 1888; *right:* The "Rattan" pattern; patented Mar. 22, 1892; both by John S. O'Connor; C. Dorflinger & Sons.

cut in the Dorflinger shop and presented to Murphy by John Dorflinger at the opening game between Connie Mack's "A's" and the New York Giants in Philadelphia in 1913. John Dorflinger had been Eddie Murphy's sponsor in his early days of baseball, and he took great pride in presenting Murphy with this handsome baseball bat in glass, richly cut with a deep polished design.

Christian Dorflinger's first design patent was issued to him on November 21, 1876. The registration covered a design for "glass bottles," and the patent illustration showed both sides of a cologne flask engraved with floral and leaf motifs.

John Sarsfield O'Connor was one of the most skillful glass cutters ever employed by Christian Dorflinger. O'Connor was born in Londonderry, Ireland, June 6, 1831. Before the Civil War he worked for Turner & Lane and E. V. Haughwout & Company, both of New York City. After his release from service in the Union Army, he returned to Haughwout's as superintendent of their plant. Haughwout went out of business just about the time Dorflinger was establishing his cutting shop in White Mills and he hired O'Connor as his foreman. O'Connor invented many machines for cutting glass that changed completely the cut glass industry. One of his inventions cut glass in curved lines instead of the usual straight-line cutting, enabling Dorflinger's to be the first to engrave glass with curved miter designs. O'Connor's "Parisian" pattern, which he patented on May 4, 1886, is a classic example of this "new" style in cutting. The "Parisian" pattern was produced in a full line of table glassware. The pattern was often modified to suit the object at hand, and for this reason differences in the design are found on pieces from this suite of glassware. The same rule applies to several cut glass patterns produced at Dorflinger's and other cut glass factories. T. G. Hawkes & Company cut a version of the "Parisian" pattern later on with single lines, or miter cuts, thus avoiding infringement on Dorflinger's patent rights.

On November 13, 1888, O'Connor registered his "Florentine" pattern, which was issued in a full line of table glassware and decorative articles.

The "Rattan" pattern was patented by John S. O'Connor on March 22, 1892. Here again the curved miter cutting is used extensively throughout the design, separating the pattern of fans, hobnails, fine hatch cutting, and brilliant rosettes into an interesting combination of motifs common to most cut glass shops. In 1890, O'Connor left Dorflinger's shop and started his own cut glass factory in nearby Hawley, Pennsylvania; later he moved it to Goshen, New York.

A trademark for Dorflinger's "Colonial" pattern was registered to the firm on April 11, 1893. On July 4, 1893, James J. O'Connor (a brother of John S.

Vase in the "Colonial" pattern; height 14 in.
Collection of Wayne County Historical Society

The "Colonial" pattern; patented July 4, 1893, by James J. O'Connor; C. Dorflinger & Sons.

The "Lorraine" pattern; patented Nov. 13, 1894, by James J. O'Connor; C. Dorflinger & Sons.

O'Connor) patented the "Colonial" pattern and assigned his rights to C. Dorflinger & Sons. This pattern was one of Dorflinger's most popular designs, according to John Dorflinger; it was also an inexpensive pattern and was produced in a wide range of tablewares and decorative articles. (According to John Dorflinger, the "flat candle holders" in this design illustrated in Dorothy Daniel's *Cut and Engraved Glass, 1771–1905*, Plate 8, are actually "table salts" produced at the Dorflinger works and illustrated in their catalogue of the 1895 period, along with other cut glass table salts. They were not produced by the H. C. Fry Glass Company of Rochester, Pennsylvania.)

James O'Connor's "Lorraine" pattern was another of Dorflinger's very popular lines and was patented on November 13, 1894. The firm was issued

"Amore" pattern bowl made at Dorflinger glassworks; diameter 8 in.

Collection of Wayne County Historical Society

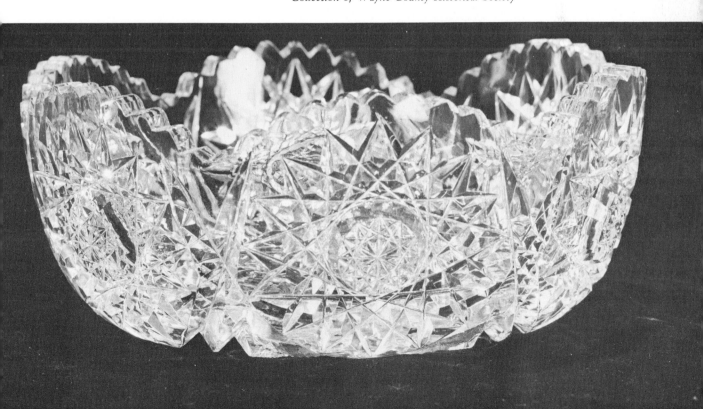

Collection of Mr. and Mrs. John C. Dorflinger;
photo courtesy of Everhart Museum, Scranton, Pa.

Left to right: Champagne glass, goblet, and punch cup in Dorflinger's "Kalana Lily" design; heights 4½ in., 5¾ in., and 2¼ in., respectively; all *ca.* 1912–21. Port wine glass etched with "Flaming Torch" design; height 4¼ in.; designed by George Locke; *ca.* 1910. Pousse-café glass; etched "Kalana Rose and Band" design; height 3⅝ in.; *ca.* 1912–21.

trademark papers for the name "Lorraine" on October 16, 1894. This was another of Dorflinger's inexpensive cut glass patterns produced in a full line of table glassware and decorative objects—vases, bowls, and so on. O'Connor stated in his patent specifications that he used a stylized version of the St. Andrew's cross in this particular design.

The following patterns in cut glass wares were found in illustrated catalogues issued by the Dorflinger Glass Works:

American
Amore
Avon
Belmont
Block Diamond
Brazilian
Brilliante
Colonial
Colorado
Cosmos
Diamond Border
Dresden
Essex
Exeter
Fan and Strawberry-Diamond
Flaming Torch (an etched design)
Flash Star
Florentine
Heavy Flute (also known as "Colonial"
    in their catalogues)

Hob Diamond
Hob Diamond and Lace
Italian Renaissance (a rock crystal design)
Kalana Lily (an etched design also produced by the Irving Cut Glass Company and La Tournous Brothers)
Lapidary (confined to knife rests only)
Large Hob Diamond
Marlboro
New American
No. 8
No. 40
No. 50
No. 147
No. 640
No. 643
No. 660
No. 1,888
Old Colony

Collection of Wayne County Historical Society

Left: "Cosmos" pattern vase; 14 in. tall; designed by Charles O. Northwood for Dorflinger glassworks; *ca.* 1910. *Right:* "Strawberry" pattern candy bowl; 10 in. long; Dorflinger glassworks; *ca.* 1895. (Note original Dorflinger label in center of dish.)

Left: Covered cheese dish in the "Russian" pattern; height 7 in.; made by C. Dorflinger & Sons; *ca.* 1890. *Right:* Cut glass rose bowl; 5½ in. tall; Dorflinger glassworks; *ca.* 1890.

Collection of Lynn Parker   *Collection of Wayne County Historical Society*

Collection of Mr. and Mrs. John C. Dorflinger;
photo courtesy of Everhart Museum, Scranton, Pa.

Left to right: Roemer glass cut in the "Old Colony" pattern with the interior of the bowl cased in green glass; height 6¾ in. Cocktail glass cut in the "Exeter" pattern, in shape No. 1,340; height 4¼ in. Claret glass cut in the "Spiral" design; height 4½ in. Roemer glass; overlay of green glass on crystal; foot cut in "Flash Star" design; bowl stone engraved in "Rococo" design; designed by Walter J. Graham; height 6½ in.; Dorflinger glassworks; *ca.* 1892.

Left: "No. 28" pattern pitcher; height 7½ in.; Dorflinger glassworks; *ca.* 1897. *Right*: Cut glass vase in the "Strawberry-Diamond" pattern; made by Dorflinger glassworks; height 6½ in.; engraved with the name "Mary R. Tracy" and dated "Dec. 28th, 1864–1879."

Collection of Mr. and Mrs. Lee Schreiber

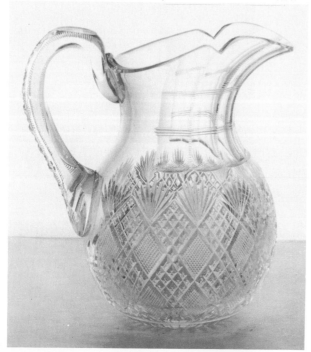

Oval and Split
Princess
Renaissance
Rock Crystal
Rococo
Royal
Russian
Savoy

Spiral
Star and Diamond
Star Bottom
Strawberry
Strawberry-Diamond
Strawberry-Diamond and Fan
Sultana
Tuxedo

Collection of Mr. and Mrs. John C. Dorflinger;
photo courtesy of Everhart Museum, Scranton, Pa.

Left to right: Water goblet; cut stem and foot; cut foliage band and "D" engraved on the copper wheel; made for Richard Deusenberry of Honesdale, Pa., *ca.* 1880; height 9⅛ in. Water goblet cut in the "Parisian" design with unusual mitered stem; height 5½ in. Goblet with copper-wheel engraving in the "Italian Renaissance" design in rock crystal technique; superb example of glass engraving; height 6½ in.; Dorflinger glassworks.

The Dorflinger trademark label consisted of the name "Dorflinger" and representations of a wine bottle and two types of stemware in an old cut glass pattern known in the trade as "Diamond Point."

Hatch & Clark
Clark & Wood
T. B. Clark & Company

In 1884, Thomas Byron Clark made the trip from Meriden, Connecticut, to Honesdale, Pennsylvania, by horse and buggy to establish a cut glass factory in Seelyville, Pennsylvania. On May 14, 1884, he wrote his sister Jane that he had arrived just the night before, and that his colt was feeling no ill affects from the trip, though, he added with obvious pride, he "drove 63 miles yesterday." The letter was written on printed stationery showing that the firm's name at that time was Hatch & Clark (George E. Hatch and Thomas B. Clark, owners).

Within two years the style of the firm had been changed to T. B. Clark & Company; Hatch had by this time established his own cutting shop in Brooklyn, New York. For a short period the firm was also known as Clark & Wood; Walter A. Wood was Clark's brother-in-law and presumably he was in partnership with Clark right after George E. Hatch withdrew from the firm. The association as Clark & Wood was short-lived, but Wood was still very active in the business as late as 1895. D. C. Osborn was the company's secretary in 1910, and had been with the firm since its inception in 1884. He continued to work for T. B. Clark & Company until it closed.

Hatch & Clark's factory in Seelyville was a two-story stone building housing all their cutting and polishing equipment. The company maintained their office, showrooms, and shipping department in nearby Honesdale, Pennsylvania. Hatch & Clark was the first and the largest cutting shop of its kind in the Honesdale area, with the exception of the Dorflinger works in White Mills, Pennsylvania. Clark established his factory in Wayne County to avail

Cut glass bottle, punch cups, and tumbler; produced by T. B. Clark & Co.

Collection of Mrs. Faith Clark Morton

himself of Dorflinger's superior glass blanks for cutting. At a later date Clark and his associates built another two-story building of stone construction along the banks of the Wallenpaupack River in Hawley, Pennsylvania, a few miles south of Honesdale, where they manufactured more fine cut glass. The company produced cut and engraved glass until the vogue for such wares waned, around 1920. Thereafter they produced mostly gold-decorated glassware until the factory closed about 1930.

Thomas B. Clark and Walter A. Wood were not practical glass cutters, but they did manage to obtain the services of several fine craftsmen, and their wares rank with the best cut glass ever produced in this country. Among the glass cutters in Honesdale and vicinity, T. B. Clark & Company was known as "the university," for many of the best glass cutters in Wayne County had learned their trade under the aegis of this firm. Henry Weed and Thomas Finnerty were Clark's most energetic and successful salesmen for many years.

Cut glass decanters and wineglasses; produced by T. B. Clark & Co.

Collection of Mrs. Faith Clark Morton

Collection of Mrs. Faith Clark Morton

Suite of cut glass table glasses; produced by T. B. Clark & Co.

Cut glass perfume bottles and a bowl; produced by T. B. Clark & Co.

Collection of Mrs. Faith Clark Morton

It has been reported that Clark purchased a cutting shop in Honesdale known as the Maple City Glass Company. We could find no official recording of this transaction in the archives of the Wayne County Historical Society, but we did find the two trademarks issued to this firm, and some illustrated catalogues of their cut glasswares. The Maple City Glass Company's trademarks, each a different representation of a maple leaf, were obviously inspired by Clark's own trademark of a similar character, which was issued to T. B. Clark & Company on June 10, 1910, and which he stated had been in continuous use by his firm since January 30, 1898. Clark's daughter confirmed that there was a Maple City Glass Company, but she denied that it was purchased by her father. Mrs. Faith Clark Morton stated that the Maple City Glass Company, like several other cut glass shops in and around Honesdale, was founded by a former employee of T. B. Clark & Company.

In addition to the leaf-shaped trademark which can often be found on Clark's cut glass, the company etched the signature "Clark," in script, on much of their wares. Trademark labels with their name and a representation of a cut glass carafe were also used by this firm.

Gaslight shade cut at Hatch & Clark factory; *ca.* 1885; diameter 8 in.

Collection of Wayne County Historical Society

Left: Cut glass jug with a sterling silver mount which was made at the Wayne Silver Company of Honesdale, Pa. *Right:* Cut glass pitcher; 11 in. tall; T. B. Clark & Co.; *ca.* 1900.

Left: The "Strawberry-Diamond and Star" pattern; patented June 1, 1886, by Walter A. Wood; *right:* The "Gothic" pattern; patented Sept. 25, 1888, by Thomas A. Baker; both for T. B. Clark & Co.

In 1895, Walter A. Wood and Thomas B. Clark established the Wayne Silver Company in Honesdale to make the fine silver fittings for their cut glasswares.

T. B. Clark & Company was listed in the *American Glass Trade Directory* as a cut glass manufacturer in Meriden, Connecticut, but we were unable to confirm this address. None of the Meriden directories for this period even mentioned Clark's company as operating so much as a showroom in that city in 1918.

Thomas Byron Clark was born in Meriden, Connecticut, on January 5, 1864; he died in Honesdale, Pennsylvania, on August 4, 1944, just one hour after leaving his office at the Wayne County Savings Bank, of which he was the president. Clark was employed by the Meriden Flint Glass Company in Meriden, Connecticut, before going to Honesdale in 1884. Horses were his greatest pleasure throughout his life.

Comparatively few cut glass designs were patented for T. B. Clark & Company when one considers their tremendous output over a period of about 45 years or more. On June 1, 1886, Walter A. Wood patented a design commonly known as "Strawberry-Diamond and Star" and assigned his rights to T. B. Clark & Company. This is obviously a variation on an old theme known in the trade as the "Strawberry" pattern.

Left: The "Pointed Star" pattern; patented Apr. 29, 1890, by William Henry Hawken; *right:* The "Maltese Cross" pattern; patented Mar. 10, 1891, by John Billard; both for T. B. Clark & Co.

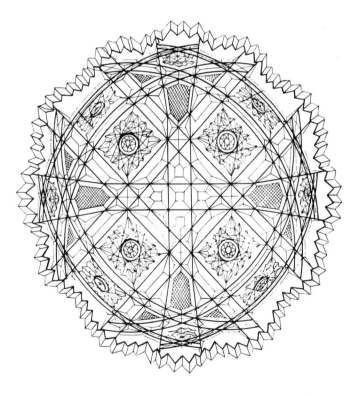

Left: The "Sea Shells" pattern; patented Apr. 12, 1892, by Walter A. Wood for T. B. Clark & Co. *Right:* The "Quatrefoil Rosette" pattern; patented Jan. 31, 1899, by Thomas B. Clark.

Left: The "Lapidary Center" pattern; patented Jan. 30, 1900, by Thomas B. Clark. *Right:* The "Cornflower" pattern; patented June 15, 1909, by Robert H. Pittman for T. B. Clark & Co.

A design known as "Gothic" was patented by Thomas A. Baker for T. B. Clark & Company on September 25, 1888. In this the designer made use of three very common motifs in cut glass—stars, crosshatching, and fan-shaped borders. Baker was superintendent of the Clark factory for many years; in fact, as late as 1913 he held this position.

William H. Hawken, later associated with the Irving Cut Glass Company in Honesdale, patented a scintillating design for cut glass and assigned his rights to T. B. Clark on April 29, 1890. In lieu of its original name, it has been designated as their "Pointed Star" pattern. In his patent enumerations Hawken stated that the design could be applied to a complete line of table-wares with some modifications. These modifications, to suit the article to be ornamented, in many cases alter the original pattern which Hawken likened to a "pointed star." Nevertheless, the various motifs which comprise the over-all design can be identified readily on other pieces in this suite of glasswares.

A very beautiful design representing a Maltese cross was patented on March 10, 1891, by John Billard for T. B. Clark & Company. Since we are unable to supply its original name, we have christened it Clark's "Maltese Cross" pattern.

"Sea Shells" is the common nomenclature given to another T. B. Clark cut glass design patented by Walter A. Wood on April 12, 1892.

Left: The "Rosette" pattern; patented Aug. 10, 1909, by Thomas B. Clark. *Right:* The "Exotic Flower" pattern; patented Jan. 15, 1924, by William P. Moran for T. B. Clark & Co.

Cut glass vase produced by Krantz, Smith & Co.; height 8 in.

Collection of Miss Marjorie Smith

On January 31, 1899, we find the first design patent for cut glass issued to Thomas B. Clark himself. As we said previously, Clark was not a glass cutter himself, but it is quite possible that he did design this and other cut glass patterns for his company. Clark's design consisted of several brilliantly cut motifs reminiscent of the ancient stained-glass windows found in some European cathedrals. For this reason we have dubbed it the "Quatrefoil Rosette" pattern.

Clark's next cut glass design was patented on January 30, 1900. In his patent papers he described the design as having a "lapidary center," and since there is no name on record for this design, we feel it appropriate to name this their "Lapidary Center" pattern.

One of the handsomest of the late floral patterns in cut glass was named the "Cornflower" pattern by Dorothy Daniel, in *Cut and Engraved Glass, 1771–1905*. It was designed and patented by Robert H. Pittman for T. B. Clark & Company on June 15, 1909. The design appears to have been made to cover the entire object, at least this is true of plates in this pattern; however, we feel reasonably certain that stemware in this design would have been unadorned around the rim of the vessel for ease of touch to the lips.

We have given the name "Rosette" Pattern to a design patented by T. B. Clark on August 10, 1909. The pattern, composed of several large cut rosettes arranged about the sides of a bowl, as is shown in the patent drawings, is coupled with many smaller rosettes and squares of fine crosshatch cutting. This pattern is rather elaborate for such a late period, but the brilliant designs were a favorite with Clark and he endeavored to keep them on the market as long as they would sell.

The last design patent for cut glass issued to this company was registered by William P. Moran on January 15, 1924. Because its proper name is not known, we have called it the "Exotic Flower" pattern. The patent illustration indicates that the plain portions of an object cut in this pattern may have been further embellished with other cut glass motifs.

Krantz & Smith Company
Krantz, Smith & Company, Incorporated
Krantz & Sell Company
G. Sell & Company

In 1893, John E. Krantz and John H. Smith entered into a partnership and established a glass cutting shop on the second floor of Wyman Kimble's factory at the foot of West 12th Street in Honesdale, Pennsylvania. Within two years their business had increased to such proportions that they required larger quarters. They built a two-story brick building for their cut glass shop at Industrial Point, which was situated at the juncture of the Lackawaxen River and Dyberry Creek in Honesdale. On August 1, 1898, it was reported that 15 men were employed by Krantz & Smith, but this number soon increased to over 120 men at the height of their business venture.

The firm established offices and showrooms in Chicago, and in New York City at 55 Park Place; in addition, they sent several experienced salesmen all over the country to sell their rich cut glass. The cut glass was sold to jewelry stores and high-class department stores. Samples were packed in large square trunks and taken to various cities where a sample room, the size of a hotel ballroom, was set up with long trestle tables, covered with black or dark purplish-red velvet, on which the cut glass was displayed to advantage. The buyers from various jewelry and department stores came to the hotel showroom and selected their cut glasswares for the entire year's anticipated sales.

On March 1, 1899, George William Sell was admitted into the firm, and

Cut glass plate produced by Krantz,
Smith & Co.; diameter 7 in.
Collection of Miss Marjorie Smith

the name was changed to Krantz, Smith & Company, Incorporated. Smith
passed away in 1908 and his interest in the company was purchased by Krantz
and Sell; at the same time the style of the firm was again changed to Krantz
& Sell Company.

In 1912, Krantz & Sell Company purchased the Barryville Cut Glass Shop
in Barryville, New York, 30 miles north of Honesdale, which was originally
built by William H. Gibbs. All kinds of cut glass articles were produced in
this auxiliary shop, where they were roughed, cut, and polished; they were
then shipped to the parent company in Honesdale, where they received final
polishing in an acid bath and were made ready for distribution. At one time
the Barryville shop employed as many as 45 people and produced from 15 to
40 barrels of glass in a week.

In the early 1920's, Krantz retired from the business when he was about
fifty years old; he sold his interest to Sell, and for a time the company was
operated solely by Sell under the old name of Krantz & Sell Company. In a
short time the name of the company was changed to G. Sell & Company.
Sell continued to manufacture fine cut glass; he also specialized in etched and
decorated glassware, such as the gilded and cut water set represented in the
Wayne County Historical Society's collection. In 1932 this large factory in
Honesdale was completely destroyed by a fire, after which Sell closed his cut
glass shop in Barryville, New York, and retired from the business as a manufacturer of rich cut glass.

John E. Krantz was born in Honesdale in 1868 and received his education in local schools. He was apprenticed in the cut glass trade at Hatch & Clark's shop in March, 1884, and stayed with this profession until his retirement from the business. He died in 1944 and was survived by his daughters Edna and Alicia (for whom the beautiful "Alicia" pattern was named).

John H. Smith was also born in Honesdale, in 1863, and passed away in 1908. He was educated in the Honesdale high school and had been employed as a glass cutter since April, 1884. At one time in his short career he was the foreman in T. B. Clark's cutting department for a period of three years. As of 1964, his daughter Marjorie W. Smith resided in Honesdale.

George William Sell also was born in Honesdale, in 1871. He received his primary education locally and then took a course in a New Bedford, Massachusetts, business college, which stood him in good stead when he entered

Left: Pitcher in the "Alicia" pattern; Krantz, Smith & Co.; *ca.* 1895. *Right:* Iridescent glass vase with etched and gold decoration made by G. William Sell; *ca.* 1920; height 11 in.; G. Sell & Co., Honesdale, Pa.

Collection of Wayne County Historical Society

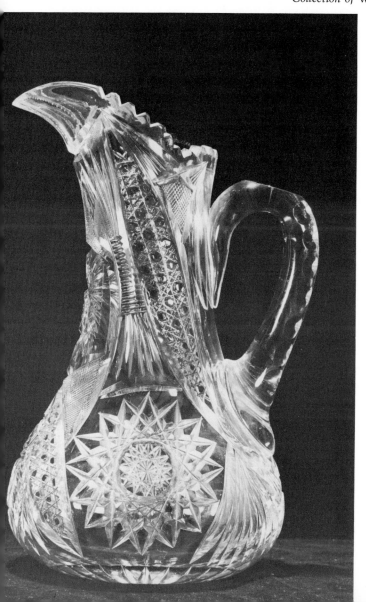

BROADWAY.
No. 1606. 6 inch Plate, $16.00 doz.

ATCO.
No. 334. Plate, $2.70

ST. ELMO.
No. 333. Bon Bon, $28.00 doz.

CROWN.
No. 2905. Celery, $4.00

ERIE.
No. 72. Pickle, $2.50

SHOHOLA.
5 in. Rd. Nappy, $13.00 doz.
6 " " 15.00 "
5 " Hdl. Nappy, 15.00 "
6 " " 17.00 "

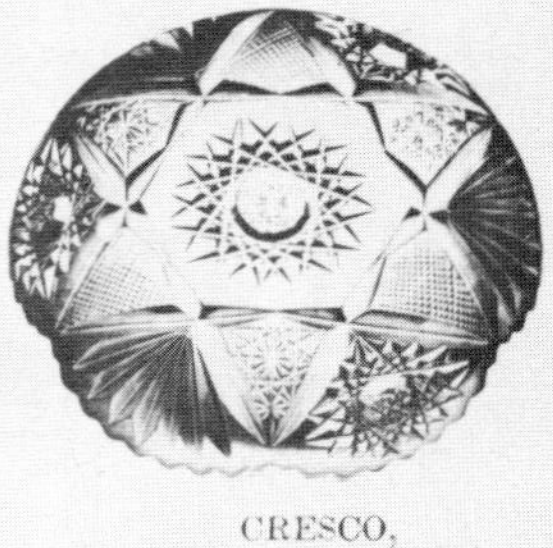

CRESCO.
5 in. Rd. Nappy, $18.00 doz.
6 " " 22.00 "
5 " Hdl. Nappy, 19.00 "
6 " " 23.00 "

ETON.
No. 877. Spoon, $2.50

CUSTER.
No. 273. Bon Bon, $2.00

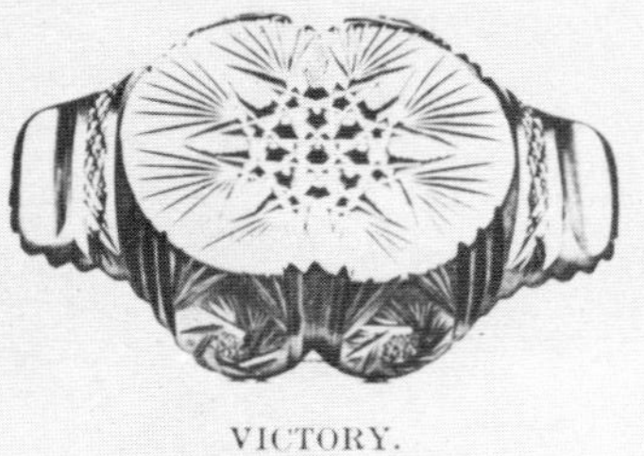

VICTORY.
No. 266. Bon Bon, $2.50

MAINE.
No. 254. Celery, $4.00

WARREN.
No. 878. Spoon, $2.50

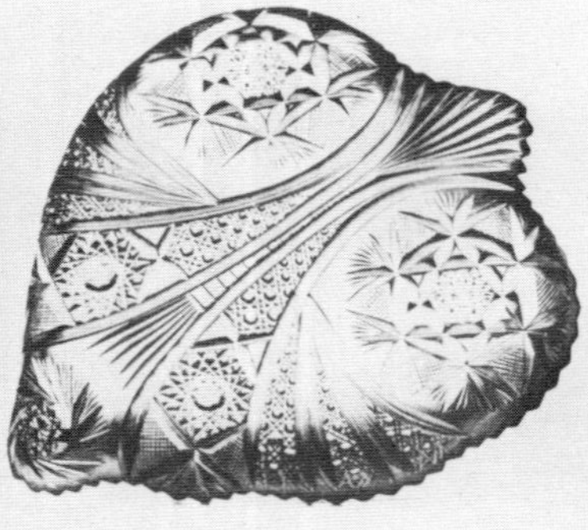

MEMPHIS.
No. 270. Dish, $2.50

BYRL.
No. 4371. Bon Bon, $2.20

ST. ELMO.
No. 37. Olive, $21.60 doz.

MAINE.
Rd. Nappy, $16.00 doz.
20.00 "
18.00 "
22.00 "

VICTORY.
No. 44
4½ in. Nappy, $14.00 doz.
Hdl. Nappy,

ALICIA.
No. 41. Bon Bon, $3.50

MAINE.
8 inch Nappy, $3.50

PARIS.
No. 4115. Celery, $3.20

GARNET.
No. 805. Celery, $3.00

Collection of Edna Krantz Yerkes and Alicia Krantz Martin
"Wheel and Star" punch bowl, glasses, and ladle; cut by John E. Krantz in 1910.

Page from an illustrated Krantz, Smith & Co., Inc. catalogue; *ca.* 1905.

into business with Krantz & Smith in 1899. Sell had been employed as a glass cutter since September, 1889.

All the patterns cut by this factory were placed on the glass blanks with stencils made of oiled paper, which made them usable for a long period. The stenciled designs were outlined with red lead and then given to the cutters who used cutting wheels of every size and shape to execute the beautiful patterns. The cutting wheels were supplied by Wyman Kimble, a manufacturer of cutting and polishing wheels to the cut glass trade, in whose building at the foot of West 12th Street Krantz & Smith had their modest beginning. Power for the cutting machines was obtained from a dammed-up stream (probably the Lackawaxen River) which was visible from the factory windows. After the articles were cut, they were given an acid bath to polish the design, dried with blowers, and polished again on a buffing wheel. In spite of the fact that the blanks used by the Krantz factory were at least one-quarter inch thick some errors were made and these were sold as "seconds." Sometimes a vase with errors in the top part was cut off for a smaller vase and thereby made salable.

An illustrated catalogue of the cut glass wares produced by Krantz, Smith & Company, Incorporated, issued about 1905, listed well over 250 patterns made by this company. Undoubtedly many of these pieces were among those lost in the devastating flood experienced in Honesdale in 1942; but since this firm's wares were so widely distributed, there is a strong possibility that some of the patterns will be found in antique shops throughout America.

In 1910, Krantz made a magnificent punch bowl and set of glasses for his wife Alice, commemorating their twentieth wedding anniversary. This monu-

Cut glass pitcher and glasses with gold-decorated tops; pitcher 11 in. high; tumblers 4 in. high; G. Sell & Co., Honesdale, Pa.; *ca.* 1920.

Collection of Wayne County Historical Society

mental cut glass artifact is now jointly owned by his daughters and we are fortunate to have a photograph of it for our illustrations. The bowl has a capacity of some two gallons and is comprised of two bowls; one bowl stands on a pedestal six inches high and is nine and one-half inches in diameter. This is turned upside down and serves as a stand for the larger bowl, which is one-half inch thick, six and one-half inches deep, and thirteen and three-quarter inches in diameter. Each bowl has six large wheels and stars cut into the glass and these are surrounded by panels of more cut stars. The matching footed cups which accompany the punch bowl are three and one-quarter inches high and have the same diameter. A sterling silver ladle with a six-inch cut glass handle completes the set. The design was known as "Wheel and Star" at the Krantz factory.

Gibbs, Kelly & Company
William H. Gibbs & Company
Barryville Cut Glass Shop

William Henry Gibbs and Michael J. Kelly opened a glass cutting shop in the W. W. Weston Building on Race Street in Honesdale, Pennsylvania, in July, 1895. Two months later Frank Steinman joined the firm and it was known as Gibbs, Kelly & Company.

Gibbs, Kelly, and Steinman were very fine craftsmen, well trained in the art of cutting glass in the intricate patterns so popular between 1880 and 1905. They were also ambitious, and it was not long before their factory grew to such proportions that they occupied the entire building. They employed about 30 hands at that time and had established sales offices in New York City at 35 Warren Street. Since all the members of the firm were practical glass cutters and knew how to produce the most brilliant designs in rich cut glass, their products were second to none in the trade at that time.

Kelly and Steinman established their own cut glass shop on West 11th Street in Honesdale, and William Gibbs became sole owner of the original company. At a later date Kelly and Steinman moved out of Honesdale and established another cutting shop, this time known as the Peerless Cut Glass Company, in Deposit, New York. Gibbs continued the firm under the name of William H. Gibbs & Company, with the financial backing of another partner, William G. Sell. At this period the concern occupied smaller quarters in another section of Honesdale. Gibbs moved again in 1909, opening a shop in Hawley, Pennsylvania, a few miles south of Honesdale.

Collection of Wayne County Historical Society   *Collection of Mrs. J. H. Tumlinson;*
former collection of Mrs. Charles E. Gibbs

Left: Cruet made at Gibbs, Kelly & Co.; *ca.* 1900; height 6½ in. *Right:* Two-part punch bowl produced by Gibbs, Kelly & Co.; height 9½ in.; diameter of bowl 9¼ in.

Gibbs built another factory in Stroudsburg, Pennsylvania, around 1911; it was located on the corner of Scott and Stone Streets. Thomas Walker, who had been working for Gibbs while he was in Hawley, came to Stroudsburg in 1911. When Gibbs opened his cut glass shop, he asked Walker to be his foreman and he accepted. Miss Lottie DePue, a resident of Stroudsburg, came to the Gibbs factory as floor lady in 1911 and continued with the firm until 1928, when it was sold to Arbogast & Stackhouse. Miss DePue recalled that the Gibbs shop produced a fine grade of cut glass, and at the height of their business the factory employed 100 people. O. P. Hoffman, another Stroudsburg resident, remembered that the Gibbs cut glass factory was operating at "full blast" in 1912, for he was married in June of that year and received many Gibbs cut glass articles as wedding presents.

After Gibbs sold his cut glass factory to Arbogast & Stackhouse, he went into the gunsmith and upholstering business and worked in this field until his death on October 26, 1939.

During the depression years, Arbogast & Stackhouse changed from lead crystal blanks to figured lime glass blanks. The cheapness of their product, and the decline in popularity suffered by the cut glass business, forced them to go into the wholesale hotel and restaurant supply business. About 1950 they sold out to Francis Smith, who continued to operate the hotel supply business under the name of the Stroudsburg Glass Company.

In the 1918 issue of the *American Glass Trade Directory*, William H. Gibbs & Company was listed as a manufacturer of cut glass, with shops in Stroudsburg, Pennsylvania, and Barryville, New York. Gibbs did build another cut glass factory in Barryville, New York, about 1910, but it was sold to the Krantz & Sell Company in 1912. While Gibbs owned the factory it was known as the Barryville Cut Glass Shop. The two-story wooden building was located along Halfway Brook, from which it derived power for its cutting and polishing wheels. The Libbey Glass Company supplied blanks for punch bowls, salt and pepper shakers, nappies, stemware, and many other types of glassware for this auxiliary plant.

Diamond-shaped bowl in the "Rose" design; produced by William H. Gibbs & Co., Honesdale, Pa.; diameter 10½ in.; width 8½ in.

Collection of Charles P. Huber

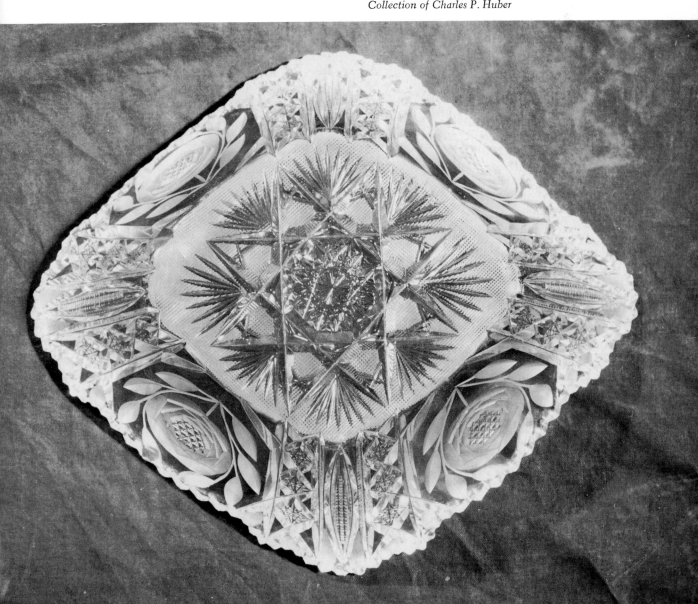

William Henry Gibbs was born in Indian Orchard, Wayne County, Pennsylvania. At an early age he was apprenticed to a glass cutter at the Dorflinger works in White Mills, in April, 1882. He followed his trade by working in cut glass shops in New York City, Pittsburgh, Pennsylvania, Wheeling, West Virginia, Corning, New York, and Toledo, Ohio. He was the general superintendent of the Gibbs, Kelly & Company factory.

Michael J. Kelly was born in Ireland and came to the United States in 1881, landing just about the time President James A. Garfield was assassinated. He learned the glass cutting trade in Meriden, Connecticut, and afterward was employed at Monaca, Pennsylvania (possibly working for the Phoenix Glass Company), New Bedford, Massachusetts (at either the Mt. Washington Glass Company, Smith Brothers, or the Blackmer Cut Glass Company), and Toledo, Ohio (possibly for Libbey). For many years he was a foreman at the old Bergen & Niland cut glass factory in Meriden, Connecticut. During his association with Gibbs, Kelly & Company, he held the position of general salesman.

Frank Steinman was born in Brooklyn, New York, and received his early training in glass cutting at one of the several cutting shops in that area. He was a foreman for Whitall, Tatum & Company in Millville, New Jersey, and was employed as a glass cutter in factories in Monaca, Pennsylvania, and Toledo, Ohio, before going to Honesdale. Steinman was the bookkeeper for Gibbs, Kelly & Company.

On November 7, 1899, a design patent for a beautiful cut glass bowl was registered by William Henry Gibbs of Honesdale, Pennsylvania. The pattern consists of three large and brightly cut rosettes, with panels of brilliantly cut

Design patent for cut glassware issued Nov. 7, 1899, to William H. Gibbs.

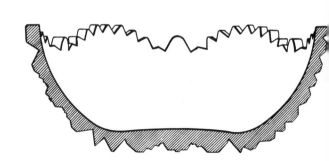

buttons arranged four in a panel between the rosettes. The bottom of the bowl is decorated with another large and brilliantly cut rosette. There is nothing unique about Gibbs's design, for it combines two very popular motifs in cut glass of the Brilliant Period. The bright-cut and diamond-faceted buttons are clearly associated with the popular "Chair Bottom" or "Harvard" patterns. A very similar design can be seen in pieces signed by the Taylor Brothers cut glass shop of Philadelphia, Pennsylvania.

A bowl purchased from William H. Gibbs & Company in Honesdale many years ago appears to be a variant of the "White Rose" pattern patented by the Irving Cut Glass Company of the same place. In this instance the petals of the rose and the leaves have been left unpolished, giving them a matlike finish, while the center of the blossom is represented by coarse brilliant cutting, not quite so finely executed as the centers of the Irving Cut Glass Company's "White Rose."

A cruet in the collection of the Wayne County Historical Society combines patterns common to most American cut glass shops of this period, as well as those of Gibbs, Kelly & Company. A handsome two-part punch bowl shown in our illustrations was originally in the collection of Mrs. Charles E. Gibbs. It too combines two popular cut glass patterns of the late period in an elegant design.

The Irving Cut Glass Company, Incorporated

In the year 1900, six men, all first-class glass cutters, formed the Irving Cut Glass Company, Incorporated, of Honesdale, Pennsylvania. The corporation consisted of George H. Reichenbacher, president; Eugene V. Coleman, John Gogard, William H. Hawken, George Roedine, and William H. Seitz. When Reichenbacher died in 1910, his son Royal L. Reichenbacher, then the firm's bookkeeper, managed the business office for a number of years. In 1910, Eugene V. Coleman was secretary, and William H. Seitz was treasurer of the company.

The firm started in an old one-story wooden building located on the south side of West 13th Street, between West Street and Spring Street (the latter is now called Westside Avenue). In the beginning the partners themselves did all the cutting, as the company was not financially able to hire glass cutters. It was a struggle at first to keep the business alive, and the owner-operators of the little cut glass shop drew the small weekly sum of $6.00 for almost two years. For those men with families to support, these were not the easiest months of their lives.

But soon the business began to prosper, and larger quarters were needed as

Covered butter dish in the "Zella" pattern; Irving Cut Glass Co.; plate diameter 8 in.; height of top 5½ in.
Collection of Mrs. Homer H. Smith

Cut glass lamp; Irving Cut Glass Co.; height 22 in.
Collection of Mrs. Homer H. Smith

well as additional helpers. A plot of ground at the foot of Irving Cliff, on the east side of Park Street, near the armory and along the Dyberry River, was purchased. On this lot a two-story brick building, 200 feet long and 40 feet wide, was erected. The Irving Cut Glass Company occupied these quarters until the factory was closed in the early 1930's.

George H. Reichenbacher was born at Cherry Ridge, Pennsylvania, on February 10, 1869; he passed away on February 28, 1910. He was the son of Johannes and Elizabeth Reichenbacher. He and his wife Mary A. Staengle Reichenbacher had two sons: Royal L. Reichenbacher and Charles Reichenbacher. In 1918 the Reichenbacher sons purchased the Clinton Cut Glass Company in Aldenville, Pennsylvania, and renamed it the Elite Cut Glass Manufacturing Company.

Eugene V. Coleman was born in Uniondale, Susquehanna County, Pennsylvania, on April 27, 1872, one of five brothers and two sisters. He attended public school in Uniondale and in nearby Forest City. After working a while in Forest City, Pennsylvania, he moved to Honesdale, where he learned the trade of glass cutting at T. B. Clark & Company. At the outbreak of the Spanish-American War, Coleman enlisted in Company E, 13th Pennsylvania Infantry, and served with that group until March 11, 1899. After being mustered out of the army, he resumed his trade at the T. B. Clark factory. On September 12, 1901, Coleman married Margaret M. Evans and they had three children: Eugene L. Coleman, Jessie M. Coleman, and Gerald D. Coleman. Eugene V. Coleman was president of the Irving Cut Glass Company from about 1916 until the factory closed in 1933. He died on November 14, 1934.

William H. Hawken was the designer of all the cut glass patterns produced at the Irving cut glassworks. An interview with his daughter, Mrs. Homer H. Smith, revealed that her father had worked in the trade since he was nineteen years old and that he had "blown glass," and "cut and designed glass," which

Cream and sugar set; Irving Cut Glass Co.; height 4 in.

Collection of Mrs. Homer H. Smith

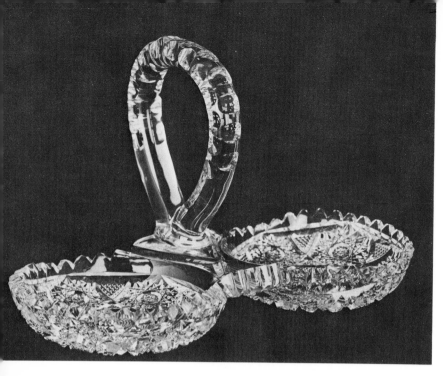

Double, handled cut glass nappy; Irving Cut Glass Co.; height 6 in.; diameter 11 in.

Collection of Mrs. Homer H. Smith

would indicate that he was well founded in every aspect of the industry. She also confirmed a report from Mrs. William H. Seitz that the Irving Cut Glass Company sold their wares to all parts of the world. Hawken was born in England in 1876 and was just six months old when he was brought to America by his parents. He had only seven years of primary schooling before he had to leave and go to work. Hawken learned his glass cutting trade at "the university," Clark's factory in Seelyville, which is now the site of the Hussco Shopping Center. Hawken first learned how to blow glass, then to cut and design it. His daughter said that "his designing came as a God-given talent," for he had no formal training for this sort of work at all. William Hawken died in March, 1942.

William H. Seitz was born in Honesdale, Pennsylvania, on August 4, 1870, and died in Larchmont, New York, on March 9, 1947. He too learned his trade with T. B. Clark & Company, and was so proficient in the cutting and engraving of glass that he was chosen as one of the men from the Honesdale area to go to the World's Columbian Exposition in Chicago in 1893 to demonstrate the manufacture of rich cut glass. When he returned to Honesdale, he continued in this work with the firm of Gibbs, Kelly & Company until he joined with Coleman, Gogard, Hawken, Reichenbacher, and Roedine in the Irving Cut Glass Company. For a good many years Seitz was the treasurer.

The Irving Cut Glass Company advertised "American Rich Cut Glass, Colored and Gold Decorated Glass" and sold their wares all over the United States and as far abroad as Johannesburg, South Africa, Spain, China, and Japan. When orders for their glassware came from China, the company clerk would take them to the local Chinese laundryman to have them translated. Gerald D. Coleman, the son of Eugene Coleman, told the author that when orders came from Japan, they were always accompanied by some small gift of an urn, vase, or bowl, which his father took home to the family; their last large order came from Japan. William H. O'Neil, bookkeeper and export manager for this concern for more than 10 years, told us that they sold great quantities of rich cut glass to an importer in London, England.

On May 13, 1913, William H. Hawken patented a cut glass design which we have named the "Pinwheel" pattern because the original designation for this design has not been found. The illustration of this design from the patent papers shows a combination of the "Buzz-saw," or "Pinwheel," motif in combination with brilliant cutting and simple representations of leaves and stems. The top of the bowl has been cut with a combination of several designs related to patterns found on other parts of the bowl.

The Irving Cut Glass Company's most famous pattern was their "White Rose" design, which was patented by Hawken on January 11, 1916. According to Mrs. William H. Seitz, Hawken's "White Rose" pattern kept the company going for quite a while. Hawken's design differs but a little from several others manufactured after 1916; the petals of the rose are left in a "gray" finish, the center of each flower being represented by a small cut button, as

Left: Cut glass lamp manufactured by Irving Cut Glass Co.; height 18½ in. *Right:* "Carnation" pitcher manufactured by Irving Cut Glass Co.; height 9 in.

Collection of Gerald D. Coleman   *Collection of Mrs. Homer H. Smith*

Left: The "Pinwheel" pattern; patented May 13, 1913; *right:* The "White Rose" pattern; patented Jan. 11, 1916; both by William H. Hawken for Irving Cut Glass Co.

Left: "White Rose" goblet; manufactured by Irving Cut Glass Co.; height 4½ in. *Right:* Vase in the "White Rose" pattern; Irving Cut Glass Co.

Collection of Gerald D. Coleman   *Collection of Wayne County Historical Society*

"Rose Combination" covered butter dish, signed "Irving"; height 6 in.; diameter of plate 8 in.

is shown in our illustrations. A good trade was also done with their "Rose Combination" pattern, which was a blend of Hawken's "White Rose" pattern with brilliantly cut ornaments. The rose design was also used on their light engraved wares, which, for the most part, were cut on pressed blanks. Demer Brothers, Libbey, and others produced a similar rose pattern.

A catalogue of the Irving Cut Glass Company's wares illustrated patterns bearing the following names:

C.B.C. Daisy (meaning "Chair Bottom Combination" and the plainer "Daisy" pattern)
Daisy
Doris
Elk
Empire
Eureka
Harvard
Helen
Iowa
Juliette
June
Keystone

Page from an original Irving Cut Glass Co. catalogue showing various cut glass designs; *ca.* 1910.

May	Victrola
Norwood	Zella
Panama	

This list by no means includes a complete compilation of their patterns in cut glass, for the firm operated for about 33 years. Some articles made by this company were signed with the name "Irving" in script etched lightly into the glass in a conspicuous place. Much of their finer wares were cut on Dorflinger blanks, but in the late period they worked on figured blanks purchased from the H. C. Fry Glass Company and the Libbey Glass Company; the workers called these pressed blanks "pig iron."

Herbeck-Demer Company
Demer Brothers Company

The cut glass works known as the Herbeck-Demer Company was active in Honesdale, Pennsylvania, from about 1904 to 1911. It was owned and operated by Emil Herbeck and John F. Demer (and perhaps one or more of Demer's brothers). Very little is known of the company's work except for two designs patented by Emil Herbeck (December 5, 1911) and his wife, Louise C. Herbeck (December 26, 1911). Both designs are floral patterns used in combination with other cut glass designs. Since their original names

Left: The "Floral" pattern; patented Dec. 5, 1911, by Emil Herbeck; *right:* The "Lotus" pattern; patented Dec. 26, 1911, by Louise C. Herbeck; both Herbeck-Demer Co.

 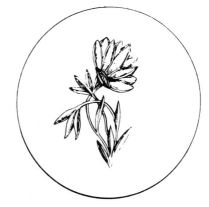

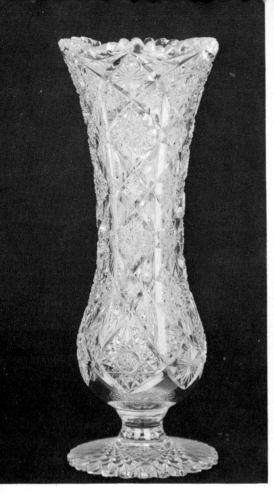

Left: Cut glass vase in the "Stratford" pattern; produced by Herbeck-Demer Co.; height 12½ in. *Right:* The "Pond Lily" pattern tray; diameter 14 in.; Demer Bros. Co.; *ca.* 1912.

are unknown, we have dubbed them Herbeck's "Floral" pattern and the "Lotus" pattern.

A magnificently cut tall vase in their "Stratford" pattern, now in the Wayne County Historical Society's collection, attests to their capability to cut patterns usually found in the earlier productions of the Brilliant Period.

About 1911 the Demer brothers formed their own cut glass company and located it in Hallstead, Pennsylvania. The firm consisted of Joseph, Jacob, Henry, Frank, Fred, and Philip Demer. Two sisters were also working in the factory at that time. Joseph Demer headed the firm as president for several years. The *Montrose Democrat,* for October 25, 1912, reported that "Demer Brothers Company are running their cut glass factory in this place to the full extent, the employees working until 9:30 P.M. every evening except Saturday. The large number of orders on hand makes this necessary, the rush will continue till after the holidays." The works continued running at full capacity until the outbreak of World War I; it was listed as a cut glass manufacturer in the *American Glass Trade Directory* in 1918, but soon thereafter they ceased operating.

Frank Demer patented his "Pond Lily" pattern for the company on November 26, 1912. In his specifications he referred to the design as representing "a pond lily with stems and leaves." The design was often used in combination with other cut glass designs, as is shown in our illustration of a tray in this pattern, which was made by Demer Brothers Company and presented to the Wayne County Historical Society.

On May 12, 1914, Henry Demer patented Demer Brothers Company's "Rose" pattern. This design predates the "White Rose" pattern patented in 1916 by William H. Hawken for the Irving Cut Glass Company of Honesdale, Pennsylvania. Demer Brothers Company's "Rose" pattern differs from similar rose designs in the respect that there are realistic serrations along the edge of the rose leaves. In all probability Henry Demer's "Rose" pattern was also used in combination with other cut glass motifs, but even so, the identification can be made with ease if one looks for "the difference." We should add that Demer suggested in his patent enumerations that his rose design was to be "cut, or otherwise impressed" on the glass articles. This implies that some of the pieces in this pattern may have been produced from pressed blanks on which his design was molded into the surface of the glass; this was a common practice in the cut glass trade dating from about 1890.

Left: The "Pond Lily" pattern; patented Nov. 26, 1912, by Frank Demer; Demer Bros. Co. *Right:* The "Rose" pattern; patented May 12, 1914, by Henry Demer; Demer Bros. Co.

Feeney & McKanna
McKanna Cut Glass Company

William P. Feeney and John J. McKanna, manufacturers of fine cut glass, established their works on March 12, 1906. The Feeney & McKanna cutting shop was located in a new two-story building, 39 by 70 feet in size, at 1008 Main Street in Honesdale, Pennsylvania. Eight years after the company was formed McKanna purchased Feeney's interest in the business and continued to manufacture beautiful cut glass under the name of the McKanna Cut Glass Company. For some unexplainable reason, the 1918 issue of the *American Glass Trade Directory* continued to list the company as Feeney & McKanna.

In a letter addressed to the Wayne County Historical Society, William McLaughlin, who had a long and intimate association with many of the old cut glass manufacturers in Honesdale, revealed that William P. Feeney had perfected the acid polishing of cut glasswares which had considerably cut down the need for hand polishing. According to McLaughlin, Feeney had designed several good patterns in which the "Buzz Star" design had been incorporated, making it one of the most popular cut glass motifs of its time.

During World War I, it was difficult for the firm to purchase blanks, and cut glass was a luxury few people could afford; nevertheless, McKanna continued to employ between 20 and 25 first-rate cutters. Feeney & McKanna,

The "Rose-bud" pattern; patented June 20, 1916, by John J. McKanna.

and their successors the McKanna Cut Glass Company, purchased their heavy blanks for cutting deep-engraved patterns from the H. C. Fry Glass Company, the Libbey Glass Company, the McKee Glass Company, the Fostoria Glass Company, the United States Glass Company, the Westmoreland Specialty Company, the Corning Glass Works, and the Williamsburg Flint Glass Company. Blanks for their light wares, on which shallow cutting was employed, were purchased from the A. H. Heisey Company, the Mound City Glass Company, and the Central Glass Company. The blanks from the Central Glass Company came with gold bands decorating the rim of each article. The Duncan & Miller Glass Company supplied this factory with light blanks for marmalade and candy jars. Most of the oil and vinegar cruets, and some of the cologne bottles and decanters were imported; the tops of the bottles in each case were numbered to correspond with numbers near the handles of the cruets and decanters.

During an interview with Kathleen McKanna, she related to the author that she used to go to the factory after school and on Saturdays to help out in the office or the wash room, where the glass was given its final cleaning. She also helped to wrap and stamp the glass before it was packed with excelsior in large barrels supplied by her father's cooperage. The packing and shipping rooms were located in the basement of the factory building.

In December, 1927, the firm advertised that their entire stock was being offered for sale at cost, and suggested that people buy their cut glass for Christmas gifts at bargain prices. The McKanna Cut Glass Company went out of business entirely very soon after that date. The factory building was sold on October 16, 1930, and was remodeled to accommodate a combination barber shop, bowling alley, and billiard parlor. Not long after the decision to close the factory was made, an order was received from Her Majesty the Queen of the Netherlands, for a complete set of cut glass in their "Rose-bud" pattern. The order was sent to Mrs. John McKanna by the Bach Art Store of Rotterdam, and inasmuch as the concern was no longer cutting glass, the order was turned over to John Gogard, formerly associated with the Irving Cut Glass Company. Gogard filled the Queen's order to her entire satisfaction.

"Rose-bud" ice tub.
*Collection of Misses Kathleen
and Helen McKanna*

"Rose-bud" plate in light ware.
Collection of Misses Kathleen and Helen McKanna

Souvenir "Rose-bud" paperweight.
Author's Collection

John McKanna patented his "Rose-bud" pattern on June 20, 1916. In the patent illustration only the representation of the rose was shown, but the design was also combined with other cut glass motifs; this was especially effective on large pieces in this suite of glassware. A souvenir paperweight was issued by the company with their "Rose-bud" pattern engraved on the top of the weight. The recipient's name was usually engraved on the underside of the paperweight. McKanna's "Rose-bud" pattern is distinguished from similar designs (Irving's "White Rose" pattern and Demer Brothers'

"Poinsettia" sugar bowl.
Collection of Misses Kathleen
and Helen McKanna

Left: "Poinsettia" handled nappy. *Right:* Octagon plate in the "Ida" pattern.
Collection of Misses Kathleen and Helen McKanna

"Rose") by the fine line cutting used on the petals and the brilliant diamond-cut rosette in the center of the flower. A representation of their "Rose-bud" pattern enclosed in a wreath and ribbon, and the name "Rose-bud" was used as one of McKanna's trademark labels while the firm operated as the McKanna Cut Glass Company.

About two years later McKenna introduced his "Poinsettia" pattern. The elongated petals of the Christmas flower were represented by fine line cutting and a diamond-cut button formed the center of the blossom. Large pieces in this suite of glass were often cut with other designs in combination with the poinsettia flower, a case in point is the handled nappy shown in our illustration. McKanna also used his "Poinsettia" design as a trademark. The paper labels were printed with the blossom surrounded with a wreath and ribbon, exactly like that he used for his "Rose-bud" trademark, and the name "Poinsettia."

The "Ida" pattern was another popular cut glass design produced at the McKanna factory, and it was issued in a full line of tablewares. A heavy cut design in a sunburst pattern, and a floral design simulating a daisy with heavy cut designs around the top of the bowl or vase, were still other patterns produced by the McKanna Cut Glass Company. A few years before McKanna's death in 1926, the light wares were in greater demand than the heavy cut glass, and a great deal of this work was produced; also some light wares with gold bands around the rim of the articles.

John J. McKanna was born in Honesdale, Pennsylvania, on August 7, 1864, the son of Patrick and Anna McKanna, and was one of nine children. After receiving his education in the Honesdale school, he entered his father's long-established cooperage business on Main Street. When his father died, John and his brother Frank continued the family business as McKanna Sons. While he was yet engaged in the cooperage trade, John McKanna entered the cut glass business with William P. Feeney. In April, 1892, John McKanna married Letitia Hollywood, a local Honesdale belle, and they had four daughters. McKanna died on February 25, 1926, but the cut glass business was carried on by two of his daughters, Kathleen and Hortense. At one time in the firm's history, Hortense H. McKanna was the president and her father the secretary and treasurer. After the factory closed, Hortense went with Stern Brothers, a department store in New York City. She left this position to accept one in the glass department at Ovington's, on Fifth Avenue in New York City, and remained with this firm for a number of years. Hortense H. McKanna died in March, 1952; her sister Kathleen in 1964 lived in Honesdale, Pennsylvania.

Crystal Cut Glass Company

The Crystal Cut Glass Company of Honesdale, Pennsylvania, was headed by Dr. Pierson B. Peterson, a local resident. The factory was located at the foot of West 14th Street in the former Kelly & Steinman factory. The firm was listed in the *American Glass Trade Directory* in 1918, and was a member of the National Association of Cut Glass Manufacturers. We could not determine an opening and closing date for this cut glass shop but newspaper clippings referred to the Crystal Cut Glass Company as early as 1913; it may have closed shortly after 1918.

Union Cut Glass Company

One of the oldest residents of Honesdale, Pennsylvania, told us that the Union Cut Glass Company's factory was located on the corner of West 13th and Spring Street (now Westside Avenue) in Honesdale, and that this company afterward became the Irving Cut Glass Company and relocated at the foot of East Park Street. Unfortunately our informant could not remember the names of the men involved in this company, and we were unable to connect it directly to the parties who founded the Irving Cut Glass Company.

Wayne Cut Glass Company

The corporation known as the Wayne Cut Glass Company was established in Honesdale, Pennsylvania, some months before January, 1905. On January 16, 1905, corporation papers were issued to the concern listing the following directors: John Riefler (who became very rich during World War I producing acetates in Tanners Falls, a village above Honesdale), John H. Weaver (a hotel owner in Honesdale), John Kuhbach of Honesdale, J. Samuel Brown (a local mortician and retail furniture store owner), Frank J. Meyers, and Frank P. Kimble, both of Honesdale.

Left to right: Cut glass cruet, syrup jug with silver top, tumbler, and goblet; made by Wayne Cut Glass Co. of Towanda and Honesdale, Pa.; *ca.* 1910.

The Wayne Cut Glass Company's factory was located on East Park Street in Honesdale and probably continued at that location even after they established another cut glass shop, also known as the Wayne Cut Glass Company, in Towanda, Pennsylvania (about 100 miles from Honesdale).

The Towanda factory was opened in the summer of 1910 and continued until 1918; it was a four-story building located on the corner of Main and Elizabeth Streets, and formerly housed the Humphrey Brothers shoe factory (whether it actually occupied the entire building is unknown). Lloyd C. Rosencrans, who originally came from Honesdale, left the Corning Glass Company and came to Towanda in 1910 as the Wayne Cut Glass Company's traveling representative. Rosencrans traveled by train from Boston down the east coast to Jacksonville, Florida, then across the south as far west as San Antonio, Texas. He covered the mid-western area including Duluth, Minnesota, and Chicago, Illinois, then on home to Towanda. His samples were all packed in five large trunks, each especially fitted with compartments to accommodate individual pieces of glass in his line of cut wares.

John Kimble of Honesdale was the first manager of the Towanda works; he was followed by a German, Henry Preumers. Rosencrans was superintendent at the time the factory closed in 1918.

A report in the *Daily Review*, Towanda's local newspaper, dated May 2, 1914, stated:

At the annual meeting of the Wayne Cut Glass Company (held at Towanda, May 1, 1914) the following officers were elected: President, Cortez H. Jennings; First Vice President, W. Worth Jennings; Second Vice President, Henry Preumers. Mr. Preumers, who has been in charge of the factory for over a year, was also elected secretary-treasurer, and general manager of the company. J. S. Brace and J. H. Weaver of Honesdale, Pa., declined re-election to the offices they have been holding, feeling that the Towanda men should guide the company since it is now located here. Seventy-five men are now employed in the plant, which moved here from Honesdale in 1910.

We were able to obtain some illustrations of the cut glass made by the Wayne Cut Glass Company in Towanda; these are from the collection of Rosencrans' widow, Mrs. Martha M. Rosencrans. Silver fittings were used on some of the cut wares produced by this factory. Mrs. Rosencrans had a jewel box with a silver rim and a syrup pitcher fitted with a handsome silver top. Floral designs included eight- and ten-petaled daisies, chrysanthemum and star, carnations and butterflies, and several others. Sherbet glasses, dresser sets with hair receivers, jewel boxes, powder boxes, pitchers, iced-tea glasses, baskets, celery and relish trays, goblets, tumblers, candlesticks, vases, and fruit bowls and dishes on legs, were among the many articles in cut glass produced by this factory.

Raymond H. Fender, former secretary of the National Association of Cut Glass Manufacturers, confirmed that the Wayne Cut Glass Company was a member in good standing in the association as late as 1915. The firm was listed in the *American Glass Trade Directory* in 1918 as a cut glass manufacturer. Obviously the company continued operating until 1918 or 1920, at least in Honesdale, if not in Towanda, Pennsylvania.

John S. O'Connor
J. S. O'Connor—American Rich Cut Glass
American Cut Glass Company

In 1890, John Sarsfield O'Connor erected a handsome and commodious glass cutting factory at the foot of the Wallenpaupack Falls in Hawley, Pennsylvania. The four-story building was built of native bluestone and still stands today. About 200 frames were operating, and some of the most beautiful cut glass made in America came from these works. The factory building was eventually sold to the Maple City Glass Company.

In 1900, O'Connor opened another cut glass shop in Goshen, New York, at 224 West Main Street. According to a report published by O'Connor's granddaughter, Mrs. John B. Connelly of Goshen, New York, both the Goshen, New York, shop and the factory in Hawley, Pennsylvania, boasted a large sign identifying them as "J. S. O'Connor—American Rich Cut Glass." In 1903 the glass factory in Goshen narrowly escaped destruction by a fire that caused an estimated loss of $5,000. O'Connor's property was willed to his four daughters, who sold the premises to Macksoud Brothers of Brooklyn, New York, for a dress factory in 1919.

In 1902, John S. O'Connor opened another cut glass factory in Port Jervis,

Collection of Wayne County Historical Society   *Collection of Mrs. Letitia Cusick Connelly*
Left: Claret glass in the "Napoleon" pattern; cut at the factory of John S. O'Connor, Hawley, Pa.; height 4½ in.; green top, crystal stem and foot. *Right:* Ruby and crystal punch bowl in the "Star" pattern; 16 in. tall; presented to Mary O'Connor Cusick by her father John S. O'Connor.

New York, occupying quarters which formerly housed the E. P. Farnum store and mill. This cutting shop, known as the American Cut Glass Company, was under the supervision of O'Connor's son, Arthur E. O'Connor. The Port Jervis factory was closed in 1903 and its equipment divided between the cut glass factories in Hawley and Goshen. Arthur O'Connor returned to his father's shop in Goshen and became its sales manager; his son-in-law, Thomas P. Cusick, was foreman of the Goshen operation.

It was in the Goshen, New York, cutting shop that many young men, upon finishing school, learned their trade of glass cutting. The works were equipped with every modern convenience known to the trade at that time, and were designed with the safety of its workers uppermost in O'Connor's mind. It was here that a magnificent crystal and ruby cut glass punch bowl was made. This handsome wassail bowl was so large and heavy that a special leather halter had to be made to hold it. A former employee of the cutting shop told Mrs. Connelly, "That was extra special—it was being cut for the boss's home." O'Connor's cutting shop in Goshen used crystal blanks that were imported from France because they came up to the high standards he always strived to maintain. Presumably the factory in Hawley worked on blanks supplied by the Dorflinger glassworks in nearby White Mills, Pennsylvania.

Undoubtedly John S. O'Connor designed a great many new patterns for his glass cutting shop, but the only one we could find that had been patented

Left: Kerosene lamp combining "Double Star and Hatch" design with fan-shaped cutting through the rim; height 25 in.; cut at J. S. O'Connor shop. *Right:* "Bowling-pin" decanter in "Star" pattern; a trophy cut at the J. S. O'Connor cut glass factory in Goshen, N.Y. for a bowling tournament between Goshen and Tuxedo Park, N.Y.; height 15 in.; *ca.* 1903.

Collection of Mrs. Letitia Cusick Connelly

is known as their "Princess" pattern. This pattern was registered by Arthur E. O'Connor on February 19, 1895, and assigned to his father. It resembles O'Connor's "Parisian" pattern in many respects, for it employs a great many curved miter cuts in the all-over design. Since the patent indicates that the O'Connors, father and son, were residing at Hawley, Pennsylvania, at the time it was issued, we can assume that the "Princess" pattern was first cut there, though most assuredly it was a production item in their Goshen, New York, shop too.

John Sarsfield O'Connor was born in Londonderry, Ireland, on June 6, 1831. He came to New Orleans, Louisiana, with his parents, where his father established a jewelry business. Later the family moved to New York City, where young John entered into the glass cutting trade as an apprentice in Turner & Lane's cutting department. He finished learning his art at the old E. V. Haughwout & Company shop. When the Civil War erupted, John and his two brothers enlisted in the Union Army, in which he was a first sergeant in Company F, 69th Regiment. After the war he returned to his trade and was made superintendent of the cutting shop at E. V. Haughwout & Company. From there he went to work for Christian Dorflinger in White Mills, Pennsylvania. O'Connor is credited with having designed the Dorflinger cutting department; he also designed some of Dorflinger's finest cut glass patterns—"Parisian," "Florentine," "Rattan," and many others. O'Connor invented a vacuum device which sucked up the ground glass, which had previously been inhaled by glass cutters, thus greatly lowering the mortality rate in this trade. He also invented the hardwood polisher and several other aids to the glass cutting trade. His "Parisian" pattern was the first cut glass design to use a circular cut, and for this he had designed special cutting wheels;

The "Princess" pattern; patented Feb. 19, 1895, by Arthur E. O'Connor for the John S. O'Connor cut glass shop in Hawley, Pa.

Decanter cut in "Star and Big Four" pattern; wineglasses, *left to right:* "Star and Big Four" pattern; cordial glass and wineglass in "Big Four" (variant of old "Strawberry-Diamond") pattern; height of decanter 13½ in.; J. S. O'Connor, manufacturer.

previous to O'Connor's invention, all cut glass patterns were engraved in a straight line.

A trademark label consisting of the initials "O.C." and the words "Hawley, Penna." was used by O'Connor for many years. It is quite possible that similar labels were used by the factories in Goshen and Port Jervis, New York.

Keystone Cut Glass Company
Wall & Murphey

In 1902, Richard Murphey, George Murphey, Theodore Wall, and Delbert J. Branning, formed the Keystone Cut Glass Company in Hawley, Pennsylvania. According to John Dorflinger, the only practical glass cutter in this group was "Del" Branning; the others supplied the needed capital to operate the cutting shop and shared their holdings in the stock with Branning. The factory operated with great success until about 1918, when the lack of business, caused in part by World War I, forced them out of business.

The Keystone Cut Glass shop was always known locally as "pork and beans" because they employed a lot of help from nearby Pike County and paid them in part each weekend with salt pork and dried beans from a company store. These Pike County "wood burners," as they were sometimes known, burned wood instead of coal because they lived in the midst of forests. The area, incidentally, was overrun with rattlesnakes. Today the territory is a plush resort area and many families who were once in modest circumstances are now well off, having sold some of their land for lakeside cottages in the now famous Pocono Mountains region.

Delbert J. Branning was born on February 1, 1866, at Damascus, Pennsylvania. At the age of fourteen he took his first trip down the Delaware River on a lumber raft. These boyhood adventures ended when he was apprenticed to a glass cutter at the Dorflinger works in White Mills. After a three-year apprenticeship, he moved to New Bedford, Massachusetts, where he worked for the Pairpoint Corporation. Branning also worked for several other cutting shops before he returned to Hawley in 1902 to join with the Murpheys and Wall in the Keystone Cut Glass Company. Incidentally, Theodore Wall was the grandfather of the famous golfer, Art Wall.

It appears that after the Keystone shop closed, Theodore Wall and George Murphey operated another cut glass factory known as Wall & Murphey, for their company was listed as a manufacturer of cut glass in the 1918 edition of the *American Glass Trade Directory*.

Branning's first wife was Myra Daniels of White Mills, Pennsylvania. She was the daughter of Frank Daniels, an early bookkeeper in Eugene Dorflinger's general store in White Mills. John Dorflinger's mother was a practical nurse and was in attendance when Branning's first son, Leon, was born. Delbert Branning's second wife, Augusta Goldbach of Hawley, Pennsylvania, bore him three children—Ruth, Mary, and Delos.

Left to right, top row: "Masonic"; "Eureka"; second row: "Jermyn"; "Liberty"; bottom row: "I. X. L."; "Wyoming"; all patterns from an original Keystone Cut Glass Co. catalogue; *ca.* 1910.

324

The Keystone Cut Glass Company purchased their blanks for cutting from
the Corning Glass Works and Dorflinger. An old catalogue showing photographs of the company's many beautiful patterns did not include any illustrations of pieces in patterns patented by Branning between 1911 and 1913;
we concluded from this that they were probably produced before 1911.
Branning registered his design for a "Fan-scalloped Dish" on February 28,
1911, in the name of his son, Delos, who at that time was only eight years
old. The undecorated portion of the bowl shown in the patent drawing was
cut in any kind of pattern suitable for such a vessel. The lamp shown in our
illustration has been decorated with Branning's "Fan Scallop" border around
the base of the shade, where it fits into the supporting metal ring.

On March 4, 1913, Delbert Branning registered two designs for a cut glass
dish. The first design patent illustrated a shallow bowl cut with a floral design arranged as a wreath around the perimeter of the vessel. The center of
each flower was engraved with small diamond cutting, while the petals were
composed of fine line cutting in a pattern resembling a pinwheel. The second
design patent obviously covered the same type of vessel, for all it showed in the
illustration was one of the flowers in the center of the bowl. The latter design
may well have been used in conjunction with other cut glass patterns produced
by this firm.

Miss Mary Branning told the author that her father designed a beautiful
"Rose" pattern; however, he was unable to secure the sole rights to such a

Left: "Fan-scalloped Dish"; design patented Feb. 28, 1911, by Delos J. Branning. *Right:*
design for cut glass tableware patented Mar. 4, 1913, by Delbert J. Branning.

Cut glass lamp decorated with Branning's "Fan Scallop" design; height 22 in.; Keystone Cut Glass Co.

Collection of Mrs. Delbert J. Branning and Miss Mary Branning

"Rose" cut glass fruit bowl; diameter 9 in.; height 4½ in.; Keystone Cut Glass Co.
Collection of Mrs. Delbert J. Branning and Miss Mary Branning

Left and right: "Romeo" cream and sugar set with two handles; creamer has two pouring lips; height of creamer 4½ in. *Center:* "Rose" covered butter dish; height 6 in. All made at Keystone Cut Glass Co.; *ca.* 1910.

design "because it would infringe on a patent for handles or anything that was raised on glassware." Branning's "Rose" design is not unlike the "Rose" patterns patented by William Hawken and Henry Demer. A design for an automobile headlight, with patriotic emblems and the legend "U.S.A.," was issued to Branning on November 12, 1918, but this was never put into production.

"Pluto"; cut glass pitcher, height 10¼ in.; goblets, 6 in. tall; Keystone Cut Glass Co.

Before Branning's death in 1951, he and his wife would give away pieces of his cut glass to family friends as wedding gifts. Among the valuable pieces still in the family collection is a cut glass lamp with hanging prisms, about 20 inches tall; a beautifully cut vase 18 inches high; some large pitchers and decanters, whiskey glasses, a cigar jar, several rose bowls, celery dishes and other tablewares, all produced at the Keystone cutting shop. The articles shown in the illustrations were all cut by Branning himself.

Maple City Glass Company

The factory occupied by the Maple City Glass Company in Hawley, Pennsylvania, was formerly owned by the John S. O'Connor cut glass company and it was sold some years after O'Connor moved to Goshen, New York. Dan Osborne was the manager of the Maple City Glass Company's cutting shop. The concern was reported to have sold out to T. B. Clark & Company, but Clark's daughter told us that this was not correct. Just how long the business

Left: Electrolier in the "Temple" pattern; Maple City Glass Co.; from the No. 10 catalogue; *ca.* 1910. *Right*: Electrolier in the "Aladdin" pattern; from an original Maple City Glass Co. catalogue; *ca.* 1910.

Vases, *left to right:* "LaKonta," "Pansy," "Axtell," "Lanier," and "Solano"; Maple City Glass Co.; *ca.* 1910.

Nappies in various designs and shapes; *left to right*, top row: "Weldon," "Fortuna," "Seward"; bottom row: "Fenmore," "Bradford," "Thyrza"; from an original Maple City Glass Co. catalogue; *ca.* 1910.

Celery dishes; *left to right,* top row: "Seward," "Manchester"; bottom row: "Shelocton," "Valdez"; from an original Maple City Glass Co. catalogue; *ca.* 1910.

Bowls; top row, *left to right:* "Hampton," "Saxman"; center: "Emerald"; bottom, *left to right:* "Thyrza," "Catalpa"; from an original Maple City Glass Co. catalogue; *ca.* 1910.

was in operation could not be determined, but evidently long enough to have issued ten illustrated catalogues (No. 9 is in the Landauer Collection in the New York Historical Society; No. 10 is in the Metropolitan Museum of Art).

The Maple City Glass Company had representatives in New York City, Baltimore, Boston, Buffalo, and Indianapolis; their export trade was handled by the Inter American Drug & Trading Company at 130–132 Pearl Street in New York City.

Most of the cut glass shown in their two catalogues were designs of the Brilliant Period and appeared to be of good quality. They registered two trademarks—each a different representation of a maple leaf—which they etched lightly into each piece of their cut glass, making it a rather simple matter for collectors to identify articles made at this factory.

Wangum Cut Glass Company
Monoghan Brothers

Very little could be found about the Wangum Cut Glass Company, also known as Monoghan Brothers, of Hawley, Pennsylvania, except that they were operating in 1918, according to a listing of this firm in the *American Glass Trade Directory* for that year; they were also listed as members of the National Association of Cut Glass Manufacturers at that time. For one year, 1917/18, Thomas A. Calahan of Meriden, Connecticut, was employed by this firm as manager and chief designer, but he returned to Meriden and entered the employ of the J. J. Niland Company.

The Brilliant Cut Glass Company

The Brilliant Cut Glass Company was listed in the *American Glass Trade Directory* in 1918 as operating in Hawley, Pennsylvania, but a check of the records in that town produced no further information on the concern. Since this was near the time of the great decline in the cut glass industry, we presume that this firm had a very short life.

Other Cut Glass Shops in the Honesdale Area

Besides the factories already mentioned, we found traces of some lesser-known cut glass producers in the Honesdale area: the Enterprise Glass Company, Honesdale; the Honesdale Union Cut Glass Company, which operated until at least 1918 and were members of the National Association of Cut Glass Manufacturers; the Kupher Glass Company, whose factory was located

Cut glass tumbler engraved by Fred Leibig for the Owanda Glass Co., Honesdale, Pa.
Collection of Wayne County Historical Society

in Honesdale at East 13th and East Streets; the Owanda Glass Company, Honesdale (this factory burned down in 1908); Shields & Knapp of Hawley; the Linke Colored Glass Shop in Seelyville; and the Penn Cut Glass Company in Prompton, Pennsylvania, a small community about four miles from Honesdale (the Penn Cut Glass Company's plant burned down about 1930).

333

Clinton Cut Glass Company
Elite Cut Glass Manufacturing Company

The village of Aldenville, Pennsylvania, was the home of the Clinton Cut Glass Company and their successor the Elite Cut Glass Manufacturing Company. Aldenville is a small place, with one store, a post office, a feed mill, and several houses. There are two churches and a cemetery, and the only street is the main road that runs from the north end of town to the south end, where the glass factory was located.

The Clinton Cut Glass Company was founded by Charles C. Wilmarth in 1905. It was located on the bank of the Lackawaxen River just below a small dam which provided the water power to turn the cutting wheels and the dynamo for lighting. Six men were employed by this company: Charles C. Lozier, manager; Glenn G. Wilmarth, bookkeeper; Frank Lent, Forest Van Wert, James Stranahan, and George Wulff.

Charles Wilmarth died on March 1, 1917, and his son Glenn Wilmarth took charge of the factory until April, 1918, when the business was sold by the executors of his father's estate to Royal Reichenbacher and his brother Charles Reichenbacher. The Reichenbacher brothers renamed the firm the Elite Cut Glass Manufacturing Company, and operated this cutting shop until 1924, when it closed for good. John Maurer, Edd Greogar, William Ritter, Ira Wright, and William Gray were associated with the Reichenbacher brothers in this cut glass factory.

Royal L. Reichenbacher was born in Honesdale, Pennsylvania, on November 11, 1892, and died on February 2, 1951. He was employed as a bookkeeper by the Irving Cut Glass Company in Honesdale while his father was president of that concern. After his father's death in 1910, Reichenbacher assumed the management of the business office of the Irving Cut Glass Com-

Cream and sugar set made by Clinton Cut Glass Co. of Aldenville, Pa.; height 2¾ in.; width 5 in.

Collection of Wayne County Historical Society; gift of Mrs. Olga Stiles

Collection of Miss Ruth E. Reichenbacher

Left: Footed rose bowl in the "Hearts and Flowers—Rose" pattern; diameter 8 in.; height 7½ in.; *Right:* Bowl in the "Rose" pattern; diameter 9 in.; height 4½ in.; Elite Cut Glass Manufacturing Co.; *ca.* 1920.

pany. He was married to Christina Hilda Knorr and had two daughters, Ruth E. Reichenbacher and Norma E. Reichenbacher (Mrs. Lester Kieft). Reichenbacher was not associated with any other cut glass manufacturer after the dissolution of the Elite cut glassworks in 1924.

Charles J. Reichenbacher was born in 1895 in Honesdale, and died in 1958. His wife Violet Guest Reichenbacher bore him two sons: Charles J. Reichenbacher and Edward V. Reichenbacher.

The original names for some of the patterns cut by the Elite works were given to us by Miss Ruth E. Reichenbacher; the company's "Rose" pattern was obviously influenced by Reichenbacher's association with the Irving Cut Glass Company, since it resembles in many ways William Hawken's "White Rose" pattern. "Hearts and Flowers—Rose" is another pattern adapted from a combination of miter-cut designs and engraved floral patterns. Miss Reichenbacher could not tell us if her father's cut glass ever bore any identifying marks.

P. H. Hughes
Wickham & Hughes
Wickham-Branning Cut Glass Company

The *American Glass Trade Directory* listed the cutting shop of Wickham & Hughes among the cut glass manufacturers operating in Scranton, Pennsylvania, in 1918. The company was formed before 1918 by Howard Wickham and P. H. Hughes. In this same directory P. H. Hughes was listed separately as a manufacturer of cut glassware. A thorough check of the Scranton city directories give no indication that either of these cutting shops ever operated in that community, though this fact was indicated in the listings found in the *American Glass Trade Directory*; apparently both cut glass shops had a very short business life.

Wickham later joined forces with Delbert Branning in the Wickham-Branning Cut Glass Company in Scranton, Pennsylvania. This partnership was formed in 1920 and was dissolved in 1924. Branning was associated with the Keystone Cut Glass Company of Hawley, Pennsylvania, until it closed about 1918.

S. H. Klinghoff

The S. H. Klinghoff glass shop in Scranton, Pennsylvania, was listed in the *American Glass Trade Directory* under manufacturers of cut glass in 1918, but the Scranton city directories and other public references contained no record of this firm. Obviously the business was not in existence for very long.

Luzerne Cut Glass Company

One of the directors of the National Association of Cut Glass Manufacturers, O. S. Atterholt, operated the Luzerne Cut Glass Company of Pittston, Pennsylvania. The factory was located on Delaware Avenue in West Pittston, and probably closed around 1930. It was listed in the *American Glass Trade Directory* in 1918, but may have been operating for at least a few years before that date.

Pioneer Cut Glass Company

In 1905, George Schiesler and Andrew Michell formed the Pioneer Cut Glass Company in Carbondale, Pennsylvania. Edward Morrison, living in 1964, in Jermyn, Pennsylvania, started with this company when he was fourteen years old and remained in their employ until they closed in 1920. World War I prevented this company, as well as many other cut glass shops in America, from obtaining the fine lead glass blanks they had been using for their cut glass products. Michell and Schiesler were members of the National Association of Cut Glass Manufacturers and were listed in the *American Glass Trade Directory* as cut glass manufacturers in 1918.

Becker & Wilson
Mahon & Wilson

The cutting shop of Becker & Wilson was established in Brooklyn, New York, some time before 1898 by Charles Becker, a German glass cutter, and Joseph Wilson. About 1903, they moved to Montrose, Pennsylvania, and in 1908 they relocated in New Brunswick, New Jersey, at 3 Union Street. Just before the factory was closed Joseph Wilson bought out his partner and operated the works himself until 1914. The business in Montrose, Pennsyl-

337

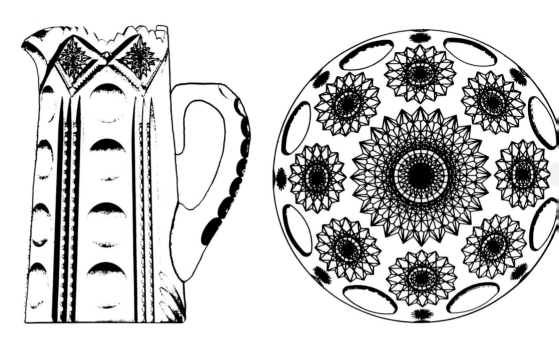

Left: The "Box Panel" pattern; patented Feb. 15, 1898, by Joseph Wilson for Becker & Wilson. *Right:* Design patent for Joseph Wilson's "Star" pattern issued to him Dec. 22, 1903.

Compote and pitcher cut by Joseph Wilson; compote, height 9 in., diameter 9½ in.; pitcher 10 in. high.

Collection of Mrs. G. W. Kinzer

vania, was replaced by a partnership consisting of Frank H. Wilson (Joseph Wilson's brother) and Leo P. Mahon.

Frank Wilson, Sr., father of Joseph Wilson and Frank Wilson, Jr., was born in Windy Nook, Gateshead, Durham, England, and learned his trade of glass cutting in English cut glass factories. He came to the United States with his family on the steamer *Hecla* arriving on September 17, 1872, and worked for the New England Glass Company in East Cambridge, Massachusetts.

Left: Cut glass vase made by Joseph Wilson according to his patented design dated Dec. 22, 1903. *Right:* Lamp cut by Joseph Wilson; height 20 in.

Collection of Claude B. Wilson   *Collection of Mrs. G. W. Kinzer*

Joseph Wilson was born on May 17, 1867, at Bathgate, Linlithgow, Scotland. He married Susan Ellen Buck of Sugar Hill, New York, at Burdette, New York, on November 21, 1888. The family Bible lists their four children who were born in various places in the United States, indicating that Wilson was working in these areas at that time; Claude B. Wilson was born in New Brighton, Pennsylvania, in 1889; Iona B. Wilson in Brooklyn, New York, in 1892; Pearl J. Wilson in Toledo, Ohio, in 1893; and Eola P. Wilson, in Corning, New York, in 1897, at which time Joseph Wilson was working with his father in Frank Wilson & Sons.

Joseph Wilson's eldest child, Claude, reported that his father worked in Corning, New Brighton, Brooklyn (where he worked for the Shotton glass cutting shop), Providence, Rhode Island, Toledo, Ohio, New Brunswick, New Jersey, Jeannette, Pennsylvania (for the Jeannette Glass Company), Blairsville, Pennsylvania, and Norristown, Pennsylvania, where he lived with his daughter. He died on October 12, 1946.

During the 15 or 20 years Wilson was in business for himself, he registered only two design patents for cut glass. The first is dated February 15, 1898, and is a rather simple pattern compared to others of this period. The illustration accompanying Wilson's patent enumerations shows a pitcher cut with punties and prismatic panels in vertical stripes and with brilliantly cut "box panels" around the top. The design was adapted for use on an entire suite of cut glass articles for table and decorative use—bowls, vases, and tazzas of all shapes and sizes. At the time of the patent, Wilson resided in Brooklyn, and we conclude from this that the design was produced by Becker & Wilson at that time.

Butter dish cut by Joseph Wilson; height 6½ in.

Collection of Mrs. G. W. Kinzer

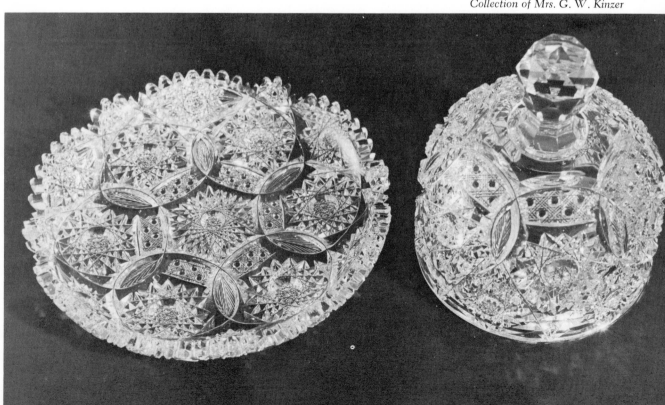

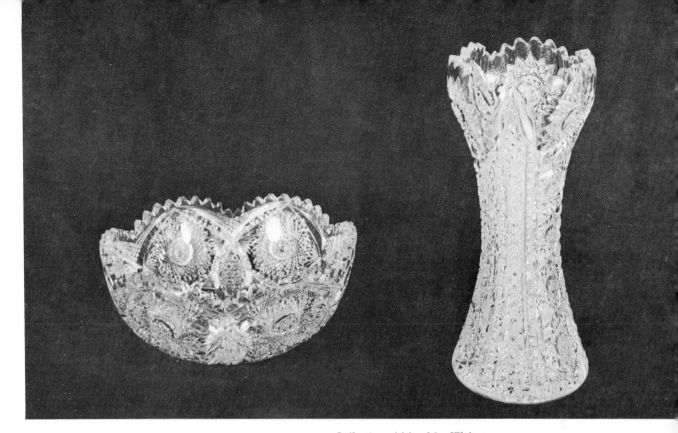

Cut glass bowl, diameter 8 in., and vase, height 9½ in.; made by Herbert E. Walton for his wife while he was foreman at Becker & Wilson, Montrose, Pa.

Wilson's second patent for a cut glass design was issued to him on December 22, 1903. The family described this as their father's "Star" pattern. The design consists of round punties, small stars, and brilliantly cut rosettes in various sizes, as is shown in the patent drawings, and in a tall vase in the collection of Claude B. Wilson. Joseph Wilson was living in Montrose, Pennsylvania, at this time and we believe the pattern was originated at his factory there.

Tunkahannock Glass Company

A long-time resident of Tunkahannock, Pennsylvania, George L. Roberts, remembered that the Tunkahannock Glass Company operated a cutting shop in that town in the period between 1894 and 1906. He used to visit the factory to watch them cut glass. No record of the cut glass concern now exists in the town's archives; however, Dorothy Daniel, in *Cut and Engraved Glass, 1771–1905*, states that the factory was sold in 1898 to Benjamin Franklin Crawford by J. S. Edsall. A closing date for this firm could not be determined, but it probably shut down a few years before World War I.

The Eygabroat-Ryon Company, Incorporated
The Ryon Cut Glass Company

Soon after the turn of the century, W. H. Ryon and Fred Eygabroat formed the Eygabroat-Ryon Company in Lawrenceville, Pennsylvania. In the beginning, W. H. Ryon was the president, Fred Eygabroat, vice president, and a man named Harry Pittman was secretary and treasurer. A short time thereafter their stationery showed that W. P. Ryon was vice president and treasurer and A. S. Brant was secretary. The company was incorporated under the laws of the State of Delaware in 1903 (the papers were filed on June 25, 1902) by Edward A. Ryon, Leonard E. Wales, and Joseph P. Wales. In addition to the factory in Lawrenceville, they maintained a cutting shop in the Heermans & Lawrence Building in Corning, New York. Some years before the company was closed (some time after 1905), W. H. Ryon bought Eygabroat's interest in the firm and it then became known as the Ryon Cut Glass Company.

At the peak of its productivity, the Eygabroat-Ryon Company employed most of the working population of Lawrenceville. The factory was located on Main Street and occupied a two-story frame building with smaller buildings

The Eygabroat-Ryon Co., Inc. cut glass factory as it appeared in 1905.

Photo courtesy of Wallace E. Ryon

342

built off the main structure. The water for the boilers and cutting wheels was taken from the Tioga River, which ran directly behind the factory buildings. The company went into bankruptcy in 1913, but all creditors were paid 100 cents on the dollar.

Besides the brilliantly cut patterns represented by objects in the collection of Wallace E. Ryon, the Eygabroat-Ryon Company cut designs in the floral patterns so popular in this late period of cut glass production. An inventory of their stock, written on the firm's old stationery, came into the author's hands, along with original sketches and rubbings of their patterns. From these we determined that the following designs were made by this company:

Adams	Narcissus
Bergamot	Nelke ("Carnation")
Bouquet	Pansy
Clematis	Peony
Dahlia	Pittman
Daisy	Poinsettia
Dawn	Primrose
Fuschia	Roses
Gardenia	Sweet Pea
Iris	Tulip
Jonquil	Vintage (a pattern of grapes and leaves)
Lotus	Violet
Marigold	

Rare champagne bucket cut in the "Chair Bottom" ("Harvard") pattern; produced at the Eygabroat-Ryon Co., Inc. *ca.* 1905; height 12 in.

Collection of Wallace E. Ryon

There are also various combinations of flowers, birds, and butterflies, as well as combinations of flowers and fanciful scrolls. In a great many instances floral designs were blended tastefully with brilliant cutting in the old style.

Alfred Kreibig and Henry Kreibig were the designers of most of the floral patterns mentioned above. Alfred Kreibig's sketchbook came into our hands, along with many rubbings of their cut glass designs taken directly from plates and other articles produced at the factory in Lawrenceville and their subsidiary cutting shop in Corning. All Alfred Kreibig's sketches bore notations in German indicating where transparent colored stains were to be applied to the cut patterns, and some of the sketches in his book were handsomely tinted. Although the colored stains may have been fired on the glass at a low temperature, this did not make it a permanent decoration, and much of Eygabroat-Ryon's cut glass no longer retains this feature. One of the last glass cutters who worked for the company, William Holton, died in the summer of 1963; the names of other employees cannot now be determined.

A rather large order from the Pittman Company, written in pencil on the firm's stationary, was among the Kreibig papers and sketches. It listed the following items made by the Eygabroat-Ryon Company: nappies, spoon holders, sugar and cream sets, compotes, vases, trays, baskets, plates and dishes in several sizes, celery vases, butter sets, decanters, bowls, stemware, ice-cream sets, pitchers, cologne bottles, and horse-radish containers. Undoubtedly the company manufactured a great many other useful and decorative articles in common use at that time. A champagne bucket in Wallace E. Ryon's collection is the only one in cut glass we have ever seen, but this need not indicate that such an article is unique in this medium.

Stage Brothers Cut Glass Company
Stage-Kashins Cut Glass Company

On November 24, 1914, the articles of incorporation of the Stage Brothers Cut Glass Company were issued to Lee (Leigh) W. Stage, James H. Miller, and William E. Barnes, all residents of Lawrenceville, Pennsylvania, where the factory was located on Mechanic Street, just east of Main Street. The initial capital stock of the company was $7,500, divided into 75 shares, with a par value of $100 each; however, the incorporation papers indicated that only 10 per cent of this amount, or $750, was actually in the company's treasury, an indication that this was not a very large concern. The business had been established as early as 1911 by Leigh Stage and his brother Everett, and was in operation only a few years when, according to Everett Stage's daughter,

Collection of Mrs. John J. Butla

Left: Punch bowl and stand; height 14 in.; cut by Everett Stage; *ca.* 1914. (Note similarity to Maple City Glass Co.'s "Temple" pattern.) *Right:* "Strawberry" lamp cut by Everett Stage; height 20 in.

Covered cigar jar in the "Kennelworth" pattern; height 10¼ in. Bonbon dish decorated with "French Stars," "Silver Diamond," and in the center a pinwheel star with a "French Star" in the center; diameter 8 in. Decanter decorated with "Hobnail Stars," "Chair Bottom" ("Harvard") pattern, and "Silver Diamond" pattern; neck cut with "Lapidary" pattern, "Star" bottom; height 9 in. All three objects cut by Everett Stage; *ca.* 1914.

Collection of Mrs. John J. Butla

Pair of vases in the "Chair Bottom" ("Harvard") pattern; height 14 in.; cut by Everett Stage.
Collection of Mrs. John J. Butla

Mrs. John J. (Adeliene) Butla, the factory burned down. Nevertheless, the Stage Brothers Cut Glass Company was listed in the *American Glass Trade Directory* in 1918; shortly thereafter we could find no indication that the company continued operating beyond the early 1920's.

The Stage-Kashins Cut Glass Company operated in Lawrenceville, occupying a building on the corner of James and Cherry Streets. Everett Stage had purchased his brother's interest in the former concern and went into the cut glass business with Herman Kashins of Brooklyn, New York; Kashins was formerly a salesman for the Stage Brothers Cut Glass Company. Everett T. Stage was president and treasurer of the newly formed concern; his wife Lillian J. Stage was secretary. Articles of incorporation for the Stage-Kashins Cut Glass Company were filed on November 25, 1914 (one day after the Stage Brothers Cut Glass Company was incorporated) and validated on December 22, 1914. This company started with a capital stock of $5,000, but only $2,000 was in cash. Kashins did not stay with the company for more than a few years. Thereafter Stage and his wife carried on the business by themselves, selling just enough stock in the company to keep officers on their board of directors. In 1942, Stage's daughter, Adeliene Stage Butla, bought stock belonging to the firm's secretary and treasurer at that time, and held these offices in the concern until 1949, when her father's health failed and he was forced to retire. The factory building and equipment were sold about 1952. On September 17, 1954, Everett Stage passed away.

In the beginning, Stage-Kashins Cut Glass Company manufactured heavy, brilliantly cut glassware and continued to do so until the beginning of World War I in 1914. It soon became impossible to get potash and other materials needed for the manufacture of the heavy glass blanks from abroad, and so the company had to resort to cutting figured blanks for a few years to keep their doors open. Then they turned to manufacturing lightware—tableware, dinner sets, and so on, in both the gray (mat finish) and rock crystal (bright cutting).

From the collection of Adeliene Stage Butla we illustrate some cut glass pieces made by her father for his own use. These objects are more elaborately cut than most pieces produced by the Stage-Kashins Cut Glass Company.

Laurel Cut Glass Company

The Laurel Cut Glass Company of Jermyn, Pennsylvania, was listed as a member of the National Association of Cut Glass Manufacturers, and as cut glass manufacturers in the *American Glass Trade Directory* for 1918. At one time, around 1917, they were associated with the Cut Glass Corporation of America (Quaker City Cut Glass Company).

Allen Cut Glass Company

In 1905, William Allen left his position as manager of the apprentice shop for J. Hoare & Company of Corning, New York, and established his own cut glass factory, the Allen Cut Glass Company, in Johnstown, Pennsylvania. Allen had been in charge of the 20 frames assigned to apprentices in the Hoare shop for several years after he had become a master glass cutter himself in 1895. The first official indication of the Allen Cut Glass Company's existence appears in the 1907 *Johnstown Directory*. At that time the factory was located at 11 Lewis Street, and William Allen was listed as a "manufacturer of cut glass." R. L. Polk & Company's *Johnstown Directory* for 1913/14 listed Allen and his wife as residing at 542 Horner Street, and indicated too that he was associated with the Allen Cut Glass Company, the factory at that time being located at Wood near Cedar Street.

In 1915, Allen was still listed as president of the firm, with Perley Smith, vice president, and E. P. Riley, secretary and treasurer. The concern was then at Messenger Street, corner of Elder Street, in Johnstown. Percy A. Rose succeeded Allen as president of the Allen Cut Glass Company in 1920; Samuel Lenhart was vice president, and M. D. Bearer was secretary and treasurer. The factory's address was then at Messenger Street, corner of Elder Street. William Allen was noted as manager of the company in 1920.

The "Lotus Flower" pattern; patented July 15, 1913, by William Allen for Allen Cut Glass Co.

After 1925, the firm was no longer listed in the directories; however, Allen was included in their compilation, with the designation "salesman" after his name.

The only cut glass design patented by the Allen Cut Glass Company was registered in the name of William Allen as assignor to his own firm, and was dated July 15, 1913. In lieu of its original name, we have designated this their "Lotus Flower" pattern. It is a simple floral design, very much like a late cut glass pattern produced by Libbey, and was probably cut on pressed glass blanks.

McKee Glass Company
McKee-Jeannette Glass Works

The McKee Glass Company was one of the oldest glass-producing firms in America. J. & F. McKee was its name in 1850. By 1853 the style of the company was changed to McKee & Brother. In 1865 they traded as McKee & Brothers. The McKee brothers were associated with James Bryce, as Bryce, McKee & Company around 1850; they severed their connections with Bryce about 1854. In 1889 the factory was moved from Pittsburgh to Jeannette, Pennsylvania, and ten years later they joined the glass combine known as the National Glass Company. In 1903 the McKee Glass Company was re-formed after they had left the National Glass Company.

On November 29, 1904, McKee registered their trademark "Prescut" (reissued October 10, 1905). In 1908 they adopted the term "rock crystal" for an imitation cut glass they were producing. The company is presently a division of the Thatcher Glass Manufacturing Company of Jeannette, Pennsylvania.

McKee's imitation cut glasswares were illustrated in their trade catalogue of the 1908 period under such names as "Aztec," "Carltec," "Rotec," "McKee," "Colonial," "Liberty," "Fentec," "Glentec," "Doltec," "Martec," "Nortec,"

McKee's designs. *Left to right, top row:* "Carltec" (usually signed "Prescut") handled compote, 4 in. high; half-pint oval creamer; oval sugar basket, length 5½ in.; *second row:* "Fentec" covered butter dish, spoon holder, creamer, covered sugar bowl; *third row:* "Glentec" nappy, "Doltec" nappy (diameter 8 in.), "Martec" footed orange bowl (separate foot); *fourth row:* "Plytec" cracker bowl, "Nortec" oil bottle with stopper, "Quintec" biscuit jar and cover, "Sunburst" covered butter dish; *bottom row:* "Valtec" covered sugar bowl, "No. 98" sugar and creamer, "Innovation Cut Glass Line, No. 407" bowl.

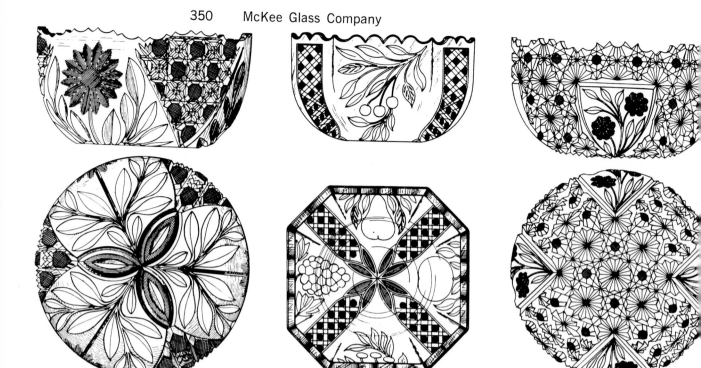

Left to right: McKee's designs: "Innovation Cut Glass Line, No. 410"; patented Apr. 10, 1917; "Innovation Cut Glass Line, No. 411"; patented June 18, 1918; "Innovation Cut Glass Line, No. 412"; patented Oct. 7, 1919; all by M. A. Smith.

Left to right: "Innovation Cut Glass Line, No. 411½"; patented Oct. 7, 1919; Cut glass dish patented Apr. 10, 1917; "Prescut" or "Innovation Cut" line of table glassware; patented May 24, 1921; all by Maurice A. Smith for McKee Glass Co.

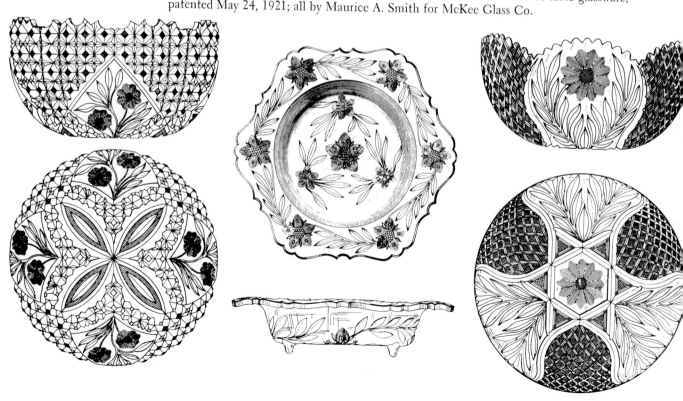

McKee's "Virginia" design; both cut wreath and cut floral decorated; plate in cut wreath; sugar and creamer in cut floral.

"Plytec," "Quintec," "Sunburst," "Valtec," and a "Chair Bottom" design combined with plain portions which they called their "No. 98" design. The catalogue indicated that all these designs were marked "Prescut."

About 1919, McKee introduced their "Innovation Cut Glass Line" with an illustrated catalogue showing their various patterns in pressed and lightly engraved wares: pattern "No. 407," "Beacon" (their pattern "No. 410," which was patented by Maurice A. Smith on April 10, 1917); pattern "No. 411" (a combination of "Chair Bottom" with engraved fruits; patented by Maurice A. Smith on June 18, 1918), pattern "No. 412" (a combination of the "Daisy and Button" pattern with engraved flowers and leaves; patented by Maurice A. Smith on October 7, 1919); "Virginia" (combining a pattern of "Bull's-eye" with light engraving of flowers and leaves; also the same pattern with laurel wreath engraving).

Other designs for pressed and cut wares were patented by this firm. These include a design for a lightly engraved dish patented by Maurice A. Smith on April 10, 1917. Smith registered the shape for McKee's orange bowls on June 19, 1917 (this form was used in their Innovation Cut Glass Line and can be found in all their patterns in this line). Smith patented an elaborate design consisting of diamond cutting in combination with engraved flowers and leaves on October 7, 1918 which was another of McKee's Innovation Cut Glass Line patterns. On May 24, 1921, Smith combined the old-fashioned "Strawberry-Diamond" pattern with a stylized flower and leaf motif for the Innovation Cut line. Smith's last design, dated January 23, 1917, was for a simple flower and leaf pattern which was shown in the patent illustration in

Maurice A. Smith's design for a simple cut glass vase manufactured by McKee Glass Co.; patented Jan. 23, 1917.

Electroliers in "Prescut" and "Innovation Cut" patterns; from an original McKee
Glass Co. catalogue; *ca.* 1918.

a vase form. The McKee Glass Company added nothing of quality to American cut glass, but they did manage to produce a prodigious amount of pressed
and lightly cut glassware which collectors will have no difficulty finding.

United States Glass Company

The United States Glass Company was formed in 1891 by several manufacturers of pressed glass tablewares. [For a history of the firm see A. C. Revi,
American Pressed Glass and Figure Bottles (New York, Thomas Nelson &
Sons, 1963).] Throughout their career they produced crystal blanks for many
cutting shops in America, but by 1910 they began producing their own cut
glasswares, using pressed figured blanks.

On March 14, 1916, Reuben Haley patented four cut glass designs for this
firm. We call the first one "Flowers and Butterflies"; the second, "Peonies and
Butterflies"; the third, "Asters"; and the fourth, "Peonies and Daisies." There

Left: The "Flowers and Butterflies" pattern; *right:* The "Peonies and Butterflies" pattern; both patented Mar. 14, 1916, by R. Haley for United States Glass Co.

Left: The "Asters" pattern; *right:* The "Peonies and Daisies" pattern; both patented Mar. 14, 1916, by R. Haley for United States Glass Co.

Left: The "Starflowers" pattern; patented Feb. 20, 1917, by R. Haley for United States Glass Co. (Note the similarity in design patented Apr. 10, 1917, by M. A. Smith for McKee Glass Co.) *Right:* Design for an engraved vase patented Aug. 30, 1921, by Bror Johnson for United States Glass Co.

is nothing particularly fine or distinctive about these patterns, and the designs were primarily intended for a cheaper market than most cut glass manufacturers were serving at that time.

On February 20, 1917, Haley patented two designs for footed glass dishes that were cut with shallow floral patterns; on this same date he registered a cut glass design which we have named "Starflowers" in lieu of its original designation.

Bror Johnson patented a design for an engraved pattern for glassware on August 30, 1921, which he assigned to the United States Glass Company.

In 1918, when this concern was at the height of its cut glass production, Marion G. Bryce was president of the firm; Ernest Nickel, secretary and treasurer; George Dougherty, sales manager; and Reuben Haley was general manager of the works. The company operated 11 furnaces with 150 melting pots, and a mold shop.

Pittsburgh Cut Glass Company

The Pittsburgh Cut Glass Company appears in the Pittsburgh, Pennsylvania, city directories from 1910 to 1921; their address was 503 Phipps Power Building, 24 Cecil Way. In 1915, and for several years following, they list three men associated with the company but do not distinguish their official positions: William M. Carey, Michael M. Liston, and Brenton Lydey. By 1919, these names no longer appear in the directories, and in 1921 the name of Henry Scott is the only one associated with the Pittsburgh Cut Glass Company; 1921 was also the last year an entry for the company appeared in the directories.

Crown Cut Glass Company

In June, 1903, the Crown Cut Glass Company of Pittsburgh, Pennsylvania, advertised in the *Ladies Home Journal* that for $1.50 they would send—"prepaid anywhere East of the Mississippi—a beautiful heart-shaped cut glass bonbon dish, 5 inches in diameter, and made of pure crystal glass, beautifully cut." The illustration which accompanied this advertisement showed a lovely piece of cut glass with a large brilliant rosette in the center of the dish and radiating prism cutting emanating from the rosette to the edge of the article.

Crown Cut Glass Co.'s advertisement in the *Ladies Home Journal* for June, 1903.

Send $1.50 To-Day and we will send you — prepaid, anywhere East of the Mississippi —this beautiful *Cut Glass Bonbon or Olive Dish*, 5 inches in diameter, made of pure crystal glass, beautifully cut.

This is a special offer to introduce to you the most brilliantly beautiful cut glass ever made in America.

CROWN CUT GLASS CO.
Pittsburgh, Pa.

355

Unfortunately, we were unable to find out anything further about this cutting shop. The lack of documentation in Pittsburgh sources indicated to us that the firm operated for a very short time.

Tarentum Glass Company

The Tarentum Glass Company was formerly known as Richards & Hartley Flint Glass Company. When this company was first established as Richards & Hartley, it was located in Pittsburgh, Pennsylvania. In 1884 they moved their works to Tarentum, Pennsylvania, and were once a part of the glass combine known as the United States Glass Company.

In 1918 the Tarentum Glass Company was listed as a manufacturer of cut glass in the *American Glass Trade Directory*; H. M. Brackenbridge was president of the concern; with J. W. Hemphill, vice president; L. Hartley, secretary and treasurer; H. S. Potter, general manager and sales manager; and H. Walker, factory manager. At that time the works were operating only one furnace with a 14-pot capacity, one-day tank, and a mold-making shop.

Only one cut glass design was registered for the Tarentum Glass Company; on February 13, 1906, Joseph M. McMahon registered his "Star Flower and Fans" pattern, which was probably produced from pressed glass blanks manufactured by the Tarentum Glass Company.

The "Star Flower and Fans" pattern; patented Feb. 13, 1906, by Joseph M. McMahon for Tarentum Glass Co.

The Phoenix Glass Company

As early as 1886, the Phoenix Glass Company of Monaca, Pennsylvania, advertised "art glassware, etched, engraved, cut and decorated goods" in the *Crockery and Glass Journal*. The firm cut glassware continually until about 1930. In the later years of their cut glass production they confined their output to such wares as shades, globes, and domes for hanging lamps and ceiling fixtures.

In 1902, William Dorflinger reported to the American Association of Flint and Lime Glass Manufacturers that in 1884, the Phoenix Glass Company made fine flint glass for cutting, and ran a cutting shop of about seventy frames. They had a capacity of four tons of best metal a week, and ran successfully until 1890, when they discontinued that branch owing to exactions and annoyances from the Glass Makers' Union.

Cut, etched, and engraved glass lampshades from the illustrated catalogue issued by Phoenix Glass Co.; *ca.* 1918.

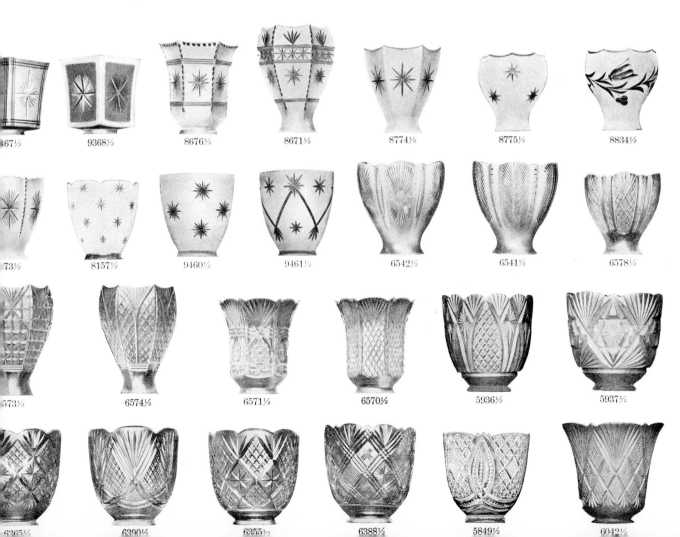

867½   9368½   8676½   8671½   8774½   8775½   8834½

73½   8157½   9460½   9461½   6542½   6541½   6578½

573½   6574½   6571½   6570½   5936½   5937½

6365½   6390½   6355½   6388½   5849½   6042½

Deidrick Glass Company

The Deidrick Glass Company of Monaca, Pennsylvania, produced some cut and engraved glassware in the first quarter of the twentieth century. Most of their engraved pieces were combined with a silver deposit decoration and sold under the trade name "Silvart," which they registered on July 25, 1916.

Fry & Scott
The Rochester Tumbler Company
H. C. Fry Glass Company

Some time before 1867, Henry Clay Fry and William A. Scott established a glass factory in Pittsburgh, Pennsylvania, known as Fry & Scott. During this early period of Fry's activities in the glass trade, he patented a design for a cut glass pattern consisting of large flutes and angular, or sharp-pointed, projections, as is shown in his patent illustration. The patent, dated November 3, 1868, was assigned to "himself, Frank Semple, and John D. Reynolds," and obviously these men were also associated with Fry in his first glass business.

For a time Fry was a traveling salesman for the William Phillips Glass Company of Pittsburgh, and also was the manager of the O'Hara Glass Works under the direction of James B. Lyon.

In 1872, Fry was president of the Rochester Tumbler Company. This concern was formed in the spring of 1872 and employed 90 men; it specialized in the manufacture of pressed and cut glass tumblers. At the height of its production it employed 1,100 people and produced 75,000 dozen tumblers a week or 150,000 tumblers a day. J. Howard Fry was secretary of the company for many years.

The Rochester Tumbler Company was succeeded by the H. C. Fry Glass Company, which was organized in 1901. Besides a fine grade of cut glassware, the H. C. Fry Glass Company manufactured oven glass, etched wares, pressed and blown crystal blanks for cutting, and numerous glass specialties, all known throughout the trade for their excellent quality.

In 1925 the company suffered financial reverses and went into receivership. It continued this way until 1933, when it was again reorganized. In 1934 it closed down completely.

358

For many years the high lead content of Fry's glass made it a very desirable product for cut glass manufacturers throughout the country to use for deep miter cutting and intricate designs. The clarity of the metal lent itself well to the elaborate patterns of the Brilliant Period. Later Fry began to manufacture pressed blanks which were lightly touched-up on the cutting and polishing wheels to simulate the finer cut glass products. This latter innovation was one of the reasons for the downgrading of American cut glass and its inevitable rejection by a quality-minded buying public.

Henry Clay Fry was born on September 17, 1840, near Lexington, Kentucky, where he also received his education. In 1857 he established himself in the glass trade in Pittsburgh. During the Civil War, Fry and his brother George enlisted at the same time as privates in the Fifteenth Regiment, Pennsylvania Cavalry, and took part in all the engagements of the Army of the Cumberland until they were mustered out in 1864. At this time he returned to Pittsburgh and was again active in the glass trade before going to Rochester, Pennsylvania, in 1872, as president of the Rochester Tumbler Company. Fry was active in civic affairs in Rochester; in 1883 he organized the First National Bank and was its president until 1926. He was also president and a director of the Duquesne Light Company, and was a director and officer in several other organizations in and around Rochester. Fry died in his home on Jackson Street and New York Avenue in Rochester on January 3, 1929. His oldest son, Henry Fry, Jr., was a colonel in the Air Force during World War I.

Cut glass design patented Nov. 3, 1868, by Henry C. Fry.

Fry's monumental punch bowl, consisting of 6 pieces, and 12 footed cups.
Photo courtesy of Lillian Nassau

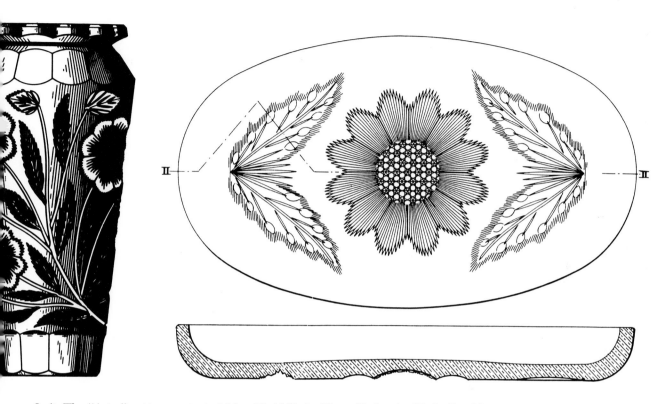

Left: The "Aster" pattern; patented May 18, 1909, by Harry Haden for H. C. Fry Glass Co. *Right:* The "Daisy" pattern; patented Nov. 25, 1913, by Harry Buckley for H. C. Fry Glass Co.

For the most part, Fry's designs favor the public's taste for the more simple style of cutting which was popular in the late period of cut glass, but many of his products were designed in the style of the old Brilliant Period as evidenced by a magnificent punch bowl consisting of six separate parts and twelve elegant footed cups. This handsome ensemble was exhibited at the Lewis and Clark Exposition at Portland, Oregon, in 1905, where it won the Grand Medal of Honor award.

On May 18, 1909, Harry Haden patented a floral design for cut glassware which we have named the "Aster" pattern. The patent was assigned on issuance to the H. C. Fry Glass Company.

Fry's "Daisy" pattern was patented by Harry H. Buckley on November 25, 1913. The design consists of a daisylike flower with fine prism-cut petals and a brilliantly cut center. The leaves of the flower have been ornamented in a style typical of this late period.

On November 14, 1916, Solon L. Parsons registered a design patent for the H. C. Fry Glass Company for a glass dish that appears to have been intended as a pressed glass article; however, the pattern is one found on some cut glass

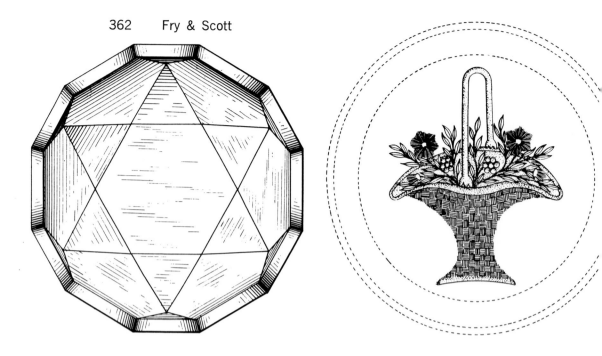

Left: Solon L. Parsons' design for a glass dish; patented Nov. 14, 1916; H. C. Fry Glass Co. *Right:* The "Flower Basket" pattern; patented Feb. 20, 1917, by F. L. Andrews for H. C. Fry Glass Co.

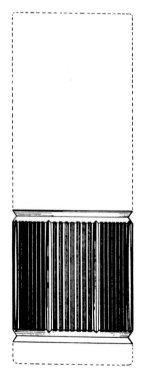

Left: The "Prism" pattern; *right:* The "Prism and Flute" pattern; both patented Mar. 20, 1917, by F. L. Andrews; H. C. Fry Glass Co.

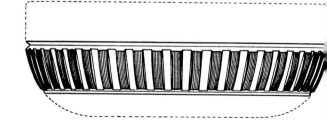

objects of the 1915–1920 period and could very possibly have been intended to represent a cut glass bowl of a very simple design.

A beautiful representation of a basket of flowers formed the major portion of a design patent for cut and engraved glassware issued to Fred L. Andrews and the H. C. Fry Glass Company on February 20, 1917. The following month, on March 20, 1917, Andrews was issued two more patents for cut glass designs which we have named "Prism" and "Prism and Flute."

Many pieces of signed Fry glass were produced from pressed crystal blanks. The most common patterns are those of a floral design used in combination with a version of the popular "Harvard" pattern, also known in the trade as "Chair Bottom." Still other pressed blanks with a variant of the "Russian" pattern were used in combination with floral or geometric designs which were easily engraved or cut into the plain portions of the figured blanks.

The name "Fry" can be found lightly etched in the surface of the glass in fancy script on much of this company's output. On April 22, 1913, they registered their trademark "Golden Glow" for glass reflectors; and on October 17, 1916, Fry was issued another trademark consisting of the name "Fry" above a shield. Still another of their identifying trademarks is the name "Fry" and the word "Quality" enclosed in a shield-shaped emblem.

It could be said that Harry Fry, Jr. was among the first collectors of cut glass in America. Many pieces of cut glass in Fry's private collection were manufactured by other glass factories. After his death these articles were erroneously attributed to his father's company; the fact that some of these pieces bore the trademark of a cutting shop other than Fry's was evidently overlooked.

Keystone Tumbler Company

In February, 1897, John Conway, August Heller, John Moulds, James T. Conlan, and Charles Bentel formed the Keystone Tumbler Company of Rochester, Pennsylvania, with a capital stock of $75,000 and became the firm's first directors. The factory employed 360 people, and the plant worked some 35 pots of glass. The factory produced mostly pressed tumblers, jelly glasses, beer mugs, and fine blown lead crystal tumblers. These latter wares were usually decorated by engraving, sandblasting, gilding, etc.; however, the cutting shop at this factory did produce great quantities of tumblers with deep miter cutting typical of the Brilliant Period.

The Keystone Tumbler Company was located in Rochester along the lines of the Pittsburgh, Fort Wayne, and Chicago Railroad. It passed out of existence in 1905.

Dithridge Flint Glass Company

In 1881, Edward D. Dithridge, Jr. purchased a factory in Martins Ferry, Ohio, which he named the Dithridge Flint Glass Works. In 1887 the factory was moved to New Brighton, Pennsylvania, where they manufactured blown lead glass, both cut and engraved. The company operated until 1891. They had a 16-pot capacity and ran 75 cutting frames. The company also supplied several small and large cutting shops around the country with lead crystal blanks.

Cut Glass Manufacturers in West Virginia

Photo courtesy of Oglebay Institute, Mansion Museum, Wheeling, W.Va.
The Sweeney punch bowl; height 4 feet 10 in.; weight 225 lbs.

Sweeney & Company
M. & R. H. Sweeney
M. & T. Sweeney

Thomas Sweeney, Jr. founded a glass factory in North Wheeling, Virginia (now West Virginia) about 1830, in which his brothers joined him. The plant was operating in 1831 and produced a very fine grade of flint glass which they cut and engraved. The Wheeling directory for the year 1839 reported:

> The Flint Glass Works of M. & R. H. Sweeney, with the cutting and grinding establishment appended, turn out glassware exceedingly transparent, and manufacture articles of the best quality and workmanship. They are made in every pattern, and receive every variety of beautiful finish, cut, plain and pressed. These works yield an annual product of $70,000 . . . and 60 hands are employed.

By 1844 the name of the firm had changed to M. & T. Sweeney. It was during this time that the famous Sweeney punch bowl was made. This was a monumental piece of cut glass made from an original design by Thomas Sweeney for his hero Henry Clay. At the time, it was the largest piece of cut glass ever produced, and many people called it "Sweeney's Folly" until it won the Grand Prize in the first International Exhibition, held in the Crystal Palace, London, in 1851. This bowl is now in the British Museum, but a second copy was made for Henry Clay; and a third punch bowl in the same design was produced for Michael Sweeney, and when he passed away in December, 1875, it was enshrined, at his request, in a granite tombstone which his family placed over his grave. This latter version of the Sweeney punch bowl stands 4 feet, 10 inches high, and weighs 225 pounds; it has a capacity of some 21 gallons of liquid. It is entirely of cut glass in a simple flute pattern, and originally long cut prisms hung from the rim of the bowl. In more recent years the punch bowl was removed from the graveyard and it now is a handsome addition to the collection of the Oglebay Institute, Mansion Museum, Wheeling, West Virginia.

Hobbs, Barnes & Company
Hobbs, Brockunier & Company

In 1845, John L. Hobbs and James B. Barnes, former employees of the New England Glass Company, came to Wheeling, Virginia (now West Virginia), and purchased the Excelsior Glass Works; they operated as Hobbs, Barnes & Company. By 1863 the company had lost by death both Barnes and his son, and it was reorganized as Hobbs, Brockunier & Company, with John L. Hobbs, Sr. and John L. Hobbs, Jr. being joined by their former book-keeper and office manager, Charles W. Brockunier.

Hobbs, Brockunier & Company were especially noted for their pressed glass wares, but in 1879 the *Crockery and Glass Journal* reported that they were considered to be the largest producers of cut glass in America. In 1878 the cutting shop alone did a business of over $300,000. Obviously not all of this amount was represented by fancy bowls and tablewares, for the company was known for its fine cut crystal chandeliers, lamp globes and shades.

The Central Glass Company

The Central Glass Company in Wheeling, West Virginia, was established in 1863 by eight glass blowers who were former employees of Hobbs, Barnes & Company. The firm was a large producer of pressed glasswares for many years, but they also cut glass on their own lead crystal blanks.

A fuller account of Sweeney & Company, Hobbs, Brockunier & Company, and the Central Glass Company can be found in the author's book, *American Pressed Glass and Figure Bottles* (New York, Thomas Nelson & Sons, 1963).

Cut Glass

Distributors

in Maryland

and Washington, D. C.

American Wholesale Corporation
(Baltimore Bargain House)

On March 14, 1922, and March 21, 1922, the American Wholesale Corporation (also known as the Baltimore Bargain House) of Baltimore, and Cumberland, Maryland, registered trademarks for "cut glass of all kinds." The trademarks consisted of the firm's initials "A.W.C.," and their full name "American Wholesale Corporation (Baltimore Bargain House)." The company operated at several locations in Baltimore and sold as wide a range of merchandise as does Sears Roebuck & Company, and Montgomery Ward & Company today; they were, in fact, a retail and mail-order house and published several catalogues showing not only cut glasswares, but just about every kind of household commodity used at that time. Obviously they did not produce their own cut glass products, and it is quite possible that they sold imported cut crystal as well as domestic wares.

Lansburgh & Brothers, Incorporated

Lansburgh & Brothers, Incorporated, of 420 Seventh Street N.W., Washington, D.C., registered their trademark for "cut glass of all kinds" on May 20, 1924. Their name "Lansburgh & Bro." appeared on their cut glasswares since September 25, 1922. Matt Hanse of the Lotus Glass Company told the author that the Lansburgh company did not produce their own cut wares.

Cut Glass Manufacturers in Ohio

Fostoria Glass Company

The Fostoria Glass Company, one of the largest, oldest, and best-known producers of handmade glassware in the United States, was established in Fostoria, Ohio, in December, 1887, by W. S. Brady and L. B. Martin. The factory was located at 307 South Vine Street. In 1889, Martin was listed as president of the firm. Within four years after it was established in Fostoria, the company was forced to move, for the supply of natural gas had given out. In 1891 the company located in its present site, Moundsville, West Virginia, in the Ohio Valley; at this time Brady was president and Martin vice president. Around 1910, with W. A. B. Dalzell and C. B. Rose at the helm, Fostoria also became known for twisted work, deep cut tableware, and etched glassware. Today Fostoria's Moundsville plant covers more than eight acres and employs some 500 skilled craftsmen.

The *Fostoria City Directory* for 1889/90 listed the Fostoria Glass Company as "wholesale manufacturers of fine cut and pressed glassware," with "special attention given to novelties."

Fostoria Glass Specialty Company

The Fostoria Glass Specialty Company was established in 1899 by J. B. Crouse, Henry A. Tremaine, B. G. Tremaine, and J. Robert Crouse (son of J. B. Crouse). The factory was located in Fostoria, Ohio, on an extension of Railroad Street (now 4th Street) and South Poplar, adjacent to the Baltimore & Ohio Railroad tracks, in a one-story brick building with a large floor space. They produced their first glass in 1901. By 1907 the company had prospered and two factories were in operation, having a daily capacity of 5,000 pounds of glass each. The company employed 700 men, and the monthly payroll exceeded $30,000, a goodly sum in those days. At this time the firm was building another glass factory in Fostoria at a cost of $75,000. E. O. Cross was general manager of the company and his assistant was Homer Black. James Goggin supervised the manufacture of the glass and J. A. Ryan had charge of the finishing department.

Trademarks issued to the firm indicate that they were in the process of being absorbed into the General Electric Company as early as 1912. During this period E. O. Cross was the president of the Fostoria Glass Speciality Company and all patents and trademarks issued to the firm in his name were assigned to the General Electric Company of New York City. Eventually, General Electric took over the works and moved them to Cleveland and Niles, Ohio, about 1917.

An illustrated catalogue of the firm's wares showed their line of "Clearcut" shades for electric lights and lamps in frosted crystal with bright cut designs. The company also made beautiful cut glass punch bowls, decanters, compotes, bowls, lamps, and other table and decorative wares in the traditional manner of American cut glass shops of this period. The cut glass shop was a separate unit in the Fostoria Glass Specialty Company; it was under the direction of John Valley, who later went to Toledo, Ohio, where he manufactured artistically engraved and decorated mirrors under the name Valley Glass and Mirror Company. The Fostoria Glass Specialty Company also made some beautiful iridescent glass in every way similar to the lustered glasses made by the Tiffany Furnaces and the Steuben Glass Works; these wares were sold under the trade name "Iris" (trademark registered on August 6, 1912).

As far as we could determine, the factory known as the Fostoria Cut Glass Company, of Fostoria, Ohio, which was listed in the 1918 issue of the *American Glass Trade Directory*, was another name for the Fostoria Glass Specialty Company's cut glass shop.

Tiffin Cut Glass Company

The Tiffin Cut Glass Company was a small concern with expert glass cutters producing fine quality cut glassware. Its limited amount of capital probably accounted for the few years it was able to operate, from about 1910 to 1915. In 1911, H. H. Close was president of the company; F. W. Lehnert, vice president and manager; and F. X. Close, secretary and treasurer. The cutting shop was located at 150 Union Street, in Tiffin, Ohio. Otto M. Yeager was listed in the 1911/12 *Tiffin City Directory* as a glassworker employed by this firm; he was also one of the officers of the company.

In 1913/14, Fred W. Lehnert was the president of the Tiffin Cut Glass Company, and William H. Kildow was secretary and treasurer. No more listings of the company could be found after 1914, and Yeager's family confirmed that the factory stopped operating about the beginning of World War I.

Marion Glass Manufacturing Company

In 1917, the Marion Glass Manufacturing Company was located at 126 Olney Avenue in Marion, Ohio. The officers of the firm were George L. Kraatz, president; R. E. White, secretary; and R. H. Robinson, treasurer. The firm was listed as a cut glass manufacturer in the 1918 *American Glass Trade Directory*.

In 1920, the concern moved to 125 Leader Street in Marion; George L. Kraatz was still president and general manager, and L. J. Zachman, secretary and treasurer. M. C. Gambrill succeeded Zachman as secretary-treasurer in 1922. A year later Gambrill's place was filled by Rex H. Robinson. In 1934, Robinson became vice president and general manager of the firm; Paul T. Blair was treasurer. Robinson became president and general manager in 1942; and Waldo E. May was treasurer of the company. In 1945, Ray E. Eaton succeeded May as treasurer. Frank S. McNeal was named president of the company in 1950, with H. Marr McNeal as vice president. In 1959, Mrs. Mary McNeal was listed as secretary. The entry for the firm in the 1960 city directory appears without any further changes in the principals.

We found no indication of this company's wares among the public records; however, it is more than possible that their early designs were mostly floral patterns, and that they later were engaged in the manufacture of light cut wares and decorated glass products.

Imperial Glass Company

Edward Muhleman organized the Imperial Glass Company in Bellaire, Ohio, in 1901. The factory was two years in the building and it was not until early in 1904 that they began producing pressed glassware in great quantities. By 1918, V. G. Wicke was president and sales manager; J. F. Anderson, vice president; J. Ralph Boyde, secretary; and A. T. Muhleman, auditor. C. F. Morris was factory manager.

The Imperial Glass Company was listed as a manufacturer of cut glass in the *American Glass Trade Directory* in 1918, but their wares were produced from pressed and figured blanks which they sold under the trade name "Nucut" (trademark registered September 15, 1914). The company is still one of the leading manufacturers of pressed glass tablewares and novelties in America. In 1964 the company was directed by Carl Gustkey.

Other Cut Glass Shops in Ohio

Aetna Glass and Manufacturing Company

From 1879 to 1890 the Aetna Glass and Manufacturing Company in Bellaire, Ohio, advertised that they also produced "fine cut and etched wares."

Barnes, Fanpel & Company

Barnes, Fanpel & Company, also of Bellaire, produced some cut glass in the early days of their existence.

National Glass Company
Rodefer-Gleason & Company

The old National Glass Company (later Rodefer-Gleason & Company) manufactured engraved and cut glass on a small scale in their Bellaire works.

The Bellaire Goblet Company

The Bellaire Goblet Company of Bellaire and Findlay, Ohio, cut and engraved pressed glass blanks, mostly goblets, tumblers, and mugs. In C. L. Poorman's *History of the Upper Ohio Valley* (1890), it was reported that

The "Dunkirk" pattern; patented July 13, 1897, by Herman Schreiber; assigned to Ohio Flint Glass Co.

the Bellaire Goblet Company leased the Ohio Glass Works in March, 1879. This could possibly have developed into the Ohio Flint Glass Company of Bellaire, Ohio, for which we have a recorded patent for a cut glass design issued to Herman Schreiber of Dunkirk, Indiana, dated July 13, 1897. The design consists of fan-shaped motifs surrounding a center of brilliantly cut palmettes, fans, and fine hatch cutting. Dorothy Daniel, in *Cut and Engraved Glass, 1771–1905*, named this pattern "Dunkirk." A thorough search of the Bellaire city records failed to show any evidence of this firm's existence in that city, and we are inclined to believe that it had a very short business life.

The LaBelle Glass Company

The LaBelle Glass Company in Bridgeport, Ohio, manufactured engraved wares on pressed blanks about 1875.

The Elson Glass Company

In 1882, the Elson Glass Company of Martins Ferry, Ohio, is reported to have made some cut wares.

A. H. Heisey & Company

Augustus H. Heisey founded his own glass company in Newark, Ohio, in 1895. Previously he had been associated with the King Glass Company and George Duncan & Sons, as well as other glass concerns. Heisey's sons, George Duncan Heisey, Edgar Wilson Heisey, and Thomas Clarence Heisey, joined their father in his business, each son succeeding to the presidency of the concern at one time or another. In May, 1958, the Imperial Glass Company in Bellaire, Ohio, acquired the name and molds of A. H. Heisey & Company and continue to produce some of their patterns in pressed glasswares.

On June 27, 1899, Augustus H. Heisey patented his design for a glass vessel. The patent illustration shows a pitcher with vertical panels of fine cutting alternating with vertical panels of thumbprints, or "bull's-eye" depressions. The style of the decoration and the ornamented handle of the pitcher indicate that the patent covered a cut glass design. We have named it the "Diamond and Bull's-eye Panels" pattern.

A. H. Heisey & Company supplied cut glass shops all over the country with pressed and figured blanks which they identified with their trademark "Plunger Cut" (registered January 30, 1906). Sometimes their blanks bore

The "Diamond and Bull's-eye Panels" pattern; patented June 27, 1899, by A. H. Heisey.

their trademark, an "H" within a diamond-shaped figure. Several design patents for these pressed blanks were issued to the firm, including the following:

July 21, 1908. Design for a jar, by Clyde S. Whipple

May 10, 1910. Sugar bowl ("Greek Key" pattern), by Andrew J. Sanford

July 4, 1911. Footed dish ("Greek Key" pattern), by Andrew J. Sanford

September 12, 1911. Sugar bowl ("Greek Key" pattern), by Andrew J. Sanford

January 23, 1912. Sugar bowl ("Greek Key" pattern), by Andrew J. Sanford

March 5, 1912. Bowl ("Loop" pattern), by Andrew J. Sanford

July 2, 1912. Nappy, by Andrew J. Sanford

July 9, 1912. Sugar bowl, by Thomas C. Heisey

July 9, 1912. Cream pitcher, by Thomas C. Heisey

December 16, 1913. Pitcher ("Loop" pattern), by Edgar W. Heisey

June 2, 1914. Uneeda Biscuit dish with handles, by Andrew J. Sanford

August 25, 1914. Footed bowl, by Andrew J. Sanford

November 24, 1914. Nappy, by Andrew J. Sanford

March 16, 1915. Oblong dish, by Andrew J. Sanford

February 8, 1916. Bowl, by Andrew J. Sanford

February 15, 1916. Basket with handle, by Andrew J. Sanford

February 22, 1916. Basket, by Andrew J. Sanford

February 22, 1916. Oval dish, by Andrew J. Sanford

February 22, 1916. Oval dish, by Andrew J. Sanford

April 24, 1917. Oval dish, by Andrew J. Sanford

September 25, 1917. Basket, by Andrew J. Sanford

March 8, 1921. Syrup jug, by Andrew J. Sanford

March 8, 1921. Syrup jug, by Andrew J. Sanford

March 8, 1921. Syrup jug, by Andrew J. Sanford

March 8, 1921. Covered jar, by Andrew J. Sanford

March 21, 1922. Syrup jug, by Andrew J. Sanford

March 24, 1925. Nappy, by Edgar W. Heisey

May 25, 1926. Nappy, by Thomas C. Heisey

December 23, 1930. Glass plate, by Thomas C. Heisey

Lotus Cut Glass Company
Lotus Glass Company

The Lotus Cut Glass Company was established in Barnesville, Ohio, in July, 1911, with an initial capital investment of about $2,700. C. M. Cole was president; Jack Colpetts, vice president; and N. M. Boswell, secretary. Colpetts and Boswell had been partners in a monument business and were not practical glass cutters. C. J. Goodenaugh, formerly of White Mills, Pennsylvania, was hired as the firm's foreman and chief cutter, and in a sense he was a partner, having invested $750 in the concern.

At first light wares were cut at the Lotus cut glassworks. The company tried to teach girls to do this type of cutting but it did not work out. Finally, they hired five good glass cutters; one of these was a man named Matt Hanse. He took over the works as manager of the cutting department when Goodenaugh left the company. Hanse is one of those self-made men, and in reminiscing with him about "the old days," he described himself as somewhat of a "tramp," since in his youth he worked first one place and then another, changing jobs at will. He finally settled down in Barnesville and in 1964 he was the sole owner of the Lotus Glass Company, successors to the Lotus Cut Glass Company. Hanse's factory continues to turn out a fine quality of light cut glassware, mostly tablewares and decorative articles. The factory is still in its original location, adjacent to the Baltimore and Ohio Railroad tracks.

On April 13, 1920, the Lotus Cut Glass Company registered their trademark, the name "Lotus" in fancy script, and stated that this trademark label had been in use by the firm since July 1, 1911.

Sterling Glass Company
Joseph Phillips & Company
Phillips Glass Company
Sterling Cut Glass Company

The Sterling Glass Company was founded in Cincinnati, Ohio, sometime before 1904. Joseph Phillips was the president until 1910. After 1910 he served as a salesman for the company until 1913, when he entered into a cut glass business with Joseph Landenwitsch (it was known as Joseph Phillips & Company). Phillips and Landenwitsch continued their operations for a short period, 1913 to 1918; thereafter the directories in Cincinnati list Phillips as a salesman for glassware and the Rookwood Pottery Company.

Joseph Landenwitsch became president of the Phillips Glass Company in 1919 and retained this position for several years.

The Sterling Glass Company went out of business in 1950, but some of the employees reorganized it under the name Sterling Cut Glass Company. This latter concern is still operating in Cincinnati, Ohio.

Only one design patent for cut glass wares was issued to the Sterling Glass Company. It was registered in the name of Joseph Phillips on August 9, 1904. From the illustration shown in the patent papers it would appear to be cover-

Joseph Phillips' design for a cut glass dish; patented Aug. 9, 1904; assigned to Sterling Glass Co.

ing more than one design. The left side of the illustration shows two large star-rosettes in combination with what appears to be a representation of feathers or stylized palm fronds. The right side shows two different treatments of the "Star and Laurel Wreath" pattern found in other cut glass designs of about this same period. It is hardly likely that collectors will find this pattern exactly as shown in the patent illustrations; however, the possibility does exist that it was Phillips' intention to combine these familiar cut glass decorations into one design.

The Eclipse Tumbler Company
The Findlay Cut Glass Company

The Findlay Cut Glass Company started out in Lansing, Michigan, as the Eclipse Tumbler Company, and operated there for only one year—1912. The works were located at 1221 Center Street and were under the management of John L. Randall, who in 1911 was associated with the Michigan Cut Glass Company. The Eclipse Tumbler Company specialized in the manufacture of cut glass tumblers at that time and advertised that they produced "the finest cut glass on the market."

In November, 1912, John L. Randall and F. G. L. Warner of the Eclipse Tumbler Company came to Findlay, Ohio, and discussed with the Findlay Business Men's Association the possibility of moving their cut glass works to that community. A month later the plant's site in the Chicago Block on North Main Street in Findlay had been chosen for their cut glass factory, and in the latter part of January, 1913, their machinery was shipped to the new works from Lansing, the town of Findlay having raised the necessary $700 to cover these expenses. At the same time eight workers and their families moved to Findlay.

On January 13, 1913, John L. Randall, Henry F. Hartman (both practical glass cutters), and H. Roy Bonnell came to Findlay to get the factory ready for the machinery. At this time the new name for the company had been announced in the local newspaper as the Findlay Cut Glass Company. It was incorporated at Columbus, Ohio, on January 20, 1913, with a capital stock of $9,800. Incorporators were F. J. Moon, J. L. Randall, H. F. Hartman, H. R. Bonnell (in 1911 the latter was associated with the American Cut Glass Company in Lansing, Michigan), and F. G. L. Warner, all of whom had been connected with the firm when it was operating in Lansing as the Eclipse Tumbler Company.

The following list of officers were elected by the stockholders of the Findlay

Cut Glass Company: president, J. L. Randall; vice president, F. G. L. Warner; second vice president, F. J. Moon; third vice president, H. R. Bonnell; secretary, Wurt W. Warner (F. G. L. Warner's son); and treasurer, H. F. Hartman.

On January 23, 1913, six cutting wheels were started grinding at the Findlay Cut Glass works commencing the first cut glass operation in that community. The plant was started at only half of its capacity, but the remaining six cutting frames were soon made operative.

On February 1, 1913, provisions for an additional 15 cutters were being made, and an electric engine replaced the outmoded gas engine which had provided power to the factory's cutting wheels. A few weeks later it was reported that every machine in the factory was operative and that the company was planning to open a retail store at 627 North Main Street for their cut glasswares. Cut glass tumblers were sold in the store at fifty cents a dozen. At this time the factory was operating at full capacity from early morning until eight o'clock each evening, but in March, 1913, the company reported only 14 cutters were working in their shop.

By September, 1913, the Findlay Cut Glass Company was shipping their cut glass wares to every state in the union except Arizona, and five new cutting frames had been added to increase their production. The Fair Department Store in Chicago, Illinois, was buying a large portion of the Findlay cutting shop's production, and the 25 cutters, under Hartman's direction, were working full time to fill their many orders. In November, 1913, Wurt W. Warner, who was in charge of the office, reported that they were then employing 30 cutters, and that their sales manager, his father F. G. L. Warner, had just returned from a five-week selling trip covering five states.

In January, 1914, a report to the stockholders of the Findlay Cut Glass Company revealed that they had had a very prosperous year. At this time a change in the list of officers of the firm was published: F. G. L. Warner, president; J. L. Randall, vice president; W. W. Warner, secretary; H. F. Hartman, treasurer. The directors of the concern consisted of the previously named officers and M. J. Warner. F. G. L. Warner continued as sales manager of the company and Wurt Warner managed the office; Hartman supervised the work in the cutting shop and in the acid department, where the cut glass received its final polishing.

By July, 1914, it became apparent that the Findlay Cut Glass Company would require larger quarters, and space for this was acquired in the Kerr Building at 448 East Sandusky Street in Findlay. G. B. Crane, the owner of the premises, made extensive repairs to the building, providing a large sample room for the Findlay Cut Glass Company to display their wares to the public. The move to the Kerr Building was made on July 31, 1914, and business was resumed a few days later. The office was in the west room, the center room housed the retail trade department, and the east side of the building was used as the factory. At this time 20 men were employed, besides the officials of the company, and their yearly output averaged from 800 to 1,000 barrels of cut glass. Their blanks were reportedly purchased from companies in Pennsylvania, possibly from the H. C. Fry Glass Company, where tumbler blanks were produced in huge quantities.

On November 17, 1914, the Findlay Cut Glass Company reported that they were in their busiest season of the year getting ready for the Christmas trade. Several large orders were shipped to the west. Albert Townsend of Lansing, Michigan, came at this time to take up his duties as a glass cutter at the Findlay Cut Glass Company's factory.

In January, 1915, a separate concern for handling the Findlay Cut Glass Company's sales was formed; it was known as the Warner Cut Glass Company, and the officers of this new firm were F. G. L. Warner, president, and Wurt W. Warner, secretary and treasurer (the Warners kept their stock holdings in the Findlay Cut Glass Company). The retail shop was discontinued at this time and all the company's business was carried on outside Findlay. A year later, on January 25, 1916, the directors of the Findlay Cut Glass Company held their annual meeting and F. G. L. and W. W. Warner re-entered the firm and were elected to the board of directors; evidently the Warner Cut Glass Company was dissolved at this time. In January, 1916, the officers of the Findlay Cut Glass Company were F. G. L. Warner, president; B. E. Traver, vice president; Wurt W. Warner, secretary; and Henry F. Hartman, treasurer.

In May, 1917, a deed of assignment was filed by F. G. L. Warner as president of the Findlay Cut Glass Company to Henry F. Hartman. The property of the company was turned over to Hartman, and was reported to be worth only $1,500, all of which included personal property. On May 12, 1917, the company listed assets of $833.22, and debts totaling $8,348.45; of this amount $486.68 was owed to a Pittsburgh glasshouse for blanks. By the end of May, 1917, permission was granted by the courts to dispose of part of the firm's assets to settle some of their debts; only $849.75 was realized. By the time all claims were settled by the company, there was a balance of only $188.07. In August, 1918, the last of the firm's business was finished, and Judge H. O. Dorsey declared the insolvency case at an end. In 1918 the Findlay Cut Glass Company was still listed in the *American Glass Trade Directory*, but obviously the concern was no longer in this business.

On January 27, 1922, the marriage of Henry F. Hartman, "cut glass manufacturer of St. Louis," and Ida E. Kobe of Findlay, Ohio, was announced in the Findlay *Morning Republican* newspaper. In April of that same year Hartman established a cut glass shop in Findlay at 110 Center Street; most of his trade was to retail customers. On February 13, 1931, it was reported that Hartman moved his cut glass business to 121 North Main Street in Findlay, where he specialized in glass and silverware.

Henry Hartman learned his glass cutting trade at the Missouri Glass Company in St. Louis, Missouri, as a teen-age boy. At that time, according to Hartman, it was the finest wholesale glass and china concern west of the Mississippi River. Hartman participated in cut glass exhibitions in Detroit, Michigan, and at the Louisiana Purchase Exposition held in St. Louis in 1904.

One of the patterns Hartman especially mentioned in an interview published in 1953 was named "Aster." He recalled that six dozen salad plates in this pattern were cut every 60 days at the Findlay Cut Glass Company's shop for O'Neil's Department Store in Akron, Ohio. The Findlay Cut Glass Company manufactured mostly heavy cut wares, which were sold at wholesale all over the country, but before the firm went out of business the light cut wares were coming into vogue and these comprised a good portion of their output.

Sunshine Cut Glass Company
Vetter Cut Glass Manufacturing Company

The Sunshine Cut Glass Company of Cleveland, Ohio, was founded sometime previous to 1916. The firm manufactured novelty wares of an inferior grade in cut glass. In 1917, Theodore R. Vetter was listed as the firm's vice president. In 1925, Vetter was recorded as superintendent of this company, which had a capitalization of $10,000. In 1928 he was listed as department manager.

In 1916, Vetter organized the Vetter Cut Glass Manufacturing Company in Cleveland, and was noted in the records as sole owner of the business. At the same time he was also connected with the Sunshine Cut Glass Company. The Vetter cutting shop produced a superior grade of cut glass. Later he discontinued making these fine wares because the cost of labor had gone up and they could not compete with other manufacturers. The firm turned their efforts to the manufacture of pressed and other glasswares—mirrors and plate-glass store windows, employing about 25 expert glaziers. In 1954, Vetter sold out to Milton Gross. The firm was owned and operated by Robert M. Yates and Peter C. Sanelli in 1964.

Rare celery boat cut and decorated in 1915 at Vetter Cut Glass Manufacturing Co., Cleveland, Ohio; flowers painted with yellow and lavender stain.

Collection of Wayne County Historical Society; donated by Theodore R. Vetter

One fine example of Vetter's cut glass is in the Wayne County Historical Society's collection in Honesdale, Pennsylvania. It was given by Vetter because Honesdale was where he got his start in the cut glass trade. Some of the cut design is stained with transparent mineral colors.

The George H. Bowman Company

The George H. Bowman Company was established in Cleveland, Ohio, in 1888, succeeding the famous C. A. Selzer Company of the same city. The principal owners of the concern were George H. Bowman, president; F. T. Bowman, vice president; R. Peck, secretary; A. Engler, treasurer; and F. F.

Left: The "Daisy Chain" pattern; an engraved design for use on pressed blanks; *right:* The "Leaf and Forget-me-not" pattern; both patented Mar. 22, 1921, by W. T. Osborne for George H. Bowman Co. (The basket and the covered jar were pressed blanks supplied by A. H. Heisey & Co.)

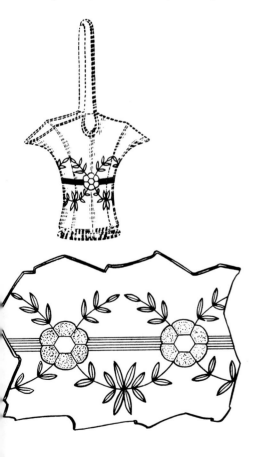

Pfifferkoon, general manager. The Bowman store was primarily engaged in the wholesale and retail trade in china, glass, and pottery; it was located on Euclid Avenue next door to the May Company store. Three floors were devoted to retail showrooms, where they sold imported bone china as well as sturdy domestic wares. The store was considered one of the biggest in the business and reportedly did an annual business of some millions of dollars.

For some time in the 1920's Bowman operated a toy factory on Cleveland's West Side. In 1932 the Cleveland store was closed. In 1933 the hotel department of the George H. Bowman Company was taken over by the Kemp-Engler Company (Samuel S. Kemp, a former Bowman employee, was head of this company, which later became S. S. Kemp & Company).

After he sold his shop in Cleveland, Bowman opened another in Salem, Ohio, under the same name. In 1964, his daughter still operated the family business, and its name has been changed to "The Fiesta Shop." Bowman was president of the Summit China Company, the Alliance Vitrified Glass Company, and was a director of the Guardian Trust Company. He was born on December 30, 1868, and died on October 17, 1960.

The George H. Bowman Company was listed as a manufacturer of cut glass in the glass directories for the period from 1910 to 1918. The firm maintained a small cutting shop in Salem, Ohio, where they produced a fine grade of light cut stemware and decorative articles. On March 22, 1921, William T. Osborne assigned two cut glass designs to Bowman's company. The patent illustrations indicate that these were engraved on pressed blanks which were supplied to them by A. H. Heisey & Company.

Condon Glass Company, Incorporated
Condon Cut Glass Company

James J. Condon was listed in the Toledo, Ohio, trade directories as a manufacturer of cut glass specialties as early as 1916. In July, 1916, the Condon Glass Company was incorporated with a capital of $5,000. The firm did business at 576 Oakwood Avenue in Toledo. Edwin A. Machen was the president of the newly incorporated business and James J. Condon was secretary and treasurer. In 1918 the firm was known also as the Condon Cut Glass Company, "manufacturers of cut glass specialties," with quarters in the "rear of 576 Oakwood Avenue." In 1919, Condon maintained a home furnishings and glassware outlet in room 315 of the Nasby Building in Toledo; the Condon Glass Company was also located in the Nasby Building, at this time occupying room 430.

From 1921 to 1923 James J. Condon and his wife Lydia Condon were manufacturers' agents, with offices at 127 Michigan (1921/22) and 135 Michigan (1923). Obviously the Condon Cut Glass Company ceased to exist as such after 1920.

Condon worked as a glass cutter for the Libbey Glass Company from 1905 to 1907. He was associated with the Corona Cut Glass Company from 1908 to 1914.

The Corona Cut Glass Company

The Corona Cut Glass Company first appears in the Toledo, Ohio, city directories in 1906, with Samuel Heinzelman as president and James Jay Condon, secretary-treasurer. In 1911 "High Grade Light Cutting Exclusively" was added to their listing, indicating that the firm did not produce any heavy, brilliantly cut glassware of the type now sought after by collectors. Instead, only glassware with some light wheel-cut engraving was produced by the Corona Cut Glass Company from 1911 until it closed, sometime around 1920.

On February 14, 1911, the company was incorporated with a capital of $15,000, and was located at 624 Jackson, Toledo, Ohio. In 1914, Harry L. Kelly of Chicago, Illinois, was president of the company, James J. Condon, secretary, and Robert H. Loosely, treasurer. Loosely was secretary and treasurer of the company in 1915 and succeeded to the presidency in 1916, maintaining his position until the firm closed. In 1917, C. B. Kishler was secretary and sales manager of the Corona Cut Glass Company. From 1905 to 1907, Condon and Heinzelman were working for the Libbey Glass Company as cutters. Condon later formed his own company, the Condon Glass Company, and in 1915, Samuel Heinzelman was listed as a glass manufacturer.

On January 23, 1912, the Corona Cut Glass Company was issued a trademark representing a total eclipse of the sun and showing a firey corona radiating from the perimeter of the round orb. The name "Corona" appears in the center of the darkened sun. James J. Condon signed the papers as a member of the firm and stated that this mark had been used continuously in the business since May, 1906. It is quite possible that the company produced heavy cut glass from 1906 to 1911 (and perhaps even after that date), since the trademark papers indicate that labels bearing their trademark were used for "cut glassware and engraved glassware."

Long Cut Glass Company

No record of the Long Cut Glass Company could be found in the Toledo, Ohio, city records; however, it was listed in the 1918 issue of the *American Glass Trade Directory* under cut glass manufacturers. The small shop was operated by James F. Long, possibly at his residence, 820 Buffalo, Toledo, Ohio. Long was employed as a glassworker at the Libbey Glass Company in 1893; he was listed as a glass blower the following year.

Ohio Cut Glass Company

According to Matt Hanse, a former employee of the Ohio Cut Glass Company and now proprietor of the Lotus Glass Company, Barnesville, Ohio, this cut glassworks was established in Bowling Green, Ohio, by Pitkin &

The "Palm-leaf Fan" pattern; patented Apr. 5, 1904, by Thomas Singleton for Ohio Cut Glass Co.

Brooks, of Chicago, Illinois, and manufactured both heavy and light cut wares. During Hanse's employment at the Bowling Green cutting shop, William P. Feeney was in charge of the factory. Feeney had once been associated with Feeney & McKanna in Honesdale, Pennsylvania, and was an employee of the Elmira Glass Company of Elmira, New York. Showrooms were maintained in New York City by the Ohio Cut Glass Company until it burned down in March, 1912.

Only one cut glass design was patented in the name of the Ohio Cut Glass Company. On April 5, 1904. Thomas Singleton, of Bowling Green, Ohio, registered his design for a cut glass pattern resembling an ornately woven palm leaf fan. The main feature of the design was a large brilliantly cut rosette placed at one extremity of the article, and radiating from this rosette were four panels containing alternately spaced rosettes and cross-hatch cutting. The illustration which accompanied the patent papers shows only one half of the design as applied to a round dish or plate. Singleton's association with the Ohio Cut Glass Company was preceded by a term of employment with the Mt. Washington Glass Company and its successor, the Pairpoint Corporation of New Bedford, Massachusetts, for whom he patented several cut glass designs. It is quite possible that Singleton managed the Ohio Cut Glass Company for Pitkin & Brooks previous to Feeney's association with this company.

Cut Glass Manufacturers in Indiana

Wright Rich Cut Glass Company

The Wright Rich Cut Glass Company was established in Anderson, Indiana, around 1904 by Thomas W. Wright. In the city directory for 1906/07 the officers of the firm were shown as George W. Wright, president; S. Hunter Richey, secretary; and Thomas W. Wright, treasurer. The factory was located at 1627–1631 Ohio Avenue (corner of McKinley). By 1914 or 1915 the company had gone out of the cut glass business and was re-established as the Wright Metal Manufacturing Company, and was listed at the same address as the cut glass factory.

Thomas W. Wright was the mainstay of the company; his son George W. Wright acted as president, and his son-in-law S. Hunter Richey was always listed in the public records as secretary of the concern.

From John L. Forkner's *History of Madison County* we learned that Thomas W. Wright was born in 1849 near Matlock, Derbyshire, England. He worked as a foreman in the shovelworks of Edward Lucas & Sons, near Sheffield, England. Wright came to America in 1872, and in 1889 started a shovel factory in Beaver Falls, Pennsylvania—the Wright Shovel Company. The shovel business outgrew the building it occupied in Beaver Falls and the plant was moved to Anderson, Indiana, in 1891. In 1900 this factory was taken over by the Ames Shovel & Tool Company and presumably Wright went into the cut glass business shortly thereafter.

Most pieces of Wright cut glass bear their trademark, the name "Wright," lightly etched in script on the object.

Warsaw Cut Glass Company

In 1911, Oscar Johnson and John Carlson of the Johnson-Carlson Cut Glass Company, Chicago, Illinois, founded the Warsaw Cut Glass Company in Warsaw, Indiana. (The incorporated name was Johnson-Carlson Cut Glass Company, Incorporated.) Their new factory building, which still stands today, was located at 505 South Detroit Street. At one time the firm employed 65 people, 40 of whom were expert glass cutters.

Turry Johnson, brother of Oscar Johnson, was president of the Warsaw Cut Glass Company; Oscar Hugo was the secretary; and Carl Hugo was superintendent of the works. The firm operated until the depression years and, about 1930, closed down for a time. In 1933 Oscar Hugo operated the Warsaw Cut Glass Company on his own; in 1957 he sold it to the present owners, Jackson T. Dobbins and his wife Mildred. Dobbins joined the Warsaw Cut Glass Company as an apprentice on June 4, 1914; he has been in the cut glass business now for more than fifty years. When World War I broke out, Oscar Hugo was called into service and his apprentice, Jackson T. Dobbins, was trained to take over his position until he returned.

In the early 1920's the heavy cut glass productions gave way to the light cut wares which the Warsaw Cut Glass Company continues to manufacture today.

Central Cut Glass Company

An industry that played a very important part in the life of Walkerton, Indiana, was the Central Cut Glass Company. This enterprise, which employed as many as 100 skilled workers, was brought to Walkerton through the efforts of local citizens who generously purchased $6,500 worth of stock at $1.50 a share. A cement block building, 30 by 200 feet, and two stories high, was erected on Tennessee Street. The brothers Joseph Roseen and Herman Roseen, of Chicago, Illinois (also owners of the Central Cut Glass Company in Chicago), were president and treasurer of the company, respectively.

The factory was well equipped and one of the most modern in its appliances. It began operations in August, 1910, with a staff of 50 men under the direction of Oscar W. Eckland, general manager of the works. The product manufactured was of a superior grade, and soon the name and fame of Walkerton was spread abroad as a cut glass center.

Local men who were active in securing the factory included George P. Ross, D. W. Place, Thompson Turner, M. B. Slick, A. D. Swank, J. E. Bose, T. H. Daughtery, and D. W. Brubaker. C. E. McCarty was the general overseer of the construction of the buildings.

The new cut glass industry was short-lived. On the night of February 19, 1919, fire of an unknown origin broke out in the building, and before effective assistance could be given by the local fire department, the factory had been gutted and its contents completely destroyed.

The Central Cut Glass Company purchased its blanks from several sources in this country. Some pieces were plain, others were pressed blanks. The best pieces were cut on plain lead crystal blanks by expert glass cutters, while the cheaper wares were manufactured from pressed and figured blanks by apprentices. One of the factory's workers reported that their best-selling designs were known as "Rex Hob," "Rex Buzz," "May Rose," "June Rose," "Yosemite," "Illinois," "Iona," and "Pineapple," and there were many others whose names she could not recall. The sample rooms and sales offices were maintained at the parent company's facilities in Chicago.

Hoosier Cut Glass Company

In 1921 the Hoosier Cut Glass Company was organized with Grant Baugher and Roy Hostetler as owners. It was located in the old Atwood Pickle factory building, which stood near the intersection of Virginia Street and Road Six in Walkerton, Indiana. It was in operation for about five years.

Pitkin & Brooks

In 1911, Pitkin & Brooks of Chicago, Illinois, opened another cut glass factory in Valparaiso, Indiana, on what was then called Main Street (now known as Lincolnway) on the west end of town. Pitkin & Brooks operated until some time in 1918, according to some of the workers still living (in 1964) in Valparaiso. William P. Feeney and Frank W. Lesch ran the factory and employed the following men and women: Charles H. Gilliland, lightweight glass engraver; George Lofte, polisher; Howard Jackson, heavyweight engraver; Knute Sundin, polisher; Carl Wahlberg, acid dipper; Ora Williams, heavyweight engraver; Byron Soliday, lightweight engraver; Ben McKean, heavyweight engraver; Al Broviak, polisher; Charles Coyer, buffer; Amelia Siemion, heavyweight engraver; Cecelia Siemion, inspector and washer; Ida Gustafson Curran, heavyweight engraver; Florence Gustafson Gilliland, heavyweight engraver; Clara Harbeck Leffler, washer; Irene Sundin, washer; Ruby Bronson Wahlberg, heavyweight engraver; Lucille Sundin, heavyweight engraver; Earl Ruth, lightweight engraver; and John Gast, lightweight engraver. In our research of the American cut glass industry this is the first mention of a factory employing women as cut glass artists. Blanks for cutting were supplied by the parent company from Chicago, Illinois.

After World War I, Frank Lesch opened his own cutting shop, the Frank Lesch Company, at the corner of Brown and Franklin Streets in Valparaiso.

Fruit bowl designed and cut by Frank W. Lesch at his shop in Valparaiso, Ind., *ca.* 1920; diameter 8 in.; height 3½ in.

He employed Charles H. Gilliland and Byron Soliday. The factory burned down on January 23, 1927, with a loss of about $3,000. Lesch continued in the business, renting a small shop on Lincolnway in the downtown section of Valparaiso, with Charles Gilliland as his only employee. This shop finally closed about 1930.

Chade Monogram Glass Company

Charles H. Gilliland opened a cutting shop, the Chade Monogram Glass Company, at 455 Locust Street in Valparaiso, and operated it from 1930 to 1940 as a part-time hobby and vocation. He employed Robert Moe as a salesman. After 1940, Gilliland moved the shop into his home and continued making some cut glass as a hobby; his health forced him to give up the business entirely. Gilliland was a fine artist and designed many beautiful and unusual patterns. He was once chief of police of Valparaiso.

Cut Glass Manufacturers in Michigan

Osborne, Boynton & Osborne
H. F. Osborne Company

The firm of Osborne, Boynton & Osborne, of Detroit, Michigan, were listed as manufacturers of cut glass in some issues of the *American Glass Trade Directory*; however, this company did not actually cut glassware. In 1908 the city directories listed the concern as wholesale crockery and glassware distributors. At this time Archibald L. Osborne, Harvey F. Osborne, and George H. Boynton were the owners of the business, which was located in Detroit at 71–75 Jefferson Avenue. In 1914 the name of the firm changed slightly to Osborne, Boynton Company; Harvey F. Osborne, president; Charles Sinclair, secretary; and George H. Boynton, treasurer. In 1916, Fred J. Moultier was vice president and A. E. Schlieder, secretary and treasurer. In 1918 a major change took place within the company and it became known as the H. F. Osborne Company, with the same list of officers it had in 1916. Because of a reclassification of street numbers the address after 1921 was 316 West Jefferson. By 1938 the officers of the H. F. Osborne Company were Charles M. Osborne, president; Wendell H. Buck, vice president and treasurer; and Aaron D. Slaver, secretary.

Simms Modern Cut Glass Company
Crystal Mirror and Glass Company

The Detroit, Michigan, city directory for 1918 listed the Simms Modern Cut Glass Company, 120 Milwaukee Avenue East, with Joseph Simms, president; Oscar Peterson, vice president; and Alban C. Woodward, secretary. The firm advertised "cut and engraved tableware, trays, door-knobs and panels, beveling, miter, experimental and scientific work, lenses, designers and cutters of special work." Joseph Simms first appeared in the 1904 directory as a "glass cutter" living at 519 Baker Street in Detroit. In the 1927/28 directory Joseph A. Simms was listed as manager of the Crystal Mirror and Glass Company at 446 East Woodbridge, Detroit.

August Knez was president of the Crystal Mirror and Glass Company in 1928/29 with Oscar Peterson, vice president; and Joseph A. Simms (or Sims), secretary and treasurer. In 1935 the Crystal Mirror and Glass Company officers were Harold P. Ruble, president; Eldon Simms (or Sims), vice president; Joseph A. Simms (or Sims), secretary and treasurer. This was the last listing for Joseph Simms and the Crystal Mirror and Glass Company in the city directories.

Detroit Cut Glass Company

The Detroit Cut Glass Company was mentioned in the *American Glass Trade Directory* in 1918 as a manufacturer of cut glasswares, but a careful search of the Detroit city directories and the *Michigan Gazetteer and Business Directory* showed no listing for this concern. The cutting shop may have been a very small operation, and may also have had a very short business life.

Michigan Cut Glass Company

The Michigan Cut Glass Company was founded in Lansing, Michigan, about 1906. The officers of the firm were T. Rogers Lyons, president; Thomas Kinney, vice president; Herbert J. Flint, secretary-treasurer; and John J. Mauer, general manager. In 1908, Lyons was still president of the company, with F. H. Williams, vice president; Archibald M. Emory, secretary; and Warren F. Sullivan, treasurer.

The factory was located at 302 Mill Street from the time the business was established until its closing; offices and showrooms were located at 116 North Washington Avenue in Lansing. By 1910, Warren F. Sullivan had succeeded to the presidency of the firm and in 1911, Edgar J. Bush was managing the Michigan Cut Glass Company. The firm was dissolved in the latter part of 1911, when Bush established his own cut glass business in Lansing, the Bush Glass Company.

The Michigan Cut Glass Company produced a very fine line of heavy miter-cut glass, using imported lead crystal blanks. About the time the firm went out of business there came on the market the cheap lime glass blanks with patterns pressed into the glass. Competition from these cheaper wares forced the Michigan Cut Glass Company to close their doors.

Bush Glass Company
Bush Cut Glass Company
Lansing Cut Glass Works (Company)

Edgar J. Bush, formerly manager of the Michigan Cut Glass Company, started his own cut glassworks in Lansing, Michigan, at 312 Wall Street, in the latter part of 1911. Harris E. Thomas, a very successful attorney, was persuaded by Bush to join him in this business venture. Thomas was considered to be quite wealthy and was financially interested in many industrial firms in Lansing; he took no active part in the cut glass business. It was

Cut glass lamp made at the Bush Glass Co., *ca.* 1913.

Collection of Lynn A. Kosht

Bush's plan to produce cut glass from pressed and figured blanks, since these wares had found a large market in this country in the latter part of the cut glass era; the firm also produced a limited amount of fine cut glass made with imported lead crystal blanks.

In 1913, Bush was listed as the manager of the Bush Glass Company (Harris E. Thomas, owner). Bush was succeeded late in 1913 by Lynn A. Kosht, who told the author that Bush was in failing health at this time. In October, 1915, Kosht was succeeded by Thomas' brother-in-law, Fred Boosinger, as manager of the cut glass shop.

The Bush Glass Company was a small business employing about eight or ten cutters full time. The factory was in a basement, with one story above it of wooden construction, and had about 50 by 100 feet of floor space. The McKee Glass Company of Jeannette, Pennsylvania, supplied this firm with their pressed glass blanks.

Late in 1916 the Bush Glass Company discontinued the manufacture of cut glasswares. At this time the name of the firm was changed to the Lansing Cut Glass Works and the plant was moved to 500 East Michigan Avenue in Lansing. After this change they operated mainly as a retail outlet for glass and chinawares. In 1918, Albert J. Esselstyne succeeded Boosinger as manager of the company. The city directories for 1920 indicate that the Lansing Cut Glass Works were the distributors of "exclusive glassware and crockery." In 1921 the company was not listed in the directories and their address at 500 East Michigan Avenue was vacant.

The *American Glass Trade Directory* for 1918 listed the Buch [Bush] Cut Glass Company of Lansing, Michigan, and presumably Bush did carry on in the cut glass business; however, we could find no official record of this business in the Lansing directories for this period.

Cut Glass Manufacturers in Illinois

American Cut Glass Company

About 1897, William C. Anderson organized the American Cut Glass Company in Chicago, Illinois. Public records indicate that his shop was located at 300 West Jackson Boulevard. Before establishing his own cut glassworks, Anderson had been employed by the New England Glass Company, W. L. Libbey & Son, Proprietors, and continued with this firm when it reestablished itself in Toledo, Ohio, as the Libbey Glass Company. Anderson was foreman of Libbey's cutting department and patented several cut glass designs for the firm both before and after it moved from Cambridge, Massachusetts, to Toledo, Ohio. In 1899, Anderson was president and manager of the American Cut Glass Company; in this capacity he probably was responsible for most, if not all, of their cut glass designs.

Left: The "Fan Border" pattern; *right:* The "Star Rosetta" pattern; both patented May 18, 1897, by W. C. Anderson for American Cut Glass Co.

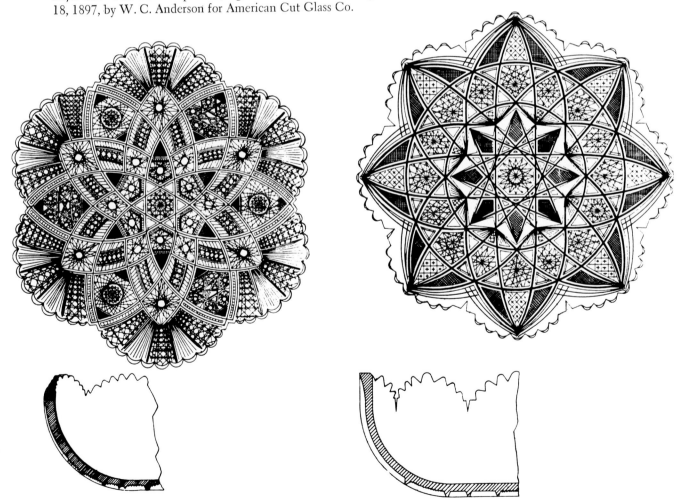

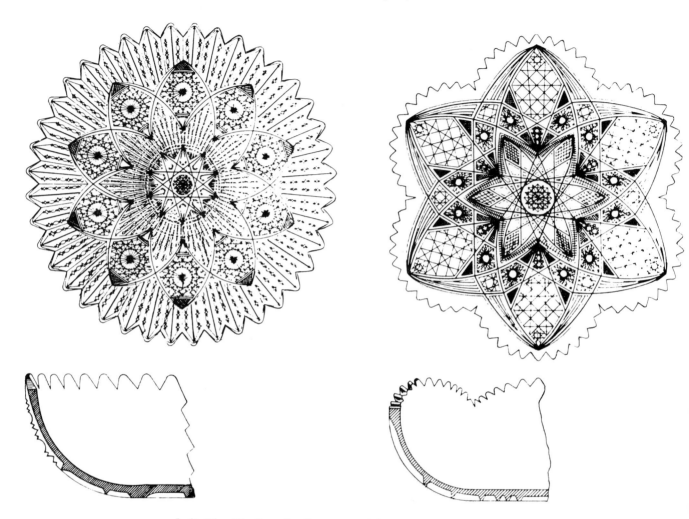

Left: The "Radiant Star" pattern; *right:* The "Kite" pattern; both patented May 18, 1897, by W. C. Anderson for American Cut Glass Co.

Soon after the turn of the century the American Cut Glass Company moved their factory to Lansing, Michigan, but they remained a corporation under the laws of the State of Illinois. In 1904, Anderson was still president and manager of the company, which was situated at 710 East Kalamazoo Street in Lansing. The last listing for Anderson and his wife Mary was dated 1914; at this time Patrick J. Healy served as vice president of the corporation. Healy later became president of the Capital Casting Company in Lansing. The American Cut Glass Company was listed in the *American Glass Trade Directory* as late as 1918, with offices in Chicago, Illinois (where they maintained showrooms to service the Midwestern market) and Lansing, Michigan. Thereafter we could find no trace of the company, and presumably they went out of business about 1920.

Several handsome cut glass designs were registered at the Patent Office by William C. Anderson and assigned to his firm, the American Cut Glass Com-

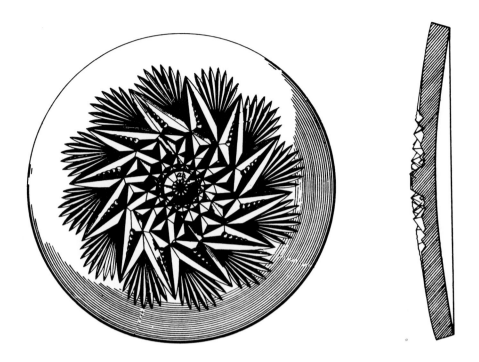

The "Pin Wheel" pattern; patented Feb. 28, 1899, by P. H. Healy for American Cut Glass Co.

pany. Four patterns in the traditional style of the Brilliant Period were patented on May 18, 1897. The first design consisted of an arrangement of "fans decorated with prisms, prismatic studs, and checkering." This design we have named "Fan Border." The second design consisted of a "many-pointed star for a border and surrounded by an octagon, each point of the star having a checkering, etc." This design we have designated "Star Rosetta."

Left: The "Triumph" pattern; *right:* The "Lansing" pattern; both patented Jan. 19, 1904, by W. C. Anderson for American Cut Glass Co.

Left: The "Jewelled Star" pattern; patented Mar. 8, 1904; *right:* The "Mary" pattern; patented Apr. 5, 1904; both by W. C. Anderson for American Cut Glass Co.

Anderson's "Radiant Star" pattern consisted of a "ten-pointed star" in combination with simple prismatic cutting. The fourth pattern we have named "Kite" because of Anderson's reference to this design's "kite-shaped fields" in his patent specifications.

On February 28, 1899, Patrick H. Healy patented the American Cut Glass Company's version of the "Pin Wheel" pattern in cut glass. Healy described the design as being a "twelve-pointed star formed by twenty-four splits and grooves." The simplicity of Healy's design could indicate that it was used in connection with other cut glass motifs common to many of its contemporaries.

The first design patent issued to the firm after it had moved to Lansing, Michigan, was dated January 19, 1904; it was an elaborate pattern which we have named "Triumph," and was designed by William C. Anderson. On this same day Anderson registered another design; because we do not know its original name, we have called it "Lansing."

"Jewelled Star" is the name given to still another beautiful cut glass design patented by Anderson on March 8, 1904. On April 5, 1904, Anderson patented a design which we have named "Mary" in honor of his wife. The patent specifications covering the "Mary" pattern stated that the firm was located in Detroit, Michigan, at this time, but a careful check of public records in that city indicated this was in error. Later patents issued to the company all showed that they were located in Lansing, Michigan.

On March 26, 1907, Anderson registered a less complicated design for cut glass; we have called it "Amelia" to make identification of the pattern easier

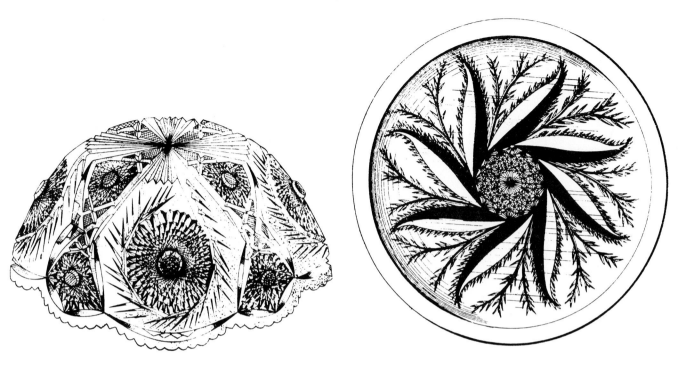

Left: The "Amelia" pattern; patented Mar. 26, 1907; *right:* The "Fern" pattern; patented May 30, 1911; both by W. C. Anderson for American Cut Glass Co.

for collectors. The last design patent issued to the American Cut Glass Company was registered by Anderson on May 30, 1911, and consisted of a pin-wheel effect formed of petallike swirls alternated with fernlike representations. This pattern we call "Fern."

Burley & Tyrrell Company

The Burley & Tyrrell Company was one of the largest wholesalers of glass and china in the Midwest from about 1870 to 1920. Its business was located in Chicago, Illinois, at 145–147 State Street in 1899, and at that time it was known as Burley & Company, with Frank E. Burley, president; Hugh Irvine, vice president and treasurer. In the same directory was listed Burley & Tyrrell, wholesale distributors of crockery, glass, and chinaware, 42–44 Lake Street; John Tyrrell, president and treasurer; M. A. Cheney, vice president; and Ferdinand P. Armbruster, secretary. From 1891 to 1897, the Burley & Tyrrell Company occupied quarters at 77–79 State Street and 145–147 State Street in Chicago. The *Book of Chicagoans* listed the firm of Burley & Tyrrell at 720 Wabash Avenue from 1905 to 1917; thereafter no listing for the company could be found. The building this concern occupied in its last years of business (720 Wabash Avenue) also housed some glass cutting shops and china decorating establishments which furnished Burley & Tyrrell with much of their fine stock. The company also imported wares to be sold to retail outlets throughout the country.

Koch & Parsche
Edward J. Koch & Company
Koch Cut Glass Company
Midland Cut Glass Company

Edward John Koch, a manufacturer of rich cut glass, was born in Chicago, Illinois, on August 27, 1861. In 1875, Koch began his business career in the employ of Burley & Tyrrell at a salary of $2.00 a week; in 1889 he became a traveling salesman for the Mt. Washington Glass Company of New Bedford, Massachusetts, at that time one of the leading manufacturers of cut glass in America. Koch remained with the New Bedford firm until 1898. On January 1, 1899, he established his own cut glass business under the style of Edward J. Koch & Company. In May, 1889, Koch married Pauline Meier, daughter of E. F. Meier, former president of the St. Louis (Missouri) City Council, and one of the most prominent queen's ware merchants in St. Louis.

The *Lakeside Directory* in 1899 listed Koch as president of Koch & Parsche, 40 State Street, Chicago. In 1907 this same source indicated that he was president of Edward J. Koch & Company, 40 and 42 State Street, Chicago. In 1912 the Koch Cut Glass Company appears in the *Lakeside Directory* for the first time, with Edward J. Koch, as president, and Arthur E. Meier, as secretary; this time their address was 182–184 North State Street, Chicago.

From 1912 to 1914 the Koch Cut Glass Company maintained a factory in Elgin, Illinois. The directories there listed Edward J. Koch, president; Thomas Singleton, manager; and a Mr. Miller, secretary (no name or initials for Miller were shown). During 1913/14 A. J. Meier was listed as secretary of the company. The 1918 issue of the *American Glass Trade Directory* listed the Koch Cut Glass Company of Chicago, Illinois, and indicated that their showrooms and sales offices were located there for the convenience of buyers.

In 1917, Edward J. Koch became president of the Midland Cut Glass Company of Chicago, Illinois. They had offices and showrooms at 115 East

Left: The "Hobstar and Wreath" pattern; patented May 20, 1902, by E. J. Koch. *Right:* The "Rose Window" pattern; patented May 3, 1910, by A. E. Meier for Edward J. Koch & Co.

South Water Street, in room 601. Koch's name appeared in the 1923 issue of the *Lakeside Directory* as a cut glass manufacturer operating at 1556 North Wells, Chicago. No closing date could be found for the firm, but we believe it ceased operating about 1926.

On May 20, 1902, Edward J. Koch registered his design for a cut glass pattern known as "Hobstar and Wreath"; the pattern has a striking resemblance to one patented on April 8, 1902, by F. C. Parsche, and consists of a wreath almost entirely enclosing a hobstar motif, together with a miter-cut representation between the branches of adjacent wreaths, the lower ends of the wreaths being enclosed by lines which surround a central figure.

Koch also registered a trade name "Koch-Kut" for his cut wares produced from pressed or figured blanks.

Arthur E. Meier patented a brilliant cut glass design for Edward J. Koch & Company on May 3, 1910. We have named this one "Rose Window" because of its resemblance to the stained glass windows found in medieval European cathedrals. The design consists of consecutive circles of brilliant hobstar motifs interspersed with kite-shaped representations.

F. X. Parsche & Son Company

Frank (Franz) X. Parsche was born in Meisterdorf, Bohemia, in 1847. When he was twelve years old, he started a five-year apprenticeship as a copper wheel engraver. At the age of eighteen he left Bohemia and went to Edinburgh, Scotland, where he worked for the Edinburgh and Leith Glass Company. Parsche was a specialist in engraving figures, faces, and armorial designs and received much royal patronage. He left Scotland in 1873 for New York City and worked for a time in a cutting shop in Brooklyn. In 1874 he answered an advertisement placed in a New York City newspaper by Burley & Tyrrell of Chicago for a top engraver of glass; Parsche worked for them for two years before opening his own cutting shop in Chicago in the Krantz Building on State Street in 1876; that same year his son Frank C. Parsche was born, and at the age of fourteen he joined his father in the glass business.

Chicago's *Lakeside Directory* for 1891 listed Frank X. Parsche and Frank C. Parsche as glass engravers living at 1819 Briar Place and having their business at 40 State Street. They started to manufacture heavy cut glasswares in 1892, all of which was hand polished in the traditional way. In 1893, Parsche had a booth at the World's Columbian Exposition in Chicago, where they sold engraved glass and solicited orders for special designs.

Edward J. Koch joined the Parsche firm in 1893 and formed a cut glass business known as Koch & Parsche. During this time all their blanks were obtained from the Mt. Washington Glass Company (later Pairpoint). When the Thatcher Brothers developed one of the first successful acid-polishing methods for cut glass, about 1894, the hand-polishing technique was abandoned and the new acid-polishing method adopted by Koch & Parsche. Between 1895 and 1905 the concern experienced a rapid growth and moved to four different locations in Chicago; the last was at 524–528 Orleans Street. Koch took over the premises at 40 State Street when he established his own cut glass company in 1907.

In 1907 the firm appears in the records as F. X. Parsche & Son Company, manufacturers of cut glass, located at 524–528 Orleans Street in Chicago. The 1912 issue of Chicago's *Lakeside Directory* revealed that they were "cut glass and china decorators" and that they had moved their business to 1432–1434 Orleans Street. The firm was listed in the *American Glass Trade Directory* as late as 1918. In 1918 the company moved to smaller quarters at 3511 North Clark Street; their last move occurred in 1944, when they located at 3374 North Clark Street, a site they still occupy, although they no longer produce cut glass of any kind. The Parsche Studios presently specializes in grinding chipped stemware, cut glass, and so forth; they also do custom lamps to order. Frank X. Parsche died in 1929; his son, now eighty-eight years old, and his grandson, Donald C. Parsche, still operated the business in 1964.

414

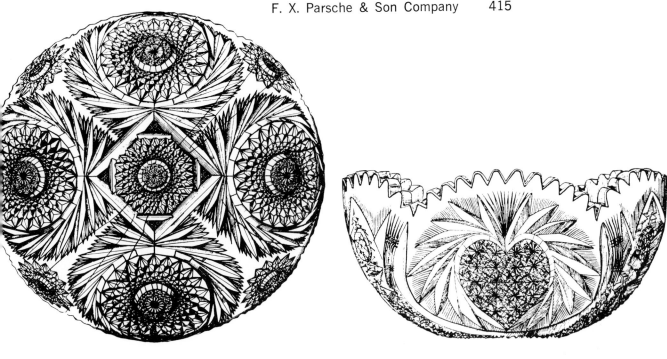

Left: The "Pinwheel" pattern; patented Apr. 8, 1902; *right:* The "Heart" pattern; patented May 14, 1907; both by F. C. Parsche.

Most of the cut glass produced by the Parsche company was manufactured between 1900 and 1918. Besides the usual tablewares and decorative pieces, they also manufactured cut glass bar bottles, and various special designs were made for certain distillers. Frank X. Parsche designed the original Chapin & Gore monogram. Many thousands of bottles were made for the Sunny Brook distillers. Ornate mirrors and decorated china in fairly large amounts were also produced at the Parsche shop. Between 1918 and 1932, cut crystal stemware was the company's biggest seller, but after 1932 this business fell off greatly and they "darn near starved," according to Donald C. Parsche. The last stemware was cut by this concern about 1952.

During the Brilliant Period, cut glass blanks were obtained from several sources—the Pairpoint Corporation, the Union Glass Works, the Steuben Glass Company, the H. C. Fry Glass Company, and from Baccarrat and St. Louis in France, and the Val St. Lambert glassworks in Belgium.

Frank C. Parsche patented two cut glass designs; the first one is dated April 8, 1902, and has been verified as being produced by F. X. Parsche & Son Company; it was called the "Pinwheel" pattern and consisted of a large rosette enclosed in a wreath formed by crossed sheaves or feathers. Parsche's second design, which he called the "Heart" pattern, was patented on May 14, 1907. It consisted of a brilliantly cut heart-shaped motif surrounded by a wreath; in between the heart and wreath designs are beautifully cut rosettes and buttons. Parsche's "Heart" pattern has affinities to designs patented by

Pitkin & Brooks (1907), and M. E. Scheck (1907), both Chicago cut glass manufacturers, and to the "Thistle" pattern produced by the Buffalo Cut Glass Company of Batavia, New York.

Pitkin & Brooks

On January 1, 1872, Edward Hand Pitkin went into the glass and china business in Chicago, Illinois; one month later, on February 1, 1872, he was joined by Jonathan Williams Brooks, Jr., and together they formed a whole-sale glass and china business known as Pitkin & Brooks. The firm was incorporated in 1891; their offices and showrooms were located in Chicago at 56–62 Lake Street. Brooks was president of the firm from 1891 to 1901, and vice president from 1902 until his death in 1910. In 1897, Edward Pitkin was listed in Chicago's *Lakeside Directory* as vice president of Pitkin & Brooks; from 1902 until 1918 he served as president of the corporation. Ralph E. Smith appears as secretary and treasurer of Pitkin & Brooks in the 1899

Left: The "Rosette and Buzz Star" pattern; patented July 17, 1900, by W. H. Shanley; *right*: The "Heart and Hob Star" pattern; patented Jan. 22, 1907, by H. H. Buckley; both for Pitkin & Brooks.

listings of this firm in various business directories. At the turn of the century, Pitkin & Brooks were reputed to be one of the largest wholesale distributors of crockery, pottery lamps, and glassware in the Midwest. In 1905 the business was relocated at the corner of Lake and State Streets in Chicago. We could not determine a closing date for Pitkin & Brooks, but their name no longer appeared in the usual publications for china and glassware manufacturers and distributors after 1920.

Edward Hand Pitkin was born in Saratoga, New York, on June 9, 1846; he died in Chicago, Illinois, on April 24, 1918. He was the son of Joshua and Caroline (Hand) Pitkin. After receiving his education in the public schools in Cleveland, Ohio, and Chicago, Illinois, he served in the Civil War as a private in Company K, 132d Illinois Volunteers. In 1871, Pitkin married Lillie Elizabeth Morey and they had five children. Pitkin began his business career in the employ of Burley & Tyrrell as an office boy. Afterward, for two years, he was in the employ of Johnson & Abbey, until early in 1872, when with J. W. Brooks, he established Pitkin & Brooks. In 1905 the *Book of Chicagoans* listed Pitkin as president of the Chicago Flint & Lime Glass Company of Chesterton, Indiana.

Jonathan Williams Brooks, Jr. was born in Norwich, Connecticut, on September 6, 1847, the son of Jonathan Williams, Sr. and Delia A. (Cary) Brooks. He was educated at Farmer's College, College Hill, Ohio, and was married in Chicago, Illinois, on August 12, 1876, to Mary L. Raymond. The Brookses had seven children. Brooks began his business career on May 8, 1864, in the china and glassware business; in 1872 he and Edward Pitkin founded their business. Brooks died in 1910.

Left: The "Korea" pattern; *right:* The "Wild Daisy" pattern; both patented Oct. 21, 1913, by W. P. Feeney for Pitkin & Brooks.

Conserve dish in the "Phena Star" pattern; cut by W. P. Feeney for Pitkin & Brooks; design patented Feb. 3, 1914; diameter 7½ in.
Collection of Wayne County Historical Society

William H. Shanley of Chicago, Illinois, registered a cut glass design on July 17, 1900, and assigned it to Pitkin & Brooks. Shanley's design combines two popular cut designs of the Brilliant Period—the "Rosette" and "Buzz Star." Ralph E. Smith and Frank L. Pitkin signed Shanley's patent papers as witnesses.

On January 22, 1907, Harry H. Buckley, a manufacturer's agent in Chicago, registered a design for cut glass and assigned it to Pitkin & Brooks. Buckley's "Heart and Hob Star" pattern is very similar to a cut glass design patented by M. E. Scheck and F. X. Parsche & Son Company of Chicago, and the Buffalo Cut Glass Company's "Thistle" pattern.

Pitkin & Brooks maintained a cutting shop in Bowling Green, Ohio, under the name of the Ohio Cut Glass Company. Before the factory burned down in 1912, William P. Feeney was its manager.

Shortly after Pitkin & Brooks opened their cut glass factory in Valparaiso, Indiana, William P. Feeney patented three designs for them. The first two patents are dated October 21, 1913; we have named them "Korea" and "Wild Daisy." The "Phena Star" pattern was registered by Feeney on February 3, 1914; he presented the Wayne County Historical Society of Honesdale, Pennsylvania, with a small conserve dish in this design. Feeney's three designs are so simple as to suggest that they may have been used in combination with other cut glass patterns.

Some of Pitkin & Brooks cut glass articles bear their trademark, the letters "P & B" within a diamond-shaped enclosure. In one collection we came across two celery trays of identical cut design; one was marked with the Pitkin & Brooks trademark, the other was signed "Fry." Since there was nothing unusual about the pattern, we believe no patent or copyright privileges were involved in this instance. Obviously one copied from the other; or one company supplied both dishes, each with a different trademark.

Roseen Brothers Cut Glass Company
Central Cut Glass Company
Roseen & Collins

Herman Theodore Roseen and his brother Joseph established Roseen Brothers Cut Glass Company in Chicago, Illinois, in 1904; they sold out to the United States Cut Glass Company in 1905.

In 1906, Herman T. Roseen and Andrew Swanson founded the Central Cut Glass Company in Chicago, employing about five cutters. By 1916 their business had increased steadily and they were operating 200 frames in their cut glass factory. The firm was listed in several business directories as one of the largest manufacturers of cut glass in America. The factory was located at 3479 North Clark Street and they maintained showrooms in room 511 at 29 East Madison. Herman Roseen was listed as president of the concern from 1917 to 1925; he was also a director of the Output Company of America, of Chicago, Illinois. On August 17, 1915, Roseen patented a dipping device for polishing several pieces of cut glass in an acid solution at one operation. Herman Roseen came to the United States from Sweden in 1898 and became a naturalized citizen in 1903.

About 1925 the firm's name was changed to Roseen & Collins. Until this time they had manufactured only heavy cut glass; thereafter they produced light cut wares and fine rock crystal glassware. The company closed in 1932.

Output Company of America

The Output Company of America, Chicago, Illinois, was listed in the *American Glass Trade Directory* in 1918 as a manufacturer of fine cut glassware. No recording of the firm appeared in any of the public records from 1914 through 1923; but the *Book of Chicagoans* for 1917 indicated that Herman T. Roseen was a director of this concern (he was also associated with Roseen Brothers Cut Glass Company and the Central Cut Glass Company). Roseen's association with this company could indicate that it might have handled wares produced by other cut glass manufacturers.

M. E. Scheck & Company

Max E. Scheck of Chicago, Illinois, operated a small cut glass shop in his home at 911 West 21st Street in 1907. In 1908, M. E. Scheck & Company was listed in the *Lakeside Directory* as cut glass manufacturers; at this time Scheck was associated with Gustave Erickson, and the business was located at 315 Englewood Avenue. Aside from the listings found in the *Lakeside Directory* for 1907/08 as a cut glass manufacturer, we could find no further mention of them in the trade and business directories for this period. Mrs. Scheck ran a millinery business in their home at the same time.

The "Butterfly and Heart" pattern; patented Dec. 3, 1907, by M. E. Scheck.

On December 3, 1907, Scheck registered a design patent for cut glass. The design consisted of a heart-shaped motif surrounded by a feathery wreath in combination with a brilliantly cut stylized butterfly, as is shown in the patent drawing. Scheck's cut glass design resembles somewhat the heart designs patented by Pitkin & Brooks, F. X. Parsche & Son Company, and the "Thistle" pattern produced by the Buffalo Cut Glass Company. We have dubbed Scheck's design the "Butterfly and Heart" pattern.

420

Monarch Cut Glass Company
Heinz Brothers

The Monarch Cut Glass Company was a partnership organized in 1901 by Richard, Emil, and Otto Heinz, and Herman and Frank Kotwitz. Their factory was located in Chicago, Illinois, at the corner of Union Street and Carroll Avenue. In 1902 the Heinz brothers bought out the Kotwitz brothers and operated the business in Chicago as Heinz Brothers. The firm was incorporated for $50,000. Richard Heinz was president; Otto Heinz, vice president and sales manager; Emil Heinz, secretary and treasurer; and Herman Schmidt and Herman Eichman plant foremen.

In 1905 they built a factory at 13th Street and Indiana Avenue in St. Charles, Illinois, and commenced operations in August of that year. Heinz

"Imperial" bowl, diameter 8 in.; "Feathered Star" sugar and cream set, height 2⅝ in.
Collection of Otto W. Heinz

Brothers were considered one of the largest cut glass manufacturers in the Midwest, their trade extending over the United States, Canada, and parts of Europe. Salesrooms were maintained at St. Charles and Chicago; Spokane, Washington; Helena, Montana; Memphis, Tennessee; San Francisco, California; Berlin, Germany; and St. Petersburg, Russia.

There were 100 frames operating in the Heinz Brothers factory and the most modern machinery then known to the craft was used by their artist-engravers. An average of from 80 to 100 persons were employed, about one tenth of whom were women; the women were wrappers and examiners of the glass.

Most of the cutters came from other cut glass shops around the country, but there were many St. Charlesans to whom the Heinz Brothers taught the craft working in their factory. More than 600 different articles in cut glass were made by the Heinz plant. There was nothing in cut glass tableware that could not be made at this factory. The yearly volume of business reached $90,000 to $100,000, with a payroll amounting to $40,000, a high rate for business earnings and for wages in 1905. Emil Heinz was in charge of the factory; Otto Heinz managed the company's sales offices; and Richard Heinz acted as the firm's executive head.

The Heinz brothers were associated with the cut glass industry most of their lives. All were employed with Pitkin & Brooks and the American Cut Glass Company for many years before going into the business for themselves.

In 1908, Richard Heinz passed away and Otto Heinz became president of the concern. Emil Heinz was vice president; Herman Schmidt, secretary and treasurer; and Herman Eichman plant superintendent. The factory was operated until 1927, when the real estate was sold and the corporation dissolved.

Illustration of a Heinz Bros. cut glass pitcher from a newspaper advertisement; *ca.* 1905.

One illustration of this firm's extensive production was taken from an old newspaper advertisement. The designs cut on this handsome pitcher are typical motifs of the Brilliant Period in cut glass. The other pieces illustrated are from the collection of Otto Heinz.

C. E. Wheelock & Company of Peoria, Illinois, were distributors of the cut glasswares produced by the Heinz Brothers; consequently, some of their wares may be found bearing Wheelock's trademark label "Radiant Crystal." Otto Heinz confirmed that the C. E. Wheelock Company was one of their customers, but they did not sell Heinz wares exclusively. No labels or trademarks of any kind were used by the Heinz Brothers factory to identify their cut glass—an unhappy circumstance that makes it almost impossible for collectors to identify their glass.

United States Cut Glass Company

In 1905 the United States Cut Glass Company purchased the Roseen Brothers Cut Glass Company of Chicago, Illinois. The 1908 trade directories listed this concern at 315 Englewood Avenue in Chicago, with Albert L. White as president. By 1912 the United States Cut Glass Company had relocated their offices at 2219 South Halstead, Chicago, and was under the direction of Herman E. Kotwitz. In 1914, Kotwitz continued in the cut glass business at the South Halstead Street location under the name of the Western Cut Glass Company. Kotwitz was formerly associated with the Heinz brothers in the Monarch Cut Glass Company from 1901 to 1902. No mention of the United States Cut Glass Company was found in the business recordings after 1912/13, and it was at this time that Kotwitz took over the firm and changed its name to the Western Cut Glass Company about 1914.

Western Cut Glass Company

About 1914, Herman and Frank Kotwitz, and Herman Kotwitz' brother-in-law Harry Baumann, organized the Western Cut Glass Company of Chicago, Illinois; the firm had previously been known as the United States Cut Glass Company. Herman Kotwitz had been in the cut glass business as early as

1901. He was once associated with the Heinz brothers in the Monarch Cut Glass Company. In 1902 the Heinz brothers bought out Herman and Frank Kotwitz' interest in the Monarch Cut Glass Company; at this time the Kotwitz brothers operated their own cut glass shop in Chicago on Jackson Boulevard. Later Herman and Frank Kotwitz moved to the Burley & Tyrrell Building at 2219–2239 South Halstead, corner of 20th Street, in Chicago. It was at this location that Kotwitz became affiliated with the United States Cut Glass Company, about 1912. By 1914 he had established the Western Cut Glass Company, remaining in the same location in the Burley & Tyrrell Building.

Herman Kotwitz was not a practical glass cutter but his daughter, Mrs. Lillian Kotwitz Stehlin, remembered that he knew enough about the trade to instruct others in both the cutting and polishing processes. He also did most of the acid polishing himself, because he did not wish to subject any of his employees to the dangers encountered in this operation. As his business increased, he had to delegate this job to others, but for years he worked to perfect the acid formula that suited his purposes best. Most of the Western Cut Glass Company's designs were created by Herman Kotwitz himself.

The showrooms of the Western Cut Glass Company were hung with dark velvet drapery and hangings, and the ceiling was painted a dull black to focus the buyer's attention on the cut glasswares. The company produced both heavy and light cut glass at this time, and much of it was sold to Marshall Field & Company in Chicago. Two of their most popular designs in the light wares were a sunburst pattern, which was repeated three times on the article, and a pattern of grapes and leaves, the grapes in a gray (mat) finish, with leaves and tendrils in bright cutting. Imitations of Kotwitz' grape pattern appeared on the market soon after it was introduced, much to his chagrin;

Left: Heart-shaped cut glass dish presented to Anna Baumann as an engagement gift by Herman Kotwitz. *Right:* Fluted trefoil-shaped bowl; diameter 9½ in.; Western Cut Glass Co.

Collection of Mrs. Lillian Kotwitz Stehlin

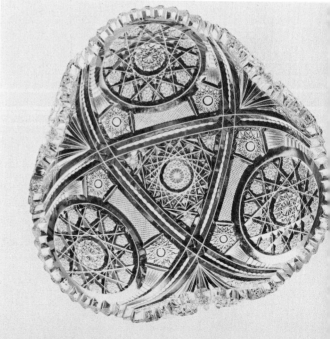

Footed bowl in late floral design, diameter 12¼ in.; relish dish, length 13 in.; Western Cut Glass Co.

Collection of Mrs. Lillian Kotwitz Stehlin

he was concerned that some of these inferior imitations might be attributed to his company.

Several pieces of cut glass made by Kotwitz' company are owned by his daughter, Lillian K. Stehlin. A small heart-shaped dish which she cherishes was presented to her mother by Herman Kotwitz the day he proposed marriage, saying, "With this dish I give you my heart." When the children were growing up, Kotwitz gave each of his daughters a small heart-shaped pendant of brilliantly cut crystal dangling from a long chain. Mrs. Stehlin still treasures this memento of her father's work. Other pieces of cut glass made by the Kotwitz shop are shown in our illustrations.

The Western Cut Glass Company went out of business about 1918, the year Kotwitz retired from business life.

Hermann Eduard Kottwitz was born on April 10, 1874, in Zezenow, Pomerania, Germany. At the age of fourteen he came to America, and on April 19, 1897, he became a naturalized citizen; at the same time he Americanized his name to Herman Edward Kotwitz. As a young man, Kotwitz worked days and went to school at night at a college in Chicago. He followed this program for a number of years. Kotwitz married Anna Baumann in Chicago, Illinois, on October 28, 1903, and they had seven children, four of whom were living in 1964. Herman Kotwitz died on May 15, 1936, at Wauwatosa, Wisconsin.

H. H. Buckley

The *Lakeside Directory* for 1912 listed Harry H. Buckley, 6th floor, 542 West Jackson Boulevard, Chicago, Illinois, as a manufacturer of cut glass. He was, in fact, only an agent for cut glass factories in the Midwest. In 1907, Buckley patented a cut glass design for Pitkin & Brooks of Chicago, and in 1913 he registered some designs for cut glassware in the name of the H. C. Fry Glass Company of Rochester, Pennsylvania.

Chicago Cut Glass Company

The *American Glass Trade Directory* included the Chicago Cut Glass Company in its list of cut glass manufacturers for the year 1918. The firm also had a membership in the National Association of Cut Glass Manufacturers, yet nothing concerning the Chicago Cut Glass Company could be found in the business listings and recordings in Chicago, Illinois. Quite obviously this was a small concern and may not have been in existence for more than a year or two at the most.

Crystal Cut Glass Company

The glass industry's directories from 1893 to 1905 listed the Crystal Cut Glass Company of Chicago, Illinois, but a careful search of the business records in Chicago from 1893 to 1907 failed to show any evidence that such a company existed in that city during that period. They were not listed as members of the National Association of Cut Glass Manufacturers.

Empire Cut Glass Company

The *Lakeside Directory* for 1912 listed Frank B. Tinker as manager of the Empire Cut Glass Company of Chicago, Illinois, with showrooms at 28 East Madison Street, room 806. This was also the showroom for the Rochester Cut Glass Company at that time, so we can assume that Tinker was simply the sales representative for these two cut glass factories. No indication of the firm's factory location could be found in any of the existing public records. In 1914 this same location was occupied by the Cut Glass Products Company under a new manager.

Cut Glass Products Company

The Cut Glass Products Company maintained a showroom in room 806, at 28 East Madison Street, Chicago, Illinois. (In 1912 these same quarters were occupied by the Empire Cut Glass Company.) Frank E. Davis was listed as secretary of the Cut Glass Products Company. In 1918 the company's existence is reaffirmed by a listing in the *American Glass Trade Directory*. The concern's name leads us to believe that it served as a wholesale outlet for several small cut glass factories operating in and around the Chicago area.

Englewood Cut Glass Company

In 1917, Victor Gustavson's name appeared as a cut glass manufacturer in the Chicago, Illinois, *Lakeside Directory*. The Englewood Cut Glass Company was listed in the 1918 issue of the *American Glass Trade Directory*; and in 1923 it was again noted in the *Lakeside Directory* in connection with Gustavson's name. At this time the business address was given as 6355 South Halstead Street, Chicago, Illinois.

Golden & Jacobson
Golden Novelty Manufacturing Company

On August 15, 1911, Charles D. Golden, president of the Golden Novelty Manufacturing Company of 126 North Union Avenue, Chicago, Illinois, patented a design for a cut glass lamp. We have named this pattern "Scarab." In this case only the shade of the lamp is made of cut crystal, and its form is such that it probably has often been mistaken for a cut glass bowl.

The Golden Novelty Manufacturing Company was originally known, in 1895, as Golden & Jacobson; the change in the firm's name occurred in 1897. Golden's company was not a manufacturer of cut glass, for the *Lakeside Directory* listed them for several years as wholesale and retail purveyors of clocks and silverware, as well as of glass and china goods.

The "Scarab" pattern; patented Aug. 15, 1911, by C. D. Golden.

Johnson-Carlson Cut Glass Company

Oscar W. Johnson came to the United States from Sweden in 1892 and was employed for five years by the Johnson Chair Manufacturing Company of Chicago, Illinois. Later he learned to cut glass and he worked in this trade until 1906. In that year he and John Carlson established the Johnson-Carlson Cut Glass Company, with offices at 81 Illinois Street in Chicago. Johnson was president and treasurer of the company. He was joined in this business venture by his brother Turry Johnson, and John Carlson's brother Gustave S. Carlson.

The Johnson-Carlson Cut Glass Company established the Twin City Cut Glass Company of Minneapolis, Minnesota, in 1908, and the Warsaw Cut Glass Company of Warsaw, Indiana, in 1911. They were members of the National Association of Cut Glass Manufacturers and the Glass, Pottery, and Lamp Association. The company was operating as late at 1932, but no record of its closing date could be found.

Richard Murr

On June 26, 1906, Richard Murr, 18 Sutter Street, San Francisco, California, was issued a trademark for "cut glass" which consisted of the word "Koh-i-noor," after the famous diamond in the British crown jewels collection. The

The "Christmas Bell" pattern; patented Feb. 11, 1908, by R. Murr.

papers stated that this trade name had been used by Murr since July 1, 1905, and this may well be a close approximation of the date that his business was established. We could not determine from available records in San Francisco whether Murr manufactured his own cut glass, or simply sold such wares produced by other companies.

About 1907, Murr moved his business to Chicago, Illinois, maintaining showrooms at 56 Fifth Avenue, room 308. "Richard Murr, Glassware" appears in the 1908 issue of the *Lakeside Directory* at the aforementioned address. In 1928, Murr is again listed in the directories; this time as a "Mercantile Consultant," with offices at 332 South Michigan Avenue, Chicago. At that time he was no longer in the cut glass business.

On February 11, 1908, Richard Murr registered a design patent for a cut glass bowl in his "Christmas Bell" pattern. The design consists of a bell-shaped motif surmounted and partially surrounded by a feathery wreath, as is shown in the patent illustration.

Northwestern-Ohio Cut Glass Company

Apparently the Northwestern-Ohio Cut Glass Company maintained only sales offices and a showroom in Chicago, Illinois, at 169 Wabash, 5th floor, for we could find nothing at all beyond this fact to establish them in the trade. Their Chicago agent was Frank H. Challen.

Mills, Gardner & Company

The firm of Mills, Gardner & Company leased and operated the Heinz Brothers cut glass factory in St. Charles, Illinois, from 1913 to 1915, when they ceased operations; it was then taken over again and operated by the Heinz brothers. Otto Heinz, in later years, could not remember the Christian names of either Mills or Gardner.

In the 1918 edition of the *American Glass Trade Directory*, Mills, Gardner & Company were listed as operating in Chicago, Illinois, but no evidence of their business activities could be found in Chicago city directories. They may have maintained only showrooms in Chicago, which could account for the lack of documentation on this firm.

C. E. Wheelock & Company

C. E. Wheelock & Company of Peoria, Illinois, were wholesale and retail distributors of china, glass, and pottery wares for many years. In 1893 the firm was listed as an agent for the Libbey Glass Company's cut glass products in a small brochure which Libbey distributed during the World's Columbian Exposition in 1893. Wheelock purchased some of their cut glass from the Heinz Brothers' factory in St. Charles, Illinois, but this was not their only source of supply. On May 30, 1915, the Wheelock company was issued a trademark consisting of a representation of a padlock on which their name and the legend "Radiant Crystal—Rich Cut Glass Since 1898" were shown. Paper labels with this identifying emblem were pasted on each piece of cut glass sold by them since August 1, 1898. At the time the trademark was assigned to C. E. Wheelock & Company, they were trading at 214–216 South Adams Street, Peoria, Illinois. The specifications stated that the mark was applied to "cut glass of every description—namely, dishes, plates, pitchers, drinking-glasses, bowls, jugs, jars, flower-holders, and vases." As of 1964 the company was still in business, but no member of the Wheelock family was then connected with the firm.

Libbey's list of their agents included George H. Wheelock & Company of Elkhart and South Bend, Indiana; W. G. Wheelock of Janesville, Wisconsin; and A. W. Wheelock of Rockford, Illinois. In 1893 all the aforementioned firms handled Libbey's cut glass exclusively.

Paul Richter Company

On January 7, 1914, corporation papers were issued to the Paul Richter Company of Maywood, Illinois, the stockholders being Paul Richter, A. E. Winterroth, and Harry Bucholtz. The factory was located at 619 South 10th Avenue, corner of Washington Boulevard. In November, 1913, Fred Rau became a stockholder in the firm with Richter, Winterroth, and Bucholtz. On April 22, 1920, their capital stock was increased from $25,000 to $75,000, indicating a sharp rise in their trade; the following month they enlarged their business activities to include the sale of "pottery, potteryware, and the purchase and sale of general merchandise connected with a general mercantile business," again indicating a further increase in business.

On October 26, 1939, the sheriff of Maywood received an order from the

431

Collection of Mrs. Julian Schoffin
Fruit bowl in the "Maywood" pattern; diameter
10 in.; Paul Richter Co.

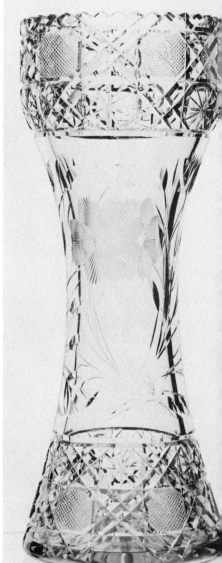

Vase in the "Flower and Harvard" pattern;
height 15 in.; Paul Richter Co.
Collection of Mrs. Julian Schoffin

Secretary of State in Springfield, Illinois, to collect the company's back taxes,
plus penalties. The corporation was officially dissolved by order of the Secretary of State on May 22, 1940.

Throughout the life of the company Richter was president. The Maywood
directories for the years 1926/27, and 1930/31, list Walter Davis as vice
president and Martin Warnecke as secretary. The dissolution papers show
that in 1940, Edward Rudolph was secretary of the company.

Paul Richter was American born. He married Lillian Bucholtz, but had no
children. One brother, Max Richter, worked for the cut glass factory. The
family, including his sister and mother, all lived side by side in one block
owned by the Richter family. One of Paul Richter's strongest supporters was
his mother. Mrs. Richter was active in the business affairs of the factory and
whenever she visited outside Maywood, she endeavored to find outlets for
her son's cut glasswares.

The Richter factory employed between 30 and 35 workers under the direction of Fred Rau, foreman. Raw blanks were purchased from the Libbey-

Basket in the "Floral" pattern;
height 12 in.; Paul Richter Co.
Collection of Mrs. Julian Schoffin

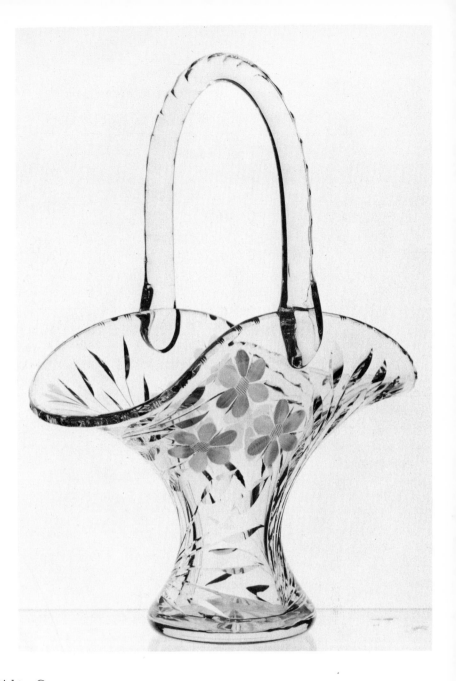

Cream and sugar set; 4 in. tall; Paul Richter Co.

Collection of Mrs. Julian Schoffin

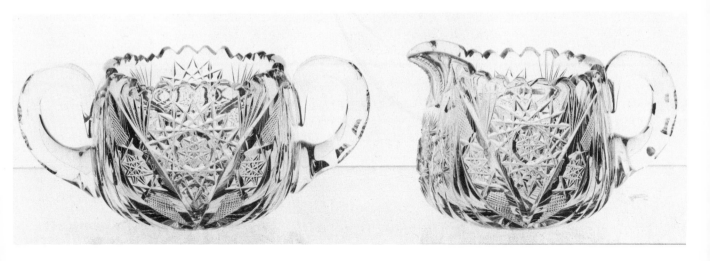

Owens Company in Toledo, Ohio. With the help of Julian (Joe) Schoffin (Edward Rudolph's brother-in-law), Richter perfected an acid bath formula which was one of the company's closely guarded secrets. Besides attending the showrooms in the front of the factory building, Mrs. Julian (Amelia) Schoffin gave the cut glass its final inspection. She recalled that only the best products left the factory; seconds were sold to residents of Maywood village. When the building occupied by the Richter cutting shop was taken over by Gordon Willey for his bicycle accessories shop, many barrels of uncut glass were found stored in the basement and were subsequently discarded.

The cut glass designs were created by Lewis Voss, Julian Schoffin, and Paul Richter himself. One of Schoffin's designs, the "Floral" pattern, consisted of a frosted four-petaled flower on a long stem, with lacey, reedlike leaves. Richter created the "Maywood" pattern, a design of large rosettes about two inches across in diameter. The quality of Richter's cut glass was excellent, according to Mrs. Schoffin, and it went under the trade name "Maywood Cut." Many pieces of Richter cut glass can be found in Maywood village homes today.

A Cut Glass Manufacturer in Wisconsin

The Kayser Glassware Company

Only one cut glass company was listed in Wisconsin. The Kayser Glassware Company of Milwaukee, Wisconsin, was listed in the *American Glass Trade Directory* in 1918, but an exhaustive search of the business and trade directories in that city failed to turn up even a trace of this concern. The firm was not even found on Milwaukee tax rolls in 1918.

*Cut Glass
Manufacturers
in Missouri*

The Missouri Glass Company
Vall, Clark & Cowen
Art Manufacturing Company

The Missouri Glass Company works were first established in St. Louis, Missouri, in 1850, by Henry T. Blow, John W. Farrell, and a Mr. Barksdale. The company was known as the St. Louis Glass Works, manufacturers of window glass. In 1854, James and Samuel Wallace, experienced glassmakers, took over the defunct St. Louis Glass Works and changed the name of the concern to the Mound City Glass Works. They manufactured green glass for common medicine bottles and a high-grade flint glass for blown tablewares. In 1859 the Mound City Glass Works was reorganized as the Missouri Glass Company, and the Wallaces took in as partners Edward Bredell, Jr., Edward Daly, and a man named Chadwick. In 1860 the company exhibited glass syrup bottles, shades, clock shades (domes), pressed and cut glass tumblers, cut goblets, gas shades, and cut glass decanters of the "most exquisite patterns." Stoppered green glass bottles for tinctures and many other such wares were also shown in their stall.

An article in the magazine *Antiques*, in August, 1943, written by Charles Van Ravenswaay, formerly director of the Missouri Historical Society in St. Louis, Missouri, stated that the firm, though it had made impressive showings, had not been successful, and that in 1863 it was finally reorganized by two men from New England, Messrs. LaSalle and Cate, under the style of Cate, LaSalle & Company. Cate and LaSalle, with some other glassmakers from the New England area, reorganized and operated the works under the name of Barry, LaSalle & Company, only to have it fail again about 1865 or 1866.

Our own research has revealed that, contrary to Van Ravenswaay's report, there is an unbroken record of the Missouri Glass Company in the St. Louis city directories from 1859 to 1911. There was reorganization of the firm from time to time, and the business also changed its address, but throughout this period—1859 to 1911—the Missouri Glass Company maintained its identity intact.

In 1868, Edward Bredell was listed as president of the firm. The company had moved to Market Street shortly after 1860. In 1870, William Somerville (or Sommerville) became president and Allen Trail was secretary. Somerville continued as president through 1900, when they moved to Olive Street, S.E., corner of 12th Street, in St. Louis. From 1901 to 1902, Stephen O. Gore was listed as president of the Missouri Glass Company. The firm moved to 801 Washington Avenue in 1906, and remained there through 1910. In 1911 the

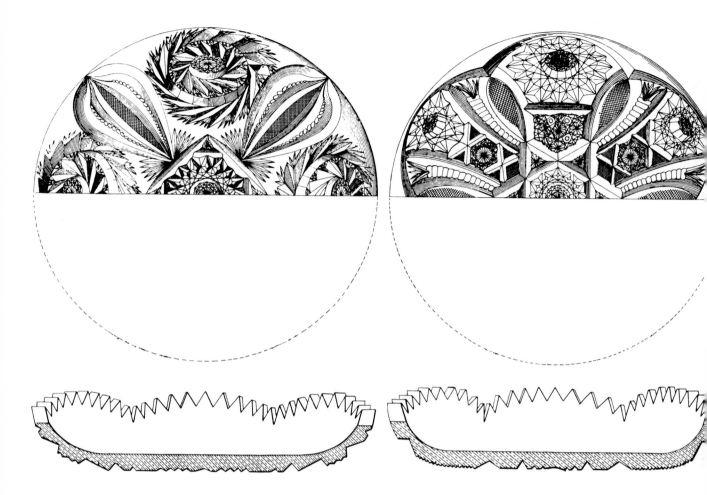

Left: The "Pears" pattern; *right:* The "Pennington" pattern; both patented May 6, 1902, by W. S. Clark for Missouri Glass Co.

last-known address of the Missouri Glass Company was given as 1723 Locust Street, St. Louis, Missouri.

The *St. Louis Directory* for 1902 listed William S. Clark at 12th Street, S.E., corner of Olive Street, in association with Yall, Clark & Cowen (cut glass manufacturers). The Art Manufacturing Company (also manufacturers of cut glass) was listed at this address too. In 1903, Clark was listed as the superintendent of the Art Manufacturing Company, at 908 Clark Avenue, St. Louis. The Art Manufacturing Company continued to be listed in the directories with Clark's name as a principal until 1904; thereafter no listing for the firm could be found. It is quite possible that the designs for cut glass assigned to the Missouri Glass Company by William S. Clark were executed at the Art Manufacturing Company's cutting shop on blanks supplied to them by the Missouri Glass Company.

William S. Clark of St. Louis, Missouri, assigned two beautiful cut glass designs to the Missouri Glass Company on May 6, 1902. Intricately cut rosettes and "pear-shaped panels" comprise the main features of one design, which we call "Pears." The center of this dish is ornamented with a small rosette surrounded by pyramidal projections, the entire central design being surrounded by a marginal cut forming a square. In his second design patent for a cut glass dish, Clark used intricately cut rosettes arranged as shown in his patent drawings, with pear-shaped arrangements of hatchwork (checkered cutting). We call this pattern "Pennington," named for G. A. Pennington, one of the witnesses to Clark's patent papers.

Bergen Cut Glass Company
Bergen-Phillips Cut Glass Company
Bergen & Son
Bergen Glass Works
Bergen Glass Company

The earliest reference to the Bergen Cut Glass Company was found in the 1912 St. Louis directories. At that time the firm was located at 4718–4720 Delmar Boulevard, St. Louis, Missouri. Charles B. Bergen was superintendent of the works and Charles B. Bergen, Jr. was listed as a glazier. In 1913 the firm's name was changed to Bergen-Phillips Cut Glass Company; Jerome J. Phillips was secretary of the company and James D. Bergen was manager. In 1914, Phillips left the cut glass business to become president of the Workman's Service Company in St. Louis. Later Phillips was the president of the Corona Typewriter Sales Company; these various positions indicate that he was not a practical glass cutter, and that his connection with the Bergen-Phillips Cut Glass Company was only a financial arrangement.

In 1921, Charles B. Bergen and Charles B. Bergen, Jr. established a cut glass business as Bergen & Son, with a shop located at 302 Market Street, St. Louis. In 1923 the company did business as the Bergen Glass Works and as Bergen & Son; their address then was 4961 Delmar Boulevard, and 304 Market Street, St. Louis. Charles U. Bergen appears in the city directories as a glass cutter in 1925, and his connection with the Bergen Glass Works is confirmed in their listings from 1927 through 1930; at this period Charles B. Bergen and Charles B. Bergen, Jr. were all in the business known as the Bergen Glass Company (Bergen & Son).

In 1937, the name Charles Bergen again appears in the public records as a glass cutter for the St. Louis Glass & Queensware Company. The president and treasurer of this firm was Ralph E. Nutting; Oscar C. Henke was secretary of the firm, which was located in St. Louis, Missouri, at 1121–1123 Olive Street. In 1938, Charles U. Bergen was the foreman of the St. Louis Glass & Queensware Company and Charles B. Bergen was assistant foreman. In 1939 the company changed its name to the Meramec Company, manufacturers of glassware, located at 1121 Olive Street, St. Louis. Ralph E. Nutting's name appears in connection with this latter company in 1939 and 1940.

Judging from the somewhat erratic listings in the city directories, it would seem that the Bergen Glass Works went out of existence some time in the early 1930's. The Bergens obviously pursued their trade with the St. Louis Glass & Queensware Company, and perhaps with their successors, the Meramec Company, though this last conclusion is not indicated in the records.

Cut Glass Manufacturers in Minnesota

Twin City Cut Glass Company

In 1908, Oscar W. Johnson of the Johnson-Carlson Cut Glass Company, Chicago, Illinois, established the Twin City Cut Glass Company in Minneapolis, Minnesota. The factory was located on the third floor of the old Exposition Building on Hampden Avenue, northeast corner of Bradford Street. In 1909 the names of Tycho H. Strandberg, Gustave Carlson, and Ernest J. Strandberg, appear in the directories as being associated with this firm. In 1910 the factory was moved to 602 North Fairview Avenue in St. Paul, Minnesota; at this time Oscar W. Johnson's name first appears in the city directory in connection with the Twin City Cut Glass Company. The firm continued at this last address until 1914, when it moved to 1905 University Avenue, St. Paul. In 1916, H. Strandberg is listed as president and treasurer of the company, and G. S. Carlson as secretary. A closing date for the factory could not be determined; however, we believe it ceased operating about 1918.

National Cut Glass Company

The National Cut Glass Company was first listed in the Minneapolis, Minnesota, city recordings in 1908, with Ernest Bersbach as president; Peter Thompson, as vice president; and Edward Otis as secretary and treasurer. They were located at 102 South Third Street. The company continued operating without any change in its principals until 1920. Thereafter all the members of the National Cut Glass Company were associated in other business enterprises; the 1922 directory listed Peter Thompson as a tailor.

Eagle Cut Glass Company

In 1908 the Eagle Cut Glass Company was founded in Minneapolis, Minnesota. At that time the president of the company was A. W. Benson; August Eckman was secretary, and Knute Eckman was treasurer. The shop was located at 1700 Washington North. A year later, Arthur Olson (later associated with the Standard Engraving & Cut Glass Company, the Queen City Cut Glass Company, and the Olson Cut Glass Company) succeeded Knute Eckman as treasurer, and Edward G. Dahl filled the position of secretary in the firm, replacing August Eckman. By 1910 all those mentioned above were associated with other firms; however, the 1918 edition of the *American Glass Trade Directory* still listed the Eagle Cut Glass Company as a manufacturer of fine quality cut glass.

The Standard Engraving & Cut Glass Company
Standard Cut Glass Company

The Standard Engraving & Cut Glass Company, also known as the Standard Cut Glass Company, was incorporated in Minneapolis, Minnesota, on August 12, 1911, and a charter was granted for a period of 30 years. At the time the charter was issued to the firm, the board of directors consisted of the following: Arthur R. Olson (who was also associated with the Queen City Cut Glass Company in Rochester, Minnesota, in 1913), president; D. D. Rider, vice president; and Charles G. Merriell, treasurer. No dissolution papers were filed for the firm prior to the expiration of their charter, in 1941, and since no further evidence of their existence can be found, it is presumed that the company was dissolved within a few years after it was formed; perhaps at the time Olson became associated with the Queen City Cut Glass Company.

On November 26, 1912, Albin Carlson of Minneapolis, Minnesota, patented his design for a cut glass vessel and assigned it to the Standard Engraving & Cut Glass Company. The patent drawings show two views of a cut glass vase in Carlson's design, which consisted of bright-cut flowers and deep miter-cut leaves and stems. This pattern we have named "Cosmos." On June 23, 1914, Carlson registered another design for cut glass. This time the design consisted of a butterfly hovering over stylized flowers resembling wild carnations. We suggest the pattern be called "Posy and Butterfly."

448

Left: The "Cosmos" pattern; patented Nov. 26, 1912; *right:* The "Posy and Butterfly" pattern; patented June 23, 1914; both by Albin Carlson for Standard Engraving & Cut Glass Co.

St. Paul Glass Company

The St. Paul Glass Company was established in St. Paul, Minnesota, in 1907. It closed in 1943. The factory, located at 54 East Indiana Avenue, was operated under the sole ownership of Harry A. Schneider. Only cutting and beveling of flat plate glass was done at this factory.

L. A. Orr Company

The L. A. Orr Company was listed under "Cut Glass" manufacturers in the 1909/10 Rochester, Minnesota, city directory. In 1917 the factory was moved from its original site at 123 South Broadway to 118 South Main Street in Rochester. Latham A. Orr, owner of the firm, was listed as treasurer of the Queen City Cut Glass Company in the 1913/14 *Rochester City Directory*. No further evidence could be found to indicate that the L. A. Orr Company operated after 1917, and it may have gone out of business, as did some other cut glass shops, at the commencement of World War I.

J. E. Reid & Company

J. E. Reid & Company established their cut glass factory in Rochester, Minnesota, on Broadway, southeast corner of 4th Street. The only listing of this firm we could find was in the 1909/10 *Rochester City Directory* under "Cut Glass" manufacturers. No closing date could be established for this concern.

The Queen City Cut Glass Company
Olson Cut Glass Company

The Queen City Cut Glass Company of Rochester, Minnesota, was located at 18–20 East Zumbro Street in 1913, according to the city directory. Arthur R. Olson was president and general manager of the concern; Kerry E. Conley, vice president; Thomas L. Phelps, secretary; Latham A. Orr, treasurer; and Charles L. White, assistant manager. The name of the firm did not appear in subsequent directories and presumably it too went out of business during World War I.

The Olson Cut Glass Company was listed in the *American Glass Trade Directory* in 1918 as a manufacturer of cut glassware. We could find no listing of this firm in the Rochester city directories, but we think it may have developed from the Queen City Cut Glass Company.

450

Cut Glass

Manufacturers

in Washington State

Washington Cut Glass Company

The cut glass industry in Seattle, Washington, had its beginning with the arrival in that city of Edward Zelasky and Antone Kusak, both natives of central Europe in the area now called Czechoslovakia, where they had been trained in the art of cutting fine glass. Zelasky came to Seattle in 1912 and opened a small glass cutting shop. In 1914, Kusak arrived in Seattle, and the two men formed the Washington Cut Glass Company. Before coming to Seattle, both men had been employed at the Fostoria Glass Company in Moundsville, West Virginia.

Local merchants patronized the newly formed cut glass company and it was soon selling all the merchandise it could produce. In 1916 the partnership was dissolved. Zelasky continued to operate under the firm's original name,

Cut glass articles from an illustrated catalogue issued *ca.* 1915 by Washington Cut Glass Co.; 10-in. vase, rose bowl, roll tray, 8-in. two-handled nappy, sugar and creamer, and 8-in. bowl.

Electric lamp cut by William J. Kokesh at Washington Cut Glass Co., *ca.* 1921. (Blank supplied by McKee Glass Co.)
Collection of William J. Kokesh

moving in 1918 to 21st Avenue South and Jackson Street in Seattle. Kusak formed his own cut glass shop in Seattle that same year.

In 1918 the Washington Cut Glass Company was listed as a cut glass manufacturer in the *American Glass Trade Directory*. When the heavy cut glasswares went out of style the firm continued cutting light wares, and in 1949 they were noted as having only four glass cutters working in the shop. Their output was almost wholly taken up by local merchants.

Before World War II, Edward Zelasky, Jr. left his father's business to form his own cutting shop. He installed the necessary machinery in the basement of his home at 6457 Empire Way in Seattle, and specialized in the production of engraved and initialed glassware until the war interrupted his work.

The 1954 *Seattle Directory* listed the Washington Cut Glass Company at 2040 Jackson Street, still under the direction of Edward A. Zelasky. He died in March, 1955, and the company was not listed in the directories again until 1960; the listing then was "Washington Cut Glass Company (Wm. J. Kokesh), 4806 27th Avenue South," and the same listing appeared in the 1961/62 issue. Kokesh was Edward Zelasky's son-in-law.

Antone Kusak came to this country in 1910; he was unknown and had no relatives or friends in America. He was befriended by Zelasky and taken into his household. In time, Kusak married Zelasky's sister, and in 1914 he was made a partner in the Washington Cut Glass Company.

In 1915, William J. Kokesh was employed as the first apprentice in the Washington Cut Glass Company and received his training from Edward Zelasky. Kokesh married Zelasky's daughter and continued working for his father-in-law until he formed his own cut glass business.

Kusak Cut Glass Company

After he severed his association with the Washington Cut Glass Company, Antone Kusak opened his own cutting shop in Seattle, Washington, in 1916. The business was located at 1303 Rainier Avenue, where orders for cut glass were filled for establishments as far away as Pawtucket, Rhode Island. Kusak had learned his trade in central Europe (present-day Czechoslovakia) and came to America in 1910, where he became acquainted with Edward Zelasky; some years later he married Zelasky's sister. For a time Kusak worked in cut glass shops in the east before joining his brother-in-law in the Washington Cut Glass Company in 1914; he had been employed by the Fostoria Glass Company in Moundsville, West Virginia, awhile earlier.

For many years Kusak made an annual pilgrimage to his native country to purchase their world-famous Bohemian crystal blanks which he cut in his own shop; he imported more than 40,000 dozen blanks each year. Original designs were engraved on the imported glass blanks by Kusak and his son Antone C. Kusak. Besides the father-and-son team, the firm employed four other expert cutters, two of whom, Yaros Kusak (no relation) and Thomas Worland, had been with the firm for 20 years in 1949. The Kusak Cut Glass Company is still cutting and engraving fine glassware in Seattle; the shop is now operated by Kusak's son, Antone C. Kusak, and his wife.

William J. Kokesh

William J. Kokesh was the first apprentice to be hired by the Washington Cut Glass Company in 1915. He still has one of the first pieces he ever made as a part of his apprenticeship—a rose bowl on which he spent four months of night work, after his chores at the shop were completed for the day.

In 1939, Kokesh wanted to cut glass to his own designs, so he purchased the equipment necessary for his trade and entered into business in the basement of his home at 4806 27th Avenue South, in Seattle, Washington. Besides the usual light cut stemware, Kokesh experimented with the sandblast method of engraving and developed this art to a very high degree. His first productions included initialed glassware and decorative lighting fixtures. By 1949 his business had grown and he was then employing three other cutters in his little shop. The firm is still doing business in Seattle, mostly with light cut wares and imported cut crystal. For the Seattle Century 21 Exposition in 1962, Kokesh made sandblasted engraved plaques with a representation of the "Space Needle," the fair's symbol for the space age.

Footed bowl; cut by William J. Kokesh during his apprenticeship with Washington Cut Glass Co., 1918.

Collection of William J. Kokesh

Seattle Cut Glass Company

The Seattle Cut Glass Company was established in Seattle, Washington, in 1917, and was located in room 511 of the Polson Building at 71 Columbia Street. At that time Peter Sibo was manager and president of the firm; in 1918, Dr. J. L. Hutchinson was listed as president and Paul F. Kowarsh as secretary-treasurer. In 1919, Joseph V. Prosser became the treasurer and manager. In that same year Kowarsh went into a partnership with John H. Digby in the Digby Cut Glass Company in Seattle. The address of the Seattle Cut Glass Company was changed in 1919 to 409 Epler Block, 813 Second Avenue, Seattle. The last entry for the Seattle Cut Glass Company was dated 1922. In 1923 Dr. Hutchinson was practicing medicine in Seattle; Paul F. Kowarsh was secretary of the Diamond Art Glass Company, Incorporated, in Seattle; and Joseph V. Prosser was a manufacturer's agent at 447 Epler Building. By 1924 Prosser had left Seattle.

Digby Cut Glass Company
Diamond Cut Glass Company, Incorporated
Diamond Art Glass Company, Incorporated

In 1919, Paul F. Kowarsh and John H. Digby established a cut glass shop in Seattle, Washington, known as the Digby Cut Glass Company; the firm at that time was located at 516 Olive Street, and produced light and heavy cut glasswares.

From 1920 to 1924 the Diamond Cut Glass Company was also listed at 516 Olive Street in Seattle. In 1923, Kowarsh was secretary of the Diamond Art Glass Company, Incorporated, and it is quite possible that this firm developed from the Digby Cut Glass Company and its successor, the Diamond Cut Glass Company, Incorporated.

Appendix A

National Association of Cut Glass Manufacturers

The National Association of Cut Glass Manufacturers was organized in Buffalo, New York, on August 17, 1911; it was incorporated in Pennsylvania on March 9, 1921, and became inactive in 1942. The purpose of the association was to promote the best interests of the cut glass trade, and to cooperate with crystal blank manufacturers to uphold the quality of American cut glass. At the first meeting of the association there were 63 members in attendance, representing about 30 firms. Meetings were held in New York, New Jersey, and Pennsylvania. The association had various presidents throughout its existence, but Raymond H. Fender was secretary from the time of the organization's inception to its very end. The last listing of the association in the *National Glass Budget's Directory* was in 1936; at that time G. William Sell was president; Thomas P. Strittmatter, treasurer; and Raymond H. Fender, secretary.

An old copy of the association's letterhead listed G. William Sell, president; F. L. Morecroft, vice president; Raymond H. Fender, secretary; and Thomas P. Strittmatter, treasurer. The board of directors consisted of O. S. Atterholt, Pittston, Pennsylvania (Luzerne Cut Glass Company); Arthur Blackmer, New Bedford, Massachusetts (Blackmer Cut Glass Company); W. E. Corcoran, Flemington, New Jersey (Empire Cut Glass Company); Raymond H. Fender, Philadelphia, Pennsylvania (Powelton Cut Glass Company); J. Howard Fry, Rochester, Pennsylvania (H. C. Fry Glass Company); Emil F. Kupfer, Brooklyn, New York (Emil F. Kupfer, Inc.); Robert A. May, Montreal, Canada (George Philips Company); J. J. McKanna, Honesdale, Pennsylvania (McKanna Cut Glass Company); F. L. Morecroft, Canastota, New York (Ideal Cut Glass Company); George W. Murphey, Hawley, Pennsylvania (Keystone Cut Glass Company); J. W. Robinson, Toledo, Ohio (formerly with the Libbey Glass Company, and later with a company of his own); G. W. Sell, Honesdale, Pennsylvania (Krantz & Sell); George E. Sherman, New Bedford, Massachusetts (Pairpoint Corporation); Thomas Skinner, Hammonton, New Jersey (William Skinner & Son); Thomas P. Strittmatter, Philadelphia, Pennsylvania (Liberty Cut Glass Works); Charles Taylor, Newark, New Jersey (Jewel Cut Glass Company); D. C. Tracy, New York City (George Borgfeldt & Company).

The following list of members in the association was compiled from memory for us by Raymond Fender:

American Cut Glass Company, Lansing, Michigan

Becker & Brisbois, Brooklyn, New York
Bergen Cut Glass Company, St. Louis, Missouri
J. D. Bergen Company, Meriden, Connecticut
Val Bergen Cut Glass Company, Columbia, Pennsylvania

Blackmer Cut Glass Company, New Bedford, Massachusetts
George Borgfeldt & Company, New York City
John A. Boyle, Brooklyn, New York
Buffalo Cut Glass Company, Batavia, New York
Burley & Tyrrell, Chicago, Illinois

Thomas B. Campbell, Brooklyn, New York
Central Cut Glass Company, Chicago, Illinois
Century Cut Glass Company, Saugerties, New York
Chicago Cut Glass Company, Chicago, Illinois
T. B. Clark & Company, Honesdale, Pennsylvania
Clinton Cut Glass Company, Aldenville, Pennsylvania
Crescent Cut Glass Company, Newark, New Jersey
Crown Cut Glass Company, Hancock, Pennsylvania
Crystal Cut Glass Company, Honesdale, Pennsylvania
Crystolyne Cut Glass Company, Brooklyn, New York
Cut Glass Corporation of America, Philadelphia, Pennsylvania (also known as the
    Quaker City Cut Glass Company)

Dorflinger & Sons, White Mills, Pennsylvania

Elmira Glass Cutting Company, Elmira, New York
Empire Cut Glass Company, Flemington, New Jersey

Figueroa Cut Glass Company, Hammonton, New Jersey
Fischer Cut Glass Company, Atco, New Jersey
Flemington Cut Glass Company, Flemington, New Jersey
H. C. Fry Glass Company, Rochester, Pennsylvania

Genessee Cut Glass Company, Rochester, New York
Gundy & Chapperton, Toronto, Canada

J. Halter & Company, Brooklyn, New York
Heinz Brothers, St. Charles, Illinois
J. H. Herrfeldt & Company, Brooklyn, New York
J. Hoare & Company, Corning, New York
Honesdale Union Cut Glass Company, Honesdale, Pennsylvania
Hunt Glass Company, Corning, New York

Ideal Cut Glass Company, Canastota, New York
Imperial Cut Glass Company, Philadelphia, Pennsylvania
International Cut Glass Company, Buffalo, New York
Irving Cut Glass Company, Honesdale, Pennsylvania

Jewel Cut Glass Company, Newark, New Jersey
Johnson-Carlson Cut Glass Company, Chicago, Illinois

Kellner & Munro, Brooklyn, New York
Kelly & Steinman, Deposit, New York
Keystone Cut Glass Company, Hawley, Pennsylvania
Kings County Cut Glass Company, Brooklyn, New York
Koch Cut Glass Company, Chicago, Illinois
Krantz, Smith & Company, Honesdale, Pennsylvania

Laurel Cut Glass Company, Jermyn, Pennsylvania
Libbey Glass Company, Toledo, Ohio
Liberty Cut Glass Works, Egg Harbor City, New Jersey
Luzerne Cut Glass Company, Pittston, Pennsylvania

G. W. McIlvain, Mt. Holly, New Jersey
Edward Mayer, Port Jervis, New York
Meriden Cut Glass Company, Meriden, Connecticut
Mills, Gardner Company, St. Charles, Illinois

John A. Nelson, Brooklyn, New York
Newark Cut Glass Company, Newark, New Jersey
Niagara Cut Glass Company, Buffalo, New York
J. J. Niland Company, Meriden, Connecticut

N. Packwood & Company, Sandwich, Massachusetts
Pairpoint Corporation, New Bedford, Massachusetts
Penn Cut Glass Company, Prompton, Pennsylvania
Philadelphia Cut Glass Company, Philadelphia, Pennsylvania
George Philips Company, Montreal, Canada
Pioneer Cut Glass Company, Carbondale, Pennsylvania
Pitkin & Brooks, Chicago, Illinois
Powelton Cut Glass Company, Philadelphia, Pennsylvania

Quaker City Cut Glass Company (see Cut Glass Corporation of America)

George Schneider Cut Glass Company, Brooklyn, New York
Thomas Shotton Cut Glass Company, Brooklyn, New York
William Skinner & Son, Hammonton, New Jersey
Statt Brothers, Philadelphia (Manayunk), Pennsylvania
John Statt, Philadelphia, Pennsylvania
Sterling Cut Glass Company, Cincinnati, Ohio

Taylor Brothers, Philadelphia, Pennsylvania
Tuthill Cut Glass Company, Middletown, New York
Twin City Cut Glass Company, St. Paul, Minnesota

Unger Brothers, Newark, New Jersey

Wangum Cut Glass Company, Hawley, Pennsylvania
Wayne Cut Glass Company, Towanda, Pennsylvania
Webster & Briggmann, Meriden, Connecticut
Wickham & Hughes, Scranton, Pennsylvania
Wright Rich Cut Glass Company, Anderson, Indiana

A poll of the membership in 1916 accounted for some 797 frames in operation; by 1918 this number had fallen off considerably, to a mere 174 working frames (there may have been a few more than this number as the poll was taken only of the members present at this meeting). In the following years there was a slight increase in the number of cutting frames operating in the United States; but by the end of the 1920's the cut glass industry was experiencing a sharp decline in the demand for their wares, as a result of the depression and a trend in the public's taste for less elaborate tablewares.

Appendix B

Trademarks and Labels for
Cut Glass Wares

Abraham & Straus, Inc.
Brooklyn, N.Y.

C. G. Alford & Company
New York, N.Y.

American Wholesale Corp.
(Baltimore Bargain House)
Baltimore, Md.

J. D. Bergen Company
Meriden, Conn.

George L. Borden & Company
(Krystal Krafters)
Trenton, N.J.
Groveville, N.J.

George Borgfeldt & Co.
New York, N.Y.

Buffalo Cut Glass Co.
Buffalo, N.Y.

T. B. Clark & Company
Honesdale, Pa.

Corona Cut Glass Company
Toledo, Ohio

Crystolyne Cut Glass Company
Brooklyn, N.Y.

467

Cut Glass Corporation of America
(Quaker City Cut Glass Co.)
Philadelphia, Pa.

Deidrick Glass Co.
Monaca, Pa.   **SILVART**

C. Dorflinger & Sons
White Mills, Pa.

O. F. Egginton Company
Corning, N.Y.

Empire Cut Glass Company
New York, N.Y.
Flemington, N.J.

H. C. Fry Glass Co.
Rochester, Pa.

T. G. Hawkes & Company
Corning, N.Y.

A. H. Heisey & Co., Inc.
Newark, Ohio

L. Hinsberger Cut Glass Company
New York, N.Y.

J. Hoare & Company
Corning, N.Y.

Hope Glass Works
Providence, R.I.

Imperial Glass Co.
Bellaire, Ohio

Irving Cut Glass Co., Inc.
Honesdale, Pa.

Lansburgh & Brother, Inc.
Washington, D.C.

Lansburgh & Bro.

W. L. Libbey & Son
(Libbey Glass Co.)
Toledo, Ohio

Libby Glass Company
Toledo, Ohio

Apr. 21, 1896

June 19, 1906

Apr. 16, 1901
(for use on pressed
[figured] blanks)

Lotus Cut Glass Company
Barnesville, Ohio

Lyons Cut Glass Company
Lyons, N.Y.

McKanna Cut Glass Co.
Honesdale, Pa.

McKee-Jeannette Glass Works
Jeannette, Pa.

PRESCUT

Maple City Glass Co.
Honesdale, Pa.

Meriden Cut Glass Company
Meriden, Conn.

Mt. Washington Glass Company
(Pairpoint Corporation)
New Bedford, Mass.

Richard Murr
Chicago, Ill.
San Francisco, Cal.

KOH-I-NOOR

J. S. O'Connor
Hawley, Pa.

Pope Cut Glass Co., Inc.
New York, N.Y.

DIAMONKUT

H. P. Sinclaire & Co.
Corning, N.Y.

Standard Cut Glass Company
New York, N.Y.

Steuben Glass Works
(Corning Glass Works)
Corning, N.Y.

L. Straus & Sons
New York, N.Y.

Taylor Brothers Co., Inc.
Philadelphia, Pa.

Thatcher Brothers
Fairhaven, Mass.

Tuthill Cut Glass Company
Middletown, N.Y.

Unger Brothers
Newark, N.J.

Van Heusen, Charles Co.
Albany, N.Y.

E. J. S. Van Houten
New York, N.Y.

C. E. Wheelock & Co.
Peoria, Ill.

Bibliography

BARRELET, JAMES. *La Verrerie en France* (Paris, 1953).

CHIPMAN, FRANK W. *The Romance of Old Sandwich Glass* (Sandwich, Mass., 1932).

DANIEL, DOROTHY. *Cut and Engraved Glass, 1771–1905* (New York, 1950).

DORFLINGER, WILLIAM. "The Development of the Cut-Glass Business in the United States," a paper read at the meeting of the American Association of Flint and Lime Glass Manufacturers, held at Atlantic City, July 25, 1902.

DUTHRIE, ARTHUR LOUIS. *Decorated Glass Processes* (London, 1908).

FIELD, KATE. *The Drama of Glass* (Toledo, Ohio, 1899).

GANDY, WALTER. *The Romance of Glass-Making* (London, 1898).

GILLINDER, WILLIAM T. "Treatise on the Art of Glass Making, containing 272 Practical Receipts" (Birmingham, England, 1894).

JARVES, DEMING. *Reminiscences of Glass-Making* (New York, 1865).

JEFFERSON, JOSEPHINE. *Wheeling Glass* (Mt. Vernon, Ohio, 1947).

MARSON, PERCIVAL. *Glass and Glass Manufacture* (London, 1918).

McKEARIN, GEORGE and HELEN. *American Glass* (New York, 1946).

PELLATT, APSLEY. *Curiosities of Glass Making* (London, 1849).

POWELL, H. J., CHANCE, H., and HARRIS, H. G. *The Principles of Glass-Making* (London, 1883).

SAUZAY, ALEXANDRE. *Marvels of Glass-Making in All Ages* (London, 1869).

WARMAN, EDWIN G. *American Cut Glass* (Uniontown, Pa., 1954).

WATKINS, LURA WOODSIDE. *Cambridge Glass* (Boston, Mass., 1930).

General Index

A complete listing of persons, places, manufacturers, book
and periodical titles. Italic numbers refer to illustrations.

Dithridge, Edward D., Jr., 364
Dithridge, J. Duncan, 147
Dithridge Flint Glass Company, 11, *11*, 147, 364
Dobbins, Jackson T., 396
Dobbins, Mildred, 396
Dobelmann, J. B., 7, 12, 268
Dodd, Samuel, 94
Doernbach, Fred, 249
Dorflinger, Charles, 270
Dorflinger, Charlotte Clemens, 266
Dorflinger, Christian, 6–7, 11, 12, 108, 149, 266–75
Dorflinger, Mrs. Christian, 268
Dorflinger, Clothilde, 267
Dorflinger, C., & Sons, *see* Dorflinger Glass Company
Dorflinger, Eugene, 267, 324
Dorflinger, Francis, 266
Dorflinger, John, 273, *273*, 277, 324
Dorflinger, Mr. and Mrs. John C., *267, 278, 280, 281*
Dorflinger, Louis J., 270
Dorflinger, William, 7, 12, 270, 357
Dorflinger Glass Company, 11, 12, 176, 217, 231, 239, 266–81, *267, 268, 270, 271, 272, 274, 275, 276, 277, 278, 279, 280, 281,* 282–3, 300, 309, 322, 324, 326, 462
Dorflinger Guards, 268
Dorsey, H. O., 385
Dorworth, George F., 264
Dougherty, George, 354
Drake, Franklin N., 200
Drake, George Washington, 199–200
Drake, George, Cut Glass Company, 199–200, *199, 200*
Dreppard, Carl, 105
Dublin, Ire., 172
Dudley, Eng., 172
Duluth, Minn., 318
Dummer, Augustus O., 9
Dummer, George, 7, 9
Dummer, George, & Company, 7, 9
Dummer, Phineas C., 7
Duncan, George, & Sons, 379
Duncan & Dithridge, 147
Duncan & Miller Glass Company, 232, 313
Dunkirk, Ind., 379

Dunham, Jacob K., 44
Dunnigan, John, 89
Durkin, Thomas, 213

E

Eachus, Iredell, 262
Eagle Cut Glass Company, 448
Ealey, Archie, 169
Earl, John, 138
Earnshaw, John R., 260
East Cambridge, Mass., 4, 19, 22, 44, 339, 407
East Honesdale, Pa., 269
East Liverpool, Ohio, 255
East River Flint Glass Works, *see* Lafayette Flint Glass Works, The
East Wareham, Mass., 51
Eaton, Ray E., 377
Ebenezer, N.Y., 221
Ebenezer Cut Glass Company, 221
Eckland, Oscar W., 396
Eckert, Frank, 249
Eckman, August, 448
Eckman, Knute, 448
Eclipse Tumbler Company, The, 383–6
Eddy, Mary Baker, 8
Edinburgh, Scot., 414
Edinburgh and Leith Glass Company, 414
Edsall, J. S., 341
Edwards, A. C., 168
Edward VIII, 273
Egg Harbor City, N.J., 248, 251, 258
Egginton, Oliver F., 172, 190
Egginton, O. F., Company, 6; *see also* Egginton Rich Cut Glass Company
Egginton, Walter E., 179, *180,* 181, 190, *191,* 193
Egginton, Walter F., 190
Egginton Rich Cut Glass Company, 172, 190–3, *191, 192*
Egypt, ancient, 1, 15
Eichbaum, William Peter, 9
Eichman, Herman, 421, 422
Eick, Peter A., 206
Eick, William B., 206, *214*
Eisenhower, President Dwight D., 176
Eisle, Edward A., 219
Eisle, Edward J., 219

Eisle & Company, 219
Eiswald, George H., 76
Elgin, Ill., 412
Eliot, William R., 94, *95,* 95
Elite Cut Glass Manufacturing Company, 303; *see* Clinton Cut Glass Company
Elkhart, Ind., **431**
Elmhurst, William Albert, 226
Elmira, N.Y., 155, 156, 158, 203, 210, 211, 391
Elmira Cut Glass Company, 155, 203, 210
Elmira Glass Company, 391
Elmira Glass Cutting Company, 462; *see also* Elmira Cut Glass Company
Elmira Heights, N.Y., 166, 208
Elmira Window Glass Works, 166
Elson Glass Company, The, 379
Elwood, N.J., 245
Emmet, Fisher, and Flowers, 4
Emory, Archibald M., 402
Empire Cut Glass Company, 231–2, 427, 461, 462
Empire Glass Company, 209
Empire State Flint Glass Works, 105, 126
Engelke, Hugo, 125
England, 1
Engler, A., 387
Englewood Cut Glass Company, 427
Enterprise Cut Glass Company, 158–66; *see also* Figueroa Cut Glass Company
Enterprise Glass Company, 333
Erckert, Earl, 221
Erckert, Frances, 221
Erckert, Louis, 221
Erickson, Gustave, 420
Erie Railroad, 200
Esselstyne, Albert J., 404
Eulalia, Princess, 26
Evans, Margaret M., 303
Evening Journal (Vineland, N.J.), 247
Everhart Museum, *267, 278, 280, 281*
Ewer, N. J., & Company, 213
Excelsior Glass Works, 234, 368
Eygabroat, Fred, 342
Eygabroat-Ryon Company, Incorporated, 342–4, *342, 343*

Index of Patterns

A complete listing of pattern names with the manufacturer's name in parentheses. Where no manufacturer is listed, a general statement regarding the pattern is to be found. Even though the pattern itself varies and there is some general discussion, the several entries are found under the one pattern name. Italic numbers refer to illustrations.